D1477374

MEN, WOMEN, AND MONEY

Men, Women, and Money

Perspectives on Gender, Wealth, and Investment, 1850–1930

Edited by

DAVID R. GREEN
ALASTAIR OWENS
JOSEPHINE MALTBY
JANETTE RUTTERFORD

OXFORD
UNIVERSITY PRESS

OXFORD

UNIVERSITY PRESS

Great Clarendon Street, Oxford OX2 6DP

Oxford University Press is a department of the University of Oxford.
It furthers the University's objective of excellence in research, scholarship,
and education by publishing worldwide in

Oxford New York

Auckland Cape Town Dar es Salaam Hong Kong Karachi
Kuala Lumpur Madrid Melbourne Mexico City Nairobi
New Delhi Shanghai Taipei Toronto

With offices in

Argentina Austria Brazil Chile Czech Republic France Greece
Guatemala Hungary Italy Japan Poland Portugal Singapore
South Korea Switzerland Thailand Turkey Ukraine Vietnam

Oxford is a registered trade mark of Oxford University Press
in the UK and in certain other countries

Published in the United States
by Oxford University Press Inc., New York

British Library Cataloguing in Publication Data

Data available

Library of Congress Cataloging in Publication Data

Data available

Typeset by SPI Publisher Services, Pondicherry, India
Printed in Great Britain
on acid-free paper by
MPG Books Group, Bodmin and King's Lynn

ISBN 978-0-19-959376-7

1 3 5 7 9 10 8 6 4 2

Contents

Preface

The chapters that comprise this book are based upon papers presented at a specially convened international workshop on wealth, investment, and gender in the nineteenth and twentieth centuries held at the Open University, Milton Keynes, UK, 16–17 June 2008. The editors would like to thank the participants and discussants at that workshop for their comments and advice on the papers presented at the time, including those whose work does not feature in this volume but whose insights and contributions have shaped the essays that do: Mark Casson, David Chambers, Philip Cottrell, Jane Frecknall-Hughes, Marco van Leeuwen, Pat Thane, and Stephanie Wyse. Cathy Playle of the Open University Business School managed the arrangements of the workshop and helped to make all the participants feel welcome.

This event was generously supported by the UK's Economic and Social Research Council as part of a wider research project on 'Women and Investors in England and Wales, *c.*1870 to 1930' (Award number RES-000-23-1435). We would like to thank the Economic and Social Research Council for funding the research and allowing us the opportunity to learn from our own efforts as well as the expertise of others who attended the workshop. The project has proved to be a rewarding and intensely collaborative interdisciplinary experience, with much of its success derived from the efforts of four first-rate Research Assistants: Steven Ainscough, Claire Swan, Carry van Lieshout, and Carien van Mourik. Such projects also rely on enormous amounts of goodwill and we would like to express particular thanks to Michael Abate for designing the project website and Marian Nicolson and Shatish Kundaiker from King's College London for their ongoing technical support. Further details about the research programme, including other published outputs, can be found on the project's website: www.womeninvestors.org.uk

Editing this book has been a pleasurable experience despite the challenges posed by working with editors and authors separated by time zones as well as continents. We would like to thank our contributors for responding constructively to sometimes voluminous editorial comments and frequent requests for information. We are indebted to them for their good humoured patience while we completed the manuscript. Eoin Dunne provided some much needed support in undertaking some of the final editorial tasks, while Ed Oliver drew the map that appears in Chapter 3 and provided helpful advice on other design matters. Finally, we would like to thank David Musson who commissioned this book on behalf of Oxford University Press and Emma Lambert whose friendly encouragement and saint-like patience enabled us to complete it.

David. R. Green, King's College London
Alastair Owens, Queen Mary, University of London
Josephine Maltby, University of York
Janette Rutterford, Open University
July 2010

List of Figures

List of Tables

List of Contributors

Graeme G. Acheson is a Lecturer in Finance at the University of Ulster, UK. His work has focused on investor behaviour, corporate structure, and the equity market in nineteenth-century Britain. Recent publications include: 'Rule Britannia!: British stock market returns, 1825–1870' (in the *Journal of Economic History* 69, 2009) and 'The death blow to unlimited liability in Victorian Britain: The City of Glasgow failure' (in *Explorations in Economic History* 45, 2008).

Steven Ainscough was a Research Assistant for the Economic and Social Research Council funded study 'Women investors in England and Wales, *c*.1870–1930', led by the editors of this book. He holds a PhD from the University of Liverpool for a thesis exploring the social, economic, and political networks of elites in nineteenth- and early twentieth-century Macclesfield. He now works as a history teacher in Lancashire, UK.

Youssef Cassis is Professor of Economic History at the European University Institute, Italy. His current research interests include the performance of European business in the twentieth century and financial crises and the shaping of modern finance, from the late nineteenth century to the present. Among Youssef's recent publications are: *Capitals of Capital: A History of International Financial Centres, 1780–2005* (2006) and *The World of Private Banking* (co-ed, 2009).

Mary Beth Combs is Associate Professor of Economics at Fordham University in New York City, USA. Her published research has focused on the impact of the British Married Women's Property Acts on shopkeeping families. She is currently working on several books, including: *Being Transformed and Transforming the World: Justice in Jesuit Higher Education* (co-ed, forthcoming); *Balances of Power: The Lower Middle Class and Married Women's Property in Nineteenth-Century Britain* (forthcoming); and *Reading the Economy: An Anthology of Literary Works in English from Chaucer to Maya Angelou* (co-ed, forthcoming).

Livio Di Matteo is Professor of Economics at Lakehead University in Thunder Bay, Ontario, Canada. His research involves the analysis of late nineteenth- and early twentieth-century Ontario probate records with an emphasis on the socio-economic determinants of wealth, life-cycle saving behaviour, wealth distribution, and portfolio composition. His most recent research has been published in *Cliometrica, Social Science History,* the *Australian Economic History Review,* and *Explorations in Economic History.*

David R. Green is Reader in Human Geography ay King's College London, UK. His research focuses on the relationships between wealth, welfare, gender, and place, and ranges from the study of middle-class investment strategies to the provision of poor relief. His latest book, *Pauper Capital: London and the Poor Law, 1790–1870,* was published in 2010.

Leslie Hannah is a Visiting Professor in the Department of Economic History at the London School of Economics, UK. He has published widely on various aspects of business history, corporate strategy, pensions, and asset management. His numerous publications include: *Barclays: The Business of Banking 1690–1996* (co-author, 2001) and *The Whig Theory of Business* (forthcoming).

Josephine Maltby is Professor of Accounting and Finance at The York Management School, University of York, UK. Her research interests include corporate governance, accounting history, and women's behaviour as savers and investors from the early nineteenth century onwards. Her most recent publications include *Women and their Money 1700–1950: Essays on Women and Finance* (co-ed, 2009).

Ranald C. Michie is Professor of History at the University of Durham, UK. His research interests all fall into the broad area of financial history. This includes the history of global securities markets, extending his publications on the London Stock Exchange to work on stock exchanges around the world. He is also interested in the history of the City of London as a financial centre as it moved from trade to finance, and from domestic to global orientations. Ranald's publications include: *The London Stock Exchange: A History* (1999), *The Global Securities Market: A History* (2006), and *Guilty Money: The City of London in Victorian and Edwardian Culture, 1815–1914* (2009).

Alastair Owens is Senior Lecturer in Geography at Queen Mary, University of London, UK. His recent work has focused on two collaborative research projects: a major study of women and investment in Britain, 1870–1930 and an investigation of the material culture and everyday domestic life in Victorian London. His recent publications include: *Gender Inequalities, Households and the Production of Well-being in Modern Europe* (co-ed, 2010); *Women, Business and Finance in Nineteenth-Century Europe: Rethinking Separate Spheres* (co-ed, 2006); and *Family Welfare: Gender, Property and Inheritance since the Seventeenth Century* (co-ed, 2004).

William D. Rubinstein is Professor of History in the Department of History and Welsh History at Aberystwyth University, UK. He has written widely on wealth-holding and elites in modern British history and on other topics including modern Jewish history and the practice of amateur history.

Recent books include: *Men of Property: The Very Wealthy in Britain Since the Industrial Revolution* (2nd edition, 2006) and *Who Were the Rich? A Biographical Director of British Wealth-Holders, Volume 1, 1809–1839* (2009).

Janette Rutterford is Professor of Financial Management at the Open University Business School, UK. Her research interests include the history of investment, equity valuation, and pension fund management. Her most recent books include: *Introduction to Stock Exchange Investment* (3rd edition, 2008) and *Women and their Money 1700–1950: Essays on Women and Finance* (co-ed, 2009).

Martin P. Shanahan is Professor at the Centre for Research and Market Analysis and Dean of Research at the University of South Australia. His research interests include comparative economic and business history with a particular focus on income and wealth distribution. His most recent co-authored publications include: 'Labour market outcomes in settler economies between 1870 and 1913' (in *Settler Economies in World History*, edited by C. Lloyd, J. Metzer, and R. Sutch. Leiden: Brill Publishers, 2010) and 'Anti-cartel or anti-foreign: Australian attitudes to anti-competitive behaviour before World War I' (in the *Australian Journal of Politics and History* 57, 2011).

Claire Swan was a Research Assistant for the Economic and Social Research Council funded study 'Women investors in England and Wales, *c*.1870–1930', led by the editors of this book. She was recently awarded a PhD from the University of Dundee for research exploring the role of Dundee investment trusts in Scottish–American business networks. She currently works for an investment management company in Edinburgh, UK.

John D. Turner has been a Professor of Financial Economics at Queen's University Belfast, UK, since 2005. Previously, he had been a lecturer at Queen's University and a Houblon-Norman scholar at the Bank of England. His main research interest is in the evolution of law, property rights, and financial institutions. His work in this area has been published in the *Journal of Economic History*, the *Economic History Review*, the *European Review of Economic History*, *Business History*, and *Explorations in Economic History*. He has recently completed an Economic and Social Research Council sponsored project examining the evolution of the British equity market in the nineteenth century. In 2010, he was the Alfred D. Chandler Visiting International Scholar at the Harvard Business School.

Carry van Lieshout is currently a PhD student at King's College London, UK. Working in collaboration with the Museum of London, her research is examining the supply and management of water and drainage in London in the eighteenth century. She was previously a Research Assistant for the

Economic and Social Research Council funded study 'Women investors in England and Wales, *c.*1870–1930', led by the editors of this book.

Carien van Mourik is a Lecturer in Accounting at the Open University Business School, UK. She was previously a Research Assistant for the Economic and Social Research Council funded study 'Women investors in England and Wales, *c.*1870–1930', led by the editors of this book. Carien's current research interest is in financial accounting theory and her recent publications include: *Globalisation and the Role of Financial Accounting Information in Japan* (2007).

1

Men, Women, and Money: An Introduction

David R. Green, Alastair Owens,
Josephine Maltby,
and Janette Rutterford

'The possessive instinct', John Galsworthy reminded his readers in the *Forsyte Saga*, 'never stands still'. From a 'self-contented provincialism' to 'a still more self-contented if less contained imperialism', he noted, the possessive instinct of the nation was always on the move.[1] In the second half of the nineteenth and early part of the twentieth century, increasing numbers of individuals became involved in owning various types of assets. Whether it was for the purchase of land at home or flotations of new companies on the stock market, loans to foreign governments or more speculative ventures in the outposts of an expanding empire, these individuals sought out ever more varied avenues for the profitable use of money. Their decisions about where to invest and in what, were taken in an increasingly international context, with the City of London acting as the switchboard for financial transfers across the globe. The individuals who invested in these different forms of wealth; the institutions, legal frameworks and infrastructures that made the circulation of capital possible; and the nature of investment both in Britain and in parts of the empire, provide the focus for this book. The chapters consider the kinds of wealth that individuals sought to possess in these different places; they focus on the choices made by individuals as well as on the institutions, legislation, and corporate practices by which those choices were regulated and through which they were channelled. Collectively, they reflect how the 'possessive instinct', as Galsworthy called it, developed in the second half of the nine-teenth century and the early years of the twentieth century.

Individual decisions regarding saving and investment need to be under-stood in the context of changes in the world economy and in this introduction

---

[1] Galsworthy, J. 2001. *The Forsyte Saga* (originally published 1906). Ware: Wordsworth Editions, 293.

we attempt to explore the nature and scope of these various transformations. We first outline macro-economic conditions, taking note of both national and international patterns of growth and rises in real incomes. We then examine the institutional arrangements and infrastructural mechanisms that encouraged and enabled individuals to participate in the widening set of financial opportunities offered by those economic shifts. Finally, we explore the demographic and cultural changes that made it more likely that individuals and households would save and invest in the expanding range of financial assets that were becoming available as a result of capitalist economic growth.

ECONOMIC GROWTH AND INVESTMENT OPPORTUNITIES: BRITAIN AND ITS EMPIRE

The nineteenth century witnessed an extraordinary transformation in the pace and scale of economic growth in the Western world. Although short-term, cyclical fluctuations continued to punctuate the rhythm of economic life, the period as a whole was characterized by sustained growth in most Western European countries and in North America. This growth subsequently extended to other regions of the world, notably parts of the British Empire, especially the settler economies in Canada, Australia, and New Zealand. It was during these years that the economic trajectories of Western countries and some of their offshoots turned sharply upwards, leading to a growing divergence from experiences in other parts of the world.[2]

The timing and extent of economic growth varied – and there were some notable reversals of fortunes, such as the Irish famine – but in Western Europe as a whole gross domestic product per capita rose some 200 per cent between 1820 and 1914, with particularly rapid expansion from the 1870s onwards.[3] In southern and eastern Europe, improvements were slower to arrive, though by the end of the period growth had also taken hold in most parts of the region.[4]

---

[2] See Clark, G. 2007. *Farewell to Alms: A Brief Economic History of the World*. Princeton, NJ: Princeton University Press, 319–27.

[3] Estimates of growth vary but see, for example, Maddison, A. 2003. *The World Economy: Historical Statistics*. Paris: OECD; Maddison, A. 2005. *Growth and Interaction in the World Economy*. Washington, DC: AEI, 6–14. Reversals also took place in other parts of the world. See, for example, Davis, M. 2001. *Late Victorian Holocausts: El Niño Famines and the Making of the Third World*. London: Verso, for a discussion of how natural events meshed with capitalist expansion to generate widespread famines in China, India, and other countries linked to Western economies.

[4] Allen, R. 2001. 'The great divergence in European wages and prices from the Middle Ages to the First World War'. *Explorations in Economic History* 38(4): 411–47; Williamson, J. 1998. 'Real wages and relative factor prices in the Third World 1820–1940: the Mediterranean Basin'. *Discussion Paper Number 1842*, Harvard Institute of Economic Research.

In the United States, growth rates gathered speed and, by the 1870s, had begun to outpace those achieved in most other Western countries.[5] Despite huge increases in population, economic improvements were driven forward in each case by enormous rises in productivity, associated with much higher levels of investment in human and physical capital and by geographical expansion into new territories. The railway network in the United States, for example, rose from 9000 miles in 1850 to 352,000 by 1910, whilst for the same period, in the United Kingdom, the volume of tonnage accounted for by steam ships rose from 168,000 to 10,443,000 tons.[6] Investment in machinery and infrastructure, together with capitalist expansion into new territories, in turn allowed an increase in output that fuelled the growth and expansion of world trade. Although short-term reversals in the rates of growth raised occasional doubts about the future prospects of economic prosperity, nevertheless the longer-term trajectory was clear. This expansion created a huge demand for capital at home and abroad; it also opened up new opportunities for investors.

In Britain by the 1850s, the capital markets that underpinned foreign expansion and domestic economic growth were already well established. While the fixed-income securities generated by the national debt were, throughout the eighteenth and early nineteenth centuries, the main alternative to land for the would-be investor, the growing number of joint-stock companies provided new opportunities for engaging with financial markets. The development of Britain's transport infrastructure, initially canals and turnpikes, but later (and more significantly) railways, was particularly important. The nominal value of domestic railway securities had reached £245 million by the end of the first 'railway mania' in 1850 and, despite setbacks such as the financial panic of 1866, rose even more rapidly in the second half of the century to £855 million in 1893, and then to £1217 million in 1913.[7] New opportunities were created in other sectors. Municipal stocks were issued to finance the great Victorian 'urban improvement' programme – the nominal value of local authority debt almost equalled the national debt by 1914.[8] However, it was the huge increase in the volume and variety of corporate securities, enabled by the continued expansion of domestic industry as well as by the advent of limited liability in the second half of the nineteenth century, that transformed the landscape of investment opportunity. Shipping, cotton

[5] See Maddison, A. 1964. *Economic Growth in the West: Comparative Experience in Europe and North America*. London: Routledge.

[6] Clark, *Farewell to Alms*, 308; Mitchell, B.R. and P. Deane 1962. *Abstract of British Historical Statistics*. Cambridge: Cambridge University Press, 218–19.

[7] Cottrell, P. 2004. 'Domestic finance 1860–1914'. In *The Cambridge Economic History of Modern Britain. Volume 2: Economic Maturity, 1860–1939*, edited by R. Floud and P. Johnson. Cambridge: Cambridge University Press, 257, 259.

[8] Wilson, J.F. 1997. 'The finance of municipal capital expenditure in England and Wales, 1870–1914'. *Financial History Review* 4(1): 31–50.

manufacturing (especially following its revival after the 1860s 'famine'), iron
and steel, food and drink (including brewing) were all sectors that saw growth
and in which there was enthusiastic take-up of limited liability.

The London Stock Exchange's role in providing finance for domestic
companies grew increasingly important over the latter decades of the nineteenth century, facilitating the development of a national capital market.
However, it is evident that prior to this period many corporate securities
were issued, brought and sold locally, as people recognized financial opportunities in the economic changes taking place around them. This also applied
to the market in real estate. Although the potential for the large-scale purchase
of land was relatively limited and rates of return on agricultural estate at best
modest, investment in housing could be more profitable, especially in rapidly
growing towns and cities. The ownership of residential and commercial
property was especially important as a way of investing money locally, as
R.J. Morris has noted in relation to Leeds merchants and industrialists around
the mid-century.[9] It was also, as David Green, Alastair Owens, Carry van
Lieshout, and Claire Swan demonstrate in their chapter, an important investment asset for those of more modest means.[10] Ownership of urban real estate
helped to insulate this group from any increase in rental costs and, indeed,
could provide a lucrative source of income.

The growth in domestic opportunities to invest was paralleled by expansion
further afield. Indeed, in a whole variety of ways it is difficult to understand
one without reference to the other. British investors keen to sink their money
into more profitable ventures than those available close to home often looked
overseas for other options. Indeed, one recent study of the evolving global
markets in sovereign bonds has speculated that 'the typical investment portfolio of a British gentleman around the turn of the twentieth century was
probably more internationally diversified than that of his great-grandson
living around the turn of the twenty-first century'.[11] Individuals had to
balance risk and rates of return in different geographical markets. Economic
policies implemented in the empire and in other parts of the world also had
clear implications for investment decisions being taken at home.

The outcomes of investors' choices were reflected in the balance of assets
held by individuals in the settler colonies, as discussed in the chapters by Livio
di Matteo and Martin Shanahan on Canada and Australia, respectively. Both
authors point out the significance of real estate in individual wealth portfolios.

---

[9] Morris, R.J. 2005. *Men, Women and Property in England, 1780–1870: A Social and
Economic History of Family Strategies among the Leeds Middle Classes.* Cambridge: Cambridge
University Press.

[10] A point also noted by Offer, A. 1981. *Property and Politics, 1870–1914: Landownership,
Law, Ideology and Urban Development in England.* Cambridge: Cambridge University Press, 136.

[11] Mauro, P., N. Sussman, and Y. Yafeh 2007. *Emerging Markets and Financial Globalization:
Sovereign Bond Spreads in 1870–1913 and Today.* Oxford: Oxford University Press, vii.

In the case of South Australia from the mid-1870s to the mid-1890s, real estate accounted for between 38 and 58 per cent of male wealth and 38–48 per cent of women's. Detailed figures for the early 1900s show that this real estate was even more important for smaller wealth-holders, accounting for some 63 per cent of men's and 54 per cent of women's net probated wealth. Men and women in Ontario between the 1870s and 1920s also held a significant proportion of their assets in land: in the frontier region of Thunder Bay approximately 45 per cent of probated wealth was accounted for by land and in the more settled area of Wentworth County the figure was closer to 35 per cent. Comparing these figures with those for England and Wales provided in the chapter by Green et al. makes it clear that individuals in these regions died with a greater proportion of their wealth held in real estate or as mortgages on land.

Such variations reflected differences in geographical conditions but were also the outcome of policies that sought to ensure access to land on the expanding colonial frontier.[12] As Martin Daunton has noted, the question as to what kind of land policy should prevail had wider implications, not just for settler economies but also for the United Kingdom.[13] By encouraging the egalitarian distribution of land in the settler colonies, the *metropole* was able to maintain a rural, albeit distant, option for the surplus British population. An outcome of this was that in the United Kingdom, where the landed interest was far more entrenched and alternative sources of income, including commerce, industry, and finance, were more widely available, the urge to break up large estates and to create a rural, freeholder class was less pressing or, indeed, less necessary. The ideology of egalitarianism on the frontier, therefore, pre-empted any attempt to redistribute land within the United Kingdom itself and made it possible for the large, landed estates to remain virtually untouched and untaxed.

But in avoiding the need to redistribute land in the United Kingdom, a different set of problems arose in relation to the economic well-being of the growing middle classes. Without access to land, how was this group, whose economic and political importance was increasing, to survive? The answer to this dilemma, apart from ensuring the possibility of land ownership overseas, was to support access to the emerging industrial and commercial economy through the ownership of shares and other kinds of financial investments. In the absence of access to land, spreading investment opportunities helped to incorporate these groups in the expansion of British capitalism, both at home

---

[12] For Canada, see Pomfret, R. 1981. *The Economic Development of Canada*. Agincourt: Methuen, 111–19. For the Australian context see, for example, Tonts, M. 2002. 'State policy and the yeoman ideal: agricultural development in Western Australia, 1890–1914'. *Landscape Research* 27(1): 103–15.

[13] Daunton, M. 2008. *State and Market in Victorian Britain*. Woodbridge: Boydell and Brewer, 128–46.

and abroad. But attracting inexperienced, risk-averse, and sometimes unwary investors into the markets depended on a number of factors including relaxing controls over investing in company shares, tightening corporate governance, and regulating the market to prevent the worst excesses of rampant speculation. The legal reform of business practices and corporate governance at home, discussed further below, which allowed a more egalitarian distribution of share ownership, was therefore the domestic equivalent of land reforms and redistributive policies in the empire. Indeed, it could be argued that the two went hand in hand.

The wider imperial and international context was important in other ways in helping to explain wealth-holding and investment in Britain. By 1900, European states controlled about 35 per cent of the world's land surface, with Britain alone accounting for nearly half the total. Where imperial control was absent in a formal sense, it was often imposed in other ways, primarily through the use of military force and diplomatic pressure. These formal and informal means of exercising imperial power provided a secure investment environment and reduced the risks of conducting business within the empire and, indeed, with foreign states. Maintaining the gold standard also helped to protect individuals against the uncertainties of investing overseas that could arise as a result of currency fluctuations. All these factors arguably helped to provide favourable conditions for investments in international and colonial ventures.

Higher rates of return were also important in encouraging British investors to look overseas, although the extent of the difference between foreign, imperial, and domestic securities should not be exaggerated. In the United Kingdom, apart from periods of recession, such as between 1877 and 1886 and from 1897 to 1909, rates of return on investments were comparable to those from further afield.[14] However, in the light of declining yields on British government securities, investors that traditionally might have bought these kinds of assets actively sought alternative opportunities. This group consisted of a substantial population of *rentier* capitalists predominantly located in London and the southern counties. It included large numbers of women for whom the safety of 'the Funds' (as government securities were sometimes known) and their guarantee of an annual income were paramount.[15] It also included institutional investors, such as savings banks, whose assets were largely composed of Consols, and trustees, whose investment activities were confined to safe if unspectacular government bonds and railway debenture

[14] Edelstein, M. 2004. 'Foreign investment, accumulation and Empire, 1860–1914'. In *The Cambridge Economic History of Modern Britain. Volume II: Economic Maturity, 1860–1939*, edited by R. Floud and P. Johnson. Cambridge: Cambridge University Press, 199; O'Brien, P. 1988. 'The costs and benefits of British imperialism 1846–1914'. *Past and Present* 120: 176.

[15] Green D.R. and A. Owens 2003. 'Gentlewomanly capitalism? Spinsters, widows and wealth-holding in England and Wales, c.1800–1860'. *Economic History Review* 56(3): 510–36.

stock.[16] The decline in the value of Consols from the late 1890s was particularly problematic for these more risk-averse and prudent investors, who, as a result, were forced to seek alternative holdings that included imperial and foreign securities as well as those in domestic companies.[17] Other groups, such as the 'gentlemanly capitalists' that feature in the important work of Peter Cain and Anthony Hopkins, more readily sought the higher rates of return offered by overseas investments. Some scholars have argued that the consequence of the actions of these individuals was to starve domestic industry of finance.[18]

The cumulative outcome of these investment decisions was that in the second half of the century there was an increase in the value of British overseas investments, from 7 per cent of national wealth in 1850 to 14 per cent by 1870, and then to 32 per cent by 1913.[19] Although the extent to which investors abandoned home-based opportunities in favour of overseas' ones is a matter of ongoing debate, expanding global markets nevertheless helped to widen and diversify investor portfolios, particularly those belonging to gentlemanly capitalists located primarily in London and the southern counties.[20]

However, as Patrick O'Brien has warned, the role of empire should not be overstated as the main destination for British investment.[21] Although Lance Davis and Robert Huttenback note that over two-thirds of called up capital on the London Stock Exchange related to foreign and imperial investment, O'Brien points out that this might have been the outcome of two sets of processes. First, much of the capital for domestic industry was raised from local sources, and in the case of small firms often from family members themselves. The issue of company prospectuses that were distributed locally and the expansion of provincial stock exchanges also tended to accentuate the importance of regional sources of capital for domestic companies.[22] As such, much of the investment in domestic industries bypassed London entirely.

---

[16] 'Consols' is an abbreviation for 'Consolidated Annuities' which were an irredeemable investment issued by the Bank of England as a government security and which paid a fixed rate of interest on the nominal value. They were by far the largest, though by no means the only, form of government security issued by the Bank of England.

[17] Offer, A. 1983. 'Empire and social reform: British overseas investment and domestic politics, 1908–1914'. *Historical Journal* 26(1): 130.

[18] The term 'gentlemanly capitalism' has generated a huge literature. For the original discussion and reflection on some critiques of the concept, see Cain P.J. and A.G. Hopkins 2001. *British Imperialism, 1688–2000*, 2nd edition. Harlow: Longman, especially 1–19. Some lines of critique are more fully developed in Daunton, *State and Market*.

[19] Edelstein, 'Foreign investment', 191.

[20] Ibid.

[21] O'Brien, 'The costs and benefits', 172–4. See also Davis, L. and R.A. Huttenback 1988. *Mammon and the Pursuit of Empire: The Economics of British Imperialism*, abridged edition. Cambridge: Cambridge University Press.

[22] See Killick, J.R. and W.A. Thomas 1970. 'The provincial stock exchanges, 1830–1870'. *Economic History Review* 23(1): 96–111.

Secondly, what happened in London was not necessarily representative of the rest of the country. Indeed, as the *Economist* noted in 1911 'London is often more concerned with the course of events in Mexico than with what happens in the Midlands'.[23] London and southern *rentier* capitalists were both distant and detached from manufacturing interests in the Midlands and elsewhere and as such the geographical focus of their investment may have been different.[24] These differences are noted by Green et al. in Chapter 3, who suggest that the composition of British wealth portfolios at death differed considerably between regions, with London and southern wealth-holders typically favouring government securities. As the relative attraction of these securities lessened, so investors in this region sought other options. The purchase of real estate – an option actively pursued elsewhere – was problematic, particularly since so much of London was in the hands of large, aristocratic landlords. Instead, wealth-holders in London and the south came to rely on expertise and information on international investment, both within and beyond the British Empire, which, as Youssef Cassis notes in Chapter 11, was mediated and coordinated by metropolitan institutions, including the major discount houses, which provided expertise in banking, investment dealing and advice, and the legal and accounting professions. As a result, investors in these regions often focused their attention on international opportunities, leaving those in the provinces to sink their money into domestic industry and other kinds of property instead.

MEN AND WOMEN WITH MONEY: A NATION OF SAVERS AND INVESTORS?

The widening set of investment opportunities that accompanied economic growth in Britain and elsewhere in the second half of the nineteenth century was paralleled by an increase in the number of investors. Although precise numbers are notoriously difficult to estimate, as Ranald Michie points out in Chapter 7, nevertheless contemporaries believed that the investing public had expanded in both number and variety. Part of the explanation for this expansion was that individuals had more opportunities to save money. In this context, rising levels of real incomes were important, especially in the second half of the century, driven by falling food prices, structural changes in the labour market, and increases in nominal wages. Where import tariffs on grain remained, the gains were slower to arrive, as happened in France and

---

[23] *Economist*, 20 May 1911: 1059.
[24] O'Brien, 'The costs and benefits', 172–3.

Germany. In Britain, where such tariffs had been removed, falls in price were greater and the increases in real wages accordingly more marked. The extent of improvement followed these shifts: in the United Kingdom, real wages between the 1870s and 1890s rose by over 1.72 per cent per annum, compared with 1.17 per cent in the United States, 1.14 per cent in France, and 1.36 per cent in Germany.[25] For the regularly employed urban working class, who stood to benefit most from falling food prices, gains in real incomes translated into better living standards and the ability to accumulate savings. The ideology of self-help promoted by the bourgeois state in various forms, not least by the imposition of a more deterrent system of poor relief after 1834, and by best-selling books, such as Samuel Smiles' *Self Help*, published in 1859, buttressed this change and provided a cultural gloss to the benefits of working-class thrift.[26]

One of the clearest manifestations of this was the growing working-class engagement with various forms of savings and mutual assistance against unemployment, incapacity, or ill health. In Chapter 8 of this volume, Josephine Maltby, Janette Rutterford, David R. Green, Steven Ainscough, and Carien van Mourik consider the range of savings schemes that developed from the nineteenth century and their relationship with investment practices. The Trustee Savings Banks, established in 1817 on the basis of earlier parish banks, were the main destination for small savers until the creation of the Post Office Savings Bank in 1861, which grew very rapidly from that date. By the 1890s, deposits in savings banks exceeded £100 million, rising to over £300 million by the early 1930s and over £500 million by the eve of the Second World War.[27] George Boyer outlines the importance of these schemes in the late nineteenth century, noting how the number of working-class savings' deposits rose from about 1.9 million in 1870 to over 7.2 million by 1911. Even allowing for a rising population, this increase reflected the growing ability and desire of individuals and households to save money over and above that needed for immediate consumption.[28] Insurance of various kinds was also of growing importance. Membership of friendly societies, for example, expanded rapidly after 1851, and by 1901, 54.5 per cent of adult males were members of an ordinary or affiliated friendly society, rising to 60 per cent

[25] Williamson, J.G. 1998. 'Growth, distribution and demography: some lessons from history'. *Explorations in Economic History* 35(3): 266. See also Hoffman, P.T., D. Jacks, P. Levin, and P. Lindert 2002. 'Real inequality in Europe since 1500'. *Journal of Economic History* 62(2): 322–55.

[26] Boyer, G.R. 2009. 'Insecurity, safety nets, and self-help in Victorian and Edwardian Britain'. In *Human Capital and Institutions: A Long-Run View*, edited by D. Eltis, F.D. Lewis, K.L. Sokoloff. Cambridge: Cambridge University Press, 46–90.

[27] Mitchell and Deane, *Abstract of British Historical Statistics*, 453–4.

[28] See Johnson, P. 1985. *Saving and Spending: Working-Class Economy in Britain, 1870–1939*. Oxford: Oxford University Press.

by 1931.[29] The two largest friendly societies – the Independent Order of Oddfellows and the Order of the Ancient Foresters – had between them over a million members by 1881.[30] Industrial branch insurance, for which premiums were collected door-to-door on a weekly basis, was a more individualistic but equally popular strategy to insure against adversity and by 1873 the Prudential was selling 11,000 policies per week, the majority to people aged 30 or younger.[31] While the act of saving or taking out insurance involved little direct interaction with financial markets and the calculative risks of investment, it can be argued that it was significant in embedding within a much wider segment of the population a familiarity with financial institutions, an understanding of concepts such as interest and economic risk, and an appreciation of the role that financial planning might play in ensuring personal and familial well-being.

This new calculative rationality was, if anything, more prevalent amongst the middle class who comprised the bulk of wealth-holders in the country. Several of the chapters explore this group's investment practices. In Chapter 3, Green et al. examine the composition of assets owned at death, paying particular attention to differences between wealth-holders in relation to the size of their estates and their geographical location. Those who perched precariously at the bottom of the wealth-owning hierarchy tended to sink their relatively modest fortunes into real estate whilst those with more to spend spread their investments to encompass shares and other kinds of financial securities. Their analysis, which ranges from the early nineteenth into the twentieth century, concludes that over this period, irrespective of the scale of wealth, individuals were increasingly drawn into a paper money economy of stocks, shares, and other securities, so that the geographical basis of their fortunes grew more extensive.

A further issue in relation to the expansion of shareholding explored by Maltby et al., focuses on whether or not British share ownership became 'democratized'; in other words, did it reach lower down the social hierarchy? They examine the relationships between different occupational groups and shareholding, concluding that despite much higher levels of savings, there was little working-class ownership of shares. Nor was there much evidence of any widening in the social make-up of middle-class shareholders. What little democratization took place from the 1870s depended to a large degree on the kinds of company securities on offer: those with less risk, notably preference shares and debentures, proved more popular for cautious investors and

---

[29] Boyer, G.R. 2004. 'Living standards 1860–1939'. In *The Cambridge Economic History of Modern Britain. Volume II: Economic Maturity, 1860–1939*, edited by R. Floud and P. Johnson. Cambridge: Cambridge University Press, 306.
[30] Ibid.
[31] Burton, D., D. Knights, A. Leyshon, C. Alferoff, and P. Signoretta 2005. 'Consumption denied? The decline of industrial branch insurance'. *Journal of Consumer Culture* 5(2): 181.

individuals with relatively little cash to invest. These more risk-averse groups included a large proportion of women who were attracted to the stock market as a way of supplementing falling incomes from fixed interest securities, noted above, and as a result of changes in their legal status arising from the Married Women's Property Acts of the later nineteenth century.

To speak of the middle class, however, is to raise questions of identity and status and here complexity blurs any simple definitions. The transition from a rural to a predominantly industrialized and urban society was reflected in shifts in the composition of the workforce, notably away from the agricultural sector and into more highly paid industrial, commercial, and service occupations.[32] This process happened fastest and went furthest in Britain, where the emergence of the middle class and their access to political and economic power in the course of the nineteenth century were decisive factors underpinning the new kinds of investment practices that are the focus of this book. Never a unified group, this middle class was comprised of individuals from a diverse range of backgrounds who had varying amounts of disposable wealth to invest and a range of social and economic motives for doing so. It included the wealthy elite who derived their fortunes from land and commerce; well-paid salaried professionals, successful manufacturers, wholesalers, and businessmen; lower ranking 'white collar' employees including clerks, technicians, and school teachers; and independent artisans and small shopkeepers – the *petite bourgeoisie* that occupied the precarious lower tier of the middling ranks.[33]

Despite an increase in the overall size of the middle class and modest opportunities for social mobility, British society remained highly unequal.[34] Indeed, in Western societies as a whole, levels of inequality tended to widen over the course of the nineteenth century, even though rising real incomes affected a growing proportion of the population.[35] Drawing on an analysis of the value of estates at death and earlier research undertaken by Peter Lindert,

---

[32] Boyer, 'Living standards', 291.

[33] There is a huge literature on the 'emergence' of the middle class during this period. For Britain and Continental Europe, see Crossick, G. ed. 1977. *The Lower Middle Class in Britain.* London: Croom Helm; Crossick, G. and H-G. Haupt eds. 1984. *Shopkeepers and Master Artisans in Nineteenth-Century Europe.* London: Methuen; Gunn, S. 2000. *The Public Culture of the Victorian Middle Class: Ritual and Authority in the English Industrial City, 1840–1914.* Manchester: Manchester University Press; Gunn, S. and R. Bell 2002. *Middle Classes: Their Rise and Sprawl.* London: Cassell; Kidd, A. and D. Nicholls eds. 1998. *The Making of the British Middle Class? Studies in Regional and Cultural Diversity since the Eighteenth Century.* Stroud: Sutton; Morris, R.J. 1990. *Class, Sect and Party. The Making of the British Middle Class: Leeds 1820–1850.* Manchester: Manchester University Press; Morris, *Men, Women and Property.* For the United States, see Blumin, S.M. 1989. *The Emergence of the Middle Class: Social Experience in the American City, 1760–1900.* Cambridge: Cambridge University Press.

[34] On the theme social mobility, see Miles, A. 1999. *Social Mobility in Nineteenth and Early Twentieth-Century England.* Basingstoke: Palgrave.

[35] For evidence of the distribution of wealth, see Bourguignon, F. and C. Morrisson 2002. 'Inequality among world citizens, 1820–1992'. *American Economic Review* 92(4): 727–44.

Green et al. demonstrate in Chapter 3 that there were pronounced inequalities in the distribution of wealth *within* the property-owning upper and middle classes in the late nineteenth and early twentieth centuries.[36] They show that the top 1 per cent of the wealth-holding population owned around a quarter of the wealth that passed at death. But middle-class wealth was also distributed in a geographically uneven way. William D. Rubinstein's analysis of income tax data for the 1860s, for example, shows that the middle classes were more numerous and generally wealthier in London compared with other towns and cities. While certain provincial capitals, such as Manchester, Leeds, or Birmingham, were home to modest-sized professional and commercial populations, many manufacturing towns outside the metropolis had comparatively few middle-class inhabitants.[37]

Within the British context, we know rather more about the rich elite than we do about the diverse group of smaller wealth-holders who comprised the large majority of the middle class. The work of Rubinstein and others has been important in uncovering the wealth and investment practices of the former group: the gentlemanly capitalists and landowners who sat at the pinnacle of the wealth hierarchy.[38] In Chapter 2 of this volume, Rubinstein builds on previous research by extending his analysis of the sources and geography of wealth among the very rich into the early twentieth century. His chapter is organized around a comparison of three cohorts of wealth-holders who died leaving probated fortunes of £100,000 or more in 1809–39, 1860–1, and 1906. Alongside evidence from probate records, Rubinstein draws together a range of biographical materials to better understand the identity of these wealth-holders, how they generated their fortunes and the extent to which their wealth enabled their participation in the social and political world of the British elite. In his conclusions, he reiterates some of the key claims of his earlier studies: that Britain's wealthiest inhabitants tended to derive their fortunes from commerce and finance – rather than manufacturing industry – and that London and the southern counties were the principal venues for generating this wealth. However, inclusion of the 1906 cohort in his study causes some modest re-assessment of these claims, since a greater proportion of wealth-holders dying in that year came from provincial towns and cities and

---

[36] Lindert, P. 2000. 'Three centuries of inequality in Britain and America'. In *Handbook of Income Distribution. Volume 1*, edited by A.B. Atkinson and F. Bourguignon. Amsterdam: Elsevier, 167–216.

[37] Rubinstein, W.D. 1977. 'The Victorian middle classes: wealth, occupation and geography'. *Economic History Review* 30(4): 602–23. Rubinstein, W.D. 1988. 'The size and distribution of the English middle classes in 1860'. *Historical Research* 61(144): 65–89; Rubinstein, W.D. 2006. *Men of Property: The Very Wealthy in Britain since the Industrial Revolution*, 2nd edition. London: The Social Affairs Unit.

[38] See *inter alia* Rubinstein, *Men of Property* and Thompson, F.M.L. 2001. *Gentrification and the Enterprise Culture: Britain 1780–1980*. Oxford: Oxford University Press.

made their money in manufacturing, or in other sectors such as food, drink, and tobacco. While finance and commerce remained the single most important source of wealth for this elite group, in relative terms, its significance declined.

Over the period covered by his chapter, Rubinstein identifies a growth in the number and proportion of the individuals who died leaving estates valued at over £100,000. This increase would seem to mirror the growth of other sectors of the British middle class. Research published by the statistician and economist Arthur Bowley has demonstrated that the proportion of non-manual income receivers rose from 16.7 per cent of all income receivers in 1880 to 26.5 per cent at the eve of the First World War in 1913.[39] By 1911, the census reveals that there were more than 1.2 million employers and proprietors (business owners) in England and Wales representing 6.7 per cent of the occupied population. But as Harold Perkin has demonstrated, it was the professional occupations that witnessed the highest rates of growth over the years that straddled the late nineteenth and early twentieth centuries. Analysis of male occupations shows that the numbers of authors and journalists, for example, more than doubled between 1880 and 1911, as did the number of dentists; those engaged in scientific pursuits increased by over 400 per cent, while the number of architects rose by around 60 per cent.[40] Moving further down the social scale, 'white collar' employment opportunities were also increasing. With the emergence of larger and more complex businesses the number of commercial clerks, for example, rose from around 181,000 in 1881 to 478,000 in 1911, reaching 1,279,000 by 1931: a sixfold increase on the 1881 figures.[41] Indeed, for much of the period covered by this book, middle-class professional employment in Britain grew at a faster rate than occupations as a whole, reflecting at least in part the increasing share of the labour force engaged in service activities.[42]

The heterogeneity that was a feature of middle-class occupations translated into a diversity of incomes, experiences, and situations. While by 1905 senior civil servants, successful manufacturers, lawyers, and clergymen might earn between £1000 and £2000 per year (and more in exceptional cases), most clerks got by on just £80 to £150 per annum. But there was variation. Statistics

---

[39] Bowley, A.L. 1920. *The Change in the Distribution of the National Income, 1880–1913.* Oxford: Clarendon Press, 7–8, 13, 22.

[40] Perkin, H. 1989. *The Rise of Professional Society: England since 1880.* London: Routledge, 79–80.

[41] Thomas, M. 2004. 'The service sector'. In *The Cambridge Economic History of Modern Britain. Volume 2: Economic Maturity, 1860–1939*, edited by R. Floud and P. Johnson. Cambridge: Cambridge University Press, 100. PP 1895 LXXX (468), *Return of Number of Males and Females in England and Wales at Censuses 1871, 1881, and 1891 under Occupational Headings*, 8–9.

[42] Thomas, 'The service sector', 99–100.

dating from 1909 on the proportion of clerks liable for income tax reveal that those working in insurance and banking did rather better than those employed by local trades and industries or by railway companies.[43] Moreover, fortunes could and did vary over time and there is a view that from 1870 to 1914 clerks' wages deteriorated as the profession became overstocked.[44]

Inequalities in incomes and wealth shaped both the financial and the social strategies of the middle class. For the professional elites the prospect of entering 'society' and thereby making a transition from the middle to the upper class was an aspiration that money could not always buy – a point underlined by Rubinstein in Chapter 2. Nevertheless, the level and nature of consumption that such a life style demanded, and the patronage that might be required in order to bridge social divides through marriage, required careful financial provision and planning. At the other end of the middling hierarchy, the *petit-bourgeois* small business owners and white collar wage earners occupied a more uncertain position. The livelihoods of this group were more exposed to the vicissitudes of the trade cycle, economic restructuring and technological change, with the consequence that their household income was often little more than that of the skilled working class, even if their social aspirations lay elsewhere. Indeed, their challenge – and one likely shared by the majority of the middle class below the more comfortable world inhabited by the higher professionals, City financiers, and manufacturing magnates – was to cope with the inherent insecurity and anxiety that, R.J. Morris has argued, was a dominant feature of bourgeois experiences in the earlier decades of the nineteenth century.[45] This meant trying to balance income and savings to take account of the uncertainties of life, such as the threat of bankruptcy or effects of ill health, and also the certainty of death, when responsibility for the remaining members of the family passed to others. Keeping appearances up and creditors at bay in good times and bad, and making provision for one's heirs, preoccupied many bourgeois households. As various studies have shown, even professionals – especially new entrants who joined their swelling ranks in the later Victorian years – were plagued by a sense of financial insecurity.[46] Regardless of whether an individual or family was struggling on

---

[43] Perkin, *The Rise*, 78, 98. For further discussion of the salary levels of different professionals, see Routh, G. 1980. *Occupation and Pay in Great Britain, 1906–1979*, 2nd edition. London: Macmillan.

[44] Anderson, G.L. 1976. *Victorian Clerks*. Manchester: Manchester University Press. For a revisionist perspective, see Heller, M. 2008. 'Work, income and stability: the late Victorian and Edwardian London male clerk revisited'. *Business History* 50(3): 253–71.

[45] Morris, *Men, Women and Property*, especially chapter 9. This argument is outlined in Szreter, S. 1996. *Fertility, Class and Gender in Britain, 1860–1940*. Cambridge: Cambridge University Press.

[46] See, for example, Digby, A. 1994. *Making a Medical Living: Doctors and Patients in the English Market for Medicine, 1720–1911*. Cambridge: Cambridge University Press, especially chapter 5.

a modest income at the bottom of the middling scale or on lavish income at the top, it seems that the need to balance credit and debt and not to let expenditure run too far ahead of income were familiar and often pressing concerns.

INVESTMENT: OPPORTUNITIES, INSTITUTIONS, AND INFRASTRUCTURES

In the second half of the nineteenth century, a period when, as Ranald Michie points out in Chapter 7, the 'individual investor reigned supreme', there were important institutional changes and infrastructural improvements that encouraged men and women to invest their money in real estate, company shares, and other forms of financial assets. Indeed, as Douglass North and other economists have recently emphasized, institutional changes are often critical in normalizing certain kinds of economic behaviour, reducing risk and uncertainty, and diminishing transaction costs, and as such they are arguably no less important an impetus for encouraging investment than the opportunities afforded by the course of economic growth itself.[47]

Changes to the ways that real estate, government securities, and shares of various types could be purchased helped to encourage a wider range of individuals to invest in these kinds of assets. In the case of real estate, the formation of permanent building societies from mid-century, which offered relatively attractive savings rates, also helped provide capital for mortgage lending. The Building Societies Act of 1874 laid the basis on which sound mortgage lending could operate and although isolated failures took place and amendments to the legal framework occurred, the system of borrowing and saving remained intact until relatively recently. As a result even those with fairly modest amounts of capital were able to purchase property.[48] Cheap advice books aimed at a popular audience, such as that published by Francis Cross, *Hints to all about how to Rent, Buy or Build House Property* (1854) and James Bishop, *The English Laws of Landlords, Tenants and Lodgers*, issued at a cost of 6d in 1858 and which ran to over 40 editions, offered specific guidance to those individuals intending to purchase housing for the purpose of generating rental income.[49] Nor was such activity confined to the middle class:

[47] See, for example. North, D.C. 1990. *Institutions, Institutional Change and Economic Performance*. Cambridge: Cambridge University Press.

[48] See Pooley, C. and M. Harmer 1999. *Property Ownership in Britain c.1850–1950: The Role of the Bradford Equitable Building Society and the Bingley Building Society in the Development of Homeownership*. Cambridge: Granta.

[49] Cross, F. 1854. *Hints to all About How to Rent, Buy or Build House Property*. London: Nelson; Bishop, J. 1858. *The English Laws of Landlords, Tenants and Lodgers*. London: Effingham Wilson.

in 1875, Samuel Smiles remarked approvingly that building societies in Leeds and elsewhere had allowed the working class to purchase houses for rent as a form of investing their savings.[50]

The other main focus of investment, and arguably of greater importance for a wider variety of individuals, was the purchase of company shares and this in turn rested on various institutional frameworks and infrastructural improvements without which it would have been impossible to mobilize savings. Here the reform of company law was significant in enticing purchasers into the market. A swathe of legislation enacted from the 1850s offered investors greater protection by establishing the concept of limited liability and thereby reducing their exposure to debt in the event of a company's failure. This promoted greater confidence in financial markets and became a critical factor in the dramatic expansion in the take-up of new security issues in the latter decades of the nineteenth century.[51]

In the banking sector, reforms instituted by mid-century helped to create stability in the system and facilitated the national integration of the capital market.[52] However, banks were slow to move to the limited liability regime that had been increasingly adopted by other companies from 1856, and even after the move, many used reserve liability and uncalled capital, which offered protection for depositors but created higher risks for shareholders. Why were bank shares nevertheless popular, and not only with the 'reckless'? This is a question posed by Graeme Acheson and John Turner in their chapter examining shareholding in a sample of 23 banks operating in the United Kingdom in the mid- to late nineteenth century. In spite of the risks associated with investment in joint stock banks, where the shareholders faced unlimited liability, they show that many individuals were perfectly willing to invest their capital in such ventures, including those groups who have frequently been regarded as 'risk-averse', such as women. Females, for example, constituted 31.6 per cent of the average shareholder constituency in their sample of joint stock banks for 1870. Acheson and Turner's conclusion is that these groups were attracted by the potentially high rate of return – the 'risk premium' offered by banks. Indeed, despite the occasional failures, such as that of the Glasgow Bank discussed in their chapter, banks generally proved to be relatively profitable investments in their own right, often yielding dividends in excess of many other kinds of domestic concerns.[53]

---

[50] Smiles, S. 1875. *Thrift*. London: John Murray, 44, 109.

[51] See Cottrell, 'Domestic finance' and Cottrell, P.L. 1980. *Industrial Finance, 1830–1914: The Finance and Organization of English Manufacturing Industry*. London: Methuen.

[52] See Black, I.S. 1995. 'Money, information and space: banking in early-nineteenth-century England and Wales'. *Journal of Historical Geography* 21(4): 398–412.

[53] For further discussion of investment in nineteenth-century banks, see Acheson, G.G. and J.D. Turner 2011. 'Investor behaviour in a nascent capital market: Scottish bank shareholders in the nineteenth century'. *Economic History Review* 64(1): 188–213.

The reform of company law from the 1850s, which introduced limited liability, widened the potential pool of investors to include those with less money and less experience, a process that was further encouraged by changes in the size of share denominations and types of shares available to purchasers. From the last quarter of the century onwards, the nominal value of shares fell, and there was a reduction in the popularity of part-paid capital. The financial panic of 1866 resulted in an epidemic of calls being made on part-paid shares, which caused difficulties for large and small investors alike. As a result, the 1867 Companies Act permitted companies to reduce their share capital by cutting nominal values or cancelling the unpaid part of partly called shares, setting off the slow and uneven movement towards lower nominal values. This continued through the century and beyond, until by 1900 the £1 share was the norm, with a movement towards 'shilling shares' by the 1920s.[54] At the same time, as Michie and Maltby et al. discuss in their chapters, there was a shift away from ordinary shares towards safer, if less profitable, preference shares, debentures, and other fixed-interest securities.[55] Preference shares were popular with company directors as well as investors. For more risk-averse investors, including women, they offered rates of return that were lower than ordinary shares but with the virtue of being guaranteed. However, because preference shares generally carried no voting rights, they were also attractive to company founders who could therefore expand their financing without diluting control.

The relationship between share type and corporate governance is a key element of Leslie Hannah's chapter in this book. He argues that company directors avoided giving power to shareholders by exercising the London Stock Exchange rule that required that two-thirds of any class of shares that were being issued should be outside board control. However, ordinary shares were often kept unlisted whilst issues on the Stock Exchange were of preference shares with limited or no voting rights, along with debenture stock. In this way, the shareholder base could be widened but control remained firmly in the hands of directors and major shareholders. Furthermore, as Brian Cheffins has recently pointed out, that process could be reinforced as United Kingdom company founders and major shareholders returned later to the market to buy more shares.[56] A potential outcome of the widening shareholder base was the

---

[54] See Jefferys, J.B. 1938. 'Trends in business organisation in Great Britain since 1856, with special reference to the financial structure of companies, the mechanism of investment and the relationship between the shareholder and the company'. Unpublished PhD Thesis, University of London, 161; and Hannah, L. 2007. 'The "Divorce" of ownership from control from 1900 onwards: re-calibrating imagined global trends'. *Business History* 49(4): 407.

[55] Essex-Crosby, A. 1938. 'Joint stock companies in Great Britain 1890–1930'. Unpublished M.Comm. Thesis, University of London, 31, 60.

[56] Cheffins, B. 2008. *Corporate Ownership and Control: British Business Transformed*. Oxford: Oxford University Press, 230.

growing likelihood of hostile takeover bids, but as Hannah argues, the use of
preference rather than ordinary shares for raising capital, together with the
dearth of good financial information on companies, and a general unwillingness
to challenge incumbent boards, helps to explain the lack of such takeover bids
until the later twentieth century.

Changes in the institutional framework within which the purchase of
company shares took place were accompanied by important infrastructural
improvements that made investment in distant enterprises both more likely
and less risky. Significant technological innovations from the mid-nineteenth
century enabled national and international integration of share and bond
prices and widened the potential geographical scope for investments. The
introduction of the telegraph in 1844 in Britain, the first undersea cable
between France and England in 1851, the replacement of pencils and paper
with the stock ticker (initially in the United States, but later elsewhere), the
opening of a transatlantic telegraph service in 1866, and the establishment of a
similar link between Britain and India in 1870 allowed the rapid transmission
of information, creating what geographers have termed 'time-space compres-
sion'.[57] At the start of the nineteenth century, it could take anything up to half
a year for news to travel across the world but by the end it took less than a
day.[58] Further integration of prices was also made possible by the expansion of
provincial stock exchanges which were particularly important for tapping into
local reservoirs of capital – a major source of funding for regionally based
domestic industry.[59] The result was the growing integration of stock market
prices both within and between national economies and the ability to respond
quickly to the impact on investment opportunities of events that might have
taken place a considerable distance away.

Certain cities became important centres for finance, channelling investment
into different activities and to different parts of the world. In Chapter 11,
Cassis examines the role of London as the world's leading financial centre
of the period. The quantitative and qualitative supremacy of the City of
London between 1870 and 1914 stemmed from the range and maturity of
the services that it offered, notably merchant banking, insurance, and a variety
of professional and information services. There were, for example, around 700
accountancy and 2000 law firms operating in the City in 1891. By 1913, the
nominal value of securities traded upon the London Stock Exchange stood at

---

[57] See Harvey, D. 1989. *The Condition of Postmodernity: An Enquiry into the Origins of
Cultural Change*. Oxford: Basil Blackwell, 240. For further discussion of some of the technologies
that underpinned emerging financial markets, see Preda, A. 2009. *Framing Finance: The Boundaries of Markets and Modern Capitalism*. Chicago, IL: University of Chicago Press, especially
chapters 4 and 5.
[58] Clark, *A Farewell to Alms*, 307.
[59] Killick and Thomas, 'The provincial stock exchanges'.

£11.3 billion – more than the New York Stock Exchange and the Paris Bourse combined. Indeed, as Cassis demonstrates, London was truly a global centre of finance: by 1914 one-third of all negotiable instruments in the world were quoted on its Stock Exchange. To the British investor, the range and sophistication of financial products and services that were available in the City were unparalleled. One particular innovation singled out by Cassis is the creation in the 1870s of the investment trust. Their growth continued in the 1880s until being temporarily halted by the Barings' crisis in 1890 and resumed in the first decade of the twentieth century. Investment trusts enabled the small investor to spread risk by buying into what was in effect a portfolio of shares and securities. By performing this kind of specialist function, London and to a lesser extent other cities such as Paris, Amsterdam, and New York – the last of which, by the 1920s, increasingly challenged the City's international pre-eminence – became lynchpins in the circulation of global capital, mediating between areas of surplus and deficit.

Infrastructural improvements were also immensely important in opening up areas for capitalist expansion and in reducing the turnover time of capital. The rapid growth of transport networks greatly improved the capacity to move both people and goods cheaply over long distances, thereby allowing the geographical expansion of capitalism into areas that hitherto had been peripheral to economic growth in the West. Capital investment from Britain and elsewhere underpinned the construction of the railway network in North and South America, and within the British Empire. By the 1870s the British railway network had been more or less completed, at which point railway construction switched overseas, notably to India. Private investors in Indian railways were guaranteed a 5 per cent return by the British government, at a time when similar investments in the United Kingdom were lucky to achieve 3 per cent. Under such favourable conditions, capital investment in Indian railways grew significantly and by 1910 the system in India had surpassed that in Britain. While the construction of railways offered new financial opportunities to investors, it was their role in fostering the economic expansion of the areas that they served that was of greatest significance in opening up possibilities for overseas investment. Improvements in shipping and refrigeration, in turn further encouraged the spread and profitability of agriculture throughout these new hinterlands.

Such changes were paralleled by the easier availability of financial information and professional expertise both at home and abroad. Investors could draw on a range of financial advice in making their decisions. For the affluent, as Michie notes in Chapter 7, there were increasing numbers of investment brokers, in both London and the provinces. There was also a growing role to be played by other professionals – both solicitors and, increasingly, accountants – as advisors and as mediators between companies and their (often disgruntled) shareholders.[60] The supply of financial information offered by professional services, in the form of investment advice, was complemented by the development of financial journalism. The nineteenth century saw the introduction of a range of financial guides and manuals as well as newspapers and journals. Six specialist publications were launched between 1876 and 1884, and a further 20 between 1880 and 1900.[61] Michie's chapter draws upon a number of these widely read periodicals: *The Investor's Monthly Manual*, *The Stock Exchange Review*, and *The 'Money-Maker' Manuals for Investors*. Their role was to complement the information offered by professional advisors, but also to act as a substitute for it, especially for those outside the traditional investor groups who were beginning to diversify their investments from cash and property into securities. Alex Preda has recently argued that in the second half of the nineteenth century 'a visible shift occurs in the vocabulary, literary genres, and the cognitive tools used to represent financial markets, as well as definitions of its object and actors'.[62] He emphasizes the way that financial knowledge was increasingly seen and presented as a science that had to be mastered by investors or their professional representatives in order to engage with markets and institutions. Certain kinds of financial information came to matter more than others, especially price trends, while manuals and guidebooks sought to distil the rules by which financial markets worked and investors should behave. These calculative and scientific discourses that were increasingly associated with finance were important in legitimating investment as a socially and professionally respectable activity, displacing eighteenth-century ideas that linked it more to speculation and gambling.[63]

But while investor manuals increasingly took on the language of rational calculation, Michie's contribution to this book emphasizes the way that novels continued to portray investment as a headlong risk and investors as naïve fools or greedy gamblers. His chapter explores this literature in order to trace changing public attitudes to investment from the mid-nineteenth century until the First World War. While his use of fiction in this way – as a barometer public opinion – is open to challenge, it leads him to conclude that there was little public sympathy for investors as they attempted to navigate the risks and temptations of financial markets. Not until the rapid increase in the investor

---

[60] See Maltby, J. 1999. '"A Sort of Guide, Philosopher and Friend": the rise of the professional auditor in Britain'. *Accounting, Business and Financial History* 9(1): 29–50 for an outline of the developing role of the auditor as advisor and mediator; and Maltby, J. 2000. 'Was the 1947 Companies Act a response to a national crisis?' *Accounting History* 5(2): 31–60 on the slow development of legislation. See also Rutterford, J. 2006. 'The world was their oyster: international diversification pre-World War I'. In *Financial Strategy: Adding Stakeholder Value*, 2nd edition, edited by J. Rutterford, M. Upton, and D. Kodwani. Chichester: John Wiley, 5–24.

[61] See Vissink, H.G.A. 1985. *Economic and Financial Reporting in England and the Netherlands*. Assen and Maastricht: Van Gorcum.

[62] Preda, *Framing the Market*, 88.

[63] Ibid., chapter 3.

population as a consequence of heavy government borrowing during the First World War, does Michie detect a shift in attitudes and, as a consequence, more direct legislative intervention to protect individuals from the kind of abuses chronicled in Victorian and Edwardian literature.

The financial thrillers of the later nineteenth century did not deter potential shareholders: they fed into a new culture of investment that Preda describes elsewhere as comprising a 'myriad of gossips'.[64] Indeed, following an approach rather different from Michie's, a range of other scholars have sought to investigate the way finance and the calculative rhetorics of exchange infused literary and other cultures in the nineteenth century. The project of such scholars has been defined broadly and ambitiously as an attempt to outline the 'culture of investment' that permeated every level of society in Victorian Britain.[65] In particularly influential work, Mary Poovey, for example, has drawn attention to the way that financial journalism and realist novels were drawn into a 'relationship of general proximity'.[66] Financial journalists drew upon literary forms and conventions, while many novelists – as Michie's chapter in this volume amply illustrates – became preoccupied by financial themes. These crossovers brought the seemingly unrelated worlds of finance and literary culture together, normalizing and naturalizing the operations of the financial world within the minds of the British public and making 'the allure of investment vivid'.[67] As finance became embedded in fictional narratives, so too it was absorbed into the personal narratives of individual lives and families.

DEMOGRAPHY AND DEPENDENCY: GENDER AND INVESTMENT OVER THE LIFE COURSE

In addition to the broader macro-economic factors associated with economic growth, geographical expansion, institutional innovations, and infrastructural

---

[64] Preda, A. 2001. 'The rise of the popular investor: financial knowledge and investing in England and France 1840–1880'. *Sociological Quaterly* 42(2): 228.

[65] See, especially, Henry, N. and C. Schmitt eds. 2009. *Victorian Investments: New Perspectives on Finance and Culture*. Bloomington and Indianapolis, IN: Indiana University Press; Poovey, M. 2008. *Genres of the Credit Economy: Mediating Value in Eighteenth and Nineteenth-Century Britain*. Chicago, IL: University of Chicago Press; Poovey, M. ed. 2002. *The Financial System in Nineteenth-Century Britain*. Oxford: Oxford University Press; and O'Gorman, F. ed. 2007. *Victorian Literature and Finance*. Oxford: Oxford University Press.

[66] Poovey, M. 2009. 'Writing about finance in Victorian England: disclosure and secrecy in the culture of investment'. In *Victorian Investments: New Perspectives on Finance and Culture*, edited by N. Henry and C. Schmitt. Bloomington and Indianapolis, IN: Indiana University Press, 39–57.

[67] Ibid., 40.

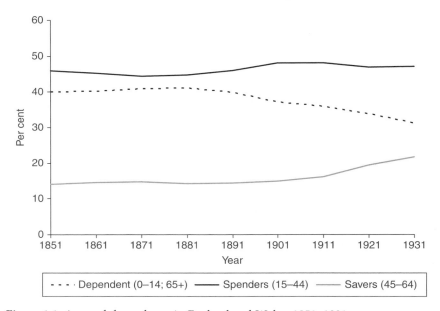

Figure 1.1 Age and dependency in England and Wales, 1851–1931

Source: Mitchell, B.R. and P. Deane 1962. *Abstract of British Historical Statistics.* Cambridge: Cambridge University Press, 12.

improvements – all of which influenced patterns of investment in the United Kingdom and abroad – we must also consider the effects of demographic processes relating to changing family size and life expectancy, and cultural shifts associated with new attitudes towards consumption. These processes – often neglected in accounts of investment in the period covered by this book – are important in understanding the demand for new financial products.

The overall capacity to save depends to some extent on the age structure and dependency ratio of a population. Improvements in longevity, falling dependency ratios, and continued economic growth – characteristics of the United Kingdom over the late nineteenth and earlier twentieth centuries – all have an impact on the overall rate of savings.[68] As Figure 1.1 shows, in England and Wales from the 1890s, the proportion of the dependent age groups – those aged 14 or younger and 65 or older – fell continuously whilst the share of the population in the prime savings age group, aged 45–64 years

---

[68] See Bloom, D., D. Canning, and B. Graham 2003. 'Longevity and life-cycle savings'. *Scandinavian Journal of Economics* 105(3): 319–38. Comparative figures for other countries can be found in Williamson, 'Growth, distribution and demography', 264.

old, rose.[69] Under such circumstances, savings rates are likely to have risen for the population as a whole.

Arguably, the most significant demographic shift likely to impact on patterns of investment was the dramatic fertility decline that began in the second half of the nineteenth century. Within Britain as a whole the number of live births per married woman fell from an average of six in 1860 to just over two in 1940.[70] This decline is in part explained by lower rates of nuptiality, especially amongst the higher social classes, as well as by lower marital fertility.[71] While often presented as a unitary, national process – one paralleled in many other European countries – more recent research has shown that the British fertility decline varied considerably depending on social class and geographical location.[72] It was more evident for all classes in better-off areas than in poorer places. In other words, wherever the middle class congregated, so fertility and nuptiality tended to decline.

Changing social aspirations and the desire for higher living standards among the middle class are often put forward as core reasons for the fertility decline in later nineteenth-century Britain.[73] In his seminal study of middle-class family planning, Joseph Banks argued that declining middle-class family sizes could be explained by new attitudes to consumption and an eagerness to maintain certain standards of living in order to cement the social status of current family members and that of future generations.[74] This required domestic consumption on an unprecedented scale in order that the family could acquire the material trappings of gentility. As Simon Szreter has pointed out, this was especially important for those engaged in professional service work where identity, reputation, and ultimately economic success depended on visual displays of wealth and status, including an address in a respectable area.[75] None of this came cheap, and obtaining the means by which these displays were achieved was a constant source of concern for those who aspired to gentility. Moreover, expressions of status ranged beyond the bourgeois

[69] Edelstein, 'Foreign investment', 201. For a discussion of age, debt, and capital accumulation, see Green D.R., A. Owens, J. Maltby, and J. Rutterford 2009. 'Lives in the balance? Gender, age and assets in late-nineteenth-century England and Wales'. *Continuity and Change* 24(2): 307–35. It is acknowledged that using age as a proxy for dependency takes no account of those who continued working beyond the age of 65.

[70] Szreter, *Fertility, Class and Gender*, 1.

[71] Ibid., 469.

[72] Ibid. See also Garrett, E., A. Reid, K. Schurer, and S. Szreter 2001. *Changing Family Size in England and Wales: Place, Class and Demography, 1891–1911*. Cambridge: Cambridge University Press.

[73] Baines, D. and R. Woods 2004. 'Population and regional development'. In *The Cambridge Economic History of Modern Britain, Volume II: Economic Maturity, 1860–1939*, edited by R. Floud and P. Johnson. Cambridge: Cambridge University Press, 31.

[74] Banks, J.A. 1954. *Prosperity and Parenthood: A Study of Family Planning Among the Victorian Middle Classes*. London: Routedge and Kegan Paul.

[75] Szreter, *Fertility, Class and Gender*, 472–4.

home. As Simon Gunn has shown in his study of the provincial middle class, a public commitment to promoting civic virtue through patronage of the arts and sciences necessitated amassing the means by which to make this possible.[76]

In many bourgeois households, saving and investing for the future started early in life. Maintaining a middle-class social position involved a significant investment in the education of children so that they too might one day attain a high-ranking professional occupation or, especially in the case of daughters, marry into the right social circle. As a result, children tended to remain in education for longer: in England and Wales the school leaving age was raised gradually from 10 in 1870 to 14 by 1918. The time spent in education rose accordingly from 4.21 years for male workers in 1870 to 6.75 by 1911 and 8.14 by 1931.[77] The growth of competitive entry to many occupations and the spread of professional qualifications meant this period of schooling was often augmented by additional years of education in one of the institutions of learning that were beginning to spring up in the late nineteenth and early twentieth centuries, including colleges and technical institutes. This invest-ment in human capital was a key reason for the decline in fertility rates among professional middle-class families, who in many cases could not afford large numbers of dependants. As a consequence, they married later (allowing more time to accumulate wealth in preparation for family formation) and limited fertility within marriage (enabling costs to be contained). Szreter suggests that white-collar employees behaved in a similar fashion, in part because they too were sucked into a culture of conspicuous consumption, but also because of the greater financial marginality of their occupational and social positions.[78] For both groups, financial prudence and sexual abstinence, therefore, went hand-in-hand.

The impact of changes in family size and life expectancy discussed above, however, also had an effect on financial planning for old age. Life expectancy rose in England from around 41 years at the middle of the nineteenth century to nearly 51 years by the 1900s and nearly 61 by the 1930s.[79] Although much of this improvement was driven by changes in infant mortality brought about by sanitary improvements in poorer urban areas, nevertheless all classes benefited. An important consequence of this demographic transition, was

[76] Gunn, *The Public Culture*. On these themes, see also Kidd, A. and D. Nicholls eds. 1999. *Gender, Civic Culture and Consumerism: Middle-Class Identity in Britain, 1800–1940*. Manchester: Manchester University Press.

[77] Broadberry, S. 2004. 'Human capital and skills'. In *The Cambridge Economic History of Modern Britain. Volume II: Economic Maturity, 1860–1939*, edited by R. Floud and P. Johnson. Cambridge: Cambridge University Press, 61.

[78] Szreter, *Fertility, Class and Gender*, 478.

[79] Office for National Statistics 2002. *Decennial Life Tables – English Life Tables: Series DS*. http://www.statistics.gov.uk/STATBASE/Product.asp?vlnk=333 (site accessed 15 June 2010).

that the burden of dependency was – at least at the macro level – rebalanced, away from the young and towards the old: fewer children cost less but increased longevity cost more. Either it was necessary to work into old age, supporting oneself and often with an eye to amassing as much capital as possible to pass on to children as an inheritance, or an individual could withdraw from work and begin to consume the family's accumulated wealth by living off savings and investments. Fewer children, and the need for them to accumulate savings during their own lifetime, further limited the range of support that could be offered to ageing parents by their offspring.

For ageing members of the middle class, the most likely source of support was therefore their own efforts. Paul Johnson has shown how the growth of retirement in England and Wales over the late nineteenth and twentieth centuries varied by occupational sector. Better-paid jobs and those which came with access to pension schemes unsurprisingly had higher numbers of retirees.[80] However, until the second decade of the twentieth century, pensions were a relatively unusual mechanism by which individuals (and their employers) could invest for old age. According to Les Hannah until the twentieth century 'for the mass of workers . . . staying on the job was the normal accepted practice in old age until incapacity intervened to force retirement'.[81] In 1881, almost three-quarters of males aged 65 and over were still in work; by 1931 the proportion had fallen to around 50 per cent (though the number of people aged 65 and older more than doubled during these years and shifted from 4.6 to 7.4 per cent of the population).[82] Hannah estimates that formally constituted public and private pension schemes contained at most a million members in 1905, amounting to around 5 per cent of the work force.[83] This would have included several groups of professional and white-collar salaried workers, such as railway clerks, banking employees, and civil servants.[84] However, Hannah additionally argues that, consistent with the pervasive bourgeois ideology of self-help, for the bulk of the middle class, financial provision in old age was regarded as a matter of personal and familial responsibility.[85]

The process of accumulating assets prior to old age in order to support a prolonged period of retirement has certainly been recognized as an important

[80] Johnson, P. 1994. 'The employment and retirement of older men in England and Wales, 1881–1991'. *Economic History Review* 47(1): 106–28.

[81] Hannah, L. 1986. *Inventing Retirement: The Development of Occupational Pensions in Britain.* Cambridge: Cambridge University Press, 7.

[82] Ibid., 123. Demographic data are taken from Mitchell and Deane, *Abstract of British Historical Statistics*, 12.

[83] Hannah, *Inventing Retirement*, 13.

[84] For a discussion of the development of middle-class pensions, see Thane, P. 2000. *Old Age in English History: Past Experiences, Present Issues.* Oxford: Oxford University Press, chapter 12.

[85] Hannah, *Inventing Retirement*, 13.

strategy of middle-ranking families. This 'life cycle' savings pattern is at the heart of Morris' model of the middle-class property cycle.[86] It describes a process whereby middle-class males in the early phases of adult life seek to accumulate property through borrowing. This is followed by a later, mid-life phase where debts are gradually eliminated but capital continues to be accumulated through investment. In old age, Morris posits a switch from active to passive forms of income generation, with middle-class men withdrawing from business to live off investments that offered a safe return, typically *rentier* style assets such as annuities. His model is based on the experiences of several industrialists active in mid nineteenth-century Leeds and therefore may not apply to the full range of middle-class individuals or to the later time frame covered by this book. However, recent research examining the relationship between age and property ownership in the latter years of the nineteenth century, based upon a larger number and much broader spectrum of wealth-holders (including both professionals and white-collar wage earners) finds evidence of a similar switch to shares and other securities – notably government annuities – as individuals age.[87] This 'capital of old age', as Morris calls it, underpinned the market for government bonds and fuelled the increasing demand for other securities that were low risk and offered guaranteed returns, such as railway debentures and preference shares.[88] These latter types of securities closely resembled Consols in offering a guaranteed, fixed-interest return and therefore attracted considerable demand from risk-averse investors seeking security of income and a trouble-free old age. They grew in importance in the later nineteenth and early twentieth centuries after the yield on government securities fell.[89]

Mary Beth Combs' chapter in this book examines the investment strategies of one important stratum of the British middle class: shopkeepers. Questioning the motives why such individuals sought to accumulate wealth, she explores whether either of the key alternatives to the life-cycle approach to wealth accumulation was prevalent among this group: the bequest strategy (where wealth is accumulated throughout the entire life course to pass on to the next generation) or the deferred-compensation strategy (where children contribute unpaid labour to the family or business in expectation of financial compensation at a later date). The study is based upon analysis of a systematic sample of 997 death duty accounts of shopkeepers who died between 1859 and 1891. Interestingly, she finds that her petit-bourgeois group did not follow the same strategy as the wealthier northern industrialists studied by Morris,

---

[86] Morris, *Men, Women and Property*, chapter 4; Morris, R.J. 1979. 'The middle class and the property cycle during the industrial revolution'. In *The Search for Wealth and Stability: Essays in Honour of M.W. Flinn*, edited by T.C. Smout. London: Macmillan, 91–113.

[87] Green, et al. 'Lives in the balance?'

[88] Morris, *Men, Women and Property*, 172–3. See also Hannah, *Inventing Retirement*, 4–5.

[89] Cottrell, 'Domestic finance', 267–8.

concluding that late nineteenth-century shopkeepers favoured an altruistic bequest motive for saving. This finding might reflect the fact that those within the lower echelons of the middle class were forced to carry on working (and hence accumulating) to ensure their own financial security as well as that of the next generation. However, the motive of inheritance and the actual mechanisms through which inheritances were provided – often via the bequest of annuities or a *rentier* style investment income – are further indicators of how middle-class life courses placed particular kinds of demands on financial markets.

Demography also had a role to play in explaining the growing significance of women in the ownership of wealth in Britain. There is a fast-growing literature on female investors in the eighteenth, nineteenth, and twentieth centuries which seeks to understand not only their relative importance in different financial markets, but also their motives for investment.[90] A further demographic phenomenon is important here: the excess of females over males, or what contemporaries termed the 'surplus woman problem'. In the mid-nineteenth century there was social and moral panic about an increasingly visible imbalance between the sexes. The 1851 census notes that there were 500,000 more women living in Britain than men. In London in that year, females above the age of 25 exceeded males by over 104,000.[91] In many other towns and cities women appeared to outnumber men significantly. This prompted concerns that too many women would be forced to remain single without a husband to provide them with financial and other support. This discourse of female dependency was common both to working-class male breadwinner cultures and to bourgeois ideals of gendered separate spheres. It was, however, middle-class women who became the focus of anxiety. Writers such as William Greg feared for these women because of the ideological difficulties they faced in independently supporting themselves: work – save for a limited number of professions such as those of governess or teacher – was regarded as something that might compromise their gentility.[92] His solution

---

[90] See Rutterford, J. and J. Maltby 2006. '"The widow, the clergyman and the reckless": women investors in England, 1830–1914'. *Feminist Economics* 12(1/2): 111–38; Maltby, J. and J. Rutterford 2006. '"She possessed her own fortune": women investors from the late nineteenth century to the early twentieth century'. *Business History* 48(2): 220–53. Laurence, E.A., J. Maltby, and J. Rutterford eds. 2009. *Women and Their Money 1700–1950: Essays on Women and Finance*. Abingdon: Routledge; Rutterford, J., D.R. Green, J. Maltby, and A. Owens 2011. 'Who comprised the nation of shareholders? Gender and investment in Britain, 1870–1935'. *Economic History Review* 64(1): 157–87; Maltby, J. and J. Rutterford eds. 2006. 'Women, accounting and investment'. (Special Issue) *Accounting, Business and Financial History* 16(1); Doe, H. 2009. *Enterprising Women and Shipping in the Nineteenth Century*. Woodbridge: Boydell and Brewer; Doe, H. 2010. 'Waiting for her ship to come in: the female investor in nineteenth-century shipping'. *Economic History Review* 63(1): 85–106.

[91] Green and Owens, 'Gentlewomanly capitalism', 513.

[92] Levitan, K. 2008. 'Redundancy, the "surplus woman" problem, and the British Census, 1851–1861'. *Women's History Review* 17(3): 359–76. See also Worsnop, J. 1990. 'A re-evaluation

was that such women should emigrate to the colonies where there were often sex imbalances of the opposite kind and where it was recognized that there might be new opportunities for financial independence – a further example of how the empire was seen as offering a safety value to relieve economic and financial pressures in Britain. Although the controversy of the 'surplus woman problem' died down after a flurry of debate in the 1850s, census evidence reveals that the differential between men and women continued to be an important characteristic of the country's demographic regime and one that was accentuated in towns and cities for the remainder of the century. This left a situation where, in spite of ideological constraints, middle-class women had to support themselves. For those with sufficient wealth, investment in shares and other securities offered one means of doing this without having to compromise their status by entering the world of work. In such instances, the search for safe and reliable investments was a priority – itself a product of gendered ways of thinking about investment and risk – with the result that women became significant consumers of low-risk investment products such as government securities, debentures, and preference shares.[93]

Further developments placed women – especially middle-class women – as key players in investment markets. A growing body of scholarship is revealing how, contrary to ideological prescription, women were active as successful entrepreneurs, business owners, and professionals.[94] In 1911, for example, women formed around a fifth of the employers and business proprietors and of managers and administrators.[95] This opening up of economic opportunities for women was a slow process, but in terms of the capacity of females of all backgrounds to engage more actively with financial markets the passing of the Married Women's Property Acts in 1870 and 1882 offered – at least in theory – economic freedom to married women who previously had not been empowered to undertake independent financial transactions. Work by Mary Beth Combs has demonstrated how passage of the 1870 Act led to women taking control of a greater share of household resources, opening up at least the potential for greater engagement with financial markets.[96] The twentieth

---

of "the problem of surplus women" in nineteenth-century England: the case of the 1851 census'. *Women's Studies International Forum* 13(1/2): 21–31.

[93] Green and Owens, 'Gentlewomanly capitalism'; Maltby and Rutterford, 'The widow, the clergyman'. On women and attitudes to risk see Rutterford, J. and J. Maltby 2007. '"The nesting instinct": women investors and risk in England, 1700–1930'. *Accounting History* 12(3): 305–27.

[94] See, for example, Kay, A.C. 2009. *The Foundations of Female Entrepreneurship: Enterprise, Home and Household, London c.1800–1870*. Abingdon: Routledge.

[95] Perkin, *The Rise*, 79.

[96] Combs, M.B. 2004. 'Wives and household wealth: the impact of the 1870 British Married Women's Property Act on wealth-holding and share of household resources'. *Continuity and Change* 19(1): 141–63; Combs, M.B. 2005. 'A measure of legal independence: the 1870 Married Women's Property Act and the wealth-holding patterns of British wives'. *Journal of Economic History* 65(4): 1028–57; and Combs, M.B 2006. '*Cui Bono?*: The 1870 British Married Women's

century saw further developments that promoted the economic independence of females, not least their entry into the labour market during the First World War.

The growing significance of women as investors and as wealth owners in their own right was not confined to Britain, as the chapters on Canada and Australia by di Matteo and Shanahan make clear. In both places, legal changes in married women's property rights that paralleled those in Britain played a part in encouraging female wealth-holding, although differences in the nature of their economies meant that the balance of assets varied. In Ontario, di Matteo notes that over time the gap between male and female wealth declined so that by the 1920s, women's probated wealth was between 60 and 70 per cent of men's, compared to between 10 and 15 per cent in the 1870s and 1880s. Such wealth, he notes, was disproportionately invested in financial assets rather than in land, a situation that he ascribes to the fact that fewer women were involved in farming. In this respect, expanding investment opportunities clearly had a gendered dimension that allowed women to increase their share of wealth relative to men. In South Australia, there was a greater emphasis on the ownership of land and the overall gains for women were less clear, although the trend towards greater equality with men was nonetheless the same. Shanahan shows that women's wealth at death rose from approximately a quarter of that of men's in the 1870s and early 1880s to between a third and a half from the mid-1880s onwards. By 1915, women comprised nearly half of all those whose estates were submitted for probate, and the average value of their estates was close to half those for men. Such findings are a useful reminder that the processes of change by which men and women engaged with the financial markets were international in scope, driven by structural economic factors, mediated by parallel processes of institutional change and ideological shifts in gender relations.

CONCLUSIONS: MEN, WOMEN, AND MONEY

Any analysis of the relationships between men, women, and money must cast its net widely and the chapters contained in this book reflect that belief. As we have argued here, macro-economic conditions helped shape the opportunities for investment but changes in demography, consumption, ideology, and institutional frameworks each played a part in influencing individual investment choices. In Britain, changes in demographic structure made it more likely that savings would be generated at the same time as individual provision

Property Act, bargaining power, and the distribution of resources within marriage'. *Feminist Economics* 12(1/2): 51–83.

for old age became more necessary and more widely accepted. The legal frameworks, technological systems, and institutional arrangements through which money was directed into investment shifted accordingly, making it easier for growing numbers of individuals to invest their savings in different kinds of securities and other forms of property. The characteristics of these individuals altered over the period as new groups of investors, notably women and those lower down the economic hierarchy, began to engage with the financial markets. Gender, in particular, was a key factor in understanding how the composition and growth of the investing population changed over the years covered by the contributions to this book.

However, that transformation was not confined to Britain alone, as the chapters that relate to Canada and Australia make clear. Regional differences in these places were accompanied by common forms of legal emancipation for women that together resulted in improvements in their economic status. As this introduction has argued, such an international dimension is by no means a geographical luxury in what is primarily a domestic story. Rather, the relationships between the *metropole* and colony – between an industrial and commercial economy in which investment in shares and financial assets became paramount, and an agricultural frontier many thousands of miles distant in which land ownership was pre-eminent – are crucial to understanding the specificity of investment practices and wealth-holding in each place. The timing of the changes in relationships between men, women, and money may have differed but the parallels and connections were nevertheless clear. In that sense, John Galsworthy's view, noted at the start of this introduction, that the possessive instinct was always on the move, was as true in relation to geography as it was in relation to gender. Tracking that movement, understanding how the nation of shareholders was transformed and the processes by which that took place, in the United Kingdom as well as further afield, are the pivots around which the chapters in this book revolve.

2

The Wealth Structure of Britain in 1809–39, 1860–1, and 1906

William D. Rubinstein

For many years I have been compiling information on everyone who died leaving a fortune of £100,000 or more in Britain between 1809 and 1914. This research builds upon, and greatly expands, the data provided in my *Men of Property: The Very Wealthy in Britain since the Nineteenth Century* (1981; revised edition 2006) and other works, which largely examined wealth-holders leaving £500,000 or more. There are more than 13,000 persons in this wider study. Having completed much of the information gathering phase of this project, I am in the process of publishing a series of biographical dictionaries which will provide comprehensive biographical information on all of the persons in this study, that is, on everyone who left £100,000 or more in Britain between 1809 and 1914. The first volume, entitled *Who Were the Rich? Volume 1: 1809–1839*, has recently appeared, published by the Social Affairs Unit, a London-based Think Tank connected with the Institute of Economic Affairs. It contains comprehensive information on all 881 persons who left £100,000 or more in the British probate records between 1809 (when the data begins in a usable form) and 1839.[1] The next volume will cover the period 1840–59, and further volumes will cover all such persons down to 1914. In this chapter, I would like to outline the data available for the economic and social historian, and then to consider the findings briefly for estates of £100,000 or more probated in 1809–39 and then for estates of £100,000 or more probated

[1] Rubinstein, W.D. 2009. *Who Were the Rich? A Biographical Directory of British Wealth-Holders, Volume 1: 1809–1839*. London: The Social Affairs Unit. I am most grateful to Michael Mosbacher and the Social Affairs Unit for sponsoring this project. I should clearly note that I had complete editorial control over the book, although it was sponsored by a 'Think Tank'.

in 1860–1 and 1906, especially for what these show about the occupational, geographical, and gender distribution of the very wealthy, and how these have changed and evolved over this period.

Something must be said here about the sources. Prior to 1858, the probating of estates in England and Wales was a monopoly of the Church of England. There were more than 40 probate courts, each with their own set of records. However, virtually all large estates were recorded in the two Prerogative Courts, of Canterbury (covering the southern two-thirds of England, and Wales) and of York (covering the northern third of England).[2] The probate act books of these courts in which probate valuations for all probated estates are given were systematically researched by me, in addition to the two lesser courts covering Lancashire, and the manuscript Scottish probate calendars, which begin in 1825. In 1858, probate in England and Wales came under the jurisdiction of the Principal Probate Registry, located at Doctors' Commons in the City of London, and then for many decades at Somerset House. All the probate calendars for the period 1858–1914 have been systematically and exhaustively searched by me to identify all estates of £100,000 or more, as have the probate calendars of Scotland (first printed in 1876) and Ireland (which began in 1858).

The valuation figures found in all of these probate records are for the gross value of the unsettled personalty of each deceased individual – that is, they exclude the land and also the value of any trust from which the decedent derived income. The main exclusion is, of course, for land, although it should be noted that many *bona fide* great landowners left personal estates of £100,000 or more. Few statistics of landownership in Britain exist until the early-mid 1870s, when Parliament compiled *The Return of Owners of Land*, which recorded the acreage and gross annual rental income of all landowners in the United Kingdom, with the exception of London, which was excluded from the *Return*. In 1883, John Bateman collated and corrected the figures in the *Return*, publishing his *Great Landowners of Great Britain and Ireland*, which included the acreage and gross annual incomes of all landowners with more than 2000 acres outside of London. In 1989, the American scholar Peter Lindert published an article on Victorian landownership, which provided equivalent figures for the great London landowners in the 1890s.[3] Notwithstanding this, the value of unsettled land continued to be excluded from the probate valuations until 1898 while the value of settled land was excluded until 1926. Thus, the data below concerning the 1809–39 and 1861 cohorts exclude all land, while the 1906 cohort excludes the value of settled land. It is, however,

---

[2] There were also a number of smaller 'peculiar' courts who had jurisdiction over probate. By the nineteenth century, most had ceased to function as courts of probate.

[3] Lindert, P. 1989. 'Who owned Victorian England? The debate over landed wealth and inequality'. *Agricultural History* 61(4): 25–51.

impossible in the 1906 case to ascertain the value of unsettled land, since the probate valuation consists only of a single global figure for the total value of the estate. As is well known, one cannot see the inventory for most estates probated at any time in England and Wales, although one can read the inventory of any estate probated in Scotland.[4] In my book *Men of Property*, I draw some inferences about the inventories of 44 wealthy Scottish estates probated between 1858 and 1939, especially between 1876 and 1902.[5]

In other respects, the valuation figures are certainly accurate, and have the enormous advantage of being objective and comprehensive: they include *all* persons of sufficient wealth to have probated estates. At the top level, they include all very wealthy persons, not merely famous or renowned business-men, and can greatly extend our knowledge of the upper classes, providing firm evidence in place of anecdote. However, the persons noted in the probate calendars – and I have extracted all of these names myself; there are no lists – provide nothing beyond their names, dates of death (after 1858), addresses, names of executors, and, occasionally, an occupational designation. All further information must be gleaned from an enormously wide variety of biographical sources, especially genealogical and similar works, local directories, and the Census (beginning in 1841) which have recently become available online.[6]

For every person listed in the biographical registers I am compiling, infor-mation has been provided on his or her name; dates; probate valuation; occupation or source of wealth; address; the name, dates, occupation, and where known, probate valuation of the father of each person in the study; similar information about their mothers; secondary, tertiary, and professional education, spouses and children; original and final religion; public offices held and honours received; miscellaneous information; and sources. Obviously, not all of this information is equally available for everyone in the study, and some is plainly unavailable in any source. The most important categories, which will be discussed in this chapter, are the occupation or source of wealth of each wealth-holder and the geographical venues in which their fortune was earned (*not* where they lived). These two categories have been divided into the following classificatory categories, which are identical to those previously employed by me in my *Men of Property* and other published work.

[4] See, however, Chapter 3 by Green et al. in this volume.

[5] Rubinstein, W.D. 2006. *Men of Property: The Very Wealthy in Britain since the Industrial Revolution*, 2nd edition. London: The Social Affairs Unit, 230–4. See also Kennedy W.P. 1987. *Industrial Structure, Capital Markets and the Origins of British Decline*. Cambridge: Cambridge University Press, which makes extensive use of the Scottish probate records.

[6] When I lived in Australia between 1976 and 1995, much of this work of identification was undertaken by my research assistant in London, Dr Carole M. Taylor, thanks to grants for this project from the Australian Research Grants Council and Deakin University. I am most grateful to them.

OCCUPATIONAL CATEGORIES AND VENUES
OF THE WEALTH-HOLDERS

As noted above, all wealth-holders are classified by their occupations and the venues in which they earned their fortunes. The categories employed derive from the *Standard Industrial Classification* which separates manufacturing industry from commerce and the service sectors.[7] They have been modified for the purposes of this study, but in general are very close to the official categories.

Occupational categories

I. Landowners

These are persons who apparently earned the bulk of their fortunes from income derived from land, including minerals and urban property. Plantation owners in the West Indies are also classified here. Persons whose fathers or grandfathers were in trade or the professions but who then purchased land would normally be classified with that trade or profession, although each case is judged on its apparent merits. Close relatives of landowners with no other apparent major sources of income are also classified here. Normally, titled landed aristocrats would automatically be classified here. However, colliery owners – businessmen who derived their incomes from working coalmines normally leased from a landowner – would not be classified here.

II. Manufacturing and industry

1. Coal mining. As noted, colliery proprietors are classified here, but the landowners who owned the land bearing the colliery or collieries (for instance Lord Londonderry) are classified in subsection I.
2. Other mining
3. Iron and steel manufacturing
4. Shipbuilding
5. Engineering and related trades
6. Chemical manufacturing and related trades
7. Cotton manufacturing
8. Woollen manufacturing
9. Other textile manufacturing
10. Construction and building

---

[7] Central Statistical Office 1968. *Standard Industrial Classification*. London: Central Statistical Office.

11. Other manufacturing

III. Food, drink, and tobacco

12. Brewing and related, including maltsting, etc.
13. Distilling
14. Tobacco manufacturing
15. Foods and foodstuffs, including non-alcoholic beverages

IV. Commerce and finance

16. Banking
17. Merchant banking – comprises international bankers
18. Other finance
19. Foreign merchants – merchants trading abroad, import–export merchants, etc.
20. Retailing
21. Other merchants, including warehousemen and 'merchants' not classified elsewhere. This category contains many wealth-holders described in directories as 'merchants' without any more specific information.
22. Insurance brokers
23. Stockbrokers
24. Shipowners
25. Other commerce

V. Publishing and miscellaneous

26. Newspaper proprietors
27. Publishers
28. Other miscellaneous

VI. Professionals, public administration, and defence

29. Lawyers and other legal professionals and officials
30. Other professionals
31. Public administration and defence, including government office holders not classified elsewhere

VII. Others

Plainly, it is often difficult to classify some wealth-holders, given the lack of information about them and the fact that some had several sources of wealth, but the above categories are certainly broadly accurate.

Venues

As noted, these are the places where the wealth-holder apparently earned or
derived most of his or her fortune, according to the best information available.
To reiterate, these venues are not necessarily where the wealth-holder lived.

1. City of London: that is, the historic 'Square Mile' centred on St Paul's
   Cathedral. Whether a business was literally in the City, or technically
   just outside of its boundaries, was sometimes difficult to ascertain. The
   Inns of Court are counted as being in the City of London.
2. Other London: other parts of central London, including Westminster,
   Mayfair, Southwark, the Docks, etc.
3. Outer London: the boundaries here are often somewhat arbitrary, but
   are roughly the coterminous with the outermost extent of the Underground system.
4. Greater Manchester, including neighbouring towns such as Bolton and
   Oldham
5. Merseyside
6. West Yorkshire – Leeds, Bradford, and surrounding towns
7. South Yorkshire – Sheffield and surrounding towns
8. West Midlands – Birmingham, Wolverhampton, and neighbouring
   towns
9. Tyneside
10. Clydeside
11. East Anglia
12. Bristol
13. Other south-west England
14. Other southern England
15. Ribblesdale, including Preston and Accrington
16. Mid-Lancashire, including Wigan and St Helens
17. Nottingham–Derby–Belper
18. Other Midlands, including the East Midlands
19. Wales
20. Teesside
21. Humberside
22. Other northern England
23. Edinburgh
24. Other Scotland
25. Belfast
26. Dublin
27. Other Ireland
28. Other and unclassified
29. Overseas and foreign, especially India and the West Indies

Some wealth-holders, most notably landowners, military officers, and most clergymen could not be assigned to any venue.

1809–39: FINDINGS AND CONCLUSIONS

Numbers and gender

What does an analysis of the 881 wealth-holders who left £100,000 or more between 1809 and 1839 tell us about the structure of wealth-holding in Britain at that time? Some distinctive patterns clearly emerge.

Of the total of 881 wealth-holders, 214 were probated in the 11-year period 1809–19, 308 in the decade 1820–9, and 359 in the decade 1830–9. There was thus a substantial rise in the number of large estates, a trend plainly consistent with the growth of the British economy at the time – although, as will be discussed, this certainly did not mean that the obvious growth areas in the British economy, especially the industrial revolution trades such as cotton spinning and engineering, were well-represented in this increase.

The great majority of wealth-holders in this study were, of course, males. Nevertheless, there were 63 women out of the grand total of 881 wealth-holders – 7.1 per cent. By decade, there were 14 women wealth-holders in the 11-year span 1809–19 out of the total of 214 (6.5 per cent), 23 out of 308 in 1820–9 (7.5 per cent), and 26 of 359 in 1830–9 (7.2 per cent). The majority were widows or 'spinsters', as unmarried women were normally described, but occasionally a married woman with a husband living left a fortune in her own right – for instance the remarkable Harriot [*sic*] Mellon, widow of Thomas Coutts the great banker and, at the time of her death, the Duchess of St Albans, whose husband did not die until 1849. More than half of the wealthy women were widows, while another substantial percentage were spinsters. Both of these categories were themselves somewhat unusual, indicating that these women inherited great wealth in their own right (or expanded the size of their inheritance), rather than receiving an annual income paid out of a settlement, which they (or their current husbands) were unable to touch apart from the income it produced, as was certainly common for many female relatives of rich men.

The great majority of women wealth-holders left estates in the £100,000–£200,000 range, rather than a higher sum. Five women, however, left estates of £500,000 or more. The wealthiest woman deceased in the period under consideration was Jane Innes (1748–1839), daughter and sister of wealthy Edinburgh bankers, who left £1,043,000. The four half-millionaires were Elizabeth Whittingstall (d.1825), who inherited a Watford maltsting and brewing fortune; Lady Harriet Holland (1744–1825), daughter of a baronet and widow of the wealthy architect Sir Nathaniel Holland; Susannah Houblon Newton (née Archer, 1753–1837), who inherited a landed fortune and married into a Huguenot mercantile family; and the above-noted Harriot Mellon (1777–1837).

Extremes of wealth

While everyone in this study was, by definition, among the wealthiest persons of their time in Britain, some were wealthier than others. Apart from the five women mentioned above, eight men left millionaire estates and 35 men left half-millionaire estates: six in 1809–19, 17 in 1820–9, and 12 in 1830–9. The eight millionaire estates were those left by the Hon. Henry Cavendish (1731–1810), the scientist, who inherited a landed fortune; Richard Crawshay (1739–1820), the ironmaster in south Wales; William Douglas, fourth Duke of Queensberry (1725–1810), 'Old Q', the notorious rake; Philip Rundell (1746–1827), goldsmith and jeweller in the City of London; Sir Robert Peel, first baronet (1750–1830), the cotton manufacturer in Lancashire and father of his namesake the prime minister; George Leveson-Gower, first Duke of Sutherland (1758–1833), landowner; William Hollond (1750–1836), who made his fortune in the Bengal Civil Service; and Nathan Mayer Rothschild (1777–1836), the great merchant banker in the City of London. Of these, the Duke of Sutherland was certainly the wealthiest, with Rothschild probably the runner-up and richest businessman. It is worth making the point again that the value of land is excluded from these figures. It is likely that several dozen landowners, chiefly landed aristocrats, died in the period 1809–39 who were worth more than £1 million if the total value of their land is included with their personalty. Many of these – perhaps the majority – do appear in this study, however, since they left at least £100,000 in personalty.

Among the 35 male half-millionaires, 12 were active in the City of London, primarily as merchants, and six active chiefly in other parts of London. Seven were landowners who left personal estates in the half-millionaire class. Two (William Crawshay, 1764–1834, and Jonathan Peel, 1752–1834) were industrialists or manufacturers in the new industrial areas, and one (Thomas Leyland, 1752–1827) was a banker in Liverpool, but provincial businessmen were rare at this level of wealth. The remainder chiefly earned their fortunes overseas, usually in the West Indies or India.

Occupational distribution

Table 2.1 shows the occupational distribution of the wealth-holders for the 1809–39 period. It includes, where known, the most important occupation or source of wealth of each of these individuals, who include women and foreigners leaving large estates in Britain.

The most striking finding of this occupational breakdown of the wealth-holders is, of course, the crucial importance of commercial and financial wealth, rather than manufacturing and industrial wealth. This conclusion was also reached in my previous study of the rich who left £500,000 or more, *Men of Property*.[8] Although Britain was experiencing the world's first industrial revolution at that time, industrialists constituted only a small percentage of the wealthiest British people. The 'conservative' nature of Britain's wealth structure at that time is also evident from the very large number of wealthy landowners – even *without* the value of their land being included in the valuation figures – and the remarkable number of wealth-holders in the public administration and defence categories, many of whom were a part of the world of 'Old Corruption', or East India Company and military or naval figures as well as government civil servants and office holders. If the landowners listed above are omitted, and only the known non-landed wealth-holders included (a total of 612 persons), 15.7– per cent were industrialists or manufacturers, 6.7 per cent in the food–drink–tobacco categories, 54.7 per cent in commerce and finance, 0.8 per cent in publishing, and 21.9 per cent in public administration and defence.

Venues

These are arranged by the geographical venues in which each wealth-holder earned his or her fortune (not where he or she lived), and bearing in mind that many wealth-holders – landowners, military, and most clerical figures, for example – cannot readily be assigned to a venue. The results are shown in Table 2.2.

As with the occupational distributions of the wealth-holders – and, indeed, even more emphatically – the 'conservative' nature of Britain's wealth structure at this time is absolutely plain from the locational analysis, with London accounting for two-thirds of all large fortunes, and another one-eighth earned overseas in the empire and other trading entrepôts. In contrast, the new industrial cities and regions of Britain were the venues for only a small percentage of British fortunes. In provincial Britain, traditional and long-established trading and manufacturing areas such as Bristol and East Anglia were more likely than Manchester and Birmingham to have been the scene of

---

[8] Rubinstein, *Men of Property*.

Table 2.1 Occupations of known wealth-holders, 1809–39

	1809–19	1820–9	1830–9	Total	%
I. Land	50	54	70	174	22.1
II. Manufacturing and industry					
1. Coal mining	1	1	0	2	0.3
2. Other mining	2	2	1	5	0.6
3. Iron/steel	3	2	7	12	1.5
4. Shipbuilding	2	2	2	6	0.8
5. Engineering	1	0	0	1	0.1
6. Chemicals	4	3	2	9	1.1
7. Cotton	2	4	5	11	1.4
8. Woollens	1	4	0	5	0.6
9. Other textiles	5	3	2	10	1.3
10. Construction	2	1	7	10	1.3
11. Other manufacturing	4	10	11	25	3.2
Total	27	32	37	96	12.2
III. Food–drink–tobacco					
12. Brewing and related	4	11	9	24	3.1
13. Distilling	1	5	4	10	1.3
14. Tobacco	0	1	1	2	0.3
15. Foods	4	0	1	5	0.6
Total	9	17	15	41	5.2
IV. Commerce and finance					
16. Banking	24	21	31	76	9.7
17. Merchant banking	2	0	2	4	0.5
18. Other finance	3	2	3	8	1.0
19. Foreign merchants	25	44	27	96	12.2
20. Retailing	6	7	11	24	3.1
21. Other merchants	31	19	38	88	11.2
22. Insurance	2	3	1	6	0.8
23. Stockbrokers	6	9	11	26	3.3
24. Shipowners	1	0	3	4	0.5
25. Other commerce	1	1	2	4	0.5
Total	101	106	129	336	42.7
V. Publishing					
26. Newspapers	0	1	1	2	0.3
27. Publishers	0	1	2	3	0.4
28. Miscellaneous	0	0	0	0	0.0
Total	0	2	3	5	0.6
VI. Professionals and public administration					
29. Professions: law	10	13	24	46	5.9
30. Other professionals	5	15	17	37	4.7
31. Public administration/defence	17	17	17	51	6.5
Total	32	45	58	134	17.0'
Overall total	219	256	312	786	

Source: see text.

Table 2.2 Geographical venues of wealth-holders, 1809–39

Venue	1809–19	1820–9	1830–9	Totals	%
1. City of London	81	95	108	284	44.8
2. Other London	37	34	53	124	19.6
3. Outer London	5	6	3	14	2.2
Total for London	*123*	*135*	*164*	*422*	*66.6*
4. Greater Manchester	3	6	5	14	2.2
5. Merseyside	1	4	11	16	2.5
6. West Yorkshire	0	0	0	0	0.0
7. South Yorkshire	0	1	0	1	0.2
8. West Midlands	3	0	4	7	1.1
9. Tyneside	1	1	3	5	0.8
10. Clydeside	0	3	0	3	0.5
11. East Anglia	5	7	4	16	2.5
12. Bristol	3	4	9	16	2.5
13. Other south-west England	1	8	1	10	1.6
14. Other southern England	2	3	6	11	1.7
15. Ribblesdale	0	0	0	0	0.0
16. Mid-Lancashire	0	0	0	0	0.0
17. Nottingham–Derby–Belper	0	0	0	0	0.0
18. Other Midlands	0	8	5	13	2.1
19. Wales	3	1	4	8	1.3
20. Teesside	0	0	0	0	0.0
21. Humberside	0	4	0	4	0.6
22. Other northern England	0	1	2	3	0.5
23. Edinburgh	0	1	6	7	1.1
24. Other Scotland	0	0	0	0	0.0
25. Belfast	0	0	0	0	0.0
26. Dublin	0	0	1	1	0.2
27. Other Ireland	0	2	0	2	0.3
28. Foreign/overseas:					
West Indies	6	9	5	20	3.2
India	9	12	17	38	6.0
Portugal	3	4	2	9	1.4
Europe	1	0	2	3	0.5
North America	0	2	1	3	0.5
China	0	1	1	2	0.3
Total foreign/overseas	*19*	*28*	*28*	*75*	*11.8*
Total	*164*	*217*	*253*	*634*	

Source: see text.

large fortunes. If anything, this understates the importance of London for Britain's wealth elite at this time, for virtually all major landowners (not included with these statistics) spent much of each year in London and had houses there, as did many wealth-holders whose fortunes were earned elsewhere.

1860–1: FINDINGS AND CONCLUSIONS

Two subsequent groups of wealth-holders have also been examined, albeit more skeletally than the 1809–39 group. The first of these includes estates of £100,000 or more probated in 1860–1, and the second, estates of £100,000 or more probated in 1906. These years have been selected as representative, and there is no reason to suppose that they are anomalous in any way.

The 1860–1 group comprises 122 individuals, 61 in each year. Nearly all were deceased between mid-1859 and the end of 1861, the zenith of the mid-Victorian 'Age of Equipoise' just before the 'cotton famine' occasioned by the American Civil War and the beginning of the real challenge to British industrial leadership which began around 1870. These two years occurred 35 years after the first railways, when British factory capitalism was probably at its zenith, and a generation or two after the 'Age of Reform' eliminated the most blatant examples of 'Old Corruption'. These trends should, presumably, be reflected in the patterns found among the 1860–1 cohort. Information about these wealth-holders was gathered primarily from local directories and genealogical guides and, more recently, from comprehensive census data now available for all censuses 1841–1901 on www.ancestry.com, as well as from many other sources. Some salient information was obtained on the great majority of the persons in the 1860–1 group, although there remained a small minority of unsolved mysteries.

One somewhat surprising fact about this cohort is that, although the annual number of estate-leavers of £100,000 or more had roughly doubled since the 1809–39 period, in 1860–1 the maximum scales of wealth do not appear to have risen at all. This group includes only one millionaire estate (George, second Duke of Sutherland (1786–1861), landowner, who left £1,137,000), and only five half-millionaires (Francis, seventh Duke of Bedford (1788–1861), urban property and landowner, £600,000 in personalty; Thomas Cotterill (1779–1860), a Birmingham linen draper and merchant, £800,000; Stephen Lyne-Stephens (1801–60), who inherited (of all things) the state monopoly on the manufacture of glasses in Portugal, and who was said (incorrectly) to be 'the richest commoner in England', £700,000; Seth Smith (1791–1860), a great London builder and the partner of Thomas Cubbitt, who then opened the famous 'Pantechnicon' storage warehouse, which claimed to be fireproof (it burned down in 1874), £500,000; and Joseph Tasker (1797–1861), a City investment banker who specialized in Latin American finance, £500,000). This situation differs from that in the United States, where there was an astronomical rise in the scales of the largest fortunes between *c*.1850 and *c*.1910. In contrast, British fortunes never rose to anything like these levels; indeed, they hardly rose at all.

For reasons of space, only a few important aspects of the characteristics of this cohort can be considered here. The occupational distribution of the 1860–1 group is set out in Table 2.3.

It will be seen that, compared with the 1809–39 group, there has been a doubling in the percentage of manufacturing and industrial fortunes. However, no relative decline is apparent in commercial and financial fortunes, the increase in manufacturing coming at the expense of professional/administrative estates – the decline of 'Old Corruption' – and of a smaller decrease in the relative percentage of landowners who left personal estates of £100,000 or more. This is pretty much as one might expect, although the number of cotton manufacturing and other textile fortunes – a total of 11 – would still probably strike many as lower than one might have expected. The fact that only 107 wealth-holders are listed here is due to the number of unknowns remaining, or to other difficulties in properly identifying the real occupational source of a fortune, as well as to foreigners with no connection to Britain who left substantial sums in this country.

The other aspect to be considered here is the geographical venue of these fortunes – again, where each estate was actually earned, not where the wealth-holder lived. As with the previous group, many wealth-holders, especially landowners, clerics, some engineering contractors, and foreigners with no connection to Britain, have not been assigned to any venue (Table 2.4).

Compared with the 1809–39 group, there have been marked changes, although again probably not as great as one might assume in advance. Most strikingly, the London percentage has declined from around two-thirds to just under half of the venues. This probably still understates the realistic importance of London in Britain's wealth structure, since virtually all great landowners lived there for at least half of the year, while many provincial wealth-holders would also certainly have resided at frequent intervals in London. Nevertheless, the decline is plainly significant. The rise of provincial fortunes, however, was geographically widespread, and did not centre in any particular city. For example, only six of these fortunes were earned in Manchester and its environs. There was also a perceptible relative decline in older, often pre-industrial centres of wealth such as East Anglia and south-west England, at the expense of newer purely industrial and manufacturing cities and towns. While this was also to be expected, the shift is, again, arguably not as great as one might have assumed.

If one contrasts the wealth-holders of London and Lancashire (Greater Manchester, Merseyside, mid-Lancashire) in the 1860–1 cohort, some other conclusions are evident. There were many more drawn from the very wealthiest among the Londoners than among the Lancastrians, with two Londoners leaving £500,000 or more (Seth Smith and Joseph Tasker); five leaving between £300,000 and £500,000 (City banker Henry Bevan (1776–1860); City merchant James Brand (d.1860); brewer Frederick Perkins (1780–1860);

Table 2.3 Occupations of known wealth-holders, 1860–1

	Number	%
I. Land	*19*	*17.8*
II. Manufacturing and industry		
1. Coal mining	1	0.9
2. Other mining	0	0.0
3. Iron/steel	3	2.8
4. Shipbuilding	0	0.0
5. Engineering	2	1.9
6. Chemicals	1	0.9
7. Cotton	3	2.8
8. Woollens	3	2.8
9. Other textiles	5	4.7
10. Construction	2	1.9
11. Other manufacturing	7	6.5
Total	*27*	*25.2*
III. Food–drink–tobacco		
12. Brewing and related	2	1.9
13. Distilling	1	0.9
14. Tobacco	0	0.0
15. Foods	0	0.0
Total	*3*	*2.8*
IV. Commerce and finance		
16. Banking	11	10.3
17. Merchant banking	0	0.0
18. Other finance	6	5.6
19. Foreign merchants	3	2.8
20. Retailing	3	2.8
21. Other merchants	16	15.0
22. Insurance	0	0.0
23. Stockbrokers	2	1.9
24. Shipowners	1	0.9
25. Other commerce	4	3.7
Total	*46*	*43.0*
V. Publishing		
26. Newspapers	0	0.0
27. Publishers	1	0.9
28. Miscellaneous	0	0.0
Total	*1*	*0.9*
VI. Professionals and public administration		
29. Professions: law	10	9.3
30. Other professionals	0	0.0
31. Public administration/defence	1	0.9
Total	*11*	*10.3*
Overall total	*107*	

Source: see text.

Table 2.4 Geographical venues of wealth-holders, 1860–1

Venue	Number	%
1. City of London	27	30.3
2. Other London	15	16.9
3. Outer London	0	0.0
Total for London	*42*	*47.2*
4. Greater Manchester	6	6.7
5. Merseyside	1	1.1
6. West Yorkshire	5	5.6
7. South Yorkshire	0	0.0
8. West Midlands	4	4.5
9. Tyneside	2	2.2
10. Clydeside	6	6.7
11. East Anglia	1	1.1
12. Bristol	4	4.5
13. Other south-west England	1	1.1
14. Other southern England	2	2.2
15. Ribblesdale	2	2.2
16. Mid-Lancashire	1	1.1
17. Nottingham–Derby–Belper	1	1.1
18. Other Midlands	1	1.1
19. Wales	0	0.0
20. Teesside	0	0.0
21. Humberside	2	2.2
22. Other northern England	0	0.0
23. Edinburgh	2	2.2
24. Other Scotland	1	1.1
25. Belfast	0	0.0
26. Dublin	1	1.1
27. Other Ireland	0	0.0
28. Foreign/overseas	4	4.5
Total	*89*	

Source: see text.

sperm whale oil manufacturer Elhanam Bicknell (1788–1861); piano manufacturer Thomas Broadwood (1786–1861)); and four more at the £200,000–
£300,000 level. In contrast, only two of the Lancastrians left as much as
£200,000, John Hargreaves (d.1860), a rather mysterious, large-scale carrier
in Liverpool, who left £400,000; and the civil engineer and railway builder
Joseph Locke (1805–60), Chief Engineer of the Manchester and Liverpool
Railway, who left £350,000.

Compared with the 1809–39 group, there was a slight rise in the percentage of women wealth-holders, with 11 female estate-leavers in 1860–1, or
9.0 per cent of the total. Given that this is only a two-year period, there was
a rise in the absolute number of women wealth-holders, although the

percentage is still obviously very small. As every female wealth-holder inherited most or all of her fortune from her husband, father, or another
relative, in times of rapid change with a significant increase in new (male)
fortunes, it is to be expected that few women would have yet inherited
substantial sums from these new wealth-holders. None of these women
wealth-holders of the 1860–1 group was among the super-rich, the wealthiest
being Elizabeth, Duchess of Cleveland (1777–1861), who left £300,000,
widow of the millionaire William, first Duke of Cleveland, who died in
1842. According to her entry in the *Complete Peerage*, she was, remarkably,
the daughter of a market gardener, Robert Russell, and was 'formerly the
mistress of Mr Coutts the banker', although her fortune came almost entirely
by inheritance from her husband.

Some conclusions may also be inferred about the nature of the social
structure of Britain's elites in 1860–1 from these data. Although landowners
were now seemingly a relatively small minority (17.8 per cent) of the wealth-
holder cohort, this is certainly quite misleading, since, as mentioned above, the
probate valuations do not include land. If the capital value of the land owned
by substantial landowners who died in 1860–1 was included, they would
almost certainly constitute a majority of all those who left £100,000. Taking
thirty years' rental (the standard figure) as a multiplier, decedents who owned
3300 acres would be worth £100,000.

The integration of the 88 non-landed wealth-holders into the traditional
upper classes and governing circles of Britain was, at the time of their deaths,
very haphazard. A small minority, it seems, purchased land on a considerable
scale, although the conclusion here must be imprecise. Only eight wealth-
holders from this group definitely had heirs with sufficient land (2000 acres
worth £2000 or more per annum in income) to be listed in John Bateman's
Great Landowners of 1883 (based upon *The Return of Owners of Land of
1872–75*) with another four or five more whose heirs or successors could
tentatively be traced in that work. Even if these figures understate the
actual number of non-landed wealth-holders of 1860–1 who became notable
landowners, or whose immediate heirs so became, it seems clear that the
great majority did not buy land on a considerable scale. This is consistent
with other research by me which has given rise to a lengthy debate on this
subject.[9] Although the purchase of land on a large scale required the
diversion of very considerable resources, other indicators of integration into

---

[9] Rubinstein, W.D. 1981. 'New men of wealth and the purchase of land in nineteenth-century
Britain'. *Past and Present* 92: 125–47. For a summary of this debate and the views of some of its
participants, see Thompson, F.M.L. 2001. *Gentrification and the Enterprise Culture: Britain
1780–1980*. Oxford: Oxford University Press, especially 45–74.

a national elite are also surprisingly meagre. Rather remarkably, only 11 of these non-landed wealth-holders were appointed as Justices of Peace, Deputy-Lieutenants of counties, or High Sheriffs of counties. These figures might well also be understatements, but it is clear that most wealth-holders certainly did not receive any such appointments. Only five of the non-landed wealth-holders served as MPs (Newcastle upon Tyne banker Cuthbert Ellison (1783–1860); Joseph Locke; Stephen Lyne-Stephens; John Ashley Warre (1787–1860), a West India merchant in London; and John Heathcoat (1783–1861), a lace manufacturer at Tiverton). Only one non-landed wealth-holder of the 1860–1 group received a peerage (the judge Sir John Campbell, first Baron Campbell (1779–1861)); and only two others received knighthoods (Sir George Carroll (1784–1860), a stockbroker who served as Lord Mayor of London, and Sir Peter Laurie (1778–1861), an army contractor who also served as Lord Mayor of London).

The majority of this group of non-landed wealth-holders were remarkably obscure. They were virtually unknown to the public in their lifetime and certainly did not enter into Society or the governing elite. Their sons and grandsons, however, almost certainly became 'gentlemen' via education at an elite public school and Oxbridge, and their daughters often married well. Yet collectively this group made little impact. Wealth-holders at the lower end of our wealth scale, those leaving between £100,000 and £200,000, were probably not wealthy or influential enough to become national figures. Nonconformists and other non-Anglicans still suffered from disabilities and prejudice. Most entrepreneurs were 'self-made' at one or two generations remove, and were often simply unsuitable or unsuited to the public life of high Society; many of these would have had no wish to leave business or even the professions (11 of the wealth-holders in this group were professionals, namely successful barristers and solicitors). Another fact of life, which remained operative for many generations, is that there were always more wealthy men and those educated as 'gentlemen' than there were (or are) positions in Britain's elites, however defined: there was not always room at the top, and neither money nor an old school tie, could guarantee upward mobility into the power elite, although obviously both helped.

1906: FINDINGS AND CONCLUSIONS

The third period to be examined here is the single year 1906. The most obvious difference between this year and its predecessors is the enormous growth in the number of estates of £100,000 or more probated in this year alone: no fewer than 301, nearly five times the number probated annually in 1860–1. The 1906 figure excludes estates probated in Ireland (which have not been surveyed after 1900), although some Irish fortunes were proved in other parts of the United Kingdom. The value of money was broadly the same in 1906 as in 1860–1, meaning that there was genuinely a substantial increase in the number of large estates. From 1898, the probate valuations included unsettled land as well as personalty (although settled land remained excluded from the valuation figure until 1926), which will have increased the overall numbers, although the overall percentage of landowners in the total declined from 1860–1.

The year 1906 was chosen as a typical year when the Edwardian plutocracy was at its peak, but before the effects were felt either of the worldwide financial panic of 1907 or for the higher rates of direct taxation imposed by Lloyd George after he became Chancellor of the Exchequer in 1908. That there was indeed an Edwardian plutocracy is evidenced by the rise in the number and size of very large estates, with 11 millionaire estates and 18 between £500,000 and £1 million left in 1906 alone. The two largest estates were those of Alfred Beit (1853–1906), the well-known 'Randlord' (Werhner, Beit & Co.), who lived in London and had offices in the City, who left no less than £8,050,000; and Sir Charles Tennant (1823–1906), the great Glasgow chemical manufacturer (and Asquith's father-in-law), whose estate of £3,146,000 made him possibly the wealthiest Scottish businessman, in real terms, in history. Nine of the eleven millionaire estates, and nine among the half-millionaire estates, were earned in London, primarily in the City, in contrast to the relative trend away from London among those lower down the wealth scale.

On the basis of the key categories discussed for the 1860–1 group, the occupational distribution of the 1906 wealth-holders is provided in Table 2.5. It will be seen that there has been a rise in the manufacturing and industry sector, as well as the food–drink–tobacco occupations, and a relative decline in commercial and financial fortunes, although these still comprise the largest single group. The classical industrial revolution trades such as cotton, woollens, iron and steel, and engineering, have considerably increased, both in absolute and relative terms. Nevertheless, these never constitute a majority of the wealthy class in Britain, even after more than a century of heavy industry and manufacturing. Landowning declined in relative terms, but there are still more wealthy landowners than any single group (with the exception of the miscellaneous category of 'other merchants'), despite the fact that settled land is not included in the valuation figures, and in spite of the agricultural depression.

The second major dimension of the wealth structure of Britain in 1906 is the occupational venues where the non-landed wealth-holders earned their fortunes. Again, it should be stressed that the data here are for where each wealth-holder's fortune was earned, not where he or she lived, and that some categories of wealth-holders, especially landowners, some professionals, and

Table 2.5 Occupations of known wealth-holders, 1906

	Number	%
I. Land	33	12.3
II. Manufacturing and industry		
1. Coal mining	6	2.2
2. Other mining	0	0.0
3. Iron/steel	14	5.2
4. Shipbuilding	2	0.7
5. Engineering	7	2.6
6. Chemicals	7	2.6
7. Cotton	13	4.8
8. Woollens	11	4.1
9. Other textiles	7	2.6
10. Construction	3	1.1
11. Other manufacturing	16	5.9
Total	*86*	*32.0*
III. Food–drink–tobacco		
12. Brewing and related	13	4.8
13. Distilling	0	0.0
14. Tobacco	1	0.4
15. Foods	5	1.9
Total	*19*	*7.1*
IV. Commerce and finance		
16. Banking	14	5.2
17. Merchant banking	6	2.2
18. Other finance	4	1.5
19. Foreign merchants	12	4.5
20. Retailing	2	0.7
21. Other merchants	35	13.0
22. Insurance	2	0.7
23. Stockbrokers	8	3.0
24. Shipowners	12	4.5
25. Other commerce	8	3.0
Total	*103*	*38.3*
V. Publishing		
26. Newspapers	3	1.1
27. Publishers	4	1.5
28. Miscellaneous	0	0.0
Total	*7*	*2.6*
VI. Professionals and public administration		
29. Professions: law	11	4.1
30. Other professionals	5	1.9
31. Public administration/defence	5	1.9
Total	*21*	*7.8*
Overall Total	262	

Source: see text.

Table 2.6 Geographical venues of wealth-holders, 1906

Venue	Number	%
1. City of London	55	23.9
2. Other London	29	12.6
3. Outer London	3	1.3
Totals for London	*87*	*37.8*
4. Greater Manchester	23	10.0
5. Merseyside	12	5.2
6. West Yorkshire	10	4.3
7. South Yorkshire	0	0.0
8. West Midlands	17	7.4
9. Tyneside	10	4.3
10. Clydeside	15	6.5
11. East Anglia	4	1.7
12. Bristol	3	1.3
13. Other south-west England	6	2.6
14. Other southern England	6	2.6
15. Ribblesdale	0	0.0
16. Mid-Lancashire	0	0.0
17. Nottingham–Derby–Belper	4	1.7
18. Other Midlands	4	1.7
19. Wales	2	0.9
20. Teesside	5	2.2
21. Humberside	2	0.9
22. Other northern England	5	2.2
23. Edinburgh	1	0.4
24. Other Scotland	5	2.2
25. Belfast	1	0.4
26. Dublin	1	0.4
27. Other Ireland	3	1.3
28. Foreign/overseas	4	1.7
Total	*230*	

Source: see text.

engineers and contractors on a national basis, cannot be assigned to a specific venue. Nevertheless, some patterns are clear (Table 2.6).

Compared with 1860–1 there was a clear relative decline in London, and a rise in most provincial centres of wealth-making, most notably for Clydeside, Manchester, and the West Midlands. This decline was relative, as there were more London fortunes in 1906 than in 1860–1. It seems likely that most of these provincial fortunes were to be found towards the minimal cut-off point in this study, with estates of around £150,000 or so common for provincial businessmen, and, as noted, a disproportionate number of millionaire and half-millionaire estates earned in London, especially the City. The figures here also certainly underestimate the real centrality of London, since very many provincial wealth-holders moved to London or the Home Counties in retirement (few moved from London to Bradford or Wolverhampton), while virtually all great landowners and aristocrats lived there for at least part of the year. A table of actual residency patterns at the time of the later life of these wealth-holders is likely to be very different, with more businessmen also found in fashionable resorts and country addresses. Nevertheless, the data here are also consistent with the rise of provincial urban elites in the late Victorian and Edwardian periods. These were neither unified nor strong enough to challenge the London-based 'Establishments', and were being steadily drawn into that Establishment, especially in the second and third generations. By 1906, much of the 'dissenting' element among Nonconformists had gone, while many political activists such as Joseph Chamberlain had already trodden the path from left to right.

The percentage (but not the absolute number) of women wealth-holders in the 1906 group declined from 1860–1, to 6.6 (20 out of 301). Most left fortunes of between £100,000 and £150,000, and clearly inherited much or all of their wealth from their husband, father, or another relative. The two wealthiest women were Ada Lewis-Hill (1844–1906), widow of the famous Society money-lender and philanthropist Samuel Lewis (d.1901), who left £1,168,000, and Lucy Cohen (1839–1906), Mayer Rothschild's sister-in-law, who left £564,000. The reasons for this relative decline in wealthy female estates are probably complicated, but might be due to the fact that there were a large number of new, relatively (as it were) small estates which had not been in existence long enough and were not large enough to produce very wealthy female heirs. For whatever reason, however, it was clearly not yet that common for a wealthy man to leave a great fortune outright to his widow or daughter.

It is arguable that the social integration of the 1906 cohort into Britain's pre-existing elite proceeded at a faster pace than it had with the 1860–1 group. Among the 250 British non-landed wealth-holders in this group (as opposed to foreigners leaving fortunes in Britain and excluding landowners), 82 could be identified as Justices of the Peace or Deputy-Lieutenants of counties, a much higher percentage than among the 1860–1 cohort. This figure of 82 is itself probably an understatement, as it is quite possible that complete information is lacking about all wealth-holders. The number of MPs among the 5 British non-landed wealth-holders of 1906 was 18, an increase from the five MPs among the 1860–1 non-landed wealth-holders at a greater than random rate. Five of the 1906 group had been given peerages, six baronetcies, and seven others knighthoods. The peers were Gathorne Gathorne-Hardy, first Earl of Cranbrook (1814–1906), ironmaster and Cabinet Minister; Sir Philip Wodehouse Currie, first Baron Currie (1834–1906), Permanent Under Secretary in the Foreign Office; Joseph Bailey, first Baron Glanusk (1840–1906), ironmaster and MP; Samuel Cunliffe Lister, first Baron Masham (1815–1906), worsted and machinery manufacturer; C.T. Ritchie, first Baron Ritchie of

Dundee (1838–1906), jute merchant and Cabinet Minister. The baronets were Sir John Austin, 1st Bt (1824–1906), maltster and MP; Sir Thomas Brockle-bank, 1st Bt (1814–1906), shipowner; Sir David Dale, 1st Bt (1812–1906), ironmaster; Sir Wyndham Portal, 1st Bt (1822–1905), paper manufacturer; Sir Charles Tennant, 1st Bt (1823–1906), chemical manufacturer and MP; and Sir Henry Wiggin, 1st Bt (1824–1905), metal refiner and MP. The knights were Sir Clinton Dawkins (1859–1905), senior civil servant in Egypt and India; Sir Frederick Peel (1823–1906), cotton fortune beneficiary and MP; Sir Thom-as Richardson (1846–1906), ship engine manufacturer and MP; Sir George Williams (1821–1905), drapery retailer and founder of the YMCA; and Sir James Thompson (1835–1906), Chairman of the Caledonian Railway. Sir Ronald Leslie-Melville, 13th Earl of Leven and Melville (1835–1906), although he owned 8800 acres in Scotland, earned his fortune of £1.3 million chiefly as a merchant banker in the City. He was made a Knight of the Thistle in 1905. As with most things, this list of title-holders can be viewed in several ways. The overwhelming majority of the non-landed wealth-holders of 1906 did not receive a title, but the likelihood that someone worth more than £100,000 in 1906 would receive one was vastly greater than the norm for the whole of the middle classes, let alone the entire adult male population.

The apparent increasing likelihood that money could be transformed into any of the recognized and recognizable markers of status was a reflection of a number of factors. Landowning per se was no longer an automatic determi-nant of high status; the Liberal party was now dominated by generally well-off businessmen and professionals and the Conservative Party increasingly so; the barriers to non-Anglican entry into Britain's elite had been largely removed. But, on the other hand, the sheer rise in the number of very wealthy men mitigated against any more than a minority being able to join the titled elite or, indeed, receive any of the formal markers of elite status. Many among the ever-increasing ranks of the wealthy were unsuitable to join the public elite, or had no wish to do so. Many, too, would have pinned their hopes for accept-ability and assimilation into the elite on their sons, increasingly sent to a public school and Oxbridge, or to marriage into the pre-existing elite by their daughters. Indeed, the public schools largely assumed the role they did in late Victorian and Edwardian society precisely to attach a marker of social respectability as 'gentlemen' to those who went there.

As noted, one of the most striking changes evident among the 1906 cohort was the relatively greater number of wealth-holders from outside London, and relative diminution in the number of London-based fortunes. To a certain extent, this is misleading, as the absolute number of London-based fortunes rose considerably, from 42 in the two years 1860–1 to 87 in the single year of 1906. As well, London still dwarfed any single venue of wealth-holding elsewhere in the country, with Greater Manchester producing 23 wealth-holders, Merseyside 12, Tyneside 10, and so on. Nevertheless, it was unquestionably true that provincial business and professional wealth was much more significant than half a century earlier. This pattern apparently mirrored the geographical distribution of middle-class *incomes* (not *wealth*) in Britain. Incomes liable to income tax (generally, those over about £150; income tax was levied between 1798 and 1815 and after 1842) showed a geographical distribution in which incomes assessed in Lancashire and Yorkshire peaked, compared with London, around 1865, and then showed a levelling off as London, where there were always more middle-class incomes than in Lancashire and Yorkshire, rose again.[10] Since wealth consists of accumulated income, with great wealth taking decades to accumulate, the 1906 statistics probably represent the importance of high mid- to late nineteenth-century provincial incomes. These income tax data show a 'swing back' to London incomes in the decade or two before the First World War (my data ceases in 1911–12), and it may be that examining the probate data at dates after the 1914–18 War would also show this, bearing in mind the fact that estate duty avoidance is likely to have increased markedly after 1918, and that the City lost something of its international pre-eminence following the Great War. Nevertheless, the contraction in Britain's traditional staple and extractive industries and the economic decline of the north of England (but not the West Midlands) and the Celtic areas after 1918 suggests that this was likely. These trends would have had very significant effects on the nature and composition of the 'Establishment', with a relatively unified and arguably successful 'Establishment' linking commercial, industrial, and landed wealth dominant between 1918 and 1945, and well able to see off the Socialist challenge before the Second World War.

---

[10] Rubinstein, W.D. 1987. *Elites and the Wealthy in Modern British History: Essays in Economic and Social History.* Brighton: Harvester Wheatsheaf, 83–118.

3

Assets of the Dead: Wealth, Investment, and Modernity in Nineteenth- and Early Twentieth-Century England and Wales

David R. Green, Alastair Owens,
Claire Swan, and Carry van Lieshout

I am the only child of parents who weighed, measured, and priced everything; for whom what could not be weighed, measured, and priced, had no existence.[1]

The money economy enforces the necessity of continuous mathematical operations in our daily transactions.[2]

INTRODUCTION

Writing at the end of the nineteenth century, the great German sociologist Georg Simmel suggested that the defining characteristic of the modern age was the all-pervading money economy. For the modern person, he noted, 'depends at any moment on a hundred connections fostered by monetary interests, without which he could no more exist than could the limb of an organic creature cut off from the circulation of its vital fluids'.[3] Money, he argued, allowed the division of labour and specialization to take place and provided

The authors would like to thank Martin Daunton and Peter Lindert for their helpful advice on an earlier draft of this chapter and the participants at an Economic and Social Research Council workshop on 'Wealth, investment and gender in the nineteenth and twentieth centuries' held at the Open University, Milton Keynes, in June 2008, for their valuable comments.

[1] Dickens, C. 1857. *Little Dorrit*. London: Bradbury and Evans. Reprinted 1999. Oxford: Oxford University Press, 17.

[2] Simmel, G. 1907. *The Philosophy of Money (Philosophie des Geldes)*. Leipzig: Duncker und Humblot. Reprinted 2004, edited by D. Frisby, 3rd edition. London: Routledge, 444.

[3] Simmel, G. 1991. 'Money in modern culture'. *Theory, Culture and Society* 8(3): 20.

the means by which products and services could be exchanged over long distances. It fostered economic relationships at a distance by dissolving the local connections between ownership and possession. An income in Berlin, Simmel observed with reference to his home town, could be derived from shares in American railroads, African goldmines, and Norwegian mortgages. He noted that increasing numbers of people had started to participate in the ever-widening circle of economic activity, and he observed how 'more and more things that appeared to be beyond exchange are pulled down into its restless flow'.[4] And just as Charles Dickens had noted the weighing, measuring, and pricing of everything in *Little Dorrit*, so Simmel commented on how 'the lives of many people are absorbed by such evaluating, weighing, calculating and reducing of qualitative values to quantitative ones'.[5]

In this chapter we investigate the extent to which increasing numbers of individuals were bound into this expanding sphere of monetary relationships through the ownership of assets. Their growing involvement, in particular, with the financial markets and the risks that these entailed, were crucial components of the emergence of the modern world of accurate measurement, rational calculation, and the assessment of risk.[6] As Alex Preda and others have pointed out, the publication of more accurate and timely information about stock market prices and the inclusion of financial information in the popular press underpinned the rise of the expert broker able to offer advice, in person and in printed form, to anyone willing to invest.[7] The growing number of advice manuals aimed at the amateur investor was further evidence of the importance of the financial sector for an increasing number of individuals. Even Samuel Beeton, publisher of *The English Woman's Domestic Magazine* and a host of other self-help manuals, aimed at the middle class, notably his wife's best- selling *Mrs Beeton's Book of Household Management*, became involved in the fad for financial advice, issuing *Beeton's Guide Book to the Stock Exchange and Money Market* in 1870.[8] As Preda has suggested, throughout the middle decades of the nineteenth century, this emergent 'knowledge

---

[4] Simmel, 'Money in modern culture', 30.

[5] Simmel, *The Philosophy of Money*, 444.

[6] For further discussion of this point, see Poovey, M. 2003. 'Introduction'. In *The Financial System in Nineteenth-Century Britain*, edited by M. Poovey. Oxford: Oxford University Press, 1–33.

[7] Preda, A. 2001. 'The rise of the popular investor: financial knowledge and investing in England and France, 1840–1880'. *Sociological Quarterly* 42(2): 205–32. For wider discussion of cultures of investment in Victorian Britain, see the essays in Henry, N. and C. Schmitt eds. 2009. *Victorian Investments: New Perspectives on Finance and Culture*. Bloomington and Indianapolis, IN: Indiana University Press; Poovey, M. 2008. *Genres of the Credit Economy: Mediating Value in Eighteenth and Nineteenth-Century Britain*. Chicago: University of Chicago Press; and Preda, A. 2009. *Framing Finance: The Boundaries and Markets of Modern Capitalism*. Chicago: University of Chicago Press. Different sources of advice are discussed by Ranald Michie in Chapter 7 of this volume.

[8] See Beeton, S. 1870. *Beeton's Guide Book to the Stock Exchange and Money Market with Hints to Investors and the Chances of Speculation*. London: Ward, Lock, Tyler.

frame', supported by a range of new cognitive instruments and institutional practices, turned financial investing into a socially desirable activity.[9] Such involvement with financial markets, of course, was not entirely new. Investment in shares and other financial instruments – notably government securities – long predated the nineteenth century. However, as Simmel had recognized in the context of social relationships and modern culture, it was the widening scope of this paper money economy and the growing dependence of middle-class households on financial assets derived at a distance through the ownership of shares and other forms of securities that constituted a distinct transformation in economic relations.

We explore this transformation by examining the assets left at death by a sample of individuals whose estates were submitted for death duties during the nineteenth century. This sample was drawn from the thousands of individuals who owned sufficient wealth at death to warrant an assessment for probate and legacy duty (or, from 1894, estate duty), and who to all intents and purposes represented more broadly the burgeoning British middle class. Their material possessions, and more significantly their financial investments – as shareholders, fundholders, depositors, and lenders – provide an insight into the way in which individuals and households were increasingly linked to the widening circle of exchange that characterized the emergence of the modern capitalist world. In doing so, this chapter extends the discussion of wealth-holders in Britain beyond the relatively narrow focus on the small set of individuals who comprised the very rich – the captains of industry, the commercial and professional elites and the landed magnates – and beyond the extent to which members of this economic elite invested their fortunes in land.[10] By contrast, we know relatively little about the mass of wealth-holders lower down the economic hierarchy who comprised the bulk of the middle class. There are few studies of the kinds of wealth owned by this group and those that exist are primarily focused on specific places at particular points in

---

[9] Preda, *Framing Finance*.
[10] For more on this group, see inter alia Cain, P.J. and A.G. Hopkins 2001. *British Imperialism, 1688–2000*, 2nd edition. Harlow: Longman; Daunton, M. 1989. '"Gentlemanly Capitalism" and British industry, 1820–1914'. *Past and Present* 122: 119–58; Rubinstein, W.D. 1991. '"Gentlemanly Capitalism" and British industry, 1820–1914'. *Past and Present* 132: 150–70. Daunton, M. 1991. 'Reply: "Gentlemanly Capitalism" and British industry, 1820–1914'. *Past and Present* 132: 170–87. and Rubinstein, W.D. 2006. *Men of Property: The Very Wealthy in Britain since the Industrial Revolution*, 2nd edition. London: Social Affairs Unit. An overview of the Gentlemanly Capitalism thesis can be found in Cain and Hopkins, *British Imperialism*. See also Chapter 2 in this volume. Important contributions to the question of land ownership include Spring, E. 1999. 'Businessmen and landowners re-engaged'. *Historical Research* 72(177): 77–88; Daunton, 'Gentlemanly Capitalism'; Rubinstein, W.D. 1999. 'Response'. *Historical Research* 72(177): 88–91; Thompson, F.M.L. 1990. 'Life after death: how successful nineteenth-century businessmen disposed of their fortunes'. *Economic History Review* 43(1): 40–61; Rubinstein, W.D. 1992. 'Cutting up rich: a reply to F.M.L. Thompson'. *Economic History Review* 45(2): 350–61; Thompson, F.M.L. 1992. 'Stitching it together again'. *Economic History Review* 45(2): 362–75.

time.[11] In this chapter we examine the assets owned by the middle class across the country as a whole for a period of more than a hundred years. To what extent were such people engaged in the wider money economy of paper investments in shares and other forms of securities? How significant were these kinds of assets compared to more concrete forms of wealth such as real estate? How did the balance of assets change over the long nineteenth century? Can we discern a growing involvement in the money economy, as Georg Simmel has suggested, and, if so, what are the implications of this pattern of ownership for understanding 'modern' society? To move beyond the interesting but rather narrow debate about 'Gentlemanly Capitalism' in which much of the discussion about British wealth-holders has been couched, we need to understand better the answers to these questions.

EVIDENCE FOR THE STUDY OF WEALTH-HOLDING: DEATH DUTY ACCOUNTS

To explore the relationships that underpinned the way in which individual wealth-holders engaged with the money economy requires understanding the composition of their wealth and this can only be achieved on a systematic basis by exploring the contents of their estates at the time of their death. The evidence used here derives from the valuations contained in the Residuary Accounts arising from the imposition of Legacy Duty upon the deceased's estate.[12] From 1796, Legacy Duty was levied on moveable property and the Residuary Accounts for the assessment of this tax provide detailed information of an individual's personal wealth up to the end of the series in 1902.[13] Unfortunately, relatively few of these Accounts have survived for each year. The dataset on which our analysis is based includes all 1446 individual accounts that remain for the period from 1870 and, for the purposes of comparison, a sample of 744 estates belonging to individuals who died in 1810, 1820, 1830, 1840, 1850, and 1860.[14]

---

[11] Key studies of wealth and property ownership among the nineteenth-century middle class include Morris, R.J. 2005. *Men, Women and Property in England, 1780–1870: A Social and Economic History of Family Strategies among the Leeds Middle Classes*. Cambridge: Cambridge University Press; and Davidoff, L. and C. Hall 2002. *Family Fortunes: Men and Women of the English Middle Class 1780–1850*, 2nd edition. London: Routledge.

[12] Legacy Duty was one of several death duties imposed on estates over the course of the nineteenth century; see: Daunton, M. 2001. *Trusting Leviathan: The Politics of Taxation in Britain, 1799–1914*. Cambridge: Cambridge University Press, chapter 8.

[13] IR19 Board of Stamps: Legacy Duty Office and Successors: Specimens of Death Duty Account, 1796–1903, The National Archives, Kew, UK.

[14] This first group of 1446 individuals reflects the number of Residuary Accounts that have been preserved between 1870 and 1902, when the series ends. This was a small proportion of the total actually submitted, the remainder having been destroyed. However, the sample itself

Over and above the sampling issues, however, there are problems associated with interpreting this kind of evidence. The first and most obvious point to note is that any evidence derived at the end of life will have an inevitable age bias towards the elderly and that this may have influenced the kinds of assets owned.[15] Research published elsewhere for the period 1870–1902 suggests that for those men who died aged 60 years or older and for women who died aged 45 or above, shares usually comprised the largest set of assets. For those who died younger, real estate tended to have been more important and for very elderly women, government securities outweighed the value of shares.[16] In relation to the wealth-holding population as a whole, therefore, the sources are likely to result in an overestimation of the relative significance of stocks, shares, and other securities. The second problem that plagues all studies that rely on taxation records is the possibility that estates were undervalued as a result of attempts to evade tax or reduce liabilities through concealment of assets, the use of trusts or by passing property via an *inter vivos* gift prior to death. It is impossible to gauge accurately the extent of each of these actions, which would have had the effect of reducing the value of recorded assets, but contemporaries appeared relatively unconcerned by such activities and thought that they had little impact on the overall assessment of estates.[17]

In spite of these limitations, the Residuary Accounts offer a unique and valuable insight into the changing composition of wealth-holding over the course of the 'long' nineteenth century, providing a rare opportunity for assessing the population's growing engagement with the paper money economy. For the period later in the century, we are able to supplement these data on the composition of personal wealth with evidence of the ownership of real estate – derived from different sets of death duty records: Succession and Estate Duty registers, discussed below – to build up a full picture of the relative importance of different kinds of assets to the fortunes of the British middle

---

appears to be representative of the broader population from which it was drawn. A comparison of the number of accounts for each county with the total number of adult deaths in 1881, for example, confirms that there is no geographical bias in the series. The R^2 coefficient is 0.9513, suggesting a very strong relationship between deaths in the county in 1881 and the number of surviving Residuary Accounts. The distribution of the gross estate valuations for our post-1870 evidence is virtually identical to that described by Peter Lindert in his analysis of a sample of probate data for 1875. The Gini coefficient (a measure of inequality) for our post-1870 sample is 0.82 and that for Lindert's data is 0.83 (the closer to 1, the higher the level of inequality); see Lindert, P. 1986. 'Unequal English wealth since 1670'. *Journal of Political Economy* 94(6): 1127–62, and further discussion below.

[15] For the sample of 1276 of the 1446 Residuary Accounts for which it was possible to establish age at death, the average age for males was 60.3 and for females 64.4.

[16] Green, D.R., A. Owens, J. Rutterford, and J. Maltby 2009. 'Lives in the balance? Gender, age and assets in late-nineteenth-century England and Wales'. *Continuity and Change* 24(2): 326–8.

[17] See Harris, W. and K.A. Lake 1906. 'Estimates of the realisable wealth of the United Kingdom based mostly on estate duty returns'. *Journal of the Royal Statistical Society* 69(4): 723–4. See also Daunton, *Trusting Leviathan*, 225.

class. The aggregate values of real and personal property liable for estate duty annually reported by the Inland Revenue allow us to continue our analysis into the twentieth century, beyond the period when the Residuary Account and Death Duty Register series end. We begin by considering the size of the nineteenth-century wealth-owning population, looking at how wealth was distributed among this group and emphasizing the significant but largely overlooked group of wealth-holders that lay somewhere between those who were super rich and those who died with assets so meagre as to escape the fiscal reach of the state. The next section examines in greater detail the changing composition of estates, charting the growing importance of stocks, shares, and other securities to nineteenth-century middle-class fortunes. We then consider what impact this had on the ownership of more traditional forms of wealth, notably land and real estate. In the final section of the chapter, we focus on the geographies of wealth-holding, examining how the emergence of the paper economy tied middle-class domestic security to the financial well-being of the British nation state and the fortunes of imperial commerce. We explore the extent to which wealth-holders in different parts of the country participated in these widening capital markets.

POSSESSIONS AND THE HIERARCHY OF WEALTH-HOLDING

In the course of the nineteenth century, the middle classes expanded. How large was this group of wealth-holders for whom the possessive instinct supposedly burned so strong? To answer this we can turn to two broad sets of evidence, the first focusing on assets of the living and the second on those of the dead. In relation to the first, in 1867, Robert Dudley Baxter estimated that the upper and middle classes, who were defined both in terms of their occupation as well as the possession of an independent income, comprised between 16 and 20 per cent of the adult population in England and Wales.[18] A few years later, Arthur Bowley estimated that the proportion of the population, excluding wage earners, who were assessed for income tax or who earned a taxable income of below £160 per annum from sources other than salaries, was some 16.7 per cent in 1880 and 26.5 per cent by 1913, although he cautioned that the basis on which incomes were assessed left room for error.[19] Notwithstanding the need for caution, these figures nevertheless

---

[18] Baxter, R.D. 1868. *National Income: The Untied Kingdom*. London: Macmillan, frontpiece, 79.
[19] Bowley, A. 1920. *The Change in the Distribution of the National Income, 1880–1913*. Oxford: Clarendon, 7–8, 13, 22. The figures refer primarily to those with a salaried income subject to income tax. He also included an 'intermediate' category of 'those who do not receive

provide a broad indication of the likely extent of wealth holders in the population at large. They also accord closely with the conclusions drawn from another source of evidence based on the proportion of the adult population that left an estate liable to probate. These data, which are described in more detail elsewhere, show that in terms of absolute numbers for England and Wales, owners of probated estates rose from 29,979 in 1858 to 56,968 by 1899.[20] In relative terms, this represented an increase from 14.2 to 17.1 per cent of those who died in each year aged over 20, a small but not insignificant rise in the proportion of the population that managed to accumulate sufficient wealth during their lifetimes to warrant probate at the time of their death.[21] In other words, those with a taxable income during their life, and those who left a probated estate at the time of their death each comprised about one in five of their respective populations. The remainder of individuals comprised the mass of wage earners who paid no tax on income during their lifetime and who, at the time of their death, either had nothing or left estates that were too small for probate.

The fortunate few, however, were by no means equally privileged and the hierarchy of wealth-holding stretched from those who owned barely enough to warrant the payment of income tax or justify the imposition of death duties to the fabulously wealthy whose fortunes were measured in the hundreds of thousands if not millions of pounds. Using data compiled by Peter Lindert, derived from the gross valuations of personal property for 1810 and 1875 for selected English counties, it is possible to establish the pattern of inequality amongst those who left personal property liable to probate. The valuations themselves were based on a variety of sources: those for 1810 on the Legacy Duty Registers together with the wills and administrations exhibited at the Prerogative Court of Canterbury and those for 1875 on the calendars of wills and administrations lodged with the Principal Probate Registry.[22] Figures 3.1 and 3.2 show the Lorenz curves for both years which tell the same story of a

---

wages, but had in all (a taxable income of) less than £150 a year prior to 1894 or £160 in or after that year', parentheses added. Most wage earners were excluded from this total.

[20] The figure for 1858 comes from the *Twenty-Second Annual Report of the Registrar General of Births, Marriages and Deaths in England*. London: Her Majesty's Stationery Office (1861), xlvi, xlvii, and that for 1899 comes from the *Forty-Second Report of the Commissioners of Her Majesty's Inland Revenue for the Year Ended 31 March 1899*. London: Her Majesty's Stationery Office (1899), 157.

[21] The figures for the numbers who died are taken from the *Twenty-Second Annual Report*, xlvi, and from the *Sixty-Second Annual Report of the Registrar General of Births, Marriages and Deaths in England*. London: Her Majesty's Stationery Office (1899), 122.

[22] See Lindert, 'Unequal English wealth'. Peter Lindert has generously made these data available online; see www.econ.ucdavis.edu/faculty/fzlinder/probate.xls (site accessed: 8 March 2010). For the 1810 sample, $n = 4243$ and for 1875, $n = 2792$. The samples are drawn from the following counties: Cambridgeshire, Derbyshire London (north of the Thames), Middlesex (excluding London), Shropshire, Staffordshire, Warwickshire, Yorkshire (East Riding), and Yorkshire (West Riding).

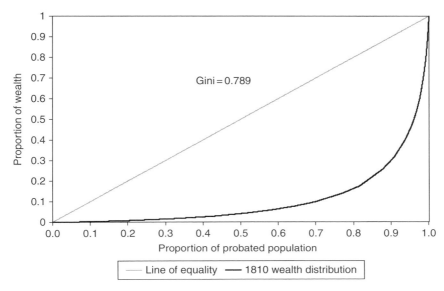

Figure 3.1 Distribution of probated wealth in selected English counties, 1810

Source: Probate data provided by Peter Lindert. Available online at www.econ.ucdavis.edu/faculty/fzlinder/probate.xls (site accessed: 8 March 2010).

Note: We are grateful to Peter Lindert for allowing us to use these data.

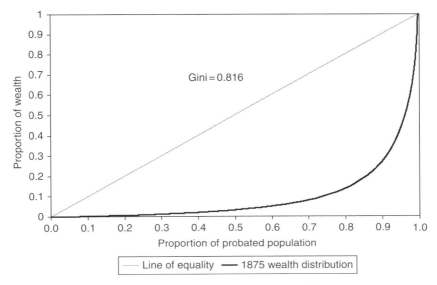

Figure 3.2 Distribution of probated wealth in selected English counties, 1875

Source: see Figure 3.1.

highly unequal distribution of wealth, with the top 10 per cent of individuals owning approximately 70 per cent of probated wealth and the top 1 per cent owning between 23 and 27 per cent of total wealth.[23] Indeed, according to Lindert, the level of inequality amongst this group of wealth-holders remained virtually unchanged throughout the nineteenth and into the early part of the twentieth century.[24]

However, whilst aristocrats, businessmen, and industrialists may have held the lion's share of wealth, the bulk of wealth-holders had more modest fortunes: throughout the century, 80 per cent of estates accounted for no more than about 10–12 per cent of the total probated wealth. For want of a better label, this 'middle class' of wealth-holders stretched from the small employer, shopkeeper, or tenant farmer who had little excess capital and for whom work continued until ended by incapacity or old age, to the professional men and minor gentry able to amass sufficient wealth in their own lifetimes to contemplate retirement funded by investment income. This class also included significant numbers of single women, including spinsters as well as widows, with small but sufficient independent incomes. The vast majority of wealth-holders, therefore, operated in quite different economic circumstances from those with incomes derived wholly or largely from the possession of landed estates or significant amounts of capital investments, or, indeed, both.

Records of personal property liable for probate duty offer some measure of the overall worth of individuals, but they provide few direct insights into the composition of fortunes. To what extent did different segments of this hierarchy of wealth-holders engage with the new financial opportunities that became available over the course of the nineteenth century?

ASSETS OF THE DEAD: THE COMPOSITION OF WEALTH

In terms of numbers sold, *Self Help*, Samuel Smiles' hugely successful gospel of thrift, hard work, and moral improvement, published in 1859, was second only to the Bible. In its first year of publication it sold 20,000 copies, and within 30 years this had risen to over 150,000, with translations into 17 different languages.[25] Over and above the merits of the work itself, its success derived in large part from the circumstances which underpinned the growing importance of the middle class and their accumulation of wealth. Economic

---

[23] The Gini coefficients are 0.79 and 0.82 respectively.
[24] Lindert, P. 2000. 'Three centuries of inequality in Britain and America'. In *Handbook of Income Distribution*, Volume 1, edited by A.B. Atkinson and F. Bourguignon. Amsterdam: Elsevier, 181.
[25] Smiles, S. 1859. *Self Help*. London: John Murray.

expansion had fostered an increasing number of professional occupations – doctors, lawyers, civil servants, bankers, financiers – accompanied by an army of clerks, teachers, shopkeepers, and small employers. The number of male white-collar employees in Britain rose from around 144,000 in 1851 to over 918,000 by 1911, with clerks alone rising from 92,000 in 1861 to over 561,000 by the end of the period.[26] Women, too, participated in the growth of white collar employment and the number of female clerks rose from virtually nothing to nearly 125,000 by 1911. The moral values and achievements prized most highly by this largely urban-based group focused around the cult of individual improvement through education, hard work, and thrift. The raft of civic institutions that sprang up in provincial towns and cities throughout the country during the nineteenth century was witness to the ethos of improvement and reform that accompanied the growing number of individuals in these kinds of occupations.[27] Alongside this emergence of an urban bourgeois 'public sphere', the accumulation of personal fortunes underpinned new attitudes of consumerism and materialism which resulted in the growing importance of the private world of the home as the site of bourgeois cultural identity and a cradle of well-being.[28] Arguably, however, the moral worth of material success was even more important than the amount of wealth itself – a fact confirmed by the immense popularity of *Self Help* – and nowhere was this more apparent than in the ways by which these middle-class values and assets could be passed on to the next generation through education and, ultimately, a timely inheritance.

Such wealth, of course, is not equivalent to income but as Peter Lindert has reminded us, 'it sheds indirect light in two ways: by showing the assets on which current property income is based, and by reflecting the wealth accumulated from earlier total incomes'.[29] It is the composition of those assets with which we are most concerned, largely for the light it can throw on the ways in which individuals engaged with the financial sector of the economy. Such engagement is evident in relation to the kinds of assets owned at the point of death, outlined in Table 3.1. Leaving aside for one moment the significance of real estate, a topic to which we return later, the evidence suggests a growing engagement with the economy of paper money. The more personal forms of wealth – including individual lending, household possessions, and stock in

---

[26] Crossick, G. 1977. 'The emergence of the lower middle class in Britain: a discussion'. In *The Lower Middle Class in Britain*, edited by G. Crossick. London: Croom Helm, 19; and Anderson, G.L. 1977. 'The social economy of late Victorian clerks'. In *The Lower Middle Class in Britain*, edited by G. Crossick. London: Croom Helm, 113.

[27] See, for example, Gunn, S. 2000. *The Public Culture of the Victorian Middle Class: Ritual and Authority in the English Industrial City, 1840–1914.* Manchester: Manchester University Press.

[28] See, for example, Cohen, D. 2006. *Household Gods: The British and their Possessions.* London: Yale University Press.

[29] Lindert, 'Three centuries of inequality', 177.

Table 3.1 Assets by value of personal estate, 1800–1935 (per cent of total)

% share	Government securities	Shares	Lending	Household	Stock	Cash	Insurance	Other	Total
1800–34 (N = 164)[a]	40.0	2.7	16.3	12.6	8.0	7.9	4.6	7.9	100.0
1835–69 (N = 580)[a]	33.0	17.4	20.6	5.1	10.3	10.1	2.5	1.0	100.0
1870–1902 (N = 1446)[a]	17.7	40.6	19.3	6.1	4.0	9.1	3.1	0.1	100.0
1903–14[b]	9.8	47.4	12.8	3.5	7.7	9.3	4.4	5.1	100.0
1920–35[b]	26.9	38.2	10.1	3.0	4.3	9.3	4.3	3.9	100.0

Source: a – Residuary Accounts, IR19; b – Inland Revenue, Annual Reports.

Note: The categories of personal estate used here are based on aggregated totals derived from the separate items noted in the Residuary Accounts. 'Government securities' refers to domestic or foreign government securities returned under the following headings in the Residuary Accounts: 'Stocks of funds including Exchequer Bills of the UK', 'Stocks or other Securities of British Colonies', 'Stocks or other Securities of Foreign States'. These categories also included municipal bonds. 'Shares' are generally corporate shares or securities, including railway shares, canal shares, and shares in ships. 'Household' includes possessions related to the household such as furniture, plate, linen, china, books, etc.; 'Stock' includes any items associated with business activity including stock, goodwill, horses, and carriages; 'Cash' includes any cash held at home or in a bank; Insurance includes any life assurance and other insurance policies; 'Other' refers to any property not included in the above.

Figures for 1800–1902 are based on individual Residuary Accounts. Those for 1903–14 and from 1920 to 1935 refer to the total number of estates assessed for estate duty in the United Kingdom. From 1922, estates in the Republic of Ireland were excluded from the totals.

trade – declined in relative importance over the period. By contrast, financial investments, including the ownership of government securities and company shares, gained in significance. At the start of the century, nearly 43 per cent of personal property by value was accounted for by government securities and by shares but by the end this had risen to around 58 per cent. However, over the period up to the First World War, the emphasis shifted from government securities to the ownership of shares particularly after 1870. As a result, by the later decades of the nineteenth century, a significant number of people became dependent on the fortunes of the stock market and increasingly reliant on the performance of British capitalism at home and abroad. Shares continued their inexorable rise until the outbreak of the First World War, at which point a massive issue of war bonds rapidly drew capital into government securities.[30] The importance of government securities after 1920 bears witness to the significance of war bonds as a form of investment in these later years.

The growing importance of financial investments was paralleled by an increase in the numbers of individuals who owned shares and government securities, albeit with some important shifts in the kinds of assets owned. Table 3.2 shows that between the first third and the last third of the century the proportion of individuals who owned shares and government securities at the time of their death rose modestly from just under 29 per cent to a little over 35 per cent of the total, with a noticeable drop in the middle of the century. However, this comparatively small overall increase hides two significant changes in the kinds of financial assets owned and their relative importance. In the first place, there was a large fall in the proportion of individuals that held government securities at the time of their death. The large majority of these holdings were British government bonds, or Consols, which accounted for over 95 per cent by value of all government securities in the period up to 1870, and for 74 per cent between 1870 and 1902. Foreign government and colonial bonds accounted for the remaining share. Given the sharp reduction in the yield on Consols during the course of the century the fall in ownership of government securities is hardly surprising.[31] As the century progressed the need to reduce the national debt was a paramount consideration for all governments leading to various attempts to redeem and consolidate the debt and to reduce dividends.[32] By contrast, the proportion of those holding shares rose steeply in the last third of the century. Changes in company law made investment in joint stock

---

[30] This mass issue of War Bonds is discussed in Wormell, J. 2000. *The Management of the National Debt of the United Kingdom, 1900–1932*. London: Routledge, 124–49. See also Chapter 8 in the present volume.

[31] Consols (sometimes referred to as Three Per Cent Consols) is the abbreviated name for 'Consolidated Annuities', the largest and most important British government security created as a consequence of consolidating various public debts in the eighteenth century.

[32] The coupon rate on Consols was 3 per cent for much of the nineteenth century but under the National Debt (Conversion) Act of 1888 this was reduced to 2¾ per cent and in 1903 it was further reduced to 2½ per cent. For further discussion, see Daunton, *Trusting Leviathan*, Chapters 5 and 7 elsewhere in this volume.

Table 3.2 Individuals holding shares and/or government securities, 1870–1902 (per cent of total)

	Shares only		Government securities only		Shares and government securities		Total with shares and government securities		Total without		Total	
	N	%	N	%	N	%	N	%	N	%	N	%
1800–34	6	3.7	36	22.0	5	3.0	47	28.7	117	71.3	164	100.0
1835–69	48	8.3	48	8.3	20	3.4	116	20.0	464	80.0	580	100.0
1870–1902	301	20.8	87	6.0	124	8.6	512	35.4	934	64.6	1446	100.0

Source: Residuary Accounts. The figures for years prior to 1870 are based on a sample of the surviving records of individuals who died in 1810, 1820, 1830, 1840, 1850, and 1860. The figures from 1870 onwards are a complete survey of all surviving records from that date forward.

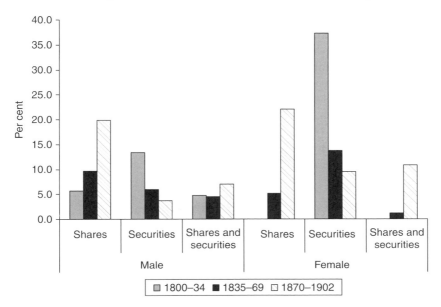

Figure 3.3 Ownership of shares and securities by gender and period in England and Wales, 1800–1902 (per cent of individuals)
Source: see Table 3.2.

companies less risky and the growing availability of smaller share denominations and partly paid up shares helped to entice new investors into the financial markets. Better financial knowledge and the spread of provincial stock exchanges similarly helped the diffusion of ownership of these kinds of investments. The outcome was that by the end of the century, as Robb has remarked, the British middle class had become 'a nation of shareholders'.[33]

This growing involvement with financial markets, moreover, was common to men and women, albeit to differing degrees (Figure 3.3). Government securities declined in importance for both groups over time, though their significance was always higher for women than it was for men. By virtue of their widespread exclusion from paid employment, many middle-class women were forced to rely on dividends for an income to a much greater extent than men and for this group the security of the Funds and the guaranteed dividend were always paramount considerations.[34] However, even their attachment to the Funds faded over time as shares became more attractive and by the end of the period, a greater proportion

---

[33] Robb, G. 1992. *White-Collar Crime in Modern England: Financial Fraud and Business Morality, 1845–1929*. Cambridge: Cambridge University Press, 3. See also Rutterford, J., D.R. Green, J. Maltby, and A. Owens, 2011. 'Who comprised the nation of shareholders? Gender and investment in Great Britain, c.1870–1935'. *Economic History Review* 64(1): 157–87.

[34] Green, D.R. and A. Owens 2003. 'Gentlewomanly capitalism? Spinsters, widows and wealth holding in England and Wales, c.1800–1860'. *Economic History Review* 56(3): 510–36.

of women than men owned shares. This process was encouraged by the growing tendency of companies to issue relatively safe preference shares, a type of investment that proved more attractive to female investors.[35] Whether they had purchased or inherited shares in their own name – practices made more likely by the passage of the Married Women's Property Acts of 1870 and 1882 – the fact remains that by the end of the nineteenth century, women, to a greater extent even than men, were tied into the ebb and flow of the financial markets for their financial well-being.[36] In that sense, their engagement with the paper economy, as well as men's, grew ever stronger.

LAND AND MONEY OR BOTH?

The counterweight to the paper economy, and one that was arguably most attractive to those with limited means, was to invest in land and housing. Unaffected by financial scandals, comparatively free of government interference, and relatively easy to understand in relation to risk and rates of return, real estate, historians have argued, was especially favoured by shopkeepers and other members of the lower middle class whose geographical scope for investment remained predominantly local.[37] Though they may have also been involved in financial investments, this was likely to have been secondary to their primary interests in bricks and mortar.

With the exception of a handful of relatively small and localized studies, analysis of the long-term composition of wealth in Britain during the nineteenth century is forced, through lack of data, to concentrate on personal estate. Freehold land was deliberately excluded from taxation at death until the Succession Duty Act of 1853 and therefore prior to that date it is impossible to assess for individuals the importance of real estate in relation to other forms of wealth-holding.[38] Aggregate figures for the country as a whole only became

---

[35] See Rutterford et al., 'Who comprised the nation of shareholders?'

[36] On this legislation and its impact, see Combs, M.B. 2005. 'A measure of legal independence: the 1870 Married Women's Property Act and the wealth-holding patterns of British wives'. *Journal of Economic History* 65(4): 1028–57.

[37] See, for example, Daunton, M. 1977. *Coal Metropolis: Cardiff, 1870–1914.* Leicester: Leicester University Press, especially 118–20; Crossick, G. 2000. 'Meanings of property and the world of the petite bourgeoisie'. In *Urban Fortunes: Property and Inheritance in the Town*, edited by J. Stobart and A. Owens. Aldershot: Ashgate, 50–78; Morris, *Men, Women and Property*, chapter 5; Offer, A. 1981. *Property and Politics, 1870–1914: Landownership, Law, Ideology and Urban Development in England.* Cambridge: Cambridge University Press, especially chapter 7.

[38] IR26 Board of Inland Revenue and predecessors: Estate Duty Office and predecessors: Registers of Legacy Duty, Succession Duty and Estate Duty, The National Archives, Kew, UK. For further discussion of these sources, see Green et al. 'Lives in the balance?' Leasehold property was subject to Legacy Duty until 1853 at which point it became liable for Succession Duty instead.

available in the Inland Revenue annual reports from 1895 onwards. Therefore, it is only from 1853, when recording started, that we can begin to piece together an individual's entire wealth portfolio by combining evidence from the Residuary Accounts with that derived from Succession Duty and later Estate Duty Registers. The evidence discussed below concentrates on the period from 1870 until 1902 for which we have compiled detailed individual inventories of wealth, including real and leasehold estate.

There is, however, one additional problem relating to the way that these assets were valued and here there are important differences between real and personal estate. The valuation of personal assets was based on the market price that prevailed at the time of assessment following the individual's death and is therefore an accurate measurement of worth. The valuation of real estate that appears in the various Death Duty Registers was more complex and usually took the form of a 'net annual value' that reflected the income that could be expected from renting out the property minus the yearly cost and encumbrances associated with its upkeep. By multiplying this value by 30 – a figure that represents a return of about 3 per cent – we can derive an approximate capital value of real estate owned by an individual.[39] This problem notwithstanding, by combining evidence from these various sets of records it is possible to question the significance of real estate compared to other forms of wealth – a topic that has hitherto only been examined for small numbers of individuals, usually drawn from the upper echelons of wealth-holders.[40]

The results of this analysis are shown in Figure 3.4 which demonstrates clearly the importance of real estate in relation to other forms of wealth. By taking into account the gross value of all estates for which we have Residuary Accounts and adding the value of real estate for those that held that kind of property, we can assess the relative importance of the different kinds of assets held by individuals at the time of their death. Although shares still accounted for about a third of individual wealth, real and leasehold estate was the next largest category, amounting to about 19 per cent of the value recorded in the Death Duty Registers. Aggregate figures from 1896 onwards suggest that even this total may have been an underestimate.[41] Between 1896 and 1902, real and leasehold estate accounted for over 29 per cent of the wealth that passed at death in the country and evidence for subsequent years, shown in Figure 3.5, suggests that although the value peaked around 1902 before declining steadily until the outbreak of war, it never fell below about a quarter of the total. After the First World War, investment in government securities associated with war bonds rose, mainly, it appears, at the expense of land.

---

[39] For further details, see Green et al. 'Lives in the balance?' 316.

[40] See n. 10.

[41] Although the series begins in 1895, the first year only refers to part of England and Wales. Subsequent years cover the United Kingdom.

Men, Women, and Money

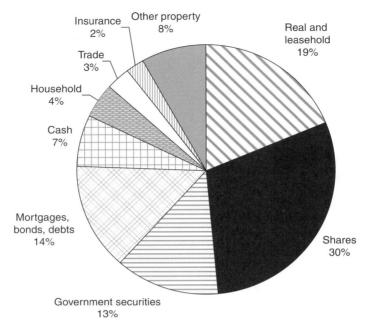

Figure 3.4 Composition of estates at death, England and Wales, 1870–1902 (per cent of gross value, Residuary Accounts sample)

Source: see Table 3.2.

Note: See Table 3.1 for definition of categories of wealth.

Nevertheless, the desire to own real estate reached deep into the social hierarchy. As the various Chartist land schemes promoted by Fergus O'Connor and others testified, the possession of land and real estate was an important element in working-class political ideology. Appearing before the 1850 Select Committee on the investments for the middle and working class, Samuel Bowley noted that 'My experience of the working men is, that they have a very great disposition to get possession of something that they can see and feel, real property'.[42] However, the legal costs of purchasing small parcels of land and houses were disproportionately high and for that reason, it was argued, those with less capital chose or were forced by necessity to seek alternative opportunities. Even the middle classes found these charges difficult to bear. Better to invest in the certainty of the Three Per Cent Consols, it was argued, than to incur the expense of acquiring property.[43]

---

[42] PP 1850 XIX (508), *Select Committee on the Report from the Select Committee on Investments for the Savings of the Middle and Working Classes; Together with the Proceedings of the Committee, Minutes of evidence, and Index*, 413.

[43] *Select Committee on Investments*, 278–87, 680–7.

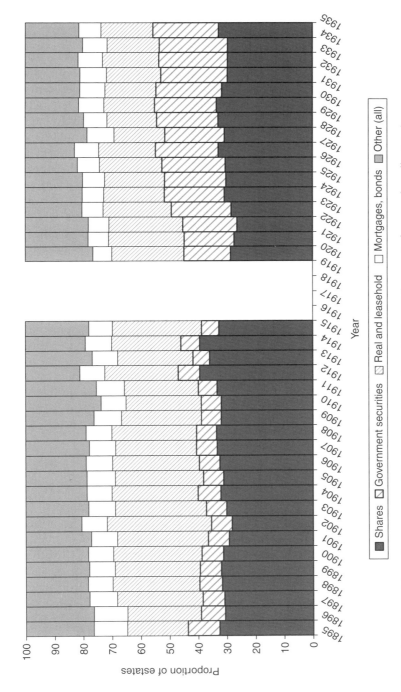

Figure 3.5 Composition of estates at death in the United Kingdom, 1895–1935 (per cent of gross value, all estates)

Source: Reports of the Commissioners of the Inland Revenue, 1895–1935.

Note: No data exist for the years around the First World War (1916–19). After 1922 the figures exclude the Republic of Ireland.

The desire to possess land and houses, however, was strong and our evidence suggests that about a third of wealth-holders possessed real or leasehold estate at the time of their death, but that this varied according to the overall size of fortunes. It is important, of course, to remind ourselves that this was still a relatively small proportion of the number who died both with and without property assessed for tax – around 4 or 5 per cent of all decedents. However, ownership of real estate was by no means restricted to the very rich. To purchase land and houses, especially freehold, required relatively large lumps of capital and those at the bottom end of the hierarchy would have found this more difficult to achieve, either because they did not have access to borrowing or because they just did not have enough money in their own names to do so.[44] As a result, less than one in five of those at the very bottom of the hierarchy owned real estate compared to between about half to two-thirds of those higher up the scale. However, for the two lower wealth bandings, real estate was still more important than shares and government securities, suggesting that when there was a choice to be made between investing in bricks and mortar or in shares and securities, it was the former that was the preferred option.[45] As wealth increased, the proportions of individuals holding a variety of different kinds of assets rose, suggesting that wealthier individuals tended to have more dispersed portfolios of wealth, either because they had more to invest in a range of options, thereby spreading risk, or because, having invested widely, they were able to maximize their income and thereby accumulate greater amounts of wealth.

In itself this is not surprising but it raises the question of the significance of real estate compared to other forms of investments for those who were able to own freehold or leasehold property. Table 3.3 shows the numbers and relative value of estates for the subset of real estate owners in our sample with and without shares and/or securities. The average wealth of those who possessed only real estate was significantly lower than those with other forms of investment, especially those who owned both shares and government securities. For this group of smaller wealth-holders, real estate was particularly important, accounting for an average of 60.3 per cent of their gross wealth compared to just 25.6 per cent for those who owned shares and/or government securities alongside land and houses. In other words, those who relied solely or primarily on real estate tended to be the less wealthy. This, in turn, suggests two life course related processes relating to capital accumulation. First, since age and wealth were positively correlated, it is likely that those with smaller fortunes who held only real estate were comparatively young – a pattern that we have

---

[44] For a discussion of lending by building societies, see Pooley, C. and M. Harmer 1999. *Property Ownership in Britain, c.1850–1950: The Role of the Bradford Equitable Building Society and the Bingley Building Society in the Development of Homeownership*. Cambridge: Granta.
[45] See Crossick. 'Meanings of property'.

Table 3.3 Real estate ownership and wealth, 1870–1902

Gross valuations (£)	Total in IR19 sample	Number with real estate	Number with shares	Number with government securities	% with real estate	% with shares	% with government securities
0–999	888	161	132	45	18.1	14.9	5.1
1000–4999	351	181	141	75	51.6	40.2	21.4
5000–9999	89	52	54	32	58.4	60.7	36.0
≥10,000	118	73	98	62	61.9	83.1	52.5
Total	1446	467	425	214	32.3	29.4	14.8

Source: Residuary Accounts, Succession, and Estate Duty Registers.

Table 3.4 The value of assets by wealth bandings, 1870–1902 (per cent of total gross estate value)

Gross estate value (£)	Shares	Government securities	Real and leasehold	Mortgages and bonds	Cash	Household	Trade	Insurance	Other property	Total
0–999	9.2	4.4	18.1	15.2	21.8	10.7	6.5	6.0	8.1	100.0
1000–4999	15.7	9.2	27.3	16.4	11.5	5.7	4.1	2.2	7.9	100.0
5000–9999	21.5	15.1	23.9	17.8	6.8	3.3	4.4	2.4	4.8	100.0
≥10,000	34.6	13.8	16.9	13.1	4.7	3.9	2.3	2.0	8.6	100.0

Source: see Table 3.3.

identified elsewhere.[46] Secondly, because the returns on land ownership were comparatively low, the life time accumulation of wealth for those who possessed only this kind of property was more limited than for those who owned a more diverse portfolio of assets, especially shares.[47] As Gavin Bell cautioned in his *Guide to the Investment of Capital*, first published in 1846, 'the purchase of land . . . is a most unprofitable investment of capital' through which an investor 'can never entertain any hope of either realising a great fortune, or rising to any eminence'.[48] This helps to account for the differences in the economic status of property owners in our sample.

This pattern is further highlighted in Table 3.4 which shows the relative importance of different categories of assets for the entire sample according to wealth bandings. For the less wealthy, many of whom – as noted above – would have been small tradesmen and retailers, assets were often associated with business, hence the importance for them of the cash economy, both as lenders and hoarders of money, and of household goods and real estate. Some of the latter undoubtedly took the form of premises or small cottage property typical of minor urban landowners or small farmers. For the middling wealth bands between £1000 and £9999, real and leasehold estate were the most significant assets, hinting at the importance of property ownership amongst the lower middle class that others have outlined in relation to shopkeepers and the petite bourgeoisie.[49] These individuals tended to invest close to home, building up their portfolio of assets, based largely on what was available in their immediate locality. As wealth increased, so shares accounted for a growing proportion of assets, although such ownership reached fairly low down the hierarchy of wealth-holders.[50] Indeed, according to Cairncross, in the second half of the century, 'retailers, professional men, skilled workers and women were all being attracted to the Stock Exchange' as well as those with larger fortunes who traditionally had made up the bulk of

---

[46] Green et al. 'Lives in the balance?'

[47] Rates of return on shares varied depending on the type of security and the sector. According to Edelstein, between 1870 and 1913 returns on domestic railways averaged between 4 and 5 per cent and on UK banks between 6 and 7 per cent. In other sectors, rates of returns were often higher. The coupons on Government Consols varied but were generally less than 3 per cent throughout the period. Returns on houses and land also varied but the contemporary view was that land and houses returned around 3 per cent net. If investors were willing to take on slum properties profits could be higher, and as much as 10–12 per cent in some parts of London. See Edelstein, M. 1976. 'Realized rates of return of UK home and overseas portfolio investments in the Age of High Imperialism'. *Explorations in Economic History* 13(3): 292; PP 1884–85 XXX (4402) *First Report of Her Majesty's Commissioners for Inquiring into the Housing of the Working Classes*, 9733.

[48] Bell, G.M. 1846. *A Guide to the Investment of Capital; or how to Lay out Money with Safety and Profit. Being a Popular Exposition of the Various Descriptions of Securities, with Hints for the Guidance of Capitalists*. London: C. Mitchell, 11.

[49] Crossick, 'The meanings of property'.

[50] Cain and Hopkins, *British Imperialism*.

shareholders.[51] Evidence from Estate Duty returns suggests that this pattern of investment changed little in the early years of the twentieth century. For this group, investment opportunities broadened, as did the geographical horizons of their involvement in the financial sector, hinted at by Georg Simmel earlier in this chapter.

MODERNITY, DOMESTICITY, AND THE GEOGRAPHY OF MONEY

Based on the estates evidence outlined above, during the course of the nineteenth and early twentieth centuries, larger numbers and greater proportions of individuals, both men and women, became increasingly engaged in the ownership of shares and other types of securities. Shares, in particular, grew in significance until the large scale take-up of war bonds during the First World War, when government investments once again provided higher rates of return. Land and houses, meanwhile, always remained important, though, in relation to the value of estates, more so for those lower down the hierarchy. In terms of numbers, perhaps as many as one in six or seven of those that died with taxable assets sank all their spare cash into owning land or houses. Nevertheless, from the evidence it is people's growing engagement with the financial markets that stands out as a key shift that occurred over the period covered by this chapter.

At the start of the nineteenth century, radicals such as William Cobbett and Henry Hunt could rail at the fortunes being sucked out of the economy by parasitical fundholders whose dividends were paid from government revenues generated by duties and increasingly from taxation. But by the late nineteenth century, this target had moved as those with money sought out more profitable, if riskier, returns from the stock market.[52] The belief that smaller investors were being drawn into the financial markets – what others have suggested might have amounted to the democratization of shareholding – was also the source of much consternation.[53] The changing regulatory framework of company law in the 1850s and 1860s and the introduction of limited liability resulted in the formation of large numbers of new joint stock companies, which in turn began to attract new kinds of investors into the market.

---

[51] Cairncross, A.K. 1953. *Home and Foreign Investment 1870–1913*. Cambridge: Cambridge University Press, 85. Cairncross notes that those with net estates of between £1000 and £5000 held 24.3 per cent of the value in stocks, funds, and shares; those valued at between £5000 and £10,000 had 36.5 per cent; and those with estates between £10,000 and £20,000 had 44.4 per cent in these kinds of investments.

[52] Daunton, *Trusting Leviathan*, 109–24.

[53] See Chapter 8 in this book for a critical review of the evidence for this suggestion.

The publication of financial information in a variety of forms and the growth of the financial press helped broaden the knowledge base of stock market investors, leading to the rise of what Alex Preda has called 'the popular investor'.[54] The *Financial News*, started in 1884, was the most successful of these ventures but by 1914 it had been joined by over 100 other titles.[55] As investments seemingly became safer – or at least the risks became better known – smaller and almost certainly less knowledgeable investors were drawn to the stock market in ever greater numbers.[56] Indeed, these trends were welcomed by many as confirmation that the fruits of capitalism could be spread further and wider than had hitherto been the case, and that this democratization of shareholding would help foster social harmony by creating a nation of investors.[57] The corollary was that the financial well-being of a growing number of individuals and families became ever more closely linked to the rise and fall of the stock market.

This transformation was not without its own dangers, for companies as well as for the individuals themselves. The widening of share ownership brought with it a class of investor different from those monied men who had underpinned many of the early ventures in the stock market. This expansion of ownership, particularly in the case of banks, gave cause for concern in the event of the need for shareholders to assume financial responsibility for company debts incurred.[58] In practice, these smaller investors were less likely to be concerned with the day to day running of the business, which in turn provided directors with a high degree of corporate control. Efforts by the state to control fraud and regulate companies need to be seen in the light of these changes.[59]

The effects of market failure and the relative vulnerability of small investors were frequently the focus of fictional plots revolving around swindlers, stock market crashes, and insolvency. From Charles Dickens' *Little Dorrit*, published in 1857, where the fall of the house of Merdle spelled financial ruin for those caught in the web of deceit, to E.M. Forster's *Howards End*, appearing in

---

[54] Preda, 'The rise of the popular investor'.

[55] Cottrell, P. 2004. 'Domestic finance 1860–1914'. In *The Cambridge Economic History of Modern Britain. Volume 2: Economic Maturity, 1860–1939*, edited by R. Floud and P. Johnson. Cambridge: Cambridge University Press, 269; see also Poovey, M. ed. 2003. *The Financial System in Nineteenth-Century Britain. Oxford: Oxford University Press*; Henry and Schmitt, *Victorian Investments*.

[56] Rutterford, J. and J. Maltby 2006. '"The widow, the clergyman and the reckless": women investors before 1914'. *Feminist Economics* 12(1/2): 111–38; Rutterford et al., 'Who comprised the nation of shareholders'.

[57] On this point, see Loftus, D. 2002. 'Capital and community: limited liability and attempts to democratize the market in mid-nineteenth-century England'. *Victorian Studies* 45(1): 102.

[58] On these themes, see Turner, J.D. 2009. 'Wider share ownership? Investors in English and Welsh Bank shares in the nineteenth century'. *Economic History Review* 62(s1): 167–92; and Acheson, G.G. and Turner, J.D. 2008. 'The death blow to unlimited liability in Victorian Britain: The City of Glasgow failure'. *Explorations in Economic History* 45(3): 235–53.

[59] See Johnson, P. 2009. *Making the Market: Victorian Origins of Corporate Capitalism*. Cambridge: Cambridge University Press.

1910, which told a tale of class relations in the context of financial insolvency, authors turned to plots that revolved around the perils of the market.[60] Such works highlight the ways in which the middle-class domestic sphere was becoming deeply penetrated by the growing involvement in the financial markets and how its welfare was increasingly dependent on the ownership of these kinds of assets.[61] The ruined shareholder, left with nothing but the paper certificate of worthless shares, cut a sorry figure in the public view, especially when the effects of failure extended into the bourgeois home and tainted those who would otherwise have remained shielded from the vagaries of the stock market and the vulgarities of having to make money.[62]

This penetration of bourgeois domesticity, moreover, was not confined to the metropolitan middle class alone. Unlike the ownership of government securities, which was heavily concentrated in and around London, share ownership was more widely dispersed around the country, as shown in Figure 3.6 which indicates the relative share of assets by value owned by individuals in each region.[63] The geographical dispersion of ownership reflected not only the broad distribution of population but also the growing integration of capital markets across the country as a whole. The emergence of an integrated national capital market in which regional interest rates moved in harmony appears to have taken place from the early decades of the nineteenth century, partly in response to government needs to raise finance for the wars against France.[64] Integration was further encouraged by the various banking reforms in the first half of the century which meant that from 1844 only the Bank of England was permitted to issue notes. By the second half of the century, therefore, note issues by country banks had disappeared in favour of a national banking system focused on London. Integration of the banking system was accompanied by subsequent improvements in communications, notably the spread of the telegraph and railway, both of which eased the flow

---

[60] See Poovey, *Genres of the Credit Economy*, especially chapter 6.

[61] This penetration of the market into the delicate gendered terrain of the bourgeois domestic sphere is explored further in Jeff Nunokawa's illuminating analysis of Charles Dickens' *Little Dorrit* and *Dombey and Son*, and George Eliot's *Daniel Deronda* and *Silas Marner*; see Nunokawa, J. 1994. *The Afterlife of Property: Domestic Security and the Victorian Novel*. Princeton, NJ: Princeton University Press.

[62] Some of these themes are developed in a literary context by Herbert, C. 2002. 'Filthy lucre: Victorian ideas of money'. *Victorian Studies* 44(2): 185–213.

[63] Dividends on government stock were traditionally paid only to those fundholders or their nominees who appeared at the Bank of England itself on dividend day (Secretan, J.J. 1833. *Fortune's Epitome of Stocks and Public Funds*, 13th edition. London: Sherwood, Gilbert and Piper, 15–16). Only later in the century was it possible to have dividends transmitted to a provincial bank. Provincial stock exchanges rarely if ever quoted government stocks. See Killick, J.R. and W.A. Thomas 1970. 'The provincial stock exchanges 1830–1870'. *Economic History Review* 23(1): 105.

[64] See Buchinsky, M. and B. Pollack 1993. 'The emergence of a national capital market in England, 1710–1880'. *Journal of Economic History* 53(1): 1–24.

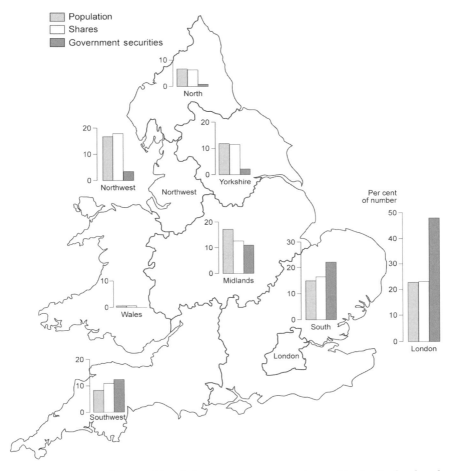

Figure 3.6 Regional ownership of shares and government securities in England and Wales, 1870–1902 (per cent of individuals)

Source: see Table 3.2.

of financial information across the country. With the diffusion of the telegraph in particular, price differentials between regional stock exchanges diminished, resulting in what geographers have termed the annihilation of space by time. The facility to move information almost instantaneously over long distances that arose as a result of the telegraph, and later the telephone, meant that decisions to buy and sell shares at a distance also became significantly easier, enticing shareholders away from a narrow regional focus to invest more in companies with a national presence and in overseas ventures.[65] These

---

[65] See Michie, R.C. 1985. 'The London Stock Exchange and the British securities market, 1850–1913'. *Economic History Review* 38(1): 66–82.

regulatory and technological changes, accompanied by the expansion of provincial stock exchanges and the growing availability of financial information which it was increasingly believed could be derived and acted upon in a 'scientific' manner, helped to draw larger numbers of shareholders from across Britain, and indeed overseas to investment markets.[66] Consequently, their money flowed not only into local share issues but also into companies operating at a distance in different parts of the country as well as those with activities abroad.

This geographical widening of ownership presented a different set of problems in relation to corporate governance from that which had prevailed when investment was primarily confined to a smaller and more local circle of investors. Personal bonds of trust and shareholder vigilance exercised through the company annual general meeting were replaced by more technocratic and formal means of control relying on the publication of audited balance sheets, the growth of specialist professionals able to offer advice and evaluate risk, and the regulation of corporate governance itself.[67] Just as Simmel had argued, that the abstract quality of money, and the facility it provided to become involved in long distance transactions in geographically separate parts of the world, profoundly altered the nature of relationships, so too did the widening spatial remit of shareholding transform the relationships between shareholders and their investments.

In the course of the nineteenth and early twentieth centuries, therefore, as Simmel had argued, the extension of the money economy was able to transform social relationships at a distance. That so many people came to rely increasingly on financial transactions may have generated a common interest in the fortunes of British capitalism that stretched not only geographically across the country but further down the social hierarchy than those gentlemanly capitalists who until recently have been the focus of much attention. But extending share ownership to a larger number of individuals, spread further down the social hierarchy and more widely dispersed around the country, raised additional questions about the provision of financial information, the probity of company directors, the nature of corporate governance, and acceptable levels of risk. These questions, of course, were not new but became more pressing as larger numbers of individuals came to depend to a greater extent on the ownership of riskier forms of financial assets. As recent events have shown, such concerns are of more than just passing academic interest.

---

[66] Alex Preda traces the creation of this 'finance society' through the embedding of different forms of institutional knowledge and technological practice. See Preda, *Framing Finance*.

[67] Pearson, R. 1992. 'Shareholder democracies? English stock companies and the politics of corporate governance during the industrial revolution'. *English Historical Review* 117(473): 840–66. See also Preda, *Framing Finance*.

4

They Lived and Saved: Examining the Savings Motives of Shopkeepers in Late Nineteenth-Century Britain

Mary Beth Combs

INTRODUCTION

During the nineteenth century, bequest saving – a more traditional method of saving that involved economic transfers from producers to dependants – gave way to life-cycle saving, a new method of saving that involved investment in financial intermediaries. A bequest motive exists if an individual accumulates assets during their working years in order to provide his or her children with an inheritance. A life-cycle motive exists if an individual accumulates assets during his or her employment in the labour market in order to finance consumption during retirement, or any period of reduced labour market earnings.[1] Social and economic historians claim that the transition from

[1] For a general interpretation of the bequest motive, see Di Matteo, L. 1997. 'The determinants of wealth and asset holding in nineteenth-century Canada: evidence from microdata'. *Journal of Economic History* 57(4): 907–34; Sundstrom, W. and P. David 1988. 'Old-age security motives, labour markets, and farm-family fertility in antebellum America'. *Explorations in Economic History* 25(2): 164–97; and Bernheim, B.D., A. Shleifer, and L.H. Summers 1985. 'The strategic bequest motive'. *Journal of Political Economy* 93(6): 1045–76. Other important studies include Ando, A. and F. Modigliani 1963. 'The life cycle hypothesis of saving: aggregate implications and tests'. *American Economic Review* 53(1): 55–84; Modigliani, F. 1988. 'The role of intergenerational transfers and life cycle savings in the accumulation of wealth'. *Journal of Economic Perspectives* 2(1): 15–40; Ransom, R. and R. Sutch 1986. 'The life-cycle transition: a preliminary report on wealth holding in America'. In *Income and Wealth Distribution in Historical Perspective*. Utrecht: University of Utrecht; Nugent, J. 1985. 'The old-age security motive for fertility'. *Population and Development Review* 11(1): 75–97; and Henretta, J. 1978. 'Families and farms: *mentalité* in pre-industrial America'. *William and Mary Quarterly* 35(1): 3–32.

bequest to life-cycle saving represents a revolution in values that had larger implications for growth and industrialization.[2]

This study considers late nineteenth-century English shopkeepers and examines the factors that may have motivated their savings decisions. In their study of savings trends, Ransom and Sutch find that the American agricultural sector made the transition from bequest to life-cycle saving in the mid-nineteenth century; parents began to save from current income during peak earning years in order to draw on those savings in old age, rather than depend on their children for old age support.[3] Moreover, their findings suggest that life-cycle saving was more conducive to economic growth than bequest saving.[4] In addition, a study of late nineteenth-century Canadian wealth-holding finds evidence to support the existence of both life-cycle and bequest saving, which indicates that country was in the midst of a transition.[5] For the specific group studied here, shopkeepers, one additional savings motive might be important to consider: deferred compensation for unpaid labour. Deferred compensation involves children undertaking unpaid labour in the shop or family household, usually while living at home, in return for compensation at a later date: sometimes at age 21, or at marriage, or after the death of one or both parents. Here I consider late nineteenth-century English shopkeepers and examine whether their saving and investment decisions exhibited a transition from bequest and/or deferred compensation to life-cycle saving.

A benefit of studying the savings behaviour of shopkeepers is the insight that might be gained about the decisions that these households made with regard to investments in the education of their children, about planning for old age support, and possibly even retirement. For example, the work of Becker and Tomes suggests that altruistic parents who have children with different abilities will invest in the education and human capital of their children differently, equating the marginal returns from investments in schooling with the returns derived from financial assets.[6] The Becker–Tomes

---

[2] The importance of saving to economic growth at the macro-level is discussed in Carter, S., R. Ransom, and R. Sutch 2004. 'Family matters: the life-cycle transition and the antebellum American fertility decline'. In *History Matters: Essays on Economic Growth, Technology, and Demographic Change*, edited by T. Guinnane, W. Sundstrom and W. Whatley. Stanford, CA: Stanford University Press, 271–327. Alter, G., C. Goldin, and E. Rotell 1994. 'The savings of ordinary Americans: the Philadelphia Savings Fund Society in the mid-nineteenth century'. *Journal of Economic History* 54(4): 735–67; Sutch, R. 1991. 'All things reconsidered: the life-cycle perspective and the third task of economic history'. *Journal of Economic History* 51(1): 271–88; and Ransom and Sutch, 'The life-cycle transition'.

[3] Ransom and Sutch, 'The life-cycle transition'.

[4] Kearl, J.R. and C.L. Pope. 1983. 'The life cycle in economic history'. *Journal of Economic History* 43(1): 149–58; and Ransom and Sutch, 'The life-cycle transition'.

[5] Di Matteo 'The determinants of wealth'.

[6] Becker, G.S. and N. Tomes 1976. 'Child endowments and the quantity and quality of children'. *Journal of Political Economy* 84(4) Part 2: S143–S162; Becker, G.S. and N. Tomes. 1979. 'An equilibrium theory of the distribution of incomes and intergenerational mobility'.

wealth model implies not only different investments in the human capital of siblings with different abilities but also a pattern of unequal transfers.[7] Looking more closely at the kinds of investments that shopkeepers made and the ways in which they bequeathed their property will help to sharpen our understanding of the decisions that members of this group took, both at the individual and the household level.[8]

Journal of Political Economy 87(6): 1153–89. This theme is further discussed in Lundberg, S. and R.A. Pollak 2007. 'The American family and family economics'. *Journal of Economic Perspectives* 21(2): 3–26.

[7] Lundberg and Pollak, 'The American family'.

[8] Given the small scale nature of most shopkeeping operations and the common practice of combining one's shop and residential premises in the same building, it is reasonable to assume that this would restrict wealth and savings strategies in distinct ways that could not be generalized to the population of savers as a whole. Elsewhere I consider the extent to which the experiences of shopkeepers from a variety of geographical locations are likely to have been typical and/or different from other small businesses and the population at large; see Combs, M.B. 2010. 'A nation of shopkeepers?' Fordham University discussion paper. Understanding the decisions of shopkeepers with regard to property holding, savings, and inheritance also will contribute to the existing wider discussion of middle-class property holding. For studies of this theme, see: Rubinstein, W.D. 1977. 'The Victorian middle classes: wealth, occupation and geography'. *Economic History Review* 30(4): 602–23; Rubinstein, W.D. 1987. *Elites and the Wealthy in Modern British History: Essays in Economic and Social History*. Brighton: Harvester Wheatsheaf; Rubinstein, W.D. 1988. 'The size and distribution of the English middle classes in 1860'. *Historical Research* 61(144): 65–89; Rubinstein, W.D. 1992. 'The structure of wealth-holding in Britain, 1809–39: a preliminary anatomy'. *Historical Research* 65(156): 74–89; Rubinstein, W.D. 2000. 'The role of London in Britain's wealth structure'. In *Urban Fortunes: Property and Inheritance in the Town, 1700–1900*, edited by J. Stobart and A. Owens. Aldershot: Ashgate, 131–48; Earle, P. 1989. *The Making of the English Middle Class: Business, Society and Family Life in London, 1660–1730*. Berkeley, CA: University of California Press; Daunton, M. 1989. '"Gentlemanly Capitalism" and British industry, 1820–1914'. *Past and Present* 122: 119–58; Floud, R. 1993. 'Britain, 1860–1914: a survey'. In *The Economic History of Britain Since 1700. Volume 2: 1860–1939*, edited by R. Floud and D.N. McCloskey. Cambridge: Cambridge University Press, 1–28; Gunn, S. 1988. 'The "failure" of the British middle class: a critique'. In *The Culture of Capital: Art, Power and the Nineteenth-Century Middle Class*, edited by. J. Wolff and J. Seed. Manchester: Manchester University Press, 17–44; Holcombe, L. 1973. *Victorian Ladies at Work: Middle-Class Working Women in England and Wales, 1850–1914*. Toronto, ON: Archon Books; Horwitz, H. 1987. '"The mess of the middle class" revisited: the case of the "big bourgeoisie" of Augustan London'. *Continuity and Change* 2(2): 269–96; Inwood, K. and S. Ingram 2000 'Property ownership by married women in Victorian Ontario'. *Working Paper No. 2000-8*, Department of Economics, University of Guelph, Guelph, ON; Morris, R.J. 1976. 'In search of the urban middle class: record linkage and methodology, Leeds 1832'. *Urban History Yearbook* 1(3): 200–22; Morris, R.J. 1983. 'The middle class and British towns and cities of the industrial revolution, 1780–1870'. In *The Pursuit of Urban History*, edited by D. Fraser and A. Sutcliffe. London: Edward Arnold, 286–305; Morris, R.J. 1980. 'Middle-class culture 1700–1914'. In *A History of Modern Leeds*, edited by D. Fraser. Manchester: Manchester University Press, 200–22; Morris, R.J. 1994. 'Men, women, and property: the reform of the Married Women's Property Act 1870'. In *Landowners, Capitalists, and Entrepreneurs: Essays for Sir John Habakkuk*, edited by F.M.L. Thompson. Oxford: Oxford University Press, 171–92; Morris, R.J. 2005. *Men, Women and Property in England, 1780–1870: A Social and Economic History of Family Strategies among the Leeds Middle Classes*. Cambridge: Cambridge University Press; Nicholas, T. 1999. 'Wealth making in nineteenth- and twentieth-century Britain: industry v. commerce and finance'. *Business History* 41(1): 16–36; Seed, J. 1992. 'From "middling sort"

A nineteenth-century English shopkeeping household may have chosen bequest saving out of benevolence – a concern for the welfare of their children (an 'altruistic' bequest motive) – or for business reasons, providing an incentive – the proceeds from the sale of the business or the business itself – for their children to care for them in old age (a 'carrot-and-stick' bequest motive).[9] One explanation of bequest saving offered by Livio Di Matteo is that young couples starting a family tend to invest much of their wealth in a home or real estate (or, for nineteenth-century shopkeepers, a business that included living space above it), which would result in less of their wealth being invested in financial assets.[10] In relation to their wealth-holding strategies, therefore, these individuals had likely decided to 'invest in their children and expect old age support from them, reducing the amount held in other assets'.[11] Thus, studies of bequest savings cite a positive relationship between total wealth and the total number of children as evidence of bequest saving, particularly if impartible settlements were not the norm.[12]

For a nineteenth-century shopkeeping couple, the rationale for a life-cycle motive would have been to accumulate assets during their years running the shop in order to finance consumption during retirement or any period of reduced labour market earnings. Specifically, a shopkeeping couple may build up wealth early in their lives by relying on markets and investing in financial assets, with a plan to live off the income stream from the rents and dividends. Or they might convert real property to personal property at retirement in order to provide themselves with an annuity that would support them into old age.[13] Savings behaviour, then, could show evidence of life-cycle saving if there is a concave relationship between age and total wealth.[14]

---

to middle class in late-eighteenth and early-nineteenth-century England'. In *Social Orders and Social Classes in Europe since 1500: Studies in Social Stratification*, edited by M.L. Bush. London: Longman, 114–35; and Shammas, C., M. Salmon, and M. Dahlin 1987. *Inheritance in America from Colonial Times to the Present*. New Brunswick, NJ: Rutgers University Press.

[9] See Di Matteo, 'The determinants of wealth'; Sundstrom and David, 'Old-age security motives', Carter, Ransom, and Sutch, 'Family matters' and Bernheim, Shleifer, and Summers, 'The strategic bequest motive'.

[10] Di Matteo, 'The determinants of wealth', 39.

[11] Ibid., 924.

[12] An impartible settlement is one in which one heir or more is favoured to the exclusion of all other claimants. For a discussion of impartible settlements and life-cycle savings, see Di Matteo, L. and P.J. George 1998. 'Canadian wealth inequality in the late nineteenth century: a study of wentworth, Ontario, 1872–1902'. *Histoire sociale–Social History* 31(1): 1–33; Di Matteo 'The determinants of wealth', 915, n. 36; Hurd, M. 1987. 'Savings of the elderly and desired bequests'. *American Economic Review* 77(3): 298–312; and Gagan, D. 1976. 'The indivisibility of land: a microanalysis of the system of inheritance in nineteenth-century Ontario'. *Journal of Economic History* 36(1): 129.

[13] Di Matteo, 'The determinants of wealth', 924.

[14] Modigliani, F. 1966. 'The life-cycle hypothesis of saving, the demand for wealth and the supply of capital'. *Social Research* 33(1): 160–217. Mathematically, a concave relationship between age and wealth would be indicated by Wealth = $B_0 + B_1 \text{age} + B_2 \text{age}^2$, where the expected

It is also possible that savings behaviour was influenced by a deferred compensation motive, which would involve the children of a shopkeeper receiving, at a later date, compensation for the unpaid labour in the shop and household that they undertook when they were younger and still lived at home. Savings behaviour could show evidence of deferred compensation if there is a positive relationship between total wealth and the number of children living in the home. Such a relationship would indicate that the children living in the home are working in the shop or helping in the home, 'earning their keep' by contributing to the total wealth of the household.

EXAMINING SAVINGS BEHAVIOUR

To study the savings motives of English shopkeepers, I collected data on wealth-holding from the Death Duty and Succession Duty Registers (hereafter registers), which run from 1796 to 1903, and the Residuary Accounts (compiled for the assessment of death duties) for England and Wales.[15] The registers consist of handwritten entries in 8000 volumes, covering all duties levied on a deceased person's estate.[16] Whether or not a will was written, the registers cover all estates worth over £20 from 1796 to 1881, and subsequently all those over £100. For tax collection purposes, it was necessary for Inland Revenue officers to determine whether a legacy was absolute, conditional, or an annuity in order to distinguish between estate that was an individual's legal property to bequeath and that which merely 'passed through' the individual as a consequence of being bequeathed by others. This allows me to

---

sign on the age term is positive and the expected sign on the age^2 term is negative. The life-cycle hypothesis implies that when a person is young, he or she contributes more income to stored-up wealth. As the person ages and either retires or works fewer hours, he or she begins to live off of that stored-up wealth, which makes the marginal contributions to wealth decline and eventually turn negative. If the statistical results indicate that B_1 is positive, statistically significant, and economically important, and that B_2 is negative, statistically significant, and economically important, then these results would provide evidence in favour of the life-cycle hypothesis.

[15] The records are located at the National Archives at Kew in London, UK: *Death Duty and Succession Duty Registers*, Class IR26, volumes for last names beginning with C or D: 1860–1890; *Residuary Accounts*, Class IR19. Unfortunately, the post-1903 registers do not survive. For further discussion of these records, see Chapter 3 in this volume.

[16] English, B. 1984. 'Probate valuations and the death duty registers'. *Bulletin of the Institute of Historical Research* 57(135): 80–91; English, B. 1987. 'Wealth at death in the nineteenth century: the death duty registers'. *Bulletin of the Institute of Historical Research* 60(142): 246; Rubinstein, W.D. 1971. 'Occupations among British millionaires, 1857–1969'. *Review of Income and Wealth* 17(4): 375–8; Rubinstein, 'The Victorian middle classes'; Collinge, M. 1987. 'Probate valuations and the death duty registers: some comments'. *Bulletin of the Institute of Historical Research* 60(142): 240–5; and Owens, A., D.R. Green, C. Bailey, and A.C. Kay 2006. 'A measure of worth: probate valuations, personal wealth and indebtedness in England, 1810–40'. *Historical Research* 79(205): 383–403.

distinguish the property that legally belonged to an individual regardless of whether he or she wrote a will.

Most registers indicate the deceased's occupation, address, spouse's name, children's names, and the number of children. The majority of entries provide information on the value of real or personal estate and some include details of more specific assets, such as clothing, jewellery, furniture, fixtures, and stock-in-trade.[17] The registers and, where they exist, the associated Residuary Accounts are the only sources from which it is possible to deduce net values of personal estates for most of the nineteenth century.[18] From 1853, when Succession Duty was introduced, the registers included a valuation, previously unobtainable, of all land, settled or unsettled. One or two reliable local men, who were known as appraisers, typically compiled the information on the property in the deceased person's estate.[19]

Inheritance tax rates were based on the type of property bequeathed and on consanguinity, or the relationship of the legatee to the deceased, and as a result the family relationship is often noted in the registers.[20] Specifically, from 1815 spouses of the deceased paid no Legacy Duty on bequests of personal estate. However, children of the deceased paid a 1 per cent tax; sisters, brothers, nieces, and nephews of the deceased paid a 3 per cent tax; and those unrelated paid 10 per cent.[21] A different kind of tax, Succession Duty, was levied on real estate and settled property, which were exempt from Probate or Legacy Duty. Like the Legacy Duty, the rates were based on consanguinity with the same percentages set from 1815 until the 1888 Customs and Inland

---

[17] Real property included immoveable property such as copyhold and freehold land; personal property included moveable property such as money, stocks, furniture, livestock, and leaseholds, as well as a subcategory called paraphernalia, which included clothing, jewellery, and other items belonging to a married women 'limited to necessaries and personal ornaments appropriate to her degree'.

[18] English, 'Probate valuations'; English, 'Wealth at death'; Collinge, 'Probate valuations'; and Owens et al. 'A measure of worth'.

[19] For additional discussions about the household inventory procedures, see Erickson, A.L. 1993. *Women and Property in Early Modern England*. London: Routledge; Scott, M. 1997. *Prerogative Court of Canterbury Wills and Other Probate Records*. Kew: Public Record Office; Buxton, S. and G.S. Barnes 1890. *A Handbook to the Death Duties*. London: John Murray; Cox, J. 1988. *Affection Defying the Power of Death: Wills, Probate and Death Duty Records*. London: Federation of Family History Societies; Cox, J. 1988. *Wills, Inventories and Death Duties: A Provisional Guide*. London: Public Record Office; Grannum, K. and N. Taylor 2004. *Wills and Other Probate Records*. Kew: National Archives; West, J. 1982. *Village Records*. London: Phillimore.

[20] Grannum and Taylor, *Wills and Other Probate Records*, chapter 8.

[21] Stamp Act, 1815 (55 Geo. III. *c.* 184). The rates are also noted in the Residuary Accounts under the 'Receipt for Legacy'. See, for example, National Archives IR19/223. See also Buxton and Barnes, *A Handbook to the Death Duties*, 18; and Grannum and Taylor, *Wills and Other Probate Records*, chapter 8. In addition to those relations listed above, aunts, uncles, and cousins of the deceased paid a 5 per cent tax; and strangers in blood paid 6 per cent. Probate duty is a tax that is paid out of the entire estate before the will is proved or, in the case of intestates, administration is granted and before the property is distributed among the legatees.

Revenue Act.[22] I use the data collected from the registers, along with a smaller, disaggregated sample of data collected from the Residuary Accounts, to examine the savings patterns of shopkeepers and to determine whether their savings and investment choices show evidence of bequest, life-cycle, or deferred compensation motives.[23] In the remainder of this section I describe in detail the data-collection procedure.

Savings decisions are revealed through information on wealth at death for male and female shopkeepers who died between 1859 and 1891.[24] I used a systematic sampling method and compiled the data by consulting each individual entry in the registers containing last names beginning with C or D. Since the register entries as a whole capture the wealth at death of individuals whose economic and social positions practically run the gamut from princes to paupers, I did not collect wealth-holding information on every individual in the registers. Rather, as noted above, I searched for particular occupations and I focused on shopkeepers. The data from the main sample on registrants dying between 1859 and 1891 capture general wealth-holding information, such as real and personal property holdings, and in some cases, more specific wealth-holding information, such as information on the value of clothing, jewellery, furniture, fixtures, and stock-in-trade.[25] In total, I collected information on the wealth-holding of 997 shopkeepers.[26]

---

[22] Customs and Inland Revenue Act, 1888 (51 & 52 Vict. *c*. 8). In 1888, the Succession Duty rates increased slightly: children of the deceased paid a 1.5 per cent tax; sisters, brothers, nieces, and nephews of the deceased paid a 4.5 per cent tax; aunts, uncles, and cousins paid a 6.5 per cent tax; strangers in blood paid 7.5 per cent and those unrelated paid 11.5 per cent. A further kind of duty, Estate Duty, was due on all estates worth more than £10,000. None of the individuals in my sample had this kind of wealth at the time of their death.

[23] The Residuary Accounts provide a breakdown of the deceased's personal estate. They were compiled to assess payment of Legacy Duty. For further discussion see below and Chapter 3.

[24] The men and women in this sample were either married, separated, or widowed and all were married before 1870. For studies of the wealth-holding of single women, see Green, D.R. and A. Owens. 2003. 'Gentlewomanly capitalism? Spinsters, widows and wealth holding in England and Wales, c.1800–1860'. *Economic History Review* 56(3): 510–36; for women investors, see Rutterford, J. and J. Maltby 2006. '"The widow, the clergyman and the reckless": women investors in England, 1830–1914'. *Feminist Economics* 12(1/2): 111–38; Maltby, J. and J. Rutterford 2006. '"She possessed her own fortune": women investors in the late nineteenth century to the early twentieth century'. *Business History* 48(2): 220–53; and for married women, see Combs, M.B. 2005. '"A measure of legal independence": the 1870 Married Women's Property Act and the wealth-holding patterns of British wives'. *Journal of Economic History* 65(4): 1028–57; and Combs, M.B. 2006. '*Cui Bono?*: The 1870 British Married Women's Property Act, bargaining power, and the distribution of resources within marriage'. *Feminist Economics* 12(1/2): 51–83.

[25] In cases where the Death Duty Registers indicated that Succession Duty had been paid at a later date, I linked the information from the noted Succession Duty Register to the information in the appropriate Death Duty Register.

[26] All individuals in the sample were married *before* the 1870 Married Women's Property Act was passed. From the early thirteenth century until 1870, English Common law held that most of the property that a wife had owned as a *feme sole* came under the control of the husband at the time of marriage; see Baker, A.H. 1990. *An Introduction to English Legal History*. London: Butterworths, 553. Not all marriages followed the law in practice. The degree to which the law

As noted above, for tax collection purposes, it was necessary for Inland Revenue officers to distinguish between property over which individuals had legal ownership and therefore could devise by will, and property in which individuals had only a life interest and therefore could not devise by will. For example, property that a wife could not devise by will included any that her husband left her for life only. The distinction between an individual who has 'legal ownership' over property and one who has only a 'life interest' in property is crucial for the study of wealth-holding, as any person who has legal ownership over some property has a degree of decision-making power with regard to that property. For example, the individual may sell this property during their widowhood or dispose of it via a will. From the Inland Revenue distinction I was able to obtain an estimate of the property that a husband or wife owned separate from his or her spouse. I used this procedure to collect wealth-holding data for the all of the men and women whose savings decisions are examined in this study.

Next, I used the data from the main sample to create a sub-sample that incorporates additional household information from the census. Specifically, I attempted to link the 997 individuals from the main sample to the census taken in the year closest to the individual's date of death. This effort establishes a linkage for 332 individuals.[27] The census links provide additional information on

---

served as a legal fiction depended on each individual marriage, and to some extent, on the regulation of property relations via the law of equity. On this theme, see Basch, N. 1979. 'Invisible women: the legal fiction of marital unity in nineteenth-century America'. *Feminist Studies* 5(2): 346–66; Davidoff, L. 1973. *The Best Circles: Women and Society in Victorian England*. Totowa, NJ: Rowman and Littlefield; Davidoff, L. 1990. 'The family in Britain'. In *The Cambridge Social History of Britain, 1750–1950*, Volume 2, edited by F.M.L. Thompson. Cambridge: Cambridge University Press, 71–129; Davidoff, L. and C. Hall. 2002. *Family Fortunes: Men and Women of the English Middle Class 1780–1850*, 2nd edition. London: Routledge; Davidoff, L. and B. Westover eds. 1986. *Our Work, Our Lives, Our Words: Women's History and Women's Work*. London: Macmillan Education. For a discussion of the circumstances under which wives married before 1870 held personal property, see Combs, M.B. 2004. 'Wives and household wealth: the impact of the 1870 British Married Women's Property Act on wealth-holding and share of household resources'. *Continuity and Change* 19(1): 141–63; Combs, '"A measure of legal independence"' and Combs, '*Cui Bono?*'. In addition there is evidence of marriages where a husband held land on behalf of his wife but permitted his wife to manage and control its uses. See Morris, *Men, Women and Property*; and Erickson, *Women and Property*. In cases where the husband held for the wife and the marriage was an egalitarian one, the law with respect to married women's property would be a legal fiction. See Shammas, C. 1994. 'Re-assessing the Married Women's Property Acts'. *Journal of Women's History* 6(1): 9–30; Shanley, M.L. 1989. *Feminism, Marriage, and the Law in Victorian England*. Princeton, NJ: Princeton University Press; Staves, S. 1990. *Married Women's Separate Property in England, 1660–1883*. Cambridge, MA: Harvard University Press.

[27] Rubinstein, 'Occupations among British milionaires'; English, 'Probate valuations'; English, 'Wealth at death'; and Collinge, 'Probate valuations'. Finding a shopkeeper in the register does not guarantee that the person will be found easily in the census. People moved. To verify names I checked that the spouse and children listed in the Death Duty Register matched those listed in the census return.

household makeup and other socio-economic factors. From this source I obtained the ages of the couple and their children and established which children were living at home at the time of the census, how many servants the family had, whether they had boarders or other family living at the house at the time of the census, and, in some cases, the number of years the couple had been married. For these 332 individuals, which I refer to as 'the census-linked sample', I was able to examine the influence of household circumstances and other factors, such as bequest, life-cycle, or deferred compensation motives on savings decisions.[28] In the sections that follow I provide a discussion of the potential importance of socio-economic factors. The majority of the sample group lived in and around Leeds, London, and Liverpool, and worked in 21 of the main occupations representative of the shopkeeping class.[29]

Finally, I used the Residuary Accounts to construct a different but smaller, disaggregated sample of information on shopkeepers' savings and investment decisions. A Residuary Account details the personal estate and monies arising from the sale, mortgage, or other disposition of real estate as directed by a testator's will. It was compiled for the purpose of the assessment of an estate for Legacy Duty.[30] The Residuary Accounts provide more detailed information than the registers about many kinds of individual investments, particularly financial investments, and they sometimes include detailed household inventories. They do not always include information on total values of real property, particularly in the case of real property that is not directed to be sold at the time of death of the testator. Information on values of real property is provided in the Death Duty, Estate Duty, and Succession Duty Registers. Thus, the Residuary Accounts, when linked to the registers, provide the most comprehensive household level data available for examining the wealth-holding decisions of the wider, property owning population in nineteenth-century Britain.[31] Each

---

[28] I also constructed a sub-sample of the census-linked sample by linking the data from the individuals in the census-linked sample to the registers of their spouses. It is possible to do this for 32 couples. This sub-sample, referred to as the 'census-spouse-linked sample', contains data on the wealth at death of wives and husbands in households that are also linked to the census.

[29] The sample includes 52 licensed victuallers, 34 grocers, 26 innkeepers, 24 merchants,17 butchers, 17 tailors, 16 bakers, 13 shopkeepers/provision dealers, 6 chemists, and at least one each in the following remaining occupations: auctioneer, bookseller, confectioner, dairyman, furniture dealer, florist, glass merchant, manufacturer, pawnbroker, shoedealer, stationer, and upholsterer. Again, a systematic sampling method was used where data were recorded for every married or widowed shopkeeper, or spouse of a shopkeeper who was listed in a random selection of registers between 1859 and 1891 containing last names beginning with C or D.

[30] See Buxton and Barnes, *A Handbook to the Death Duties*, and Chapter 3 in this volume.

[31] W.D. Rubinstein used the indices to the registers to examine the property and occupations of British millionaires, but few others have used the Death Duty Registers or Residuary Accounts (Rubinstein, 'Occupations'; Combs was the first to use the information in the registers in a large scale data study and the first to link information on wealth at death from the Residuary Accounts back to the registers and the census; see Combs, 'Wives and household wealth'; Combs, '"A measure of legal independence"'; Combs, 'Cui Bono?'). Research by David Green, Josephine Maltby, Alastair Owens, and Janette Rutterford has linked approximately 1400 Residuary

Residuary Account bears a register number which makes it possible to link it back to the relevant register. A sample of 139 shopkeepers were first found in the Residuary Accounts, then linked back to the registers, and then linked to the census. This effort establishes a complete linkage of all three kinds of manuscripts for 35 of these individuals. I use the data in this small sample to look for evidence of bequest, deferred compensation, or life-cycle savings motives that might contradict or support the empirical results.

EVIDENCE OF SAVINGS MOTIVES

The hypotheses outlined in the preceding discussion of bequest, life-cycle, and deferred compensation motives suggest that a positive relationship between the total number of children and total wealth would provide evidence in support of bequest saving; a concave relationship between age and total wealth would provide evidence for life-cycle saving; and a positive relationship between the number of sons or daughters living in the household and total wealth would provide evidence for a deferred compensation motive. Thus, a test of whether any of these motives affected savings behaviour may be modelled as a function of socio-economic variables which include the total number of children (living inside or outside the home), age, age-squared, the number of sons living in the home, and the number of daughters living in the home.

To determine whether these or other factors had an impact on savings decisions, I adopt a method that follows that used in studies by Di Matteo and Pope, who outline a determinants approach and categorize the data into choice and non-choice variables, with the remaining variation in wealth-holding decisions being a function of random forces.[32] Choice variables are socio-economic characteristics that an individual could attempt to alter.[33] For nineteenth-century shopkeepers, choice variables include the total number of children, the number of non-family members in the household (such as

---

Account entries between 1870 and 1903 to the appropriate register entry. See Green, D.R., A. Owens, J. Maltby, and J. Rutterford 2009. 'Lives in the balance? Gender, age and assets in late-nineteenth-century England and Wales'. *Continuity and Change* 24(2): 307–35 and Chapter 3 in this volume. Seminal papers on record linkage include Morris, 'In search of the urban middle class' and Lindert, P. 1981. 'An algorithm for probate sampling'. *Journal of Interdisciplinary History* 11(4): 649–68.

[32] Di Matteo, 'The determinants of wealth', 916–17 and Pope, C. 1989. 'Households on the American frontier: the distribution of income and wealth in Utah 1850–1900'. In *Markets in History: Economic Studies of the Past*, edited by D. Galenson. New York, NY: Cambridge University Press, 148–89.

[33] Di Matteo, 'The determinants of wealth', 917.

Table 4.1 Description of variables

Variable	Definition	Mean
Wealth	Total wealth at death	£1276
LWealth	Log of wealth	6.55
Age	Average age at death in years	61
Age-squared	Average age at death squared	3884
Total children in/out home	Number of children living inside and outside of home	3.27
Number of sons home	Number of sons living at home	1.10
Number of daughters home	Number of daughters living at home	1.10
Number of boarders	Number of boarders living in household	0.17
Married or widowed	1 if married, 0 if widowed	0.47
Gender	1 if female, 0 if male	0.53

Source: Death Duty and Succession Duty Registers, volumes for last names beginning with C or D: 1860–90, Class IR26, The National Archives, Kew, UK.

boarders), and marital status. Non-choice variables are fixed characteristics that an individual would not be able to alter, such as age and gender. The census for England and Wales provided information on household composition that makes it possible to examine the relationship between wealth, choice, and non-choice variables. Descriptions of the variables and data on variable means are provided in Table 4.1. I use the data collected on household composition to identify which choice and non-choice variables, if any, have the greatest impact on the total wealth of individuals. Similar data are not available in modern public records due to privacy restrictions.

I estimated total wealth with weighted least squares regression, where the weighting variable used in the analysis is the inverse of the age-specific mortality rate.[34] The weight was applied so that younger individuals, because of their lower mortality rate, would receive a heavier weight in the regression than older individuals. The weighting procedure therefore allows the data to better reflect the age composition of the population of shopkeepers at large.[35] As in Di Matteo's study of wealth and asset holding in nineteenth-century Canada, the weighted regression technique used here is applied as if the

[34] The estimation method used here follows Di Matteo, 'The determinants of wealth', 916–19.
[35] Di Matteo, 'The determinants of wealth', 907, 916–19; and Di Matteo, 'Wealth accumulation and the life-cycle'. The concern here is that heteroskedasticity may cause the least squares estimates to be inefficient. For references on weighted regression, see Magee, L., A.L. Robb, and J.B. Burbridge 1998. 'On the use of sampling weights when estimating regression models with survey data'. *Journal of Econometrics* 84(2): 251–71; and Maddala, G. 1997. *Introduction to Econometrics*. New York, NY: Wiley, 169–72. Anderson, M. 1990. 'The social implications of demographic change'. In *The Cambridge Social History of Britain 1750–1950*, Volume 2, edited by F.M.L. Thompson. Cambridge: Cambridge University Press, 16 shows that in 1911–12 the national average age at death for all occupations was 55 for females and 52 for males.

Table 4.2 Evidence of a bequest motive among mid nineteenth-century shopkeepers: weighted least squares regressions

Variable	Coefficient	
Constant	2.00	(3.58)*
Age	−0.04	(−1.36)
Age-squared	0.00	(0.75)
Total children in/out home	0.17	(4.45)***
Number of sons living at home	−0.07	(−1.08)
Number of daughters living at home	−0.17	(−2.57)***
Number of boarders in the home	0.17	(2.13)**
Married/widowed	0.28	(1.71)*
Gender	−0.15	(−0.94)

Source: see Table 4.1.

Note: The estimate of total wealth was obtained with weighted least squares estimation, where the weighting variable used in the analysis is the inverse of the age-specific mortality rate. The fully nested model estimates the factors that affect the dependent variable, the log of total wealth. Number of observations = 332. Of these 156 are men and 176 are women; 173 are married and 159 are widowed. Adjusted R^2 = 0.54.

* Significant at the 10 per cent level,
** Significant at the 5 per cent level,
*** Significant a the 1 per cent level.

adjusted data were replicated data from a sample survey.[36] The mortality rates used are based on age-specific mortality tables for nineteenth-century England obtained from research by Robert Woods and Andrew Hinde.[37]

Furthermore, to differentiate between a deferred compensation motive and a bequest motive, I control for the number of sons and daughters living at home (again, positive signs and large coefficient values would support the idea that these children may be undertaking unpaid labour in the family household or business while living at home and are thus contributing to the support of the household), as well as for the total number of children living inside and outside of the home (a positive sign and large coefficient value for this variable would support a bequest motive). All independent variables are listed in Table 4.2, which provides the results from the estimation.

The results from the estimation do not support the argument that total wealth changes with age: the coefficients for age and age-squared do not provide evidence that a life-cycle motive impacted on savings decisions. Additional support for the econometric results comes from data collected on the

---

[36] As Di Matteo, 'The determinants of wealth', 917, n. 46 explains, 'suppose the initial model is $W_i = Z_i'B + v_i$, where W_i is wealth, Z_i is the independent variable, B is the coefficient to be estimated, and v_i is the error term. If the inverse of the mortality rate is defined as a multiplier M_i, then each observation W_i, Z_i is replicated M_i times. The weighted least squares estimator is obtained by applying OLS to the transformed model: $M_i^{1/2} W_i = M_i^{1/2} Z_i'B + v_i'$.

[37] Woods, R. and P.R. Hinde 1987. 'Mortality in Victorian England: models and patterns'. *Journal of Interdisciplinary History* 18(1): 33, table 1.

retirement status of these individuals.[38] While retirement was not unheard of in late nineteenth-century Britain, the results from the data collected on English shopkeepers reveal that only 13 men in the sample were listed as retired tradespersons in the census or at the time of death as indicated by the registers. Thus, about 91.6 per cent of the men in the sample still had some connection to the business up until death.[39] In addition, 48.5 per cent of the women in the sample either bequeathed business property or had business property 'pass through them' to children after their death as directed by the wills of their husbands. These women had either established their own businesses or they had been given the power to run the family business after the death of the husband. The other 51.5 per cent of women in the sample either lived off an annuity or other property provided by the will of someone other than the husband (and thus had property to leave to the husband), or they lived off an annuity provided by the sale of the family business as directed by the will of their spouse.

That many of the wives in the sample, after the death of the husband, either ran the family business or were supported by an annuity (typically provided for them from the sale of the family business) lends further support to the claim that at least one spouse in a shopkeeping household did not retire but rather worked almost until the day one of the spouses died. Moreover, in the majority of the cases where the wife had only a life interest in the sale of the property, she therefore could not consume more than the annuity allowed (she could not sell or give away the property upon which the annuity was raised or dissave).[40] Retirement and dissaving are standard signals for a life-cycle motive for saving.[41] Most of the individuals studied here did not retire and did not dissave.

The results from the estimation of total wealth also do not seem to support a deferred compensation motive. Deferred compensation for unpaid labour in a shopkeeping household would typically involve children of shopkeepers working in the shop when they are young or when they are teenagers, who then

---

[38] In their research on the nineteenth-century United States, Ransom and Sutch, 'The life-cycle transition', found that full retirement from the labour force was more common than previously believed. Kotlikoff, L. 1988. 'Intergenerational transfers and savings'. *Journal of Economic Perspectives* 2(2): 41–58 notes that the motivation behind life-cycle saving is that 'people save to prepare for retirement when they must dissave and consume. Without periods of retirement, or at least, significant decreased labour earnings at the end of life there is no life-cycle motive for saving'.

[39] For example, William Clark was a retired draper (National Archives IR26/8499/289), Austin Dibb was a retired butcher (National Archives RG12/4478/85), and Samuel Dudley was a retired grocer and butcher (National Archives IR26/8510/1587).

[40] Individuals could and did incur debt which might, after death, consume some or all of the estate.

[41] See Davies, J.B. 1981. 'Uncertain lifetime, consumption and dissaving in retirement'. *Journal of Political Economy* 89(3): 561–77; and Kotlikoff, 'Intergenerational transfers and savings'.

leave home, and who are compensated later in life (either when they turn 21, at the time of marriage, or at the time of the death of one or both parents). Positive, large, and statistically significant coefficients for the variables 'number sons of living at home' and 'number of daughters living at home' would indicate the potential for a deferred compensation motive, supporting the idea that the son or daughter living in the home is contributing positively to household wealth. The results in Table 4.2, however, indicate that the number of sons living in the home does not seem to impact on total wealth, while every additional daughter living at home reduces total wealth by 17 per cent.

As noted above, positive and large coefficient values for the variables 'number of sons living at home' and 'number of daughters living at home' would provide evidence that the son or daughter living at home is contributing to the support of the household. Negative values, however, could indicate either an economic liability or possibly a choice on the part of parents to invest in the education and 'human capital' of their children.[42] If parents are investing in education (by allowing children to stay in school rather than work all day in the shop), then we would expect the sign on the coefficient to be negative. The opportunity cost of a grammar school or secondary school education is the lost time spent earning wages or helping in the family shop. Evidence against a deferred compensation motive, therefore, could be taken as evidence in support of the idea that parents chose to invest in the education and human capital of their children.

Evidence against a deferred compensation motive would include investments in education. To determine whether there is any evidence of investment in education that might support the empirical results, I examined the census manuscripts for school-age or teenage children listed as a 'scholar'. For some of the households in the sample, particularly those with shopkeepers who died at ages equal to or older than the national average and thus did not have young or teenage children living at home during the census year taken closest to the year of death, I also linked their registers to a second, earlier census. In such instances I linked their registers to an additional census that was taken when these individuals were still in their 30s or 40s and thus were more likely to have younger children living at home. The data from the individuals in this 'double-census-linked sample', when combined with the data from the individuals in the census-linked sample who died at ages younger than national averages, leaves a sub-sample of 218 of the total 332 individuals in the census-linked sample.

---

[42] An individual could be considered an economic liability if he or she consumes more of the household income than he or she contributes to it. An alternative example is given by the coefficient on the variable 'number of boarders in the home'. The results indicate that for every additional boarder living in the home, total wealth is expected to increase by 17 per cent.

Among the 218 households in the sub-sample of the census-linked sample, 44.5 per cent had at least one child under age 12 listed as a 'scholar', while 19.7 per cent had at least one teenage child listed as a 'scholar'. The majority of the teenage 'scholars' were 13 or 14 years old, but a few households had at least one child listed as a scholar who was 15 or 16 (five households in total) and, in one case, 18. These numbers, however, are rough estimates, and depend both on what the reporting household member and census enumerator considered to fall under the category 'scholar'. In addition, it is highly likely that these children helped in the family shop before and after school, and on days when school was not in session.[43]

To determine whether there is any evidence of a deferred compensation motive that might contradict the empirical results, I examined the census manuscripts for evidence of school-age or teenage children working in the family business. This meant finding instances where children were listed in the census as having an occupation other than that of 'scholar'. Among the 218 households in the sub-sample of the 'census-linked sample', 34.4 per cent had at least one teenage child listed in the census with an occupation, and of these households 23.2 per cent had at least one teenage child listed with an occupation that was the same as or similar to the occupation of the shopkeeping parent. Moreover, 5.2 per cent of these households had at least one child under the age of 12 working in the family business.[44] The investments of shopkeepers in the education of their children seemed to favour a grammar school education for children under age 12, followed by a transition to full-time work in the shop, training in a trade, or some other labour market work for teenagers and older children. It could be argued that these statistics support the empirical results and contradict the deferred compensation hypothesis: parents educated each of their children until age 13 or 14, then had their teenage offspring work in the shop full time or find a different occupation and contribute labour market earnings to the household in order to help repay the educational investment.[45]

The empirical results do seem to support a bequest motive. As noted earlier, evidence of a bequest motive is thought to exist if there is a positive

[43] See Winstanley, M.J. 1983. *The Shopkeeper's World, 1830–1914*. Manchester: Manchester University Press.

[44] It is possible for the percentages to add up to more than 100, as any one household might have a number of children of different ages, with each child being assigned to a different category: scholar under age 12, teenage scholar, occupation and under age 12, teenager with occupation, 20 years or older with occupation.

[45] On the other hand, it could be argued that these results support a deferred compensation motive. One might argue that parents educated each of their children until age 13 or 14, then had their teenage children work in the shop full time or find a different occupation and contribute labour market earnings to the household, and they compensated their children for their contribution at a later date. In any case, the empirical results do not support the deferred compensation hypothesis.

relationship between total wealth and the total number of children, and if impartible settlements are not typical. The coefficient for the 'total children' variable is significant at the 1 per cent level, and indicates that for every extra child, total household wealth increased by 17 per cent. Moreover, of the total decedents with children, only two estates (less than 0.01 per cent) where the decedent was testate could be classified as impartible, while only 3.5 per cent could be classified as being unequal in the amounts left to different children. Most of the testators left their property to their spouse either 'absolutely' or, more commonly, 'for life or until marriage' and then directed it to be divided 'equally among all the children' after the death or remarriage of the spouse.[46] Specifically, 12.5 per cent left their property to their spouse absolutely, and 83.9 per cent left their property to their spouse 'for life or widowhood' and then directed the property to be divided equally among all the children after the death or remarriage of their spouse.[47]

Further evidence in support of a bequest motive and against a life-cycle savings motive comes from an examination of data obtained from a small, disaggregated sample of 35 Residuary Accounts that I linked to the registers. Households with larger portions of their total wealth invested in a home or real estate instead of financial assets might be considered households that favour bequest or deferred compensation saving. Such individuals, it has been argued, choose to invest in their children and expect old-age support from them, reducing the amount held in other assets.[48] Households with larger portions of their wealth in financial assets favour life-cycle saving and would appear to rely on financial markets for old-age support. As noted earlier, the Residuary Accounts provide more detailed information than the registers about many kinds of individual investments, particularly financial investments, but they do not include information on total values of real property, as they exclude any real property that is not directed to be sold at the time of death of the testator. Information on values of real property is provided in the Death Duty, Estate Duty, and Succession Duty Registers. Thus, the Residuary Accounts, when linked to these registers, enable me to look for direct evidence, at the household level, for a particular savings motive. The 35 households in this sample preferred investments in real property to investments in financial assets. The average value of financial assets per shopkeeping household was £145, while the average value of real property was £739.

---

[46] It might be noted as well that the register-linking procedure cannot account for *inter vivos* transfers, as the registers provide a glimpse of property in the deceased person's possession at the time of death. The registers share this limitation with all other sources that identify wealth at death.

[47] Of this last group, 82.8 per cent of men and 85.7 per cent of women directed the property to be divided equally among all the children after the remarriage or death of their spouse.

[48] Di Matteo, 'The determinants of wealth', 924.

To determine the kind of bequest motive (altruistic or carrot-and-stick) behind the savings and inheritance decisions of shopkeepers, one could look to the census manuscripts for evidence of older children living at home, possibly helping in the shop and/or caring for an aging parent. Evidence from the census manuscripts examined for the census year closest to the date of death of each shopkeeper reveals that 46.8 per cent of the households in the census-linked sample had at least one employed adult son or daughter (older than 20 years) living with them. In some cases it was a widowed daughter, but in most cases, it was either an unmarried son or unmarried daughter, or some combination of older children. If savings and inheritance decisions were influenced by a carrot-and-stick kind of bequest motive, then we might expect that an adult child who lived at home, helped in the shop, and helped to care for his or her aging parents would receive a larger share of the inheritance than his or her other siblings who lived elsewhere and possibly helped their aging parents less. Yet, among this sample of shopkeepers, 96 per cent of the individuals did not favour one or more children above the rest of their offspring by leaving them a larger share of the inheritance.

Admittedly, it is difficult to know the specifics of the arrangement between parents and adult children living at home. It could be that the child is helping with the business and caring for the parent, or it could be that the parent has a child who is unmarried or widowed and has no other place to go, or it could be some combination of the two. Still, if the carrot-and-stick kind of bequest motive influenced savings and inheritance decisions, we should expect to see a larger portion of adult children who are living at home receiving more than their siblings (if the help they provided was worth more than their room and board and if they helped more than their siblings) or less than their siblings (if the help they provided was worth less than their room and board or if they provided less help than their siblings). Instead, as noted above, the data indicate that only 3.5 per cent of the estates could be classified as being unequal in the amounts left to different children.

The results provided in Table 4.2, coupled with the fact that 96 per cent of the individuals in the sample did not favour one or more children above the rest of their offspring, provide fairly persuasive evidence in favour of an altruistic bequest motive. Moreover, the results also seem to support the findings of historians who have argued that shopkeepers resisted the transition to life-cycle saving, mainly because they depended on their children's labour in the shop: 'the small shopkeeper continued to survive by relying on unpaid family help, his (*sic*) wife running the business for much of the day assisted by the children at peak periods.'[49] And in the end, it seems, almost all the children received an equal share of the inheritance.

---

[49] Winstanley, *The Shopkeeper's World*, 67.

CONCLUSION

The results presented here support an altruistic bequest motive for saving among nineteenth-century English shopkeepers. That individuals in the sample invested in at least a grammar school education for their children, did not dissave, and did not seem to favour one or more children above the rest of their offspring with regard to inheritance provides further evidence for an altruistic bequest motive. The results indicate that the shopkeepers studied here did not prefer life-cycle saving, but rather lived and saved in much the same way as Alfred Marshall had described, 'preferring to leave their stored up wealth intact for their families'.[50]

---

[50] Marshall, A. 1920. *Principles of Economics*, first published 1890. London: Macmillan and Company, cited in Menchik, P. and M. David 1983. 'Income distribution, lifetime savings, and bequests'. *American Economic Review* 73(4): 672–90. For a survey of studies with similar findings with regard to a lack of dissaving in old age, see Di Matteo and George, 'Patterns and determinants of wealth'; Kessler, D. and A. Masson 1989. 'Bequest and wealth accumulation: are some pieces of the puzzle missing?' *Journal of Economic Perspectives* 3(3): 141–52; Kotlikoff, 'Intergenerational transfers'; Modigliani, 'The life cycle hypothesis'; Ransom and Sutch, 'The life-cycle transition'; and King, M. 1985. 'The economics of savings: a survey of recent contributions'. In *Frontiers in Economics*, edited by K.J. Arrow and S. Honkapohja. Oxford: Basil Blackwell, 227–327.

5

Colonial Sisters and their Wealth: The Wealth Holdings of Women in South Australia, 1875–1915

Martin Shanahan

THE SOCIAL SETTING

The first European settlers landed in South Australia in 1834. Jeremy Bentham, the philosophical radical, had suggested their colony be called Feliciania or Liberia, such was the heady combination of optimism and utopian idealism of the founders.[1] Ignoring the claims of local native inhabitants, English, Irish, Scottish, and German immigrants, many of them religious dissenters, set about establishing a community in central southern Australia, 16,000 kilometres from London, and 800 kilometres west of the nearest settlement, Melbourne, that would rank equally with those in the Europe they had left.

The intention of the first white settlers in South Australia was to reproduce a 'superior' but still fundamentally 'English' community.[2] Adopting principles of settlement designed by Edward Gibbon Wakefield, the colony was planned by a group of Englishmen 'whose professed ideals were civil liberty, social opportunity, and equality for all religions'.[3] Such middle-class ideals emanated from the

The author would like to thank the Australian Research Council and the UK's Economic and Social Research Council for their support in undertaking and presenting this research. Thanks also to Matt Giro who provided invaluable research assistance and to the editors of this volume.

[1] Richards, E. ed. 1986. *The Flinders History of South Australia: Social History*. Adelaide, SA: Wakefield Press, 1.

[2] Ibid., 1–32.

[3] Pike, D. 1957. *Paradise of Dissent: South Australia, 1829–1857*. Melbourne, VIC: Melbourne University Press, 3. Edward Gibbon Wakefield was cofounder of the National Colonization Society in the United Kingdom. With others he outlined principles of colonization that sought to balance land, labour, and capital using proceeds from land sales to assist migrants, while selling land at fixed but affordable prices to encourage land ownership and hard work. His principles ultimately affected colonial settlement in Australia, New Zealand, the South African Cape, and

Whiggish liberalism that had developed in England in the early nineteenth century and meant that land ownership, religious tolerance, and distaste for convict settlement underpinned the settlers' approach to social policy.[4]

The decades of settlement saw significant numbers of assisted immigrants brought to the colony to enhance the growth of the fledgling population.[5] As a 'planned' colony, the authorities were also aware of the problems that might be caused by a persistent imbalance in the number of male and female immigrants of child-rearing age. While there were episodes when a disproportionate number of young men or women arrived in a single ship, exciting local comment, by the end of the century the proportion of females in the colony, had stabilized at around 49 per cent; a closer balance of males to females than in any other Australian colony.[6]

Beginning with a few canvas tents on the local beach, after 50 years, Adelaide had grown to a city of over 100,000 inhabitants.[7] Having endured early years of financial difficulty, the colony slowly prospered: wheat and wool farming expanded and the discovery of copper in 1845 and later gold increased the pace of growth. The discovery of gold in other colonies in the 1850s benefited wheat farmers and increased wool prices in the 1870s delivered further economic prosperity. Infrastructure, in the form of government buildings, roads, railways, water systems, and sewerage systems, was constructed – always with an eye to European standards and expectations. Commenting on the hospitals, asylums, orphanages, and other facilities in the 'city of churches', the visiting novelist Anthony Trollope noted that there were 'more than all the appliances of humanity belonging to four times the number in old cities'.[8]

Not everything progressed smoothly for the colony. A lack of understanding of the environment saw the expansion of wheat farming into unsustainable regions, and a subsequent retreat to more reliable areas.[9] Drought, when it

---

Brazil. See Prest, W., K. Round and C. Fort eds. 2001. *The Wakefield Companion to South Australian History*. Adelaide, SA: Wakefield Press, 575–6.

[4] McMichael, P. 1984. *Settlers and the Agrarian Question: Foundations of Capitalism in Colonial Australia*. Cambridge: Cambridge University Press, 87–8, 222–3.

[5] Richards, *The Flinders History*, 115–42. As with self-funded migrants, assisted immigration programmes ebbed and flowed depending on the economic conditions of the colony. As with other Australian states, such programmes continued well into the second half of the twentieth century.

[6] Nance, C. 1984. '"Making a better society?" Immigration to South Australia, 1836–1871'. *Journal of the Historical Society of South Australia* 12(1): 105–22; Pike, *Paradise of Dissent*, 180; Vamplew, W., E. Richards, D. Jaensch, and J. Hancock 1986. *South Australian Historical Statistics*. Monograph 3. Sydney, NSW: University of New South Wales, 13–4.

[7] Hirst, J.B. 1973. *Adelaide and the Country, 1870–1917: Their Social and Political Relationship*. Melbourne, VIC: Melbourne University Press, 227.

[8] Anthony Trollope (1872) quoted in Richards, *The Flinders History*, 17.

[9] Meinig, D.W. 1962. *On the Margins of the Good Earth: The South Australian Wheat Frontier, 1869–1884*. Adelaide, SA: Rigby Ltd.

came, pressed hard on production and water supplies. Economic fluctuations saw depressions in the 1840s and again in the 1890s.[10] Distance was a constant barrier and living conditions could be hard, especially for those whose sole source of income was their own labour, and for most women, whether in outback stations or in city bungalows, whose lives revolved around their families and the household.[11]

While some settlers held liberal social views, European attitudes about the role of men and women were also fundamental in structuring labour market opportunities. Indeed, the Wakefield system was dependent on the traditional family structure to ensure systematic colonization and land development. Almost all women married at some point.[12] As the nineteenth century progressed, women took up more and varied occupations, and from 1861 to 1911 comprised between 15 and 20 per cent of the total labour force. Most were young, single and served as domestic servants, cooks, or governesses.[13] Diversification of women's occupations was slow until the social and technological break associated with the First World War and its aftermath expanded female opportunities.

There are several possible explanations for the gradual shift in women's roles. In the case of South Australia, one suggestion has been that men's roles as providers and women's as housemakers were also subject to the practical realities of settlement in a new and harsh environment. Others have argued that the 'free-thinking' early settlers respected women's intellectual capacity and sought to supply them with the education necessary to be independent if necessary.[14] Regardless of the cause, it is true that women were first admitted to Adelaide University in 1876, and the Advanced School for Girls was established in 1879.[15] The mix of progressive social policies, traditional family values, and practical necessity meant that in South Australia in the nineteenth century, women's roles were potentially less constrained than in more traditional and established societies.

[10] Sinclair, W.A. 1985. *The Process of Economic Development in Australia*. Melbourne, VIC: Longman Cheshire.

[11] Bacchi, C. 1986. 'The "woman question" in South Australia'. In *The Flinders History of South Australia: Social History*, edited by E. Richards. Adelaide, SA: Wakefield Press, 403–32.

[12] In 1866, only 2.3 per cent of women aged under 60 had never married. By 1881, the figure was 4.1 per cent and by 1901, 9.8 per cent. For men under 60 years of age, the figures were 8.9, 14.8, and 18.6 per cent, respectively. See Bacchi, 'The "woman question"', 428.

[13] Sinclair, W.A. 1981. 'Women at work in Melbourne and Adelaide since 1871'. *Economic Record* 57(159): 344–53.

[14] Mackinnon, A. 1984. *One Foot on the Ladder: Origins and Outcomes of Girls' Secondary Schooling in South Australia*. St Lucia, QLD: University of Queensland Press.

[15] Bacchi, 'The "woman question"', 411. Although women were officially admitted to Adelaide University in 1876, they were not admitted on terms equal with men until 1894.

THE LEGAL FRAMEWORK

Included in the settlers' baggage was 'so much of the English law as [was] applicable to their new situation and the new infant colony, such, for instance, as the general rules of inheritance'.[16] Thus the legal framework around women's right to own property, the transmission of land, and the process of probate was initially identical to that in place in England in the 1830s. This meant that, at marriage for example, women delivered their property, earnings, and children to the control of their husbands. It also meant that the system for the transferral of assets at death followed English precedents.

Changes in the legal framework shaping women's property rights in Britain during the later nineteenth century were paralleled, and indeed in some cases preceded, by those in South Australia.[17] In 1845, less than 10 years after settlement, colonial legislators passed the Married Women's Conveyances Act to facilitate the transfer of property. Numerous other acts to clarify and improve women's standing with regard to marriage, divorce, and property ownership reached an important milestone for married women with the Married Women's Property Act of 1884.[18] This recognized women's right to hold assets in their own name regardless of marital status. Other changes that affected women's rights in the second half of the nineteenth century accompanied this legislation. South Australia, for example, was the first Australian colony to grant women suffrage for municipal and district councils in 1861 and for the colonial legislature in 1894.[19] Attitudes, therefore, were not set in stone and although in South Australia most women's social position was defined by their marital status, these legal changes point to a shifting landscape of rights and expectations.

It is one thing to change social policies and statutes that might have benefited women; it is quite another to make real changes to their material and social position. One source of evidence to determine the real impact of these changes in relation to women's wealth lies in the probate record. The role of the Probate Court was to oversee the payment of debts, the collection of monies owed, and the transfer of ownership of property when somebody died. This involved, among other things, determining the validity of the will, ensuring the accurate valuation of assets and liabilities, and granting a right

---

[16] William Blackstone (1809), quoted in Castles, A.C. 1963. 'The reception and statutes of English law in Australia'. *Adelaide Law Review* 2(1): 5.

[17] Daunton, M. 2001. *Trusting Leviathan: The Politics of Taxation in Britain 1799–1914*. Cambridge: Cambridge University Press, 224–55.

[18] Between 1842 and 1902, the colony passed at least 33 acts that affected property or probate laws and thereby also impacted on probate records.

[19] Full male suffrage was achieved for the lower house in South Australia in 1856. Jones, H. 1986. 'South Australian women and politics'. In *The Flinders History of South Australia: Political History*, edited by D. Jaensch. Adelaide, SA: Wakefield Press, 415.

of representation to a third party (the executor) to act on the deceased's behalf.[20] Probate was administered in South Australia from 1844, although detailed records are only available from 1876. There was no legal requirement for an estate to be processed by the Probate Court but the incentive to seek a grant of representation was the need to obtain court sanction for the transfer of property or the settlement of accounts. Clearly, where this recognition was not necessary the executors of an estate could bypass the Probate Court. Consequently, the types of estates passing through the Court were likely to be those with assets, creditors, beneficiaries, or disputants, or any combination of these. Estates with neither wealth, creditors, nor beneficiaries were less likely to have come before the Court.

The probate jurisdiction of the Court was limited to South Australian property. However, the law required an executor to sign a sworn statement attesting, 'the Nature and Value of Real and Personal Estate in South Australia...the Nature and Value of Real and Personal Estate not in South Australia' together with a 'Statement of Debts and Liabilities Still Unpaid' and a 'Statement of Monies Received and Paid'.[21] The value of property that lay outside South Australia was therefore included in the probate records lodged with the Court. The requirement that all property should be included, irrespective of where it was located, was further strengthened by the Succession Duties Act of 1893 which required executors to complete an inventory list of all assets held at the time of a person's death. These ranged from cash, clothing, furniture, and household assets to stock-in-trade, land, shares, and other financial assets. The file might also contain statutory declarations from a licensed valuer, correspondence with the tax department (usually disputing the tax due), and calculations and valuations used by the department to determine the tax.

Importantly for this chapter, when property was owned jointly, there was no need for the surviving owner to seek the authority of the Probate Court to obtain full ownership. In this situation, the transfer of property occurred automatically upon application to the Registrar-General of the Lands Titles and therefore might not have been recorded in the Probate Court. In the case of husband and wife, the husband was entitled to register as co-proprietor of land held by the wife unless the property was held exclusively for the wife's use.[22] While it was not possible to ascertain precisely the number of omissions from

---

[20] The form of grant depended on if and how the deceased had arranged his or her affairs. If a will existed naming executors, one executor was given a grant of probate. If there was a will but no designated executors, the court gave a grant of *'administration cum testamento annexo'* (administration with will annexed) to an executor it appointed. If there was no will (an intestate estate), the court granted letters of administration to an administrator.

[21] South Australian Parliamentary Papers 1892. *Legislative Council, Rules under the Administration and Probate Act, 1891*, 81(6).

[22] The Real Property Act, 1886, 49 & 50 Victoria cap 380, part 15 s. 188–90.

the probate record that resulted from the joint ownership of property, the total was probably small.[23] Fewer than 2 per cent of entries in the Succession Duty Index were for payment of duty on property transfers involving joint tenancy.[24] Evidence from the colony's statistical register also shows that the number of 'automatic' land transfers triggered by individuals' deaths was negligible.[25] Consequently, it can be assumed that for the period under review, property transferred through joint tenancy arrangements does not account for a large percentage of omitted estates.

The South Australian Parliament first passed legislation to raise revenue from probate and succession duties in 1876. The Act of 1876 introduced two duties: Probate Duty levied on the entire estate (personal and real), and Succession Duty levied on the beneficiaries of the estate. The legislation required the executor to swear to the gross value of the entire estate, not just for assets held in South Australia that may have been subject to probate. There was no minimum threshold below which estates were not required to seek probate and all South Australian residents were covered by the Act.[26]

The Probate and Succession Duty Act, passed in 1893, removed the probate tax of 1876 and altered the existing succession duty. Instead of two taxes, a single less onerous, progressive duty was to be levied on succession. As the administration of the Act was assigned to the Registrar of Probates, the transfer of property and the disclosure of assets for tax were supervised by the same body. The duty, however, was assessed and collected by the Successions Duty Office.[27] Comparatively little changed until 1914 when the

---

[23] Searches of land transfer records, the Department of Land's official correspondence, archival records of probated individuals, succession duty files, marriage records, or censuses, failed to shed much light on the extent of jointly owned land. The only information on jointly held property was recorded in the Succession Duty Index.

[24] Every index entry recorded the type of duty that was being paid: Succession Duty, Gift Duty, Deed of Gift Duty, Settlement, or Joint Tenancy Transfer Duty. A 10 per cent random sample was taken from the two Succession Duty Indexes which covered the years from 1893 to 1923. Every tenth page was examined producing a total of 4860 cases. Over 97 per cent of cases concerned Succession Duty, 1.19 per cent concerned joint tenancy, 0.74 per cent settlements, and 0.58 per cent Gift and Deed of Gift Duty. Given the small proportion of cases incurring Gift and Deed Duty, it is also presumed that such duty had only minimal influence on the number of *inter vivos* gifts.

[25] Shanahan, M. 1991. 'The distribution of personal wealth in South Australia, 1905–1915'. Unpublished PhD Thesis, Flinders University of South Australia, 192. The situation is further complicated because some estates containing jointly owned property did appear in the probate record. Reasons for this include the existence of creditors or disputants to the estate, the registration of the person's will with the Probate Court prior to their death, or the inclusion of assets other than jointly owned property in the deceased's estate.

[26] The Probate Duty was a flat payment of £1 for all estates valued at under £100, £2 for estates under £200, going to 1 per cent for estates over £500. A penalty of £50 was liable in cases of underpayment. Practical considerations, however, are likely to mean very small estates were not probated. A critical determinant appears to be whether the transfer of land was involved.

[27] Obtaining a Grant of Representation and paying Succession Duty were thus two separate acts. Although obtaining a Grant of Representation was not mandatory, the paying of Succession

Commonwealth Government introduced a tax on estates with the passage of the Estate Duty Act and the Estate Duty Assessment Act.

While the legislative framework in which the data for this chapter were collected changed over the 50 years, it did not alter so radically as to make comparisons invalid.[28] Indeed, the changes of 1876 enhanced the public record, as more detailed administrative attention was given to the value and composition of estates. Nonetheless, it is also important to acknowledge that probate records do not represent a full sample of all those who die, and the evidence they provide must be interpreted with caution.[29]

THE DATA

The body of evidence from which the data are drawn consists of approximately 38,000 probated estates held in the state archives of South Australia for the period 1877–1918.[30] Between 1880 and 1915, about one-quarter to one-third of all adults who died left an estate that was submitted for probate.[31] The probate files are stored chronologically as they were presented to the court and are currently archived in boxes that each contain approximately a hundred records.[32] Each estate record is in a separate file and consists of an

---

Duty was. This difference was used to estimate whether a significant number of people left wealth but were not probated, or whether the two processes captured significantly different numbers of people. Using the period January 1905 to March 1915, it is estimated that the total number of entries in the Succession Duty Index does not exceed 11,400 cases. This is close to the figure of 11,495 probated South Australians recorded over the same period.

[28] Nonetheless, even small legislative changes could influence probate observations, particularly at the lower end of the distribution. For example, although the Act of 1891 directed the Probate Court to aid executors in drawing up papers for estates valued at under £200, the existence of court fees for administering and processing estates could have had a disincentive effect on small estates. The observed number of small estates may also have been influenced by section 15 of the 1904 amendment to the Probate Act. This amendment allowed banks to release the balance of a man's account to his widow without the need for probate papers, provided the amount was less than £50. In the 10 years to 1915, there were 1184 South Australian estates recorded as leaving less than £50 net wealth.

[29] See Auwers, L. 1979. 'History from the mean – up, down and around: a review essay'. *Historical Methods* 12(1): 39–45; Main, G.L. 1974. 'The correction of biases in colonial probate records'. *Historical Methods Newsletter* 8(December): 10–28; Smith, D.S. 1975. 'Underregistration and bias in probate records: an analysis of data from eighteenth-century Hingham, Massachusetts'. *William and Mary Quarterly* 3(1): 100–10; Owens, A., D.R. Green, C. Bailey, and A.C. Kay 2006. 'A measure of worth: probate valuations, personal wealth and indebtedness in England, 1810–40'. *Historical Research* 79(205): 383–403.

[30] Of these the last three years are currently not open to the public.

[31] Shanahan, 'The distribution of personal wealth', 205.

[32] Adjustments were made to the data finally represented here. For example, the probate records include some people not dying in South Australia. Any estate, wherever located, came before the Adelaide Probate Court if it included South Australian assets. Estates primarily based

identifying number, the deceased's full name, and the costs and charges
levied by the Probate Office. Net and gross wealth are recorded on the back
cover of the file while inside are documents submitted to the Court by
the executor or administrator of the estate. These could include the will, the
executor's oath, correspondence with the Court, and statements from the
public trustee. The executor's oath contains information as to the name,
address, occupation, and sworn gross value of the estate. Where the gross
value as sworn by the executor does not match the figure accepted by the
court, the Court's valuation is used. For the period 1876–1905 an inventory
list of assets was included in the files, while after this date the asset list was filed
separately.

For the period 1876–95, the probate records were sampled by recording all
the files in the storage boxes that centred on 1876, 1880, 1885, 1890, and 1895.
To increase the size of the sample, one year either side of the focus year was
also recorded. The files contained both the probate record and succession
record. All cases where the testator died 'resident' outside the state were
excluded. Some South Australians held assets outside the state and in these
cases wealth was normally excluded from the probate record but included in
the succession file. To avoid any double counting, as may occur when related
people die and are probated, an effort was made to exclude the estates of sons,
daughters, wives, and widows of previously recorded estates. People
with similar surnames and addresses were traced and in cases where there
was a clear connection, the assumed dependant was omitted. In all, only 22
estates were removed from the data set to avoid double counting. A total
of 2631 estates were included in the sample from 1875 to 1896, as shown in
Table 5.1.[33]

For the period 1905–15, the entire population of probated estates was
accessed resulting in a dataset of 12,397 individual files.[34] The reason for
examining the entire population of estates for these years was the existence
of a wealth census in 1915 – the first and, to date, only census on wealth
recorded in Australia.[35] All residents in Australia over the age of 18 were
required to estimate their income from all sources and assets held in all forms

interstate and overseas were therefore included in the original records. However, the full value of
these estates was not recorded, only the value of South Australian assets.

[33] Observation figures include some missing cases. The number of files is affected by various
factors including the number of deaths, the number of probated estates, economic conditions
and the speed of the Probate Court. Note too that as the probate and succession legislation began
in 1876, the sample for this year mostly covers 1876 and 1877. A few earlier cases, where
individuals died in 1875 were recorded, presumably because of delays in obtaining probate.

[34] Of these, only 10,335 (about 83 per cent) contained complete information on gender, net
and gross wealth, and domicile.

[35] Knibbs, G.H. 1918. *The Private Wealth of Australia and its Growth as Ascertained by
Various Methods Together with a Report of the War Census of 1915*. Melbourne, VIC: McCarron
and Bird.

Table 5.1 Number of probated estates sampled, 1875–1915

Period	Number of observations
1875–7	261
1879–81	509
1884–6	610
1889–91	782
1894–6	569
1905–15	10,335*
	345[†]

Source: Probate files, GRS/1334 and Succession Duty files GRG84/9, South Australian Archives, Adelaide.

Notes: *The total population of Probate files 1905–15 was 12,397. Of these only 10,335 provided complete information on gender, net and gross wealth, and place of residence. [†]Matched subset of Probate and Succession Duty files.

in the previous financial year during the week of 6–15 November 1915. Although there are some concerns over the accuracy of the final data, they have generally been accepted as reasonable.[36] Significantly for this chapter, the reported results include information on wealth-holdings by gender as well as by state.

At the time of examining these records, however, the succession files were not stored together with the probate material. To overcome this, a randomly stratified sample of probate records was selected and matched with their corresponding succession duty files. Given the distribution of gross wealth, four strata were selected. A 1 per cent sample was taken from estates recorded between £0 and £500, a 2 per cent sample from estates worth between £501 and £2500, and a 5 per cent sample from estates valued between £2501 and £20,000. The complete population of estates valued at over £20,000 was recorded. Estates within each stratum were selected randomly identifying each estate by its official probate file number, resulting in a total of 345 individual cases where both the probate record and succession duty files were matched.[37]

---

[36] See Soltow, L. 1972. 'The census of wealth of men in Australia in 1915 and in the United States in 1860 and 1870'. *Australian Economic History Review* 12(2): 125–41; Shanahan, M. 1995. 'The distribution of personal wealth in South Australia, 1905–1915'. *Australian Economic History Review* 35(1): 82–111.

[37] To ensure a correctly weighted sample was taken from a stratum, any estate which could not be matched with its succession duty file was replaced with another also selected at random from within the stratum. This was done in 29 cases. It should be noted, however, that a complete comparison between probated estates and estates liable for Succession Duty for this 10-year period was not possible, because widows and direct heirs were exempt from Succession Duty on bequests under £500.

VALUING WEALTH

Two additional problems arise when using valuations from probate to assess patterns of wealth-holding over time and between individuals. The first concerns changes in prices that may have impacted on the real value of estates. While prices remained relatively stable between 1905 and 1915, current estimates of price changes in the late nineteenth century suggest that, particularly in the 1890s to early 1900s, there was deflation.[38] The worldwide depression of the 1890s, combined with drought (1895–1903), the severity of which had not previously been encountered in Australia, meant agricultural output and, consequently, land values fell. This means that comparisons of absolute wealth from 1876 until 1915 are difficult to make. It does not, however, invalidate cross-sectional comparisons within time periods, which is the approach taken here to evaluate the relative wealth status of women.

The problem relates to whether gross or net valuations are used as an estimate of an individual's true worth and here there are some important differences depending on the level of debt owed at the time of a person's death. Net wealth simply refers to the gross value minus funeral and administrative costs, debts, and mortgages owed at death. As discussed below, for poor estates, where debts and mortgages accounted for a larger proportion of gross wealth, the difference was of most importance. By contrast, that difference was less significant for women since they generally died owing less in terms of mortgage debt than men. Since net valuations were always liable to alteration after an estate had been valued, in the analysis that follows the gross values have been used as an approximation of an individual's worth at the time of death.[39]

GENDER AND WEALTH-HOLDING, *c*.1915

It was with some pride that commentators at the end of the nineteenth century claimed that the colonies offered greater opportunities for individuals to amass personal wealth. In 1896, for example, the chief New South Wales statistician T.A. Coghlan observed the distribution of probated estates in South Australia and noted: 'these figures show a distribution of wealth not

---

[38] Butlin, N. 1962. *Australian Domestic Product: Investment and Foreign Borrowing, 1861–1938/39*. Cambridge: Cambridge University Press, 10 (table 2) and 460 (table 269).

[39] All valuations were rounded to the nearest pound. Several asset categories were aggregated: rents were added to mortgages owing to the deceased; fixed deposits in banks were added to fixed and flexible deposits in building societies; 'lodge money' added to life insurance; 'bond' debts were entered under the general category of 'other' debts. All other assets were recorded as they appear in the Succession Duty file.

Table 5.2 Aggregate net assets in South Australia, 30 June 1915

	South Australia (£)	% of South Australia assets	% of Australian assets	Australia (£)
Males	93,992,280	60.8	10.2	921,985,433
Females	29,185,188	18.8	9.7	302,240,560
Non-residents	31,445,661	20.4	7.5	419,237,383
Total	154,623,129	100.0	9.4	1,643,463,376

Source: Knibbs, G.H. 1918. *The Private Wealth of Australia and its Growth as Ascertained by Various Methods Together with a Report of the War Census of 1915*. Melbourne: McCarron and Bird, 28.

Note: Net assets: excludes Federal, State, and Local Government property. Non-residents: includes, non-resident partnerships, trust funds (including life-assurance companies and friendly societies, adjusted to exclude amounts held by individuals), companies and institutions. Resident partnerships included in returns of individual partners.

to be paralleled in any other part of the world; in South Australia is found the widest diffusion of the individual colonies'.[40]

However, evidence from the turn of the century suggests that the extent of that diffusion varied by gender. While women in nineteenth- and early twentieth-century South Australia may have been relatively less socially re-stricted than their colonial sisters, and the legal constraints on property ownership more liberal, this did not mean that they owned the same amount of property as men. As an example of this, between 1905 and 1915, when the ratio of females to males among the living population was 49:51 and the ratio of females to males among all deaths was 46:54, the ratio of female probated estates to male probated estates was 33:66.[41] In other words, twice as many males as females were probated in this period, despite the distribution of the living and dying populations being almost equal.

Further evidence relating to the distribution of wealth among living men and women throughout Australia is provided by the wealth census of 1915.[42] Unfortunately, the distribution of assets by gender is not available for each state in the census records. As Table 5.2 shows, males held approximately three times the assets by value compared to women. Nationally, the net wealth averages were £665 for males and £367 for females although the gap was wider for South Australians at £745 and £360, respectively.[43] These averages,

---

[40] Coghlan, T.A. 1896. *A Statistical Account of the Seven Colonies of Australasia, 1895–6*, 6th issue. Sydney, NSW: Government Printers, 322.

[41] Shanahan, 'The distribution of personal wealth', 67 (table 3.1).

[42] Knibbs, *The Private Wealth of Australia*, 8–10, provides examples of the forms used in the census. A question on marital status was included, but frustratingly for this chapter, the published report did not include information about wealth-holdings by marital status. The original individual responses to the census are no longer available.

[43] Ibid., 30.

however, hide the true extent of inequality. Table 5.3 shows that just over half
(59 per cent) of the adult population aged over 18 held less than £100, with
slightly more women than men in this lower wealth-holding category. Fewer
women, however, were recorded as actually being in debt. At the other end of
the scale almost a fifth of men held assets worth over £500, while only 14 per
cent of women did so. In the very wealthiest group that owned over £5000 at
the time of their death, men outnumbered women by more than two to one.
Table 5.3 also reveals the distribution of net assets by value. The aggregate
wealth of the total population holding less than £100 was around £28 million.
Put differently, over half the Australian population held less than 3 per cent of
total wealth. Almost 4 per cent of women's wealth was held by individuals
whose assets were less than £100 or who were net debtors, while less than 2 per
cent of men were in this position. Males with assets of £750 or less accounted
for just under 15 per cent of men's total wealth, while this category represented
more than 25 per cent of women's wealth. Compared with men, therefore,
proportionately more of women's wealth was held by those with £5000 or less,
while around one-third of women's wealth was held by those with more than
that amount compared to over half of men's. As a final comparison, the figures
show that among the total population the top 0.5 per cent of wealth-holders
held 23 per cent of the aggregate net assets and the top 10 per cent around
three-quarters of all assets. Assets were distributed slightly more equally
among women than men, with the top 1 per cent of women holding almost
a third of aggregate assets and the top 10 per cent around 73 per cent, while
among men the top 10 per cent held closer to 80 per cent of aggregate male
wealth.[44]

WOMEN'S WEALTH IN SOUTH AUSTRALIA,
1876–1915

While these figures provide us with an overview of relative wealth among men
and women in Australia at the turn of the twentieth century, probate records
allow us to delve more deeply into the similarities and differences in wealth-
holding by gender. Table 5.4 shows that from 1876 until the mid-1880s, for
every female whose estate was granted probate approximately five men's
estates also received probate. Thus despite the change to property ownership
laws in 1875, it took around 20 years for the ratio of female to male estates to
change. In the sample taken from 1890, the ratio of female to male estates fell
to one for every three, and within a few years the ratio was one probated

---

[44] For a discussion of inequality in the English context, see Chapter 3 in this volume.

Table 5.3 Number of probate returns and value of net assets for resident men and women in Australia, 30 June 1915

Net assets	Number of returns			Proportion per cent			Aggregate amount			Proportion per cent		
	Males	Females	Total	Males (%)	Females (%)	Total (%)	Males (£'000)	Females (£'000)	Total (£'000)	Males (%)	Females (%)	Total (%)
Debt and nil	249,693	110,036	359,729	18.10	13.55	16.41						
Under £100	533,315	392,146	925,461	38.64	48.31	42.22	17,119	10,975	28,095	1.87	3.68	2.31
£100 < £250	198,668	115,846	314,514	14.39	14.27	14.35	31,914	18,394	50,309	3.48	6.17	4.14
£250 < £500	135,689	76,772	212,461	9.83	9.46	9.69	48,161	27,019	75,180	5.25	9.06	6.18
£500 < £750	66,101	35,895	101,996	4.79	4.42	4.65	40,282	21,696	61,978	4.39	7.28	5.10
£750 < £1000	39,746	19,905	59,651	2.88	2.45	2.72	34,331	17,164	51,496	3.74	5.76	4.23
£1000 < £2500	88,779	40,336	129,115	6.43	4.97	5.90	139,001	61,609	200,611	15.14	20.66	16.49
£2500 < £5000	37,593	12,885	50,478	2.72	1.59	2.30	130,578	44,098	174,671	14.22	14.79	14.36
£5000 < £10,000	18,176	5183	23,359	1.32	0.64	1.07	125,230	35,341	160,571	13.64	11.85	13.20
£10,000 < £15,000	5313	1362	6675	0.38	0.17	0.31	64,181	16,431	80,612	6.99	5.51	6.63
£15,000 < £20,000	2366	530	2896	0.17	0.07	0.13	40,753	9191	49,944	4.44	3.08	4.11
£20,000 < £25,000	1283	279	1562	0.09	0.03	0.07	28,770	6226	34,997	3.13	2.09	2.88
£25,000 < £50,000	2179	406	2585	0.16	0.05	0.12	74,371	13,771	88,142	8.10	4.62	7.25
£50,000 < £75,000	641	81	722	0.05	0.01	0.03	38,956	4926	43,882	4.23	1.65	3.61
£75,000 < £100,000	249	26	275	0.02	0.003	0.01	21,380	2241	23,621	2.33	0.75	1.94
>£100,000	417	49	466	0.03	0.006	0.02	83,068	9057	92,125	9.05	3.04	7.57
Total	1,380,208	811,737	2,191,945	100.00	99.999	100.00	918,090	298,141	1,216,232	100.00	99.99	100.00
Total £500 and over	262,843	116,937	379,780	19.04	14.41	17.33	820,896	241,753	1,062,649	89.41	81.09	87.37

Source: Knibbs, *The Private Wealth of Australia*, 30.

Note: Excludes interest in trust estates, assurance and annuity policies, and prospective benefits from Friendly Societies.

Table 5.4 Number of probated estates in South Australia, 1876–1915

	1876	1880	1885	1890	1895	1905–15[†]
Males	251 (80.9)	428 (84.1)	500 (82.0)	612 (78.3)	343 (60.3)	6940 (66.8)
Females	59 (19.1)	81 (15.9)	110 (18.0)	170 (21.7)	126 (39.7)	3452 (33.2)
Widow	41 (69.5)	47 (58.0)	74 (67.2)	86 (50.6)	69 (54.7)	1765 (51.1)
Married	11 (18.6)	20 (24.7)	22 (20.0)	60 (35.3)	48 (38.1)	
Spinster	6 (10.2)	9 (11.1)	7 (6.4)	19 (11.2)	3 (2.4)	
Occupation	1 (1.7)	2 (2.5)			2 (1.6)	
Not stated		3 (3.7)	7 (6.4)	5 (2.9)	4 (3.2)	1687 (48.9)
Total sample size*	310	509	610	782	569	10,392‡

Source: Probate files, GRS/1334, South Australian Archives, Adelaide.

Note: Data collected for 3-year periods (1875–7, 1879–81, 1884–6, 1889–91) except 1905–15 which covers 10 year average. Female marital status expressed as percentage of female estates. * Excludes missing files, † 1905–15 females categorized as widow and non-widow only; ‡ includes women with no record of wealth (and is thus greater than 10,335 total reported in Table 5.1).

Table 5.5 Average gross wealth of probated estates, by gender and marital status in South Australia, 1876–1915 (pounds sterling)

	1876	1880	1885	1890	1895	1905–15[†]
Average all*	2216	2581	3043	2266	2469	2283
Males	2643	2881	3358	2485	2966	2483
Females[‡]	456	663	1522	1476	1141	1156
Widow	511	708	2101	2138	969	1398
Married	300	903	483	1002	891	903
Spinster	256	347	439	569	284	

Source: Probate files, GRS/1334, South Australian Archives, Adelaide.

Note: Data collected for 3-year periods (1875–7, 1879–81, 1884–6, 1889–91) except 1905–15 which covers 10 year average. *Nominal values, total South Australian gross wealth only; [†]1905–15 females categorized as widow and non-widow only; [‡]Average for 1895 includes one 'independent' female who left over £25,000.

female estate for every two male estates, a ratio that continued into the early 1900s. Table 5.4 also reveals that widows constituted the majority of female estates, presumably because of the property they inherited from their husbands, but that married women increased in importance over the period and by 1890 comprised more than a third of all female probated estates, a proportion compatible with their share of the population as whole.[45] From 1890 to 1915, there was a gradual increase in the representation of women in the probate record, notably by married women, which is consistent with the slow shift toward more equal social and economic status between the sexes.

In terms of average gross wealth recorded in the probates, the trends are broadly similar to the numbers of estates. Table 5.5 and Figure 5.1 describe average wealth holdings by gender and marital status and show that although men initially left estates that were on average six times larger than those of women, by the mid-1880s, this ratio had fallen to approximately two to one. The story is a little more complicated within female probate estates themselves. As Figure 5.1 reveals, the average value of the estates belonging to widows increased sharply in 1885 and 1890 before falling back to levels approximately equal to those left by married women. Nonetheless, it does not appear fanciful to suggest that the Married Women's Property Act of 1884 seems to have had some impact. After the passage of the Act, the proportion of probated females increased rapidly, as shown in Table 5.4, and the average wealth of widows also rose substantially, perhaps because the wealth they enjoyed until the moment of their death was now recognized as their own. The number of married women who left probated estates also rose sharply after 1884 as did the size of their estates. As the proportion of women that were

---

[45] National and regional variation between rates of marriage thus also increase the difficulty in making interregional comparisons of wealth distribution based on probate records.

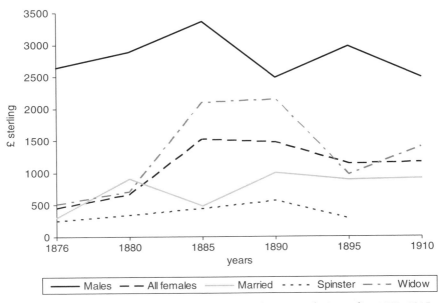

Figure 5.1 Average gross probated wealth by gender in South Australia, 1875–1915
Source: see Table 5.5.

probated had increased from 19 per cent in 1876 to over 30 per cent by 1895, a levelling in average female wealth-holdings could, perhaps, have been anticipated.

THE COMPOSITION OF WOMEN'S WEALTH

The convergence of probated wealth between men and women after 1884 was consistent with a colonial society in which opportunity for advancement was relatively open. However, it tells us little about the elements that comprised an individual's wealth at the time of their death and here some notable differences occurred. Table 5.6 illustrates the composition of men's and women's gross wealth between 1876 and 1895. In the 1870s and early 1880s, women held three to four times as much of their wealth as cash in the bank, and two to five times as much as furniture, and linen, than did men. On the other hand, men held disproportionately more of their gross wealth in assets related to income generation. For example, compared with women, they held five to seven times as much of their wealth as stock-in-trade, and up to four times as much as mortgages and debts owing. Interestingly, in real estate the pattern is less discernible, with the proportions roughly similar, or with men holding slightly

Table 5.6 Assets by gender in South Australia, 1876–95 (per cent of gross wealth)

	1876 Male	1876 Female	1880 Male	1880 Female	1885 Male	1885 Female	1890 Male	1890 Female	1895 Male	1895 Female
Cash in the house	1.00	1.77	0.23	0.34	0.89	0.30	0.71	0.49	0.36	0.91
Cash in the bank	5.55	14.98	5.56	7.14	3.94	13.32	9.69	7.23	3.27	12.64
Furniture, plate, linen, china	1.99	5.84	1.69	1.56	1.07	2.25	2.23	1.89	1.97	4.66
Wine and liquors	0.13	0.18	0.08	0.07	0.27	—	0.06	0.02	0.03	—
Horses, carriages, farm stock	4.81	3.30	2.66	3.84	4.25	0.48	5.81	1.02	2.87	0.48
Stock-in-trade	5.94	1.11	1.51	2.29	2.03	0.04	0.18	0.09	7.29	0.01
Goodwill	1.08	2.07	1.37	0.42	0.01	—	0.05	0.03	0.30	—
Leasehold estates	1.08	1.24	0.58	2.68	8.08	—	0.43	0.22	1.87	0.36
Life assurance	2.69	—	2.56	4.03	3.16	1.14	1.10	0.41	1.92	0.15
Mortgages, rent, and interest due	14.53	3.07	21.56	9.98	7.38	22.84	21.24	14.56	6.42	8.03
Bonds, bills, rates, interest due	1.34	0.06	1.21	1.54	1.36	1.79	1.38	0.59	2.40	4.17
Book and other debts due	6.05	4.54	1.62	2.54	2.39	1.13	1.07	0.47	4.38	0.99
Ships or shares in ships	0.27	1.86	0.02	2.82	0.02	0.01	0.10	—	0.68	—
Treasury bills	—	—	—	0.21	—	0.12	—	—	—	—
Government debentures	0.32	—	—	—	0.05	—	—	—	—	—
Stocks/shares in banks	4.49	11.05	4.14	5.76	4.93	4.58	5.31	4.79	4.81	5.94
Stocks/shares in companies	0.77	0.12	0.44	0.72	9.88	3.56	0.32	0.15	0.36	0.45
Dividends from stocks	0.02	0.01	0.10	0.01	0.01	—	0.02	0.02	0.02	0.05
Foreign stocks/securities	—	—	0.01	—	0.15	—	0.78	—	0.07	0.13
Real estate	37.77	38.15	52.92	47.7	44.38	44.77	40.75	51.9	57.88	47.67
Other controlled property	0.15	—	0.84	0.06	—	0.17	7.30	—	0.74	—
Property not elsewhere listed	10.02	10.63	0.91	6.29	5.73	3.49	1.48	16.13	3.34	13.35
Total	100.00	100.00	100.00	100.00	100.00	100.00	100.00	100.00	100.00	100.00
Number of observations	208	53	415	567	339	125	154	88	362	62

Source: Succession Duty files GRG84/9, South Australian Archives, Adelaide.

more of their wealth as real estate than women. This may, in part reflect the rationale for estates being probated, but it may also be because women could own real estate in their own right. It does suggest that among probated estates, land ownership was generally as important for men as it was for women; a result consistent with an economy heavily dependent on the agricultural sector.

From the mid-1880s to the mid-1890s, the gap between the relative importance of cash in the bank, and furniture and linen for men and women, narrows, as do differences in relative holdings of stock-in-trade. From around 1890, however, it is suddenly women who hold a larger proportion of their assets as mortgages and rent owing than men. This may be an important reason for the apparent jump in the aggregate wealth of women particularly widows over this period. It also suggests, however, that women were engaging more with the land market, both as owners and as lenders, a trend that is also consistent with the agricultural expansion of the colony in the late nineteenth century.

By contrast, financial holdings in terms of shares in banks and companies was relatively limited, although interestingly, with the exception of the mid-1880s, both men's and women's holdings of this kind of asset were roughly similar. Nor did either men or women hold much by way of government-backed securities, unlike their nineteenth-century English counterparts. It is not until the probate records collected for early in the twentieth century are viewed, that holdings of treasury bills or government debentures really appear in South Australian women's inventories, and even then they do not reach the proportions held by their English sisters.[46]

The ownership of different kinds of wealth, however, depended partly on the size of estates, as the evidence for 1905–15 in Table 5.7 demonstrates. For the two smallest wealth bands, there are approximately equal numbers of males and females but for estates over £2500 there are six times as many males as females. The composition of assets differed between wealth bands: for example, people recorded with net estates under £500 held no government debentures, treasury bills, dividends from stocks and shares, shares in foreign states, nor did they possess any share of a ship. All these assets, however, are

---

[46] By contrast, nineteenth-century English women with sufficient wealth also appear to have been significant holders of government debt in England. See Green, D.R. and A. Owens 2003. 'Gentlewomanly capitalism? Spinsters, widows and wealth holding in England and Wales c.1800–1860'. *Economic History Review* 56(3): 510–36; Rutterford, J. and J. Maltby 2006. '"The widow, the clergyman and the reckless": women investors in England, 1830–1914'. *Feminist Economics* 12(1/2): 111–38; and Chapters 3 and 8 in this volume. A study by Johns, L. 2006. 'The first female shareholders of the Bank of New South Wales: examination of shareholdings in Australia's first bank, 1817–1821'. *Accounting, Business and Financial History* 16(2): 293–314 suggests a high proportion of women were shareholders in colonial New South Wales. Against this, the number of shareholders involved was very small (15) and her work suggests their role was to allow male directors access to cheaper proxy voting rights.

Table 5.7 Assets by net wealth banding and gender in South Australia, 1905–15 (per cent of gross wealth)

Assets	£0–£500		£501–2500		£2501–£20,000		£20,001+	
	Female	Male	Female	Male	Female	Male	Female	Male
Cash in the house	0.14	0.24	0.26	0.32	0.56	0.44	0.01	0.03
Cash in the bank	11.46	7.17	14.92	5.50	4.33	4.53	1.79	4.46
Furniture, plate, linen, china	4.76	8.04	1.26	1.68	2.01	2.49	1.09	0.57
Wine and liquors	—	—	—	—	—	—	0.03	0.01
Horses, carriages, farm stock	—	1.50	0.05	4.19	0.02	3.85	0.20	2.29
Stock-in-trade	9.50	4.73	0.58	1.14	0.12	8.12	0.31	2.40
Goodwill	1.25	0.74	—	1.69	—	0.43	—	0.26
Leasehold estates	1.13	1.47	11.69	5.54	7.19	8.09	0.72	1.39
Life assurance	2.73	8.91	0.29	9.84	0.01	2.62	0.15	1.03
Mortgages and interest due	2.61	4.10	6.28	3.15	3.79	6.59	13.61	10.81
Bonds, bills, rates, interest due	1.13	0.82	1.34	1.52	1.42	2.75	4.69	2.14
Book and other debts due	0.28	3.60	0.78	2.92	0.05	4.62	4.13	2.60
Ships or shares in ships	—	—	—	—	—	—	—	0.49
Treasury bills	—	—	3.77	0.41	4.33	0.21	10.45	2.82
Government debentures	—	—	—	—	—	0.67	3.46	1.71
Stocks/shares in banks	0.26	—	1.12	1.87	5.16	1.60	1.62	1.59
Stocks/shares in companies	0.45	2.90	3.40	1.40	7.12	7.12	7.56	12.11
Dividends from stocks	—	—	—	#	0.02	0.01	0.04	0.05

(continued)

Table 5.7 (Continued)

Assets	£0–£500		£501–2500		£2501–£20,000		£20,001+	
	Female	Male	Female	Male	Female	Male	Female	Male
Foreign stocks/securities	—	—	—	—	—	—	1.75	0.27
Real estate	62.56	53.72	51.24	58.71	50.86	35.59	13.77	29.69
Other controlled property	—	—	—	#	0.29	0.24	3.96	1.37
Property not elsewhere listed	0.49	1.51	2.82	#	6.41	5.76	24.43	10.48
Property outside South Australia	1.25	0.55	0.20	0.12	6.33	4.27	6.23	11.43
Total gross	100.00	100.00	100.00	100.00	100.00	100.00	100.00	100.00
Debts								
Funeral expenses	−4.74	−2.33	−0.97	−0.76	−0.38	−0.32	−0.05	−0.04
Administrative expenses	−3.32	−1.80	−1.22	−1.34	−2.26	−0.95	−0.94	−1.22
Simple debts	−13.55	−27.45	−1.75	−12.60	−2.88	−9.68	−0.78	−2.31
Mortgages, bonds, other debt	−18.49	−29.87	−18.43	−31.10	−0.99	−12.07	−1.58	−2.10
Net as % of gross value of estate	59.90	38.55	77.63	54.20	93.49	76.98	96.65	94.33
Total observations	32	37	31	33	8	64	17	100

Source: Succession Duty files GRG84/9, South Australian Archives, Adelaide.

Note: # only one case.

recorded by people in the top wealth group, and to a lesser extent by people in other wealth bands. The differences in asset holdings are so marked, in fact, that it is possible to identify in which wealth category a person should be recorded simply by knowing whether they owned particular assets. For example, any person leaving assets including wine and liquors or securities in foreign states, or a share of a ship, owned an estate in excess of £20,000. A person not possessing these assets, but leaving government debentures was probably in the wealth category between £2500 and £20,000. Anyone leaving treasury bills or dividends from stock would have left over £500. It is possible that these various kinds of assets proved more lucrative forms of investment, and therefore those who owned them were likely to have died wealthy, but it is more likely that they were purchased by those who possessed wealth already and who had greater access to a wider range of opportunities and flows of information regarding profitable investments.

The main source of wealth, however, was real estate, although it tended to decline in importance as other kinds of assets became more attractive. With the exception of estates valued at over £20,000, the proportion of gross wealth held as real estate was roughly similar for men and women. In the top wealth group, however, real estate holdings among women contributed only 14 per cent to gross wealth compared to men's 30 per cent. It was not uncommon for husbands to leave the family home to the wife, together with the rights to income from stock and other financial assets, but the majority of the real estate to the children. Such patterns are consistent with the results for estates over £20,000. For example, for women in the top wealth group, treasury bills contribute over 10 per cent of their gross estate compared to 2.8 per cent of men's; the contribution of income from mortgage and interest, bonds, and bills, book and other debts, government debentures, and furniture, plate, and linen, are all higher for women. Compared to women, men in the top group possessed a greater proportion of their assets in farm stock, horses and carriages, stock-in-trade, goodwill, leasehold estates, company shares (although women owned a higher proportion of 'safer' bank shares), and property held 'outside the state'. Women in the top wealth group also tended to have a relatively high proportion of the wealth in 'property not elsewhere described', a category which encompassed assets such as personal and family trusts.[47]

A similar pattern of asset holdings, although not quite as clearly defined, occurred between men and women in the lower wealth groups. In estates between £2500 and £20,000, women generally held a higher proportion of their wealth as treasury bills, 'property not elsewhere described', shares in banks, and 'other property'. Again a higher proportion of men's wealth was

---

[47] A close reading of the Succession Duty files suggests that where women left considerable wealth (over £20,000), several possessed property and funds which reverted to their children on the testatrix's death.

associated with income generation, such as goodwill, stock-in-trade, and horses, carriages, and farming stock.

For the lower wealth bandings below £2500, real estate and cash in the bank were the two largest categories. As with women in richer groups, treasury bills, and 'property not elsewhere described', contributed a higher proportion of wealth than for males in the same group, though the overall amounts attributable to these kinds of assets were fairly low. Leasehold estates were also an important asset for those who left more than £500. For the smallest estates, however, women owned a relatively high proportion of their wealth as stock-in-trade. This can be explained by the fact that, at this wealth level, the most commonly inherited assets (other than the family home) for wives were likely to be the stocks and materials of their late husband's store, trade, or business. While they also held some cash in the bank, they typically owned little else.

INTERNATIONAL COMPARISONS: WOMEN'S WEALTH-HOLDING

There may have been greater opportunities for social mobility and the accumulation of wealth in the settler colonies compared with Britain, but the question remains as to how this compared with other, newly emerging parts of the Western world. International comparisons of wealth distributions based on probate records are difficult, not least because of differences in demographic profiles, legal definitions of wealth, mortality rates, and the administrative processes of collecting information.[48] For the decade just prior to the First World War (the only period for which comparisons with South Australia are currently available), it is known that personal probate wealth in South Australia was distributed more equally than in England, the United States, Prussia, France, Italy, or Norway, and in roughly the same measure as in New Zealand.[49] Unfortunately, there are very few comparisons that separate out

---

[48] See, for example, Lindert, P. 2000. 'Three centuries of inequality in Britain and America'. In *Handbook of Income Distribution*, Volume 1, edited by A.B. Atkinson and F. Bourguignon. Amsterdam: Elsevier, 167–210.

[49] Between 1905 and 1915 in South Australia, the Gini coefficient of wealth distribution was roughly 0.75, with the top 1 per cent holding 30 per cent of wealth and the top 10 per cent around 70 per cent. In England and Wales around 1912, the figures suggest the top 1 per cent held 66 per cent of the wealth and the top 10 per cent owned 90 per cent of the wealth. For the United States in 1912, the estimates are: the top 1 per cent held 55 per cent and the top 10 per cent held 89 per cent of the wealth. In Prussia in 1908 and France in 1909, the top 1 per cent of estates held 50 per cent of the wealth, the top 10 per cent around 80 per cent, while for Italy and Norway, the Gini coefficient was around 0.81–0.86. In New Zealand between 1910 and 1914, the top 1 per cent held around 30–40 per cent of the personal wealth and the top 10 per cent around 70 per cent. See Shanahan, 'The distribution of personal wealth in South Australia', 549.

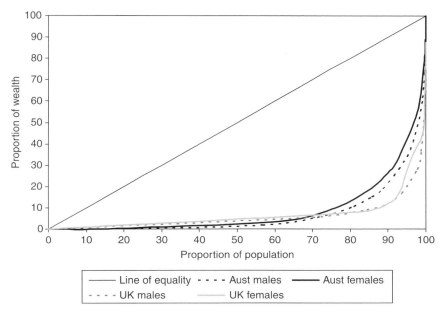

Figure 5.2 The distribution of wealth by gender in Australia, 1915, and in the United Kingdom, 1923–5

Source: Australia: see Table 5.2; the United Kingdom: see Wedgwood, J. 1929. *The Economics of Inheritance*. London: George Routledge and Sons, Appendix to chapter 1, table 4, 47.

the relative holdings, or levels of inequality of women compared to men.[50] Figure 5.2, however, presents Lorenz curves of the wealth of males and females in Australia in 1915 and for male and female estates in the United Kingdom for 1923–5. While there are significant dangers in making such comparisons (given, for example, differences in age structures, marital status, and estimation techniques), the results suggest that the distribution of probated estates among colonial sisters was more equal than among UK-based female estates a decade later.[51]

When it comes to comparing female wealth more specifically, the lack of detailed information means that broader international comparisons for this

---

[50] Most probate-based studies examine comparatively small samples of estates. Given women are underrepresented in the records until late in the nineteenth century, many reported studies have focused exclusively on male estates.

[51] The Australian figures are based on the 1915 wealth census data, while the UK results are based on probate data that have been adjusted by applying mortality multipliers. Despite concerns that such a difference in data may invalidate the comparison, it is clear that mortality multiplier adjusted probate-based estimates underestimate the distribution of wealth compared to census based studies. For a discussion, see Shanahan, 'The distribution of personal wealth', 101–5. See also Atkinson, A.B. and A.J. Harrison 1978. *The Distribution of Personal Wealth in Britain*. Cambridge: Cambridge University Press, 138–70.

Men, Women, and Money

Table 5.8 Female estates in selected 'new world' regions 1860–1939 (per cent of male estates)

Year	South Australia	Australia	New Zealand	Massachusetts, the United States	Wentworth Ontario[†]
1860				26.2	
1876	17.25				13.6
1880	23.01			36.9	27.4
1885	45.32				
1888			19.16		
1890	59.40			42.8	37.6
1895	38.47				
1896			35.49		
1906			40.99		38.7
1910	46.56				
1915*	48.32	55.19			
1916			55.67		
1924			50.47		
1932			55.06		
1939			62.74		

Source: South Australia, see text. Australia, calculated from Knibbs, *The Private Wealth of Australia*, 30–1; New Zealand from Galt, M.N. 1985. 'Wealth and income in New Zealand 1870 to 1939'. Unpublished Ph.D. Thesis, Victoria University, Wellington; 58; USA, Massachusetts from Shammas, C. 1993. 'A new look at long-term trends in wealth inequality in the United States'. *American Historical Review* 98(2): 423; Wentworth, Ontario, calculated from Di Matteo L. and P. George 1998. 'Patterns and determinants of wealth among probated decedents in Wentworth County, Ontario 1872–1902'. *Histoire sociale–Social History* 31(1): 22.

Note: *Based on wealth census of living population; [†]dates for Wentworth County, Ontario: 1872, 1882, 1892, and 1902.

period are only possible using information on the relative proportion of probated female estates, as shown in Table 5.8.[52] Despite the rather large gaps, the data suggest that in the late nineteenth century comparatively more women in South Australia may have been holding wealth than their New Zealand counterparts. The number of South Australian females estates was about half that of males, compared to around 20 per cent for New Zealand women. It was not until after the First World War that the ratio of female to male probated wealth in New Zealand reached 50 per cent. The ratio of women to men calculated from the 1915 Australian wealth census both confirms the South Australian trend, and adds the surprising finding that South Australian women may have lagged behind the national average. For the

---

[52] For New Zealand, see Galt, M.N. 1985. 'Wealth and income in New Zealand 1870 to 1939'. Unpublished Ph.D. Thesis, Victoria University, Wellington; for Massachusetts, the United States, see Shammas, C. 1993. 'A new look at long-term trends in wealth inequality in the United States'. *American Historical Review* 98(2): 412–31; for Wentworth County, Ontario, see Di Matteo, L. and P. George 1998. 'Patterns and determinants of wealth among probated decedents in Wentworth County, Ontario 1872–1902'. *Histoire sociale–Social History* 31(1): 1–33.

United States, Shammas suggests a slightly higher percentage of women were probated there than in other regions of the 'new world', particularly in the 1860s. By the 1890s, however, the relative share of probated estates left by women in Massachusetts appears to have fallen behind that of women in New Zealand and South Australia. Di Matteo reports women's relative wealth holdings in Wentworth County, Ontario, for the period 1872–1902 and also finds the proportion of women leaving probated estates increased over the period. Again, their share relative to that of men was slightly lower than that observed in South Australia. Given the spasmodic nature of these studies, and the comparatively small sample sizes involved, the results are more intriguing than conclusive but hint at some important differences between newly emerging economies as well as changes over time.

CONCLUSION

At one level, social attitudes to women in South Australia in the nineteenth century, and the consequent legislative changes to their rights to own property, access education, and vote, would appear to have had comparatively little impact on their material wealth holdings, certainly in the short term. The probate data suggest that women still came a distant second in terms of their individual wealth ownership, the relative quantity of wealth they possessed and the types of assets they controlled, compared with men. The series of data on the proportion of probated women to men in South Australia also suggests a trend to greater property ownership among women between 1876 and 1915. Changes in legislation appear to have been important in hastening this trend, particularly after the Married Women's Property Act of 1884. However, the trend is also evident in other countries and so broader, structural forces are also likely to have been a factor in helping to explain the changes.

As other chapters in this book by Di Matteo and Green et al. show, by using similar kinds of evidence based on probate records, we can begin to unravel the complexities of wealth-holding for relatively ordinary individuals in a variety of different geographical settings. In general, these were not the super rich who formed the uppermost echelons in any society but rather the bulk of wealth-holders whose fortunes were made primarily by their own efforts as they began to settle and develop in other parts of the world. In the settler colonies, and in the United States, the similarities of the evidence provide an intriguing opportunity for comparison with the United Kingdom, and although this exercise is yet at a relatively early stage, we can already begin to distinguish some important trends and differences. Comparison with the United Kingdom suggests that Australian (and probably South Australian) women were, in relation to the ownership of wealth, some way ahead of their

British counterparts. Real estate, in particular, appeared to be the key to their comparative wealth, something that was in very short supply in the United Kingdom. Comparisons with women in New Zealand, Massachusetts, and Ontario, while less detailed, also appear to suggest that South Australian women were relatively better off than those in some other 'new world' regions. Future research that explores the social, cultural, and political processes by which these differences in wealth were generated remains to be carried out, but the evidence is being gathered and a start has been made.

6

Wealth and Gender in Ontario: 1870–1930

Livio Di Matteo

INTRODUCTION

The proliferation of female property rights legislation in nineteenth-century North America, Britain, and Europe hints at common concerns and transformations in relation to women's ownership of assets. Beginning in the 1840s in the United States, during the course of the nineteenth century, married women's property laws were passed in English-speaking North America as well as in England and other parts of Europe.[1] There were several reasons that help to explain why such legislation emerged. There was a concern to protect widows and families against rapacious creditors and irresponsible husbands.[2] At the same time, early forms of married women's property law made it easier for men to protect themselves against creditors by transferring property to their wives, although subsequent revisions made it more difficult for them to do so.[3] A further driver may have been the desire to create some degree of equality of opportunity between male and female children. As Peter Baskerville has noted in the Canadian context, 'granting of more control over wealth

The financial support of the Social Sciences and Humanities Research Council of Canada in conducting this research is gratefully acknowledged. I am also indebted to the United Kingdom's Economic and Social Research Council for support in enabling me to attend the workshop 'Wealth, investment and gender in the nineteenth and twentieth centuries' at Milton Keynes, in June 2008 where a preliminary version of this chapter was presented.

[1] See Beckert, J. 2008. *Inherited Wealth*. Princeton, NJ: Princeton University Press, 93–4. For England and Wales, see Holcombe, L. 1983. *Wives and Property: Reform of the Married Women's Property Law in Nineteenth-Century England*. Toronto, ON: University of Toronto Press. Reforms were also instituted in European countries. See Beachy, R., B. Craig and A. Owens eds. 2006. *Women, Business and Finance in Nineteenth-Century Europe: Rethinking Separate Spheres*. Oxford: Berg.

[2] Beckert, *Inherited Wealth*, 95.

[3] Ibid., 7. Shammas, C. 1994. 'Re-assessing the Married Women Property Acts'. *Journal of Women's History* 6(1): 9–30 argues that many US states passed married women's property acts to protect women's property in the case of a husband's bankruptcy.

to married women allowed fathers and mothers to bequeath wealth to single daughters with more frequency since they had less to fear from acquisitive behaviour of prospective husbands'.[4] Such concerns also fed into a broader debate about economic, social, and political impediments to women's progress raised by the nascent feminist movement in Britain as well as elsewhere. Another driver of the new property laws may simply have been the increasing lifespan of women and a greater tendency to outlive husbands, fostering a need to provide surviving spouses with more secure control of family wealth.[5]

Whatever reasons underpinned the legal changes set in place during the nineteenth century, questions remain about how effective these were in enhancing women's opportunities to own wealth and this chapter seeks to address that issue. Most historians interested in economic inequality in North America have chosen to focus on other variables relating to the accumulation of wealth including occupation, ethnic origin, birthplace, urbanization, and age, and as yet there is relatively little research that focuses explicitly on gender-based wealth differences.[6] Although there has always been some

---

[4] Baskerville, P. 2008. *A Silent Revolution? Gender and Wealth in English Canada 1860–1930.* Montreal, QC: McGill-Queen's University Press, 87.

[5] For example, Bourdieu, J., G. Postel-Vinay, and A. Suwo-Eisenmann 2008. 'Aging women and family wealth'. *Social Science History* 32(2): 147 argue that in France as women came to outlive their husbands, new ways of sharing resources in the family had to be devised. According to the Civil Code of 1804, common property was split and a widow received half of it after her husband's death. The legal changes that appeared in 1891 and 1925 improved the position of surviving spouses by giving them greater usufruct rights.

[6] See for example Atack, J. and F. Bateman 1981. 'Egalitarianism, inequality and age: the rural north in 1860'. *Journal of Economic History* 41(1): 85–93; Conley, T.G. and D.W. Galenson 1998. 'Nativity and wealth in mid-nineteenth century cities'. *Journal of Economic History* 58(2): 467–91; Di Matteo, L. 1997. 'The determinants of wealth and asset holding in nineteenth-century Canada: evidence from microdata'. *Journal of Economic History* 57(4): 907–34; Di Matteo, L. 1998. 'Wealth accumulation and the life-cycle in economic history: implications of alternative approaches to data'. *Explorations in Economic History* 35(3): 296–324; Ferrie, J.P. 1994. 'The wealth accumulation of antebellum European immigrants to the U.S., 1840–1860'. *Journal of Economic History* 54(1): 1–33; Ferrie, J.P. 1995. 'The entry into the U.S. labour market of antebellum European immigrants, 1840–1860'. *Explorations in Economic History* 34(3): 295–330; Ferrie, J.P. 1999. *Yankees Now: Immigrants in the Antebellum US, 1840–1860.* New York, NY: Oxford University Press; Galenson, D.W. 1991. 'Economic opportunity on the urban frontier: nativity, work and wealth in early Chicago'. *Journal of Economic History* 51(3): 581–603; Gregson, M.E. 1996. 'Wealth accumulation and distribution in the Midwest in the late nineteenth century'. *Explorations in Economic History* 33(4): 524–38; Herscovici, S. 1993. 'The distribution of wealth in nineteenth-century Boston: inequality among natives and immigrants, 1860'. *Explorations in Economic History* 30(3): 321–35; Herscovici, S. 1998. 'Migration and economic mobility: wealth accumulation and occupational change among antebellum migrants and persisters'. *Journal of Economic History* 58(4): 927–56; Haines, M.R. and A.C. Goodman 1991. 'A home of one's own: aging and homeownership in the United States in the late nineteenth and early twentieth centuries'. *National Bureau of Economic Research, Working Paper Series on Historical Factors and Long-Run Growth* 21; Pope, C. 1989. 'Households on the American frontier: the distribution of income and wealth in Utah 1850–1900'. In *Markets in History: Economic Studies of the Past*, edited by D. Galenson. New York, NY: Cambridge University Press, 148–89; Steckel, R.H. 1990. 'Poverty and prosperity: a longitudinal study of

degree of property-holding by women, changes in the legal status of female rights to ownership of property during the late nineteenth century that enabled married women to possess property in their own name may have started to have some effect on wealth levels by the early twentieth century. These changes suggest the need to include gender as an explanatory variable in understanding the accumulation of wealth and the aim of this chapter is to focus on this issue.

While traditionally, historians have characterized these legal changes as revolutionary, new perspectives have emerged that suggest the changes were more evolutionary.[7] In Canada, Baskerville argues that in the wake of nineteenth-century property law reforms women became more significant actors in various economic and financial sectors.[8] However, the extent to which changes in the economic status of women were the result of these reforms is open to debate. Based on the records of legal cases, Anne Chambers argues that the legacy of the property law reforms in Victorian Ontario was mixed in relation to providing economic opportunities for women, though these laws were better than none at all.[9] Baskerville also notes the importance of the Married Women's Property Laws in enabling wealth accumulation on the part of women in the late nineteenth and early twentieth centuries but at the same time concedes that underlying social and cultural changes, as well as the economic force of a rising middle class, may have contributed to increases in female property-holding.[10] Whether the law led or followed changes therefore remains an open question.

This chapter addresses that issue by focusing on the timing and extent of female property ownership in late nineteenth-century Ontario in relation to changes in property rights legislation. More importantly, were female wealth increases continuous over time or were there interruptions to the process? In addition, was the increase in female property-holding a uniform trend

wealth accumulation, 1850–1860'. *Review of Economics and Statistics* 72(2): 275–85; Steckel, R.H. and C.M. Moehling 2001. 'Rising inequality: trends in the distribution of wealth in industrializing New England'. *Journal of Economic History* 61(1): 160–83; Walker, T.R. 2000. 'Economic opportunity on the urban frontier: wealth and nativity in early San Francisco'. *Explorations in Economic History* 37(3): 258–77.

[7] Salmon, M. 1986. *Women and the Law of Property in Early America*. Chapel Hill, NC: University of North Carolina Press, argues that there is a slow expansion of women's property rights in colonial America from 1750 to 1830 but there is much regional variation. Berg, M. 1993. 'Women's property and the industrial revolution'. *Journal of Interdisciplinary History* 24(2): 233–50 finds that women's property rights in England became more constricted in the late eighteenth and early nineteenth centuries but women nevertheless owned property on a relatively large scale and played important economic roles.

[8] Baskerville, P. 1999. 'Women and investment in late nineteenth-century urban Canada: Victoria and Hamilton, 1880–1901'. *Canadian Historical Review* 80(2): 191–218.

[9] Chambers, L. 1997. *Married Women and the Law of Property in Victorian Ontario*. Toronto, ON: Osgoode Society for Canadian Legal History, University of Toronto Press.

[10] Baskerville, *A Silent Revolution?* 236–47.

irrespective of geography or were there regional differences? Historical wealth micro-data from two regions of Ontario over the period 1870–1930 are used to examine these questions. The data consist of 2516 probated decedents from Wentworth County, Ontario from selected interval years and 1780 probated decedents from the Thunder Bay District in northern Ontario collected annually for the years 1885–1925. These data span the post-Confederation period from 1870 to 1930, when Canadian industrialization and urbanization increased, as did agricultural production, especially during the wheat boom era that reached its zenith in the years from 1907 to 1913.

THE EVOLUTION OF FEMALE PROPERTY-HOLDING

Nineteenth-century women's economic roles are a major theme in Canadian historical research. Early work focused on the significance of women's earnings for household income in urban areas and the ways in which women's unpaid labour on farms allowed men to participate in other wage earning opportunities.[11] More recently, attention has shifted to the way in which women were able to accumulate wealth and the various assets that comprised their growing fortunes. Baskerville has documented how the late nineteenth and early twentieth centuries witnessed a shift in wealth and assets from men to women in British North America as traditional conceptions of women's position in society were being transformed.[12] His work and that of others explores the direct economic role of women in owning assets in an effort to understand the evolution and impact of female property rights and changing opportunities.

Ontario and British North America generally lagged behind the United States in female property rights legislation. Starting in the 1840s, most American states passed legislation which allowed married women ownership and

---

[11] See, for example, Cohen, M. 1988. *Women's Work, Markets and Economic Development in Nineteenth-Century Ontario*. Toronto, ON: University of Toronto Press; Bradbury, B. 1979. 'The family economy and work in an industrializing city: Montreal in the 1870s'. *Historical Papers, Canadian Historical Association* 14(1): 71–96.

[12] Part of the shift in wealth also may have involved changes in inheritance practices as more equal division of estates amongst all children – sons and daughters – came to replace primogeniture during the course of the nineteenth century. In the case of Ontario, the shift began with the partible–impartible system in the mid-nineteenth century, well before changes in the married women's property law, which saw the farm estate bequeathed to a prime beneficiary – usually a son – who then compensated siblings. See Baskerville, *A Silent Revolution?* 55–75; Gagan, D. 1976. 'The indivisibility of land: a microanalysis of the system of inheritance in nineteenth-century Ontario'. *Journal of Economic History* 36(1): 126–46; Gagan, D. 1981. *Hopeful Travellers: Families, Land and Social Change in Mid-Victorian Peel County, Canada West*. Toronto, ON: University of Toronto Press.

control over real and personal property they had brought into the marriage.[13] Prior to this, such property had been essentially considered a gift to the husband. Subsequently, women acquired the right to dispose of property acquired during marriage by way of inheritance and ultimately to acquire, own, and dispose of property independently. In 1840, none of the 27 US states had such legislation whereas by 1880, 36 out of 38 states allowed for separate estates for married women while 31 out of 38 gave them control over earnings.[14] One impact of these laws in the United States was an increase in the percentage of female testators who appear in probate records. For example, in Bucks County, Pennsylvania, the proportion of testators who were female rose from 17 per cent in the 1790s to 38.5 per cent 100 years later.[15] Another impact was an expansion in patenting activity by women.[16]

In British North America, the New Brunswick legislature passed married women's property legislation in 1851 while British Columbia passed such laws in 1873 and 1886 and Nova Scotia in 1884 and 1898. By the end of the 1870s, married women were able to earn money and purchase but not dispose of real estate while by the end of the 1880s they could buy and sell real and personal property in any manner that they saw fit.[17] In Ontario, a variety of laws were passed in the nineteenth century in response to British legislation which sought to address women's property rights and improve their position with respect to the law especially in the event of marital breakdown.[18] These were the Married Women's Property Acts of 1859, 1872, and 1884 and the Married Woman's Real Estate Act of 1873 which allowed married women to dispose of real estate as if *feme sole*.[19] Of these, the most significant was the Married

---

[13] Shammas, C., M. Salmon, and M. Dahlin 1987. *Inheritance in America from Colonial Times to the Present*. New Brunswick, NJ: Rutgers University Press, 83.

[14] Jacobsen, J.P. 2007. *The Economics of Gender*. Malden, MA: Blackwell Publishing, 406.

[15] Shammas et al., *Inheritance in America*, 119.

[16] See Khan, Z. 1996. 'Married women's property laws and female commercial activity: evidence from United States patent records'. *Journal of Economic History* 56(2): 356–88.

[17] Baskerville, *A Silent Revolution?* 6.

[18] In England, the debate over property rights spawned numerous bills though effective legal change with respect to women's rights came with the married women's property acts of 1870 and 1882, which Ontario followed in 1872 and 1884. See Inwood, K. and S. van Sligtenhorst 2004. 'The social consequences of legal reform: women and property in a Canadian community'. *Continuity and Change* 19(1): 166. It should be noted that the Canadian colonies were innovative in enacting women's property laws in the mid-nineteenth century to deal with marriage breakdown and that English legislators were aware of this pioneering reform but the lead nevertheless passed to England. As Constance Backhouse notes with respect to the Canadian colonies: 'A spirit of legislative creativity, ably demonstrated in earlier decades, seems to have stultified by the 1870s and 1880s. In its place, a distinctly colonial mentality took root, and subservience to English precedent seems to have superseded any sense of Canadian identity.' See Backhouse, C.B. 1988. 'Married women's property law in nineteenth-century Canada'. *Law and History Review* 6(2): 231.

[19] Statutes of Ontario, 1873, 36 Vict., cap. 18. *Feme sole* referred to an unmarried woman. A married woman, on the other hand, was termed a *feme covert* or covered woman because her legal interests were 'covered' by those of her husband. See Shammas et al., *Inheritance in America*, 25.

Woman's Property Act of 1884 which enabled a married woman to dispose, by will, of any real or personal property as her separate property in the same manner as if *feme sole* without any intervention of a trustee.[20] Essentially, before 1884, any property that a woman brought into a marriage became her husband's property while after that date a woman could maintain her own separate ownership.[21]

Questions remain, however, as to the extent to which these legal changes transformed women's ability to accumulate wealth. Sceptics, such as Chambers, argue that the changes only had a limited impact because they did not recognize the economic value of domestic labour and still allowed scope for coercion by husbands when it came to female property-holding.[22] Others are more willing to accept that material changes in property ownership were related to the passage of legislation. According to Kris Inwood and Sarah van Sligtenhorst patterns of female property-holding began to change in anticipation of the 1884 legislation as the earlier reforms started to enhance the legitimacy of women's ownership of all kinds of assets.[23] Indeed, the 1872 and 1873 laws may have prompted some women to acquire real property based on the mistaken liberal interpretation of the law. Using probate records, assessment rolls, and census records, Baskerville has examined female wealth-holding in Victoria and Hamilton in the wake of property rights legislation in the 1880s. His findings suggest that in both cities women were gaining autonomy in land markets and other economic affairs although they appear to have made greater gains in Victoria, a fact that he partly ascribes to its frontier nature and the greater independence that fostered on the part of women.[24] His work on the later period from 1870 to 1930 also suggests that women acquired substantial wealth in both places, especially in relation to the acquisition of financial assets such as bank stocks. Nevertheless, locality still had a role to play and he noted that 'the difference in probated wealth held by women and men in both cities remained substantial'.[25]

Although experiences clearly differed between places, other research confirms the steady expansion of women's property-holding in this period. Kris Inwood and Sue Ingram examined the holdings of single, married, and widowed women in Guelph during the years 1871–91 and found significant

---

[20] Revised Statutes of Ontario, 1887, cap. 132. See Howell, A. 1895. *Probate, Administration and Guardianship*, 2nd edition. Toronto, ON: Carswell, 55.

[21] For a detailed account of women's property law in nineteenth-century Canada, see Backhouse, 'Married women's property law'. For an examination of marriage contracts and aspects of property law in Quebec, see Hamilton, G. 1999. 'Property rights and transaction costs in marriage: evidence from prenuptial contracts'. *Journal of Economic History* 59(1): 68–103.

[22] Chambers, *Married Women and the Law of Property*, 10.

[23] Inwood and van Sligtenhorst, 'The social consequences of legal reform', 169.

[24] Baskerville, 'Women and investment in late nineteenth-century urban Canada', 205–7.

[25] Baskerville, *A Silent Revolution?* 47.

increases in property-holding.[26] Using assessment rolls, census manuscripts, wills, mortgages, and property transfers over the period 1853–1913 in Guelph, further research by Inwood and van Sligtenhorst compared the propensity of women to hold real estate before the property rights changes of 1873 with those after the changes of 1884. While they found that women substantially increased their share of property, they still lagged behind men. Nevertheless, the evidence suggests that the property rights legislation was a factor in the rise of female property ownership, leading the authors to conclude that legal changes made female property ownership socially acceptable and 'helped legitimize the idea of property ownership by married women and to persuade both men and women of its respectability'.[27]

The impact of female property rights legislation has also been studied from a British perspective and is of relevance given the importance of British institutions to Ontario and Canada.[28] The 1870 Married Women's Property Act in Britain allowed women married after 1870 the right to own and control personal property and Mary Beth Combs links wealth-holding data to census information to assess the impact of this legal change.[29] Using evidence on wealth-holding derived from the Death Duty and Succession Registers for England and Wales, she examined three groups of shopkeeping women who died in the years 1860, 1890, and 1901–3. Combs established that women married after 1870 appeared to have shifted their wealth-holding away from real estate and towards personal property and that these women also owned a larger share of household wealth than those married before the Act.[30] In

---

[26] Inwood, K. and S. Ingram. 2000. 'The impact of married women's property legislation in Victorian Ontario'. *Dalhousie Law Journal* 23(2): 504–49.

[27] Inwood and van Sligtenhorst. 'The social consequences of legal reform', 187.

[28] With respect to the impact of other institutional arrangements on women's wealth outside the Anglo-American world, it should be noted that a study of wealth accumulation by women in France over the period 1800–1939 using individual bequest data found that over time more women died without assets but those who had assets were richer resulting in a more unequal overall distribution of wealth. See Bourdieu et al. 'Ageing women and family wealth'. In nineteenth-century France, the surviving spouse was not considered an heir but merely had rights of succession in cases where no relative entered into the inheritance. Inheritance rights of the spouse were expanded through legal reforms in the second half of the nineteenth century but the weak position of the spouse in French law persisted well into the twentieth century. See Beckert, *Inherited Wealth*, 97.

[29] Combs, M.B. 2004. 'Wives and household wealth: the impact of the 1870 British Married Women's Property Act on wealth-holding and the share of household resources'. *Continuity and Change* 19(1): 141–63; Combs, M.B. 2005. 'A measure of legal independence: the 1870 Married Women's Property Act and the portfolio allocation of British wives'. *Journal of Economic History* 65(4): 1028–57. Combs' sample included 1238 individuals from which a census-linked sub-sample of 214 was constructed.

[30] There is also British evidence suggesting that the increases in female property-holding after 1870 were part of a long-term trend that predated the property rights legislation. For example, Green, D.R. and A. Owens 2003. 'Gentlewomanly capitalism? Spinsters, widows and wealth-holding in England and Wales c.1800–1860'. *Economic History Review* 56(3): 510–36 examined the lists of fund holders at the Bank of England and found that the evidence contradicts the view of

essence, it seemed that women used their newly acquired legal independence to gain a greater measure of economic independence.

GENDER AND WEALTH IN ONTARIO

Historical context

Late nineteenth-century Ontario consisted of both industrializing and agricultural regions that offered individuals with a variety of opportunities to acquire a diverse range of assets and to accumulate wealth. Two regions provide an opportunity to explore this further: Wentworth County at the head of Lake Ontario and the Thunder Bay District at the head of Lake Superior (see Figure 6.1). The Thunder Bay District is a sprawling region that encompasses a large part of Ontario's Canadian shield region whereas Wentworth County is a relatively compact agricultural region that also included the city of Hamilton and the town of Dundas plus the adjoining rural townships of East and West Flamborough, Beverly, Ancaster, Glanford, Binbrook, and Saltfleet.[31] Relative to the Thunder Bay District, Wentworth County has a much older history of permanent European settlement dating from the late eighteenth century and by the latter half of the nineteenth century was undergoing a process of urbanization and industrialization. This growth continued and its population rose from 57,599 in 1871 to 111,706 in 1911 and reached 153,567 by 1921.

The two main urban places, Hamilton and Dundas, both aspired to be regional centres but by 1850 the former had emerged the winner and proceeded to dominate its hinterland. Hamilton's prominence as a commercial and later as an industrial centre was the result of its strategic location at the head of Lake Ontario that enabled it to reap the benefits of being a transshipment point. In this sense, Hamilton was similar to the Lakehead cities of Fort William and Port Arthur in the Thunder Bay District. The expansion of the wheat trade, especially during the boom years from 1896, when prices began to rise, to 1914, was also accompanied by the growth of other industrial sectors, notably the manufacture of iron and steel products.[32] Indeed, as

women as being at the margins of property ownership. The proportion of female investors in government securities rose from 34.7 per cent in 1810 to 47.2 per cent in 1840, suggesting that by 1840 nearly half of public creditors were women. See also Chapter 3 by Green et al. in this volume.

[31] Wentworth County was established in 1816 and in 1971 became the Regional Municipality of Hamilton-Wentworth. The historic county had an area of just over 1000 square kilometres. Thunder Bay District was established in 1871 and over time had the Districts of Kenora-Rainy River and Cochrane carved out of it and by the 1920s was just over 100,000 square kilometres.

[32] For an overview of the wheat boom debate and its impact on Canadian economic growth, see Chambers, E.J. and D.F. Gordon 1966. 'Primary products and economic growth: an empirical

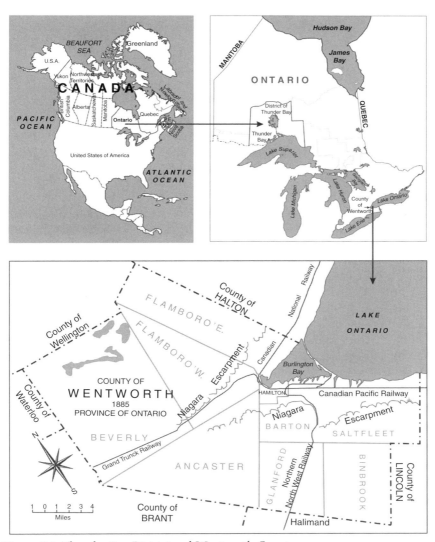

Figure 6.1 Thunder Bay District and Wentworth County

measurement'. *Journal of Political Economy* 74(4): 315–32; Pomfret, R. 1993. The Economic Development of Canada. 2nd edition. Toronto, ON: Nelson, 182–211. See also Norrie, K.H. 1975. 'The rate of settlement of the Canadian prairies'. *Journal of Economic History* 35(2): 410–27. Expanded analysis of the impact of the wheat boom includes the impact of tariffs, the value of immigrant capital and the impact on wages. See Lewis, F. 1975. 'The Canadian wheat boom and per capita income, new estimates'. *Journal of Political Economy* 83(6): 1249–57; Lewis, F. 1981. 'Farm settlement on the Canadian prairies 1898 to 1911'. *Journal of Economic History* 41 (3): 517–35; Caves, R.E. 1971. 'Export-led growth and the new economic history'. In *Trade,*

various scholars have argued, the development of Hamilton and other cities during these years was the outcome of a series of inter-linked economic changes arising more generally from the opening of the Prairies.[33]

The transcontinental railroad and the settlement of the Prairies had an even more dramatic impact on the economy of north-western Ontario and the Thunder Bay District.[34] The European settlement of the Thunder Bay District began during the fur trade when it was home to Fort William, the inland headquarters of the Northwest Company of Montreal. The decline of the fur trade led to the region's marginalization but a mining boom in the 1870s and a growing timber trade created the conditions for export-led economic growth. Improvements in transportation encouraged further growth: the opening of the transcontinental railway in the 1880s linked the region to the Prairie wheat economy and central Canada and in 1895 the locks at Sault Ste. Marie were completed, providing a deep water channel from Lake Huron to Lake Superior and from there to the industrializing and urbanizing heartland of Ontario. The Thunder Bay District was positioned between the Prairie wheat economy, from which it benefited by having its major metropolitan centre serve as êntrepot, and central Canada, where it was part of the country's wealthiest province.

The region's fortunes were directly tied to the expansion of wheat farming on the Prairies via the grain port function of the twin cities of Fort William and Port Arthur known collectively as the 'Lakehead'.[35] The growth of grain elevator storage capacity at the Lakehead from 1884 to 1915 was a direct consequence of the expanding wheat economy. From approximately 350,000 bushels of grain storage in 1884, capacity grew to 48.6 million bushels by 1915 with approximately 85 per cent of the construction after 1900. The development of local manufacturing, resource extraction, and agricultural

Balance of Payments and Growth, edited by J.N. Bhagwati, R.W. Jones, R.A. Mundell, and J. Vanek. Amsterdam: North-Holland, 403–42.

[33] See Green, A.G. and M.C. Urquhart 1987. 'New estimates of output growth in Canada: measurement and interpretation'. In *Perspectives on Canadian Economic History*, edited by D. McCalla. Toronto, ON: Copp Clark Pitman, 158–75; Urquhart, M.C. 1986. 'New estimates of gross national product, Canada 1870–1926: some implications for Canadian development'. In *Long Term Factors in American Economic Growth*, volume 51, NBER Conference on Research in Income and Wealth, edited by S.L. Engerman and R.E. Gallman. Chicago, IL: The University of Chicago Press, 9–94; Urquhart, M.C. 1993. *Gross National Product, Canada 1870–1926: The Derivation of the Estimates*. Kingston, ON: McGill-Queen's University Press.

[34] North-western Ontario consists of the Districts of Kenora, Rainy River, and Thunder Bay.

[35] Di Matteo, L. 1991. 'The economic development of the Lakehead during the wheat boom era: 1900–1914'. *Ontario History* 83(3): 297–316; Di Matteo, L. 1992. 'Evidence on Lakehead economic activity from the Fort William building permits registers, 1907–1969'. *Thunder Bay Historical Museum Society Papers and Records* 20: 37–49; Di Matteo, L. 1993. 'Booming sector models, economic base analysis and export-led economic development: regional evidence from the Lakehead'. *Social Science History* 17(4): 593–617.

development added further impetus to economic growth.[36] As a result, the district grew rapidly, especially between 1901 and 1911 when the population nearly tripled to 39,496, reaching 49,560 in 1921.

Probate data and wealth at death

The primary data source for investigating wealth in the two regions is the probate records of the Ontario surrogate courts. Under the Surrogate Courts Act, 1858, a surrogate court with the power to issue grants of probate and administration valid throughout the province was established in each Ontario county, replacing the centralized Court of Probate originally established in 1793.[37] Probate was an institutional arrangement transferring property from the dead to the living and served to grant administration over the estate of the deceased as well as to authenticate the will and provide evidence as to the character of the executor.[38] In intestate cases (without a will), the application to the court for administration was made by an interested party (usually the spouse or next of kin but sometimes a creditor), and once granted, distribution of the estate was made according to law. Executors or administrators applied for probate in the county or district where most of the deceased's property was located while non-residents would apply for probate in the district or county in which that property was situated. The key component of these records was the inventory which provided wealth data organized into 16 asset categories.[39]

Some potential drawbacks to the use of probate records should be acknowledged but these should be weighed against the fact that wealth in probate records is inventoried to a degree not found in any other Canadian nineteenth-century source.[40] First, it can be argued that probated decedents are of

---

[36] Gross regional product in the absence of the wheat boom at the Lakehead would have been 42 per cent smaller. In addition, by 1921, there were 1534 farms supporting a rural population of 7397 around the Lakehead. Forestry also employed thousands, in extraction, at sawmills, and at the three pulps mills either operating or under construction by 1921. See Di Matteo, 'Booming sector models', 611–14.

[37] Statutes of Canada, 1858, 22 Vict., cap. 93.

[38] Howell, A. 1880. *The Law and Practice as to Probate, Administration and Guardianship.* Toronto: Carswell, 155.

[39] The wealth inventory categories are: (*a*) Household goods and furniture, (*b*) Farming implements, (*c*) Stock in trade, (*d*) Horses, (*e*) Horned Cattle, (*f*) Sheep and swine, (*g*) Book debts and promissory notes, (*h*) Moneys secured by mortgage, (*i*) Moneys secured by life insurance, (*j*) Bank shares and other stocks, (*k*) Securities for money, (*l*) Cash on hand, (*m*) Cash in bank, (*n*) Farm produce of all kinds, (*o*) Real estate, (*p*) Other personal property.

[40] Discussions of Ontario probate records as historical sources of data are contained in Elliott, B.S. 1985. 'Sources of bias in nineteenth-century Ontario wills'. *Histoire sociale–Social History* 18 (35): 125–32; and Osborne, B.S. 1980. 'Wills and inventories: records of life and death in a developing society'. *Families* 19(4): 235–47. See also Siddiq, F.K. and J. Gwyn 1991. 'The importance of probate inventories in estimating the distribution of wealth'. *Nova Scotia Historical Review* 11(1): 103–17.

higher average wealth and socio-economic status, often older and therefore not representative of the general population. This potential bias is problematic if the data set is used to draw inferences about the wealth of the general population but as this chapter focuses only on the probated decedents themselves, the problem of selection bias is limited.[41] A further consideration is that the wealth data is likely to be affected by whether the individuals died unexpectedly or had been ill a long time and therefore had run down their assets. One way to deal with this problem would be to have data on the cause of death for the individuals in the data set but unfortunately this information was not available in the probate records and other sources are not reliable for this time period.[42]

Second, the presence of estate taxes may provide incentives for an executor or administrator to underestimate the wealth being inventoried. The wealth data obtained from nineteenth-century Ontario probate records does not suffer from such a bias because there were no succession duties in Ontario until 1 July 1892 when the Succession Duty Act, 1892 came into effect, and even then the Act allowed for numerous exemptions.[43] In Ontario, therefore, the presence of estate taxes provided no reason to underestimate the value of the estate for almost all decedents.

A final concern is the occurrence of *inter vivos* transfers which means that an unknown portion of wealth may be unaccounted for by the probate records. The Succession Duty Act applied even to property 'voluntarily transferred by deed, grant, or gift made in contemplation of the death of the grantor or bargainor, or made or intended to take effect, in possession or enjoyment after such death'.[44] Generally, such transfers are considered a problem if estate

[41] When studying the wealth-holding of the general population, an attempt can be made to adjust the data for potential biases based on wealth and age using the estate multiplier technique. See Di Matteo, L. and P.J. George 1992. 'Canadian wealth inequality in the late nineteenth century: a study of Wentworth County, Ontario, 1872–1902'. *Canadian Historical Review* 73(4): 453–83.

[42] A noted scholar of Ontario's civil registration of vital events statistics writes that: 'For years after 1869 Ontario's civil registration of vital events was unsatisfactory. Although its legislative provisions surpassed Quebec's, Ontario was less successful in obtaining registrations... the registrar-general estimated that registrations for 1870 captured only a fifth of the province's deaths.' By 1893, reported death rates for municipalities ranged from 26 to 2 per thousand. See Emery, G. 1993. *Facts of Life: The Social Construction of Vital Statistics, Ontario 1869–1952.* Montreal, QC: McGill-Queen's University Press, 32–4.

[43] Statutes of Ontario, 1892, 55 Vict., cap. 6. The Succession Duty Act did not apply (*a*) to any estate the value of which, after payment of all debts and expenses of administration, does not exceed $10,000; nor (*b*) to property given, devised or bequeathed for religious, charitable or educational purposes; nor (*c*) to property passing under a will, intestacy or otherwise, to or for the use of the father, mother, husband, wife, child, grandchild, daughter-in-law, or son-in-law of the deceased, where the aggregate value of the property of the deceased does not exceed $100,000.

[44] A report on the Succession Duty Act in Welland, Ontario, from the *Welland Tribune* (1 April 1892: 2) asserted that 'The act provides for evasion by transfers before death, although the fear of revival makes such attempts very rare'.

taxes present an obstacle to intergenerational wealth transmission but the evidence for Ontario suggests that they were not.

Constructing the data set

The data set for the Thunder Bay District was constructed from the annual probate records of the District of Thunder Bay Surrogate Courts for the period 1885–1925.[45] All estates bearing application dates in the years 1885–1925 were examined. A total of 1780 individuals, and data on their residence, occupation, marital status, number of children, date of death, whether they had a will, and the value of the estates by inventory category were recorded.[46] Unfortunately, variables such as age at death, date married, or immigrated to Canada were not available in the probate records.[47] The result is a 40-year time series with cross-sections of varying size. The initial years of the data set contain few estates whereas the later years contain approximately 100 estates per year. For example, the years 1885–9 account for only 28 estates and 1890–4 for only 42 estates, whereas from 1910 to 1914 accounts for 348 estates, 1915 to 1920 accounts for 520 estates, and 1921 to 1925 contains 482 estates.

The data for Wentworth County contain 444 core census-linked probated decedents for the years 1872–1902 collected previously which were then augmented with the addition of 76 decedents for 1892 and 54 for 1902 who could not be traced for the original data set but for whom data on real and personal estate and other characteristics were available from probate.[48] Age at

[45] Prior to the creation of the District of Thunder Bay in 1885, the few estates from the region were probated in the District of Algoma and were not included in this data set.

[46] For the Thunder Bay District, the number of children is simply the number of children reported in the probate records – that is, the will and supporting documents. The number of children for Wentworth County's core 444 census-linked decedents was the larger of the number of children reported in the census and the probate records. For the remainder of the data set, the number of children is the number children reported in the probate records. Since the administration of an estate was at stake, one would expect the probate papers of intestates to be more comprehensive in their references to offspring than those of testates who designated an executor. Di Matteo, L. 1990. 'Wealth holding in Wentworth County, Ontario, 1872–1892'. Unpublished Ph.D. Thesis, McMaster University, 55, finds no discrepancy between the number of children reported by testates and intestates and concludes underestimation of the number of children not to be a major issue.

[47] In future, data on age could theoretically be acquired by census-linkage as was done for Wentworth County for 1872–1902.

[48] For information on the collection of the original Wentworth County Data set of 405 census-linked observations, see Di Matteo and George, 'Canadian wealth inequality'. An additional 39 decedents for 1902 were census-linked later bringing the size of the data set to 444. For 1872 and 1882, probate only provides personal estate. Real estate data for these original census-linked estates was obtained from assessment rolls and therefore no additions were made to the data for these years. However, had these estates been utilized there would be a total of 72 for 1872 and 115 for 1882.

death is only available for the core census-linked 444 decedents and therefore is not utilized as a variable in this chapter's analysis. This increases the total data set available for 1872–1902 to 574 individuals. To this was added data for all the estates probated for the years 1907, 1912, 1917, 1922, and 1927 which adds another 1905 probated decedents with data on their residence, occupation, marital status, number of children, date of death, whether they had a will, and the value of the estates. The early years of this data set are smaller as was the case for Thunder Bay District. There are 50 observations for 1872, 79 for 1882, 230 for 1892, 215 for 1902, 277 for 1907, 332 for 1912, 380 for 1917, 483 for 1922, and 470 for 1927 for a total of 2516 individuals.[49]

WEALTH AND GENDER IN ONTARIO: COMPARISONS

The two regions chosen for analysis represent places at different points in a trajectory of economic growth, and these differences are reflected in the summary statistics of wealth shown in Table 6.1. Wealth in general was more unequally distributed in the frontier Thunder Bay District compared to Wentworth County, as suggested by the higher standard deviation in the

Table 6.1 Summary statistics for Thunder Bay and Wentworth County data sets (1900 Canadian dollars)

	Thunder Bay 1885–1925 N = 1780		Wentworth County 1872–1927 N = 2516	
Average value of wealth	$5156	(20,877)	$6796	(20,129)
Average value of real estate	$2310	(10,318)	$2383	(6521)
Average value of financial assets*	$2449	(12,652)	$3944	(16,544)
Proportion male	0.79	(0.41)	0.63	(0.48)
Proportion testate	0.46	(0.50)	0.68	(0.47)
Proportion farmer	0.09	(0.29)	0.14	(0.35)
Proportion married	0.55	(0.50)	0.50	(0.50)
Proportion widow	0.08	(0.27)	0.20	(0.40)
Proportion widower	0.09	(0.28)	0.13	(0.34)
Proportion single	0.28	(0.45)	0.17	(0.38)
Average number of children†	1.60	(2.20)	2.13	(2.40)

Source: see text.

Note: Figures in brackets are standard deviations. *For Wentworth County, financial assets were incorporated into personal property; †per probated decedent.

[49] Approximately 37 of the individuals in the 1927 data actually had an application date for probate in 1926 but their files were located within the date sequence for 1927.

former area compared to the latter. As one might expect from a more recently settled frontier region, the proportion of male decedents was substantially higher in the Thunder Bay District compared to Wentworth County. The average value of probated estates in Wentworth County data was 32 per cent higher than the Thunder Bay District with the gap accounted for mainly by the ownership of financial assets.[50] The value of real estate was approximately the same in both places. Demographic factors may have been partly responsible for the different levels of wealth: testators were likely to have been older in the Wentworth County, which had been settled for longer, than in Thunder Bay, a fact also hinted at by the larger number of children linked to decedents there. Research in a variety of places suggests that wealth tends to rise with age over the life course and therefore, in the Canadian context, an older population is also likely to have been a wealthier one.[51] Wentworth County decedents were also more likely to be testate and be employed as farmers.[52] As for marital status, the proportion of married decedents and single individuals was higher in the Thunder Bay District while Wentworth County had relatively more widows and widowers – evidence again of the likely age differences between the two sets of data. Thunder Bay District's larger share of single decedents is again a reflection of the frontier nature of the area compared to a more settled one.

WEALTH IN ONTARIO: THE SIGNIFICANCE OF GENDER

As noted above, legal changes to married women's property rights in the late nineteenth century began to have an impact on their ability to accumulate assets in their own names and under these circumstances female wealth in general was likely to have risen. This trend is evident not least in the

---

[50] Financial assets in the probate record categories are the following: book debts and promissory notes, life insurance, monies secured by mortgage, cash on hand, cash in bank, bank shares and stocks, and securities for money.

[51] See Di Matteo, 'The determinants of wealth and asset holding' for a discussion of the effects of age on wealth-holding using a set of census-linked probated decedents for all Ontario in 1892. The average age for decedents in Wentworth County in 1892 was 59.9 years while for Thunder Bay District and Rainy River Districts in the north-west it was 47.5 years. For a more detailed discussion of the life-cycle model and life-course strategies, see Di Matteo 'Wealth accumulation and the life-cycle in economic history', 300–3. For evidence of the relationships between age and wealth in Britain, see Green, D.R., A. Owens, J. Maltby, and J. Rutterford 2009. 'Lives in the balance? Gender, age and assets in late-nineteenth-century England and Wales'. *Continuity and Change* 24(2): 326–8.

[52] The agricultural sector was particularly weak in the Thunder Bay District compared to Wentworth County. Agriculture in northern Ontario was extended past the point of commercial viability due to a free land grants programme and many farms were abandoned in the 1930s.

growing number and share of female estates in the Ontario probate data set. In the Thunder Bay District, the average percentage of male probated decedents declined from 85 per cent from 1885 to 1906 to 77 per cent for 1914 to 1920 and 74 per cent for 1921 to 1925, either indicating increased female property owning or greater female longevity or both. In Wentworth County, the pattern was similar: in the period from 1872 to 1927, the proportion of male probated decedents declined from 88 per cent in 1872 to 60 per cent by 1927. In both places, therefore, women who left estates liable to probate were far more common at the end of the period than at the start.

Numbers alone, however, hide a more complex story of fluctuating fortunes depending on economic conditions in each specific place. Wealth in the Thunder Bay District grew for both men and women during the boom years from 1907 to 1913 and then collapsed dramatically with the decline being much steeper for females. This deterioration in female fortunes is reflected in the comparative differences between men and women. Over the entire period from 1885 to 1925, male wealth was two-thirds higher than that for women, averaging $5638 compared to $3393.[53]

However, these overall figures conceal some significant differences over time. Between 1885 and 1906, men's and women's wealth was approximately even, but the gender difference widened considerably during the years of economic downturn from 1914 to 1920 (see Table 6.2). The precipitous decline continued in the early 1920s for men but female wealth actually began to recover, albeit from a relatively low base. Growth during the boom era was more pronounced for males but the wealth decline during the bust period from 1914 to 1920 was far more pronounced for females. Between the periods 1885–1906 and 1914–20, male average real wealth still rose by 26 per cent whereas for females it fell by 53 per cent. The collapse in female property-holding in the Thunder Bay District was particularly pronounced when it came to the ownership of financial assets and the greater tendency for women than men to hold this kind of wealth, notably as securities and moneys secured by mortgage, may account for the change in their fortunes. This decline at the end of the boom period was also paralleled elsewhere in Canada, including Victoria, British Columbia, and may indicate that western parts of Canada were harder hit than elsewhere by the collapse of the wheat boom.[54] The early

---

[53] Thunder Bay District estate files were collected annually for the period 1885–1925 but small numbers particularly for the period prior to 1900 made aggregating into broad periods a more suitable approach. From 1885 to 1900, there are a total of 153 estates for the Thunder Bay District. For Wentworth County, the year 1892 alone has 154 census-linked estate files.

[54] According to Baskerville in his study of Victoria and Hamilton, the 'setback in women's wealth-holding following the pre-World War One boom, then, was greatest in western cities, where land speculation significantly exceeded similar behaviour in longer settled and more industrialized communities such as Hamilton' (Baskerville, *A Silent Revolution?* 50).

Table 6.2 Selected wealth statistics by gender in Thunder Bay, 1885–1925 (1900 Canadian dollars)

	1885–1906	1907–13	1914–20	1921–5
Male and female (%)				
Male	84.7	81.9	77.3	73.6
Female	15.3	18.1	22.7	26.4
Average wealth ($)				
Male	4427	9665	5572	2984
Female	4192	7572	1965	2337
Average real estate ($)				
Male	1739	4923	2468	987
Female	2299	2873	1061	1032
Average value of monies secured by mortgage ($)				
Male	460	1741	1166	123
Female	277	2730	233	352
Average real estate to average wealth				
Male	0.393	0.509	0.443	0.331
Female	0.548	0.379	0.540	0.442
Average mortgages to average wealth				
Male	0.104	0.180	0.209	0.049
Female	0.066	0.361	0.119	0.151

Source: Thunder Bay District estate files.

1920s witnessed some recovery for women but men's wealth continued to languish.

Experiences in Wentworth County, shown in Table 6.3, demonstrate both similarities and some important differences to the situation in Thunder Bay. It should be noted that the rising proportion of married women with wills combined with a decline in the proportion of widows amongst female decedents overall may also have affected average female wealth in the Thunder Bay District and Wentworth County. Generally, the widows tended to be wealthier than married women and therefore, given the life-course of wealth, a decline in the proportion of widows could have slowed the growth rate of female wealth overall. The evidence suggests that the share of women who were widows in Thunder Bay District declined substantially over time whereas the proportion of widows in Wentworth County remained stable.[55] This

---

[55] For the period 1907–13 in Thunder Bay District, 51 per cent of female decedents were married, 42 per cent were widows, and 7 per cent were single. For 1914–20, 60 per cent of female decedents were married and 29 per cent were widows and the remaining 11 per cent single. For 1921–5, 54 per cent were married, 35 per cent were widows, and 9 per cent were single. For 1872–1902 in Wentworth County, 34 per cent of female decedents were married, 52 per cent were widows, and 13 per cent were single. For 1907–27, 30 per cent of female decedents were married, 52 per cent were widows, and 17 per cent were single.

Table 6.3 Selected wealth statistics by gender in Wentworth County, 1872–1927 (1900 Canadian dollars)

	1872	1882	1892	1902	1907	1912	1917	1922	1927
Male and female (%)									
Male	88	78	72	68	64	63	58	60	60
Female	12	22	28	32	36	37	42	40	40
Average wealth ($)									
Male	8032	7148	10,691	9835	7019	8814	10,113	6947	8010
Female	1376	1531	2732	2612	4351	3937	3014	4687	4910
Average real estate ($)									
Male	3102	3043	5843	3331	2129	3476	2785	2369	2279
Female	358	475	1323	1107	1547	1406	1191	1352	2242
Average financial assets ($)									
Male	n/a	2721	3391	5299	4357	4832	6991	3966	5442
Female	n/a	774	1242	1370	2622	2376	1599	3057	3481
Average mortgages ($)									
Male	n/a	729	565	1628	640	1906	781	802	771
Female	n/a	318	376	499	865	392	572	817	899
Average real to average wealth									
Male	0.386	0.426	0.547	0.355	0.303	0.394	0.275	0.341	0.285
Female	0.260	0.310	0.484	0.424	0.355	0.357	0.395	0.288	0.457
Average financial assets to average wealth									
Male	n/a	0.381	0.317	0.539	0.621	0.548	0.691	0.571	0.679
Female	n/a	0.108	0.116	0.139	0.374	0.270	0.158	0.440	0.709
Average mortgage to average wealth									
Male	n/a	0.102	0.053	0.173	0.091	0.216	0.077	0.115	0.096
Female	n/a	0.208	0.138	0.191	0.199	0.099	0.190	0.174	0.183

Source: Wentworth County estate files.

Note: For 1872, separate categories for financial assets were not available, only aggregates for personal property.

tendency alone would have helped to account for at least some of the differences in the average value of female estates between the two regions.

Perhaps of greater importance, however, was the fact that average wealth for both men and women in Wentworth County during the wheat boom period grew relatively slowly compared to the situation in Thunder Bay, which was more directly tied to the wheat economy via its trans-shipment role for grain. This difference can also be explained, at least in part, by higher land prices during the boom period. Nominal land values in both western Canada and southern Ontario increased during the wheat boom era but land gained value more quickly in the west.[56] Nevertheless, differences occurred in relation to

[56] See Emery, J.C., K. Inwood, and H. Thille 2007. 'Hecksher-Ohlin in Canada: new estimates of regional wages and land prices'. *Australian Economic History Review* 47(1): 38.

gender. Male wealth grew relatively little during the wheat boom compared to women's and this trajectory continued during the 1920s when female average wealth carried on rising – a situation that contrasted with the relative decline that affected both groups in the Thunder Bay District.

While Baskerville argues that in the frontier region of Victoria women overall made relatively large gains during the boom period, the evidence presented here shows that over the long term the more established region provided greater and more stable long-term gains.[57] The wheat boom affected the Thunder Bay District more directly which is why there was a greater surge in wealth there in the pre-1913 period than in Wentworth County. The years from 1872 to 1912 saw average male wealth in Wentworth County rise by 11 per cent while average female wealth rose by 186 per cent. From 1912 to 1927, average male wealth in Wentworth County declined by 9 per cent while that of women rose by 25 per cent. In the Thunder Bay District, during the wheat boom period spanning 1896–1913, average male real wealth rose 118 per cent while female wealth rose 81 per cent, as shown in Table 6.2 by the change in average wealth between the period spanning from 1885 to 1906 to that from 1906 to 1913. By contrast, in the post-boom years after 1913, average male and female wealth both declined by 69 per cent, as shown by the changes between the period from 1907 to 1913 compared to 1921 to 1925. By 1927, the real average wealth of women in Wentworth County was $4910 (about 61 per cent of average male real wealth) while women in the Thunder Bay District saw average real wealth of $2337 for the period 1921–5 (about 78 per cent of average male real wealth).

Differences between places

Differing patterns of wealth accumulation between the two regions can be explained with reference to a number of factors relating to economic conditions during the wheat boom period, the impact of urbanization and industrialization, and from portfolio composition and investment choice. The interplay of these factors can be demonstrated most clearly in relation to women in both districts whose wealth frequently included a share of a deceased spouse's estate invested in mortgages and financial securities as a directive of the will. The will made by physician Henry Orton, who died in 1882, is typical of others in directing that his estate be liquidated by his executors and the monies arising from the sale be invested in good securities for his wife Annie with the interest from the investments to be paid for the education and support of the children.[58] Indeed, one of the advantages of mortgages in particular in nineteenth-century Ontario was that they, together

---

[57] See Baskerville, 'Women and investment'.
[58] Will of Henry Orton (Wentworth County Will 1745, 1882).

with any income derived, were by exemption not liable to taxation as personal property under municipal property taxes.[59] In addition, it was often easier for men to bequeath stocks, bonds, and mortgages to their wives because such financial assets could be managed more cheaply than land or businesses.[60] In the case of mortgages, what this did in essence was to more directly link financial assets to the real estate market, which could be problematic in the event of a downturn in land values as was the case in the Thunder Bay District. As a result, when both direct real estate ownership and indirect ownership via mortgages is factored in, women there had a proportionately larger share of their wealth invested in real estate. For example, as indicated in Table 6.2, during the boom period from 1907 to 1913, the ratio of average real estate to average wealth for men was 50.9 per cent whereas for women it was 37.9 per cent. However, when the average value of monies secured by mortgage is treated as a 'real estate' investment, the comparable figures become 69 per cent for men and 74 per cent for women. This compares to 39 and 55 per cent, respectively, in Wentworth County for 1907 (Table 6.3).

These differences in asset portfolios meant that when the economic bust arrived in the Thunder Bay District, women were hit hard first in their real estate portfolios (as were men) but then a second time because of their dependence on mortgages as their primary financial asset. During 1907–13, the ratio of the average value of monies secured by mortgage to average wealth for women was 36 per cent while for men it was 18 per cent. When the decline in the real average value of mortgages came between 1907–13 and 1914–20, there was a drop of 33 per cent in the average value of mortgages for men and 91 per cent for women. Interestingly enough, in Wentworth County, women reduced their dependence on mortgages just prior to the bust period.

In an attempt to see if financial assets were consistently more important for women than men, their share of wealth held in this type of property was regressed on wealth using a non-parametric technique known as LOWESS on male and female estates valued at $100,000 or less.[61] The results are presented

[59] Burley, D.G. 1994. *A Particular Condition in Life: Self-Employment and Social Mobility in Mid-Victorian Brantford, Ontario*. Montreal, QC: McGill-Queen's University Press, 131.

[60] Shammas, 'Re-assessing the Married Women Property Acts', 24–6.

[61] LOWESS is a non-parametric regression technique, which estimates a line of best-fit without assuming a specific functional form and which is also less sensitive to the presence of outliers and extreme observations than standard parametric techniques such as Least Squares Regression. In fitting LOWESS curves, the crucial decision involves the size of the smoothing parameter or bandwidth over which the locally weighted regressions used in the estimation process are estimated. Larger bandwidths provide greater degrees of smoothing while smaller bandwidths provide more variation in the final smoothed curve. For references on LOWESS, see Cleveland, W.S. 1979. 'Robust locally weighted regression and smoothing scatterplots'. *Journal of the American Statistical Association* 74(368): 829–36; Cleveland, W.S. 1985. *The Elements of Graphing*. Monterey, CA: Wadsworth; Cleveland, W.S. 1993. *Visualizing Data*. Summit, NJ: Hobart.

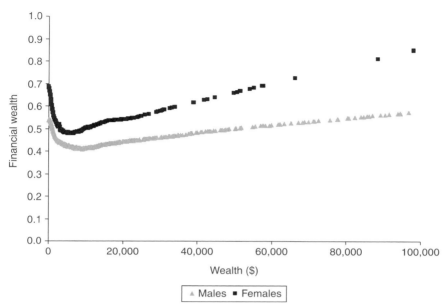

Figure 6.2 Portfolio share in financial assets by gender, Wentworth County: LOWESS SMOOTH (bwidth = 0.8)

Source: see text.

in Figures 6.2 and 6.3 and reveal that in Wentworth County women held a greater share of their wealth in financial assets than males at all wealth levels. However, both men and women reduced the proportion attributable to financial assets for estates valued below $5000 but then increased this share of wealth for those estates above $5000. In the Thunder Bay District, a similar U-shaped pattern also occurred. Eventually, the financial share of wealth rises as estate values increase but the proportion of women's estates accounted for by financial assets only began to exceed men's at the upper end of the wealth-holding spectrum. This would suggest that the high average propensity of women in Thunder Bay to hold mortgages and other financial assets was driven by wealthier women whereas in Wentworth County, the propensity to hold these kinds of assets was more evenly distributed among all women.

The tendency of women in both Thunder Bay District and Wentworth County to hold a larger share of their wealth as financial assets and particularly securities and mortgages can be explained by a number of factors. First, they were much less likely to be farmers and therefore this reduced the amount of real estate that they would own.[62] Moreover, over time the agriculture sector

---

[62] Women were, nevertheless, beginning to acquire more real estate. Baskerville argues that married women were beginning to dominate the Victoria land market and widows the Hamilton

Men, Women, and Money

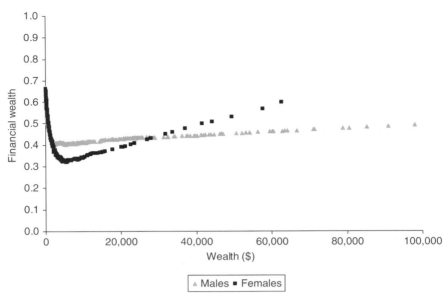

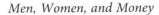

Figure 6.3 Portfolio share in financial assets by gender, Thunder Bay District: LOW-ESS SMOOTH (bwidth = 0.8)

Source: see text.

declined, as did the proportion of rural population in the wake of urbanization and industrialization.[63] In Ontario, the share of rural population fell from 78 per cent in 1871 to 39 per cent by 1931 and the proportion of men gainfully employed in agriculture similarly declined from 52.2 per cent in 1891 to 27.2 per cent by 1931.[64] In Wentworth County, this decline was evident in the fall in the average value of real estate for men which peaked in 1892 at $5843 but fell thereafter to $2279 by 1927 (see Table 6.3). The changing sectoral distribution of the workforce had a disproportionately important impact on women, larger numbers of whom began to enter the labour market in better paid and more secure forms of employment. As the share of agricultural employment fell, the proportion of gainfully employed males in trade and finance rose from 6.2 per cent in 1891 to 10.2 per cent by 1931 while the corresponding figures for females increased from 3.8 to 9.2 per cent – suggesting that relatively larger

land market in the late nineteenth century. He writes that 'land markets in both cities were becoming, albeit in slightly different ways, increasingly feminized during the later years of the nineteenth century' (Baskerville, 'Women and investment', 198). Real estate acquisition was also a feature of female wealth-holding in Thunder Bay District.

[63] The agricultural sector's share of GDP in Canada declined from 37.1 per cent in 1870 to 21 per cent by 1920. See Green and Urquhart, 'New estimates', 174.

[64] See Urquhart, *Gross National Product*.

employment gains were made by women than men. In total, there were 636,000 gainfully employed men in Ontario in 1891, which rose to 1,097,000 by 1931 – a 72 per cent increase, but this relative rate of growth was less than half that of women, the employment of which rose from 96,000 in 1891 to 249,000 by 1931 – an increase of 159 per cent.[65]

The deteriorating agricultural sector and rural land market, coupled with the rise of the financial markets, allowed women to reap the economic advantages of such changes to a greater extent than men, especially in the wake of the property law reforms. According to Baskerville, women were particularly active investors in financial assets, especially bank stocks, and he suggests that 'one could legitimately speak of the feminization of that financial market in Ontario over the course of the last half of the nineteenth century'.[66] Nor was the importance of the financial sector that underpinned women's growing wealth confined to Ontario alone. The post-Confederation period after 1867 saw a rapid rise in Canadian savings rates during which the aggregate saving ratio rose from 8.7 per cent of GDP in the 1870s to 15.7 per cent during the first decade of the twentieth century.[67] In addition, the value of financial assets in 1900 Canadian dollars between 1870 and 1910 rose from $119.2 million to $1.5 billion implying an annual growth rate of 6 per cent. Growth was especially pronounced in the assets held by chartered banks, life insurance companies, mortgage and loan companies, and trusts – precisely the kinds of investments favoured by women.[68]

The other form of financial assets that appeared to have been relatively attractive was mortgages, which in nineteenth-century Ontario were very favourably treated under municipal tax assessments. Mortgages could be particularly lucrative as an investment because their value and any interest arising were not taxed as personal estate and thus became a way of converting real property to exempt personal property. This was attractive to businessmen and widows alike.[69] Throughout the period covered by this study, as Table 6.4 illustrates, both these groups in Wentworth County and the Thunder Bay District held relatively large amounts of their wealth in mortgages. Widows' estates in the Thunder Bay District in particular recorded the highest average value of mortgages which was more than double that of widows in Wentworth County.

---

[65] Drummond, I.M. 1987. *Progress without Planning: The Economic History of Ontario from Confederation to the Second World War*. Toronto. ON: University of Toronto Press, table 2.2, 362–3.

[66] Baskerville, *A Silent Revolution?* 12.

[67] Green and Urquhart, 'New estimates of output growth in Canada', 187.

[68] See Neufeld, E.P. 1972. *The Financial System of Canada: Its Growth and Development*. Toronto, ON: Macmillan.

[69] Burley, *A Particular Condition in Life*, 131.

Table 6.4 Average value of selected assets by gender in Thunder
Bay and Wentworth County (1900 Canadian dollars)

	Wentworth County	Thunder Bay
	1882–1927	1885–1925
Women		
Wealth	3942	3402
Financial assets	2446	1671
Real estate	1993	1537
Mortgages	674	743
Men		
Wealth	8483	5639
Financial assets	4838	2663
Real estate	3021	2521
Mortgages	972	904
Widows		
Wealth	4839	5460
Financial assets	3104	3465
Real estate	1486	1720
Mortgages	910	1852
Farmers (men)		
Wealth	5454	1831
Financial assets	1638	487
Real estate	3232	1077
Mortgages	649	172
Businessmen		
Wealth	16,222	13,806
Financial assets	10,104	6080
Real estate	4310	5498
Mortgages	1276	1261

Source: Thunder Bay District and Wentworth County estate files.

Change over time

In view of the important sectoral shifts in economic activity and cyclical
fluctuations, the question remains as to whether women's wealth-holding
was continuous over the period 1870–1925 or if there were any setbacks? To
assess this, the non-parametric LOWESS technique was used to construct
wealth-year profiles using average annual wealth for males and females in
Wentworth County and Thunder Bay District. The results are presented in
Figures 6.4–6.7.[70] These show that male wealth was greater than female wealth
in both the Thunder Bay District and Wentworth County but that over time

---

[70] A particular advantage of non-parametric regression is its reduced sensitivity to extreme
observations or outliers as well as its more flexible functional form compared to a linear
technique such as Ordinary Least Squares.

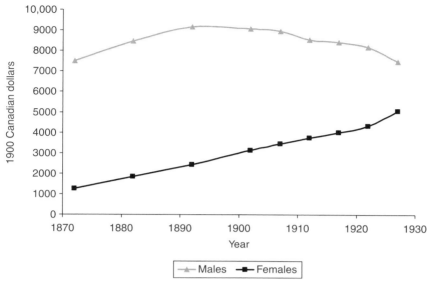

Figure 6.4 Annual average wealth by gender, Wentworth County, 1872–1927: LOWESS SMOOTH (bwidth = 0.8)

Source: see text.

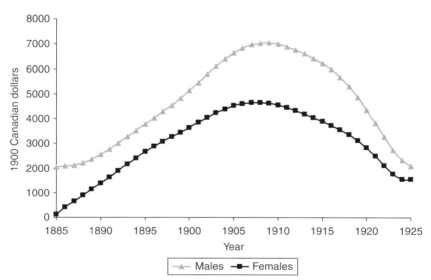

Figure 6.5 Annual average wealth by gender, Thunder Bay District, 1885–1925: LOWESS SMOOTH (bwidth = 0.8)

Source: see text.

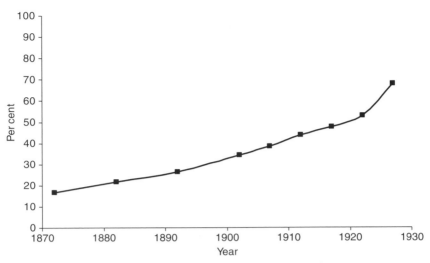

Figure 6.6 Female wealth as a share of male wealth, Wentworth County, 1872–1927
Source: see text.

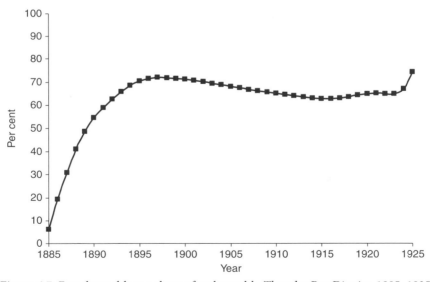

Figure 6.7 Female wealth as a share of male wealth, Thunder Bay District, 1885–1925
Source: see text.

the gap declined. Female wealth rose continually in Wentworth County over the period 1872–1927 and the average female wealth level was 67 per cent that of males by 1927 compared to about 15 per cent in 1872. In the Thunder Bay District, the increase in female average wealth as a percentage of male wealth was quite dramatic rising from just under 10 per cent in 1885 to over 70 per cent by the late 1890s and then declining to approximately 60 per cent by the First World War with a slow recovery afterwards. It appears that improvements to female property ownership relative to male property ownership occurred in both Wentworth County and the Thunder Bay District; in this respect both regions were quite similar by the 1920s.

However, the process of female wealth accumulation was more gradual in the older, more established Wentworth County compared to Thunder Bay perhaps because of the opportunities afforded by a booming economy on the resource frontier. The Thunder Bay District was sparsely populated prior to 1900 but as the frontier was developed and as population growth accelerated, numerous opportunities emerged for the acquisition of property. Such opportunities were more restricted in Wentworth County, which was already a well established and populated region by 1900, whilst from the 1890s in southern Ontario a severe recession impacted on real estate values.[71]

A final useful examination of the evidence breaks the data up according to marital status. Figures 6.8–6.11 present LOWESS wealth-year profiles using the individual level data by year for males and females and for each geographic division according to marital status.[72] In Wentworth County, LOWESS smoothed real wealth between 1872 and 1927 rises steadily for married women, widows, and single women (Figure 6.7), but widows had greater wealth than married women who in turn held more wealth than single women – not a surprising result given the standard course of the life-cycle. Between 1872 and 1927, the LOWESS smoothed real wealth of widows in Wentworth County more than trebled from $1503 to $6107, whilst that of married women rose to a similar degree from $1011 to $4306. The value of single women's estates had a much lower rate of increase, from $1388 to $3324 – a rise of only 139 per cent. Whereas widows had the highest wealth at both the start and end of the period, by 1927, the relative positions of single women and married women had reversed suggesting that the married women property laws had an effect on wealth accumulation by married women. By way of comparison, the LOWESS smoothed real wealth of married and single men in Wentworth County actually declined from 1872 to 1927 while that of

---

[71] Darroch, G.A. 1983. 'Early industrialization and inequality in Toronto, 1861–1899'. *Labour/Le Travail* 11(Spring): 31–61 notes an increase in wealth for the Toronto area during the 1880s that was ended by the recession of 1892.

[72] The use of LOWESS compensates for the presence of outliers, which could influence results if simple averages were presented.

Men, Women, and Money

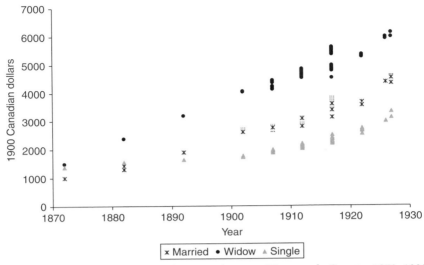

Figure 6.8 Women's real wealth by marital status, Wentworth County, 1870–1930:
LOWESS SMOOTH (bwidth = 0.8)

Source: see text.

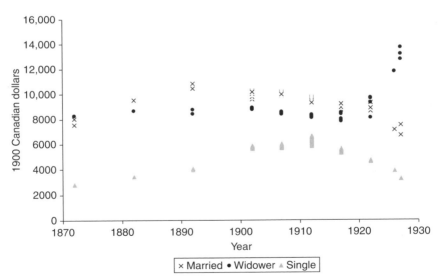

Figure 6.9 Men's real wealth by marital status, Wentworth County, 1870–1930:
LOWESS SMOOTH (bwidth = 0.8)

Source: see text.

widowers rose. For married men, the decline began after 1892 whereas for single men the decline sets in after 1912. Widowers are stable for the period 1872–1912 and then see an increase in their wealth. Again, this provides evidence supporting the view that women in the wake of the property rights legislation may have benefited more from the economic opportunities afforded by urbanization and industrialization. This also provides some support to Baskerville's view that there was a wealth transfer from men to women as a result of the property law reforms. Moreover, some of the wealth may have begun to flow back to men when they became widowers – a trend that becomes pronounced for Wentworth County widowers after 1917.

In contrast, the LOWESS smoothed results for men and women in the Thunder Bay District in Figures 6.10 and 6.11 were influenced by the boom and bust nature of the economy and are markedly different from those in Wentworth County. The wealth of single, married, and widowed women rises and then declines during the bust period. Overall, from 1885 to 1925, the LOWESS smoothed wealth of married, widowed, and single women declined, but widows experienced the sharpest drop. Married men's wealth seemed to vary most compared to widowed and single men, depending on the boom and bust. Between 1885–1906 and 1907–13, the value of average LOWESS

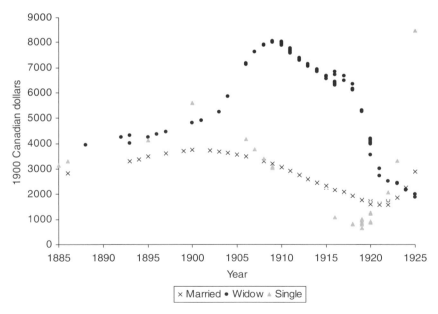

Figure 6.10 Women's real wealth by marital status, Thunder Bay District, 1885–1925: LOWESS SMOOTH (bwidth = 0.8)

Source: see text.

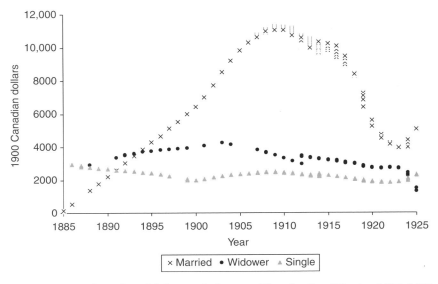

Figure 6.11 Men's real wealth by marital status, Thunder Bay District, 1885–1925: LOWESS SMOOTH (bwidth = 0.8)

Source: see text.

smoothed real wealth of widows in Thunder Bay District rose from $5210 to $7671 – a 47 per cent increase but then declined dramatically to $2416 by 1921–5. Meanwhile, that of married women declined from $3575 dollars in 1885–1906 to $2078 by 1921–5 – a fall of 42 per cent. By contrast, single women fared relatively well, and their estates rose in value, albeit modestly, from $4066 to $4976. Thus, while women initially appear to have made greater gains in Thunder Bay relative to Wentworth County, these accrued primarily to widows. Furthermore, compared to women in Wentworth County, whose wealth increased gradually throughout the period, those in Thunder Bay saw their fortunes eroded as the wheat boom ended and economic downturn set in. The impacts of these broader currents of economic change were refracted both through different types of asset holdings as well as by marital status and gender. Gains for women in one place, therefore, did not necessarily mean gains everywhere for everyone.

CONCLUSION

Improvements in women's economic status occurred in late nineteenth-century North America and were concurrent with the legal transformation of married women's property rights. In the wake of these legislative changes in nineteenth-century Ontario, particularly the 1884 Married Woman's Property Act, there was an increase in women's wealth-holding relative to men. At the same time, increases in wealth also reflected economic conditions and changes associated with urbanization, industrialization, and the decline of the agricultural sector. Important differences occurred between Thunder Bay and Wentworth County, especially when marital status is taken into account, that suggest that property and wealth acquisition by females varied both temporally and spatially. In particular, the differential impact of the wheat boom meant that there were more fluctuations in the levels of wealth-holding in the frontier Thunder Bay District. Moreover, with respect to portfolio composition, women were more inclined to hold a greater share of their wealth in the form of financial assets such as mortgages, securities, and stocks. The growth in financial asset ownership in late nineteenth and early twentieth-century Ontario shows that even 'colonial' regions were fully integrated into the financial web and apparatus of the expanding British empire.

While growth occurred in female property ownership in Ontario in the years after the Married Women's Property Act, female wealth levels nevertheless remained substantially below that of males. Levels rose continually in Wentworth County over the period from 1872 to 1927 but in Thunder Bay District, progress was less certain, especially in the early years of the twentieth century as the wheat boom came to an end. While women initially made greater gains in Thunder Bay relative to Wentworth County, these appear to have accrued primarily to widows. By contrast, all women in Wentworth County exhibited a more gradual and sustained increase in their ownership of wealth over time. The picture, therefore, is rather more complex than merely a simple rise in women's wealth over time as the legal impediments to property ownership were slowly dismantled. Such legal changes had a part to play but their effects were filtered through broader economic fluctuations and different geographies of development. Place and time, therefore as well as the law, need to be considered as variables in explaining how changes in the relationship between gender and wealth occur.

7

Gamblers, Fools, Victims, or Wizards? The British Investor in the Public Mind, 1850–1930

Ranald C. Michie

INTRODUCTION

In the years between the 1840s and 1914, there was a transformation of the composition of both investments and the investing public. No longer were investors confined to a wealthy elite largely located in London, for they were increasingly found throughout the country and among the middle classes. No longer were publicly available securities largely confined to the National Debt or mortgages on land and property, for they came to encompass the bonds issued by governments from around the world and the shares of companies operating in a huge variety of different activities. The effect of this was to increase simultaneously the risks being run by investors and the participation of those least likely to have the knowledge, connections or expertise to cope. Under these circumstances it might have been expected that legislation would have been introduced to protect investors not only from taking such risks but also from the actions of crooked bankers, fraudulent company promoters, and devious stockbrokers. This was a period when the parameters of state authority were in flux, as attitudes of laissez-faire faced growing calls for state intervention. It was also a time when the abuse of investors was being exposed in the frequent court cases over false representation.[1] E.A. Vizetelly was one who complained in 1894 that 'we are overrun with rotten limited liability companies, flooded with swindling "bucket shops", crashes and collapses rain upon us, and the "promoter" and the "guinea-pig" still and ever enjoy

---

[1] Fisher, J., J. Bewsey, M. Waters, and E. Ovey 2003. *The Law of Investor Protection*, 2nd edition. London: Sweet and Maxwell, 551–2; Powell, J.L. 1988. *Issues and Offers of Company Securities: The New Regimes*. London: Sweet and Maxwell, 97.

impunity'.[2] Certainly, claims are made that it was political concerns rather than investor protection that led to the wide ranging reforms of 1986, for example, which, driven by privatization, increased the number of investors from 3 million in 1979 to 11 million by 1990.[3] However, it was not until 1939 that the 'Prevention of Fraud (Investments) Act' was passed, and this was the first major piece of legislation aimed specifically at investor protection.[4] This long delay appears to be a puzzle as the state did play a growing role in protecting individuals from both hazards and crooks in this period, as in laws covering such areas as employment and food adulteration, and the same might have been expected for the investor.[5]

The period between the mid-nineteenth century and the 1930s was one when the individual investor reigned supreme. It was sandwiched between a time when most people were too poor to invest and one when investment became the preserve of the pension fund and professional asset manager driven by the burden and complexities of taxation.[6] Though collective investments did exist, with the growth of both insurance companies and investment trusts, it was individuals who held most of the securities in circulation at this time. It was thus the behaviour of the individual that determined the pace and pattern of public investment over those years, unrestrained by government controls or institutional regulations.[7] How investors were regarded could thus be a powerful influence upon the actions taken by government not only in terms of investor protection but also company law and market regulation. As Franks and Mayer have observed there was a 'widely held belief that, in designing investor protection legislation, a distinction should be drawn between different classes of investor'.[8] Here they were differentiating between an institution with the time and expertise to fully research a potential investment and an individual lacking both knowledge and skill. There was also a difference between the type of investment made, with some being seen to involve

---

[2] Vizetelly, E.A. 1894. 'Introduction' in Zola, E. *Money (L'Argent)*. London: Chatto and Windus, viii–ix.

[3] Lomax, D.F. 1987. *London Markets after the Financial Services Act*. London: Butterworths, 3–4; Clarke, M. 1999. *Citizens' Financial Futures: The Regulation of Retail Investment Financial Services in Britain*. Aldershot: Ashgate, 11–12, 179, 183; Morris, S. 1995. *Financial Services: Regulating Investment Business*, 2nd edition. London: FT Law and Tax, 1.

[4] Fisher et al. *The Law of Investor Protection*, 13–14.

[5] See Quinn, S.E. 1992. *Statutes Revised on Commercial Law, 1695–1913*. Bray: Irish Law Publishing.

[6] For the importance of the growth in the number and variety of investors on financial markets and governments, see Hoffman, P.T., G. Postel-Vinay, and J-L. Rosenthal 2007. *Surviving Large Losses: Financial Crises, the Middle Class, and the Development of Capital Markets*. Cambridge, MA: Harvard University Press, chapter 3.

[7] See Michie, R.C. 1992. *The City of London: Continuity and Change since 1850*. London: Macmillan, chapters 4 and 5.

[8] Franks, J.R. and C. Mayer 1989. *Risk, Regulation and Investor Protection: The Case of Investment Management*. Oxford: Clarendon Press, 161.

greater risk than others, and this would influence the degree of protection extended to investors.[9] This indicates the nature of the dilemma that existed both then and now. A balance has to be struck between the need to protect the interests of investors against the needs of those running companies to take risks and financial markets to operate with relative freedom.[10] The need for such a balance was familiar to the Victorians. Robert Lowe, when Vice President of the Board of Trade at the time of the passage of the Company Act of 1856, stated that, 'We should throw no obstacle in the way of incor-poration, as it is to the interest of the public as much as for that of the company itself that it should take place'.[11] Similarly, the enquiries into both foreign loans and the Stock Exchange in the 1870s exhibited a clear reluctance to intervene in the workings of financial markets, despite the abuses that had been exposed.[12] However, the balance did change over time. By 1933, H.B. Samuel was pressing for legislation that would protect the investor from 'the consequences of his own cupidity, folly or inexperience, or of the fraud or "arms' length" reticence, as the case may be, of those who obtain his money'.[13] That was followed by the 1939 Act and subsequent legislation which leads to the question of what changed between the mid-nineteenth century and the 1930s to produce such a changed attitude.

INVESTMENT

There was a transformation in the investment landscape from the mid-nineteenth century onwards. No longer was the investor faced with limited choice of publicly available securities as had long been the case. Instead, from the 1850s onwards there was a huge expansion in the volume and variety of securities in circulation and these were readily available to investors. News-papers contained frequent and prominent advertisements of prospectuses seeking to attract public subscriptions to the new issues being made. New issues were also retailed to investors by the stockbroking profession, which grew in size and coverage, while banks and lawyers acted as their agents

---

[9] Franks and Mayer, Risk, Regulation and Investor Protection, 7, 151–2, 162.

[10] Fisher et al. *The Law of Investor Protection*, 8; Franks and Mayer, *Risk, Regulation and Investor Protection*, 152.

[11] Quoted in Hein, L.W. 1978. *The British Companies Acts and the Practice of Accountancy, 1844–1962.* New York, NY: Arno, 129.

[12] PP 1875 XI (136) *Select Committee on Making of Contracts for Loans to Foreign States: Report*, 47; PP 1878 XIX (2157) *Royal Commission on Origin, Objects and Constitution of London Stock Exchange: Report*, 16–17.

[13] Samuel, H.B. 1933. *Shareholders' Money: An Analysis of Certain Defects in Company Legislation with Proposals for their Reform.* London: Pitman, 4–5, 9, 14, 67, 111, 329.

by feeding business to them from customers and clients. Stockbrokers also catered for those investors who wished to purchase securities already in existence and they were served not only by the London Stock Exchange, whose formal existence dated from 1801, but also by the numerous local stock exchanges that were established in all major cities from the 1830s onwards.[14] Such a growth and spread of publicity, intermediaries, and institutions would not have been required if the National Debt had remained almost the sole security available, as in the eighteenth century. Though the value of the National Debt did fluctuate, especially in times of war, it was a relatively simple security, especially after the creation of the consolidated debt, or Consols, in 1749. Consols were an irredeemable investment paying a fixed rate of interest of 3 per cent per annum on the nominal value. This interest was guaranteed by the British government and that ultimately rested upon the taxes paid by the British population.

The other securities that were popular among investors in the eighteenth century were, in many ways, variations of the National Debt. Prior to the consolidation of its debt the government had borrowed extensively from the Bank of England, the East India Company, and the South Sea Company. This made their shares proxies for the National Debt as the payment of dividends was largely based on the interest paid to them by the government on the money it had borrowed. The South Sea Company even ceased to have a trading operation, for example. Until the mid-1820s the London Stock Exchange only provided a market for these securities and even after admitting others it was not until the mid-1830s that they were given access to the main trading floor. However, in the years between the end of the Napoleonic Wars in 1815 and the outbreak of the First World War in 1914, the British government raised few new funds. The nominal value of the National Debt quoted on the London Stock Exchange rose from £853.6 million in 1853 to £1013 million by 1913, or by only around £150 million over a 60-year period.

As a result of its growing scarcity compared to investor demand, the National Debt became an increasingly unattractive investment during the course of the nineteenth century, given the demand from trustees, who were legally restricted in the investments they could make, and banks, attracted by the liquidity it offered for the employment of idle balances. Reflecting this demand was the fact that the yield on Consols fell from 3.2 per cent in 1850 to 2.5 per cent in 1896. The government also took the opportunity created by this demand to convert the debt to a lower rate of interest in 1888, making it an even less attractive investment. Thus, investors searching for a security that delivered a reliable and regular income had, increasingly, to look for an alternative. This is clear from the comments made by those who had the

---

[14] See Michie, R.C. 1999. *The London Stock Exchange: A History*. Oxford: Oxford University Press, chapters 1–3.

responsibility of advising them. In the mid-1890s the Edinburgh stockbrokers, Walker and Watson, found that 'Most trustee investments are scarce and difficult to buy at the quoted prices'.[15] By 1910, the *Investor's Monthly Manual* was of the opinion that investment in Consols was confined to those who had no other choice, such as trustees.[16] One alternative was the national debts of foreign countries but these were also the preferred investment among risk-averse investors in other parts of the world. Thus French *rentes*, which were equivalent to Consols, were largely held by French investors and the return they offered was often little different. The French were also the largest holders of Russian government bonds by the First World War. Though governments did continue to borrow extensively in the late nineteenth century, with established European countries being joined by emerging economies from around the world, the absence of major wars after 1871 did mean that the level of debt creation was relatively low. As a result the attention of British investors turned increasingly to corporate securities.

Though joint-stock companies had grown in popularity from the 1690s, in Britain most companies were small and their shares were mainly held by a limited group of people, often connected through locality, trade or marriage. Even the likes of the canals that appeared in the late eighteenth century were largely owned by investors resident in the areas that they served. This meant that those who invested in corporate securities were not drawn from the investing public generally but from those within it who were most familiar with each particular enterprise. What broke the mould were railways, though even with them there was a preference among investors for the securities issued by their local line. Due to the relatively constant nature of the passenger and freight traffic that railways carried, they generated a reliable and regular income out of which to pay interest on debt and dividends on shares. As the network expanded so did the funds raised from investors. The paid-up capital of British railways grew from £246 million in 1850, in the wake of the railway mania, to £1335 million by 1912, so offering investors new outlets. In addition, other companies that had similar characteristics to railways, such as those supplying water, gas, and later electricity or providing telegraph and telephone services, also attracted the attention of the investing public. Nevertheless, investor demand outgrew even the capital requirements of British railways and other infrastructure activities. The dividends paid on the shares of UK railways, for example, fell from an average of 4.99 per cent in 1873 to 3.34 per cent in 1900.

The inevitable consequence was a further move along the perceived risk profile, with investors finding the yields they desired among the stocks and

---

[15] Walker, J.D. and R.M. Watson 1894. *Investor's and Shareholder's Guide*. Edinburgh: E. and S. Livingstone, 23–6.
[16] *Investor's Monthly Manual*, August 1910.

shares of foreign railways. Many of these traversed large tracks of land in rapidly developing economies, often closely allied to Britain, and so had the capacity to service both the interest paid on their bonds and the dividends on their shares. This did not mean that problems did not occur from time to time as expansion outran profits and excessive risks were taken by those running the companies, but these were neither frequent nor commonplace. Again, however, British investors had to compete with those from around the world who were also looking for the ideal combination of risk and return. The United States had the world's largest railway network by the First World War but the stocks and bonds that their railway companies issued were not only largely held by US investors but they were also favoured by the Dutch, Germans, and Swiss as well as the British.[17] Thus, British investors had increasingly to seek out new securities if they were to obtain the level of return that they had been accustomed to in the past, whether from the UK National Debt and then UK railways or the national debt of foreign governments and the stocks and bonds of foreign railways.

As a consequence there was an enormous expansion in the volume and variety of securities available to the investing public, especially from the 1860s onwards. Between 1870 and 1913, new issues on the London capital market, for example, totalled £5.7 billion and among them were an increasing number of shares from the likes of British industrial and commercial companies and foreign mines and plantations. This was despite the fact that they were universally considered among the riskiest of any investments.[18] The change and the balance between 1853 and 1913 can be seen through an examination of the securities quoted on the London Stock Exchange. If this is restricted to those on which interest and dividends were payable in London it provides a rough approximation of the national portfolio. The total rose from £1215.3 million in 1853 to £9550.5 million in 1913, or by £8335.2 million, indicating the enormous growth in the securities held by the British investing public. In the process, the UK National Debt fell from 70.2 per cent of the total in 1853 to 10.6 per cent by 1913 whereas the debt of foreign and colonial governments grew from 5.7 per cent to 21.3 per cent. Despite that, it still left government debt of all kinds as a significantly smaller share of the national portfolio being

---

[17] For investment in railways, see Roth, R. and G. Dinhobi eds. 2008. *Across the Borders: Financing the World's Railways in the Nineteenth and Twentieth Centuries*. Aldershot: Ashgate, chapters 8–13, 16, and 17.

[18] For the changing nature of investment opportunities, see Michie, R.C. 1981. *Money, Mania and Markets: Investment, Company Formation and the Stock Exchange in Nineteenth-Century Scotland*. Edinburgh: John Donald; Michie, *The London Stock Exchange*; Michie, R.C. 2006. *The Global Securities Market: A History*. Oxford: Oxford University Press; and Michie, R.C. and P.A. Williamson eds. 2004. *The British Government and The City of London in the Twentieth Century*. Cambridge: Cambridge University Press. Figures on national debt, railway capital, and new issues can be found in Mitchell, B.R. 1988. *British Historical Statistics*. Cambridge: Cambridge University Press, 543–4, 601–2, 678, 685.

44.8 per cent in 1913 compared to 75.9 per cent in 1853. What made up the difference were corporate securities, especially those issued by railways. Railways alone increased from £225 million in 1853 to £4147.1 million in 1913, or from 18.5 per cent to 43.4 per cent of the total securities. Even when governments and railways are accounted for this left considerable scope for other securities, especially the shares of numerous joint-stock companies. Whereas in 1853 government debt and railways comprised 94.4 per cent of all securities quoted on the London Stock Exchange, the proportion had shrunk to 78.2 per cent in 1913. By then there were small but significant categories of other securities. Iron, steel, and coal companies were now 3.5 per cent of the total while breweries and distilleries were 1.1 per cent, and though they were mainly British there was also a sprinkling of foreign ones that had been sold to UK investors. There were also certain categories of enterprise dominated by companies operating abroad such as metal mining with 0.6 per cent of the total, oil exploration and production at 0.2 per cent and tea, coffee, and rubber plantations with 0.3 per cent. Though these were individually a very small proportion of the value of securities traded on the London Stock Exchange they did indicate how dramatically the horizons of investors had changed in the 60 years before 1914.[19]

INVESTORS

The implication of this was that investors were increasingly holding risky securities as the returns were no longer guaranteed by a government or even the revenue generated by a monopoly service such as a railway network. Instead, they were dependent upon the ability of a single company to generate sufficient income to service its debt and pay dividends. This left the investor much more at the mercy of the skill and honesty of those running the business, the competition they faced in the marketplace, the problems encountered in maintaining production, and variations in demand from consumers. Though this could be minimized by selecting companies making products with relatively inelastic demand, as with drink and tobacco, it still exposed the investor to the other risks. This helps explain the attractions of large companies with a high degree of control over the marketplace they served, as was the case with iron and steel producers, given the costs of setting up rival manufacturing facilities. Even then there was always the risk that the technology of production could be transformed or the product replaced by another. These were fundamental risks that had to be accepted by investors with little knowledge of the

[19] Michie, *The London Stock Exchange*, 88–9.

economics of the industry that generated the profits upon which their interest and dividends were dependent. Conversely, there were other investments that offered the possibilities of huge gains if successful, as was the case with mineral exploration or the introduction of a new technology. What became available in the late nineteenth century was a wide range of investments suited to all types of investors. In turn, this was matched by a transformation of the investing public, both in number and variety.[20]

Such a situation was clear to contemporaries. The magazine *Capital and Investment* observed in 1873 that 'the class of investors is constantly and rapidly increasing in number, and enterprise keeps pace with its wants'.[21] Similarly, Viscount Goschen writing in 1905 noted that 'year by year, it would seem, a larger number of persons are becoming shareholders in companies'.[22] He was in a position to know the reason why because, as Chancellor of the Exchequer, it was he who had reduced the rate of interest paid on the National Debt, and so encouraged investors to look elsewhere. This growth in the number of investors was subject to sudden jumps during speculative booms, as with the railway mania in the mid-1840s. Inevitably, these numbers shrank afterwards as gains failed to materialize. Nevertheless, there was an underlying and permanent expansion of the investing population.[23] An estimate based on a government survey of British railway companies in 1886 produced a figure of 546,438 individual names of those holding UK railway stock, with an average holding of £1521, but this is likely to include a large degree of duplication. Investors held different categories of securities in different companies. At the very least, though, the figures for the London and North Western Railway reveal a sizeable investing public as it had 19,233 holders of its debentures and 37,579 shareholders.[24] Allowing for multiple holdings would suggest a figure of between 150,000 and 300,000 for the number of investors in British railways by 1886, with the lower figure being those with major stakes.[25]

In 1901, an estimate published in the *Stock Exchange Gazette*, which was a weekly journal aimed at investors and their advisers, produced 3,369,000

---

[20] For the transformation of our knowledge of this investing public, see Laurence, E.A., J. Maltby, and J. Rutterford eds. 2009. *Women and their Money, 1700–1950: Essays on Women and Finance*. Abingdon: Routledge. For a case study of female involvement in shipping finance, see Doe, H. 2009. *Enterprising Women and Shipping in the Nineteenth Century*. Woodbridge: Boydell and Brewer.

[21] *Capital and Investment*, 15 February 1873.

[22] Goschen, G.J. 1905. *Essay and Addresses on Economic Questions, 1865–1893*. London: Edward Arnold, 232. See also Paish, G. 1909. 'Our investments in 1908'. *The Statist,* 2 January.

[23] Cairncross, A.K. 1953. *Home and Foreign Investment, 1870–1913*. Cambridge: Cambridge University Press, 84–5.

[24] PP 1886 LVIII (219) *Return showing the holding of Debenture, Preference and Ordinary Stock of Railways of United Kingdom, and Shareholders*.

[25] Irving, R.J. 1976. *The North Eastern Railway Company, 1870–1914: An Economic History*. Leicester: Leicester University Press, 154–7. The return was discussed in the *Investor's Monthly Manual*, January 1887.

shareholder names based on a survey of over 6120 companies registered under the Limited Liability acts. This excluded railways as they operated under separate acts of parliament. Consequently, this survey captured those investors who had bought the shares issued by the growing number of joint-stock companies that appealed to the public for funds. After eliminating multiples, and allowing for only one shareholder per family, this survey claimed that there were 445,000 separate investors by then.[26] However, even that figure may be a serious overestimate. The financial adviser, Henry Lowenfeld, writing in 1907, believed the average portfolio contained 15 different investments. If this ratio is applied it would reduce the number of investors in joint-stock companies to 225,000.[27] Whatever the figure, it is fairly evident that by the late nineteenth century there were significant numbers of investors who were substantial holders of corporate securities whether issued by the railways or a variety of other enterprises. The period was one that witnessed both the conversion of numerous private businesses into public joint-stock companies, especially those in industry and commerce, and the promotion of entirely new ventures hoping to exploit a new technology, a new product, or explore for minerals.[28]

The preferences of these investors were also very varied. Many appeared to favour the fixed interest securities issued by governments and railways.[29] The work done on female investors, for example, suggests that they were basically risk-averse, especially when they lived on the income produced by their investments.[30] Those who have suggested that new industries had problems obtaining finance before 1914 have accused investors of being 'risk-averse',

[26] *Stock Exchange Gazette: A Weekly Journal for Investors and their Advisers*, 30 March, 21 September, and 28 December 1901.

[27] Michie, *The London Stock Exchange*, 72–3.

[28] Alborn, T.L. 1998. *Conceiving Companies: Joint-Stock Politics in Victorian England.* London: Routledge, 146, 212–15, 238–9; Michie, *The London Stock Exchange*, 72–3.

[29] Thompson, F.M.L. 1963. *English Landed Society in the Nineteenth Century.* London: Routledge and Kegan Paul, 306; Sutherland, A. 1968. *The Landowners.* London: Blond, 45; Cannadine, D. 1977. 'Aristocratic indebtedness in the nineteenth century: the case re-opened'. *Economic History Review* 30(4): 647; Cannadine, D. 1980. *Lords and Landlords: The Aristocracy and the Towns, 1774–1967.* Leicester: Leicester University Press, 159; Vincent, J. ed. 1981. *The Later Derby Diaries: Home Rule, Liberal Unionism and Aristocratic Life in Late Victorian England.* Bristol: J. Vincent, 8–9; Wilson, A. 1954. *The History of Unilever.* London: Cassell, 160; Cairncross, *Home and Foreign Investment*, 84; Michie, R.C. 1987. *The London and New York Stock Exchanges, 1850–1914.* London: Allen and Unwin, 119–21.

[30] See Rutterford, J. and J. Maltby 2006. '"The widow, the clergyman and the reckless": women investors in England, 1830–1914'. *Feminist Economics* 12(1/2): 111–38; Maltby, J. and J. Rutterford 2006. '"She possessed her own fortune": women investors in the late nineteenth century to the early twentieth century'. *Business History* 48(2): 220–53; Acheson, G.G. and J.D. Turner 2007. '"Canny investors?" The investment behaviour of Scottish bank shareholders in the nineteenth century'. European Business History Association, conference paper, see also Chapter 9 in this volume.

preferring 'safe' stocks instead.[31] However, other evidence suggests that investors were far from being 'risk-averse'. The investigation into the London Stock Exchange, which reported in 1878, was of the opinion that investors exhibited a 'craving for high rates of interest and unreasonable profits on the investment of capital'.[32] This echoed an 1875 report that revealed the public's willingness to invest in foreign loans, despite defaults throughout the 1860s and early 1870s.[33] Those who have looked at the activities of company promoters at this time have also been surprised at the willingness of investors to buy shares in companies about which they knew little because of promises of high dividends.[34] What this reveals is that investors did not follow a single stereotype – for all types existed, ranging from the most risk-averse to the most risk taking and all gradations in between, and that changed over time depending on age and circumstances. This had always been true but the difference for the period from the 1840s onwards was that the variety of investors was matched by the variety of securities and so their preferences were now visible to all.

The fact that variety rather than uniformity existed was well known to contemporaries. In 1869 the London brokers, Bartlett Chapman, using their experience divided investors into different classes. Firstly, there were the highly risk-averse who stuck to established securities and 'who look upon all mining enterprise as a species of gambling'. Secondly, there were those who were willing to take some risk in return for a better rate of return, looking for 'say 5, 6, or 7 per cent, rather than in the more assured return of 3⅓, or a little more, sometimes, in government securities'. Finally, there were those 'who, in the hope of a lucky adventure, in the long run, will purchase shares in companies which have never declared a dividend, and which, in the estimation of less hopeful speculators, never will declare one'.[35] The Edinburgh stockbrokers, Walker and Watson, in 1894 came to similar conclusions about investors: 'if there is a wide variety among investments, there is a corresponding variety, in respect both to their requirements and their tastes, among investors themselves – compromising every shade, from the

---

[31] For one such example, see Harrison, A.E. 1981. 'Joint-stock company flotation in the cycle, motor-vehicle and related industries, 1882–1914'. *Business History* 23(1): 165–90.

[32] *Royal Commission on Origin, Objects and Constitution,* 10.

[33] *Select Committee on Making of Contracts,* 10, 28, 31, 37.

[34] Armstrong, J. 1990. 'The rise and fall of the company promoter and the financing of British industry'. In *Capitalism in a Mature Economy: Financial Institutions, Capital Exports and British Industry, 1870–1939,* edited by J.J. van Helten and Y. Cassis. Aldershot: Edward Elgar Publishing, 120. See also Turrell, R. and J.J. van Helten 1986. 'The Rothschilds, the Exploration Company and mining finance'. *Business History* 28(1): 181–205.

[35] Bartlett, W. and H. Chapman 1869. *A Handy-Book for Investors: Comprising a Sketch of the Rise, Progress, and Present Character of every Species of Investment, British, Colonial, and Foreign; Including an Estimate of their Comparative Safety and Profit.* London: Effingham Wilson, 339–40.

conservative believer in nothing but the "Funds", to the speculative investor who is content to face the risk of loss for the sake of a 10 or 20 per cent return or a prospective increase in market value'.[36]

Generally, investment advisers were of the belief that most investors sought security over yield and stability over capital gain, which would fit a period that was largely deflationary. The *Investors' Review* in 1895 was certainly of that view as was the *Investor's Monthly Manual*. It was this caution that explained the continued holding of the National Debt, despite its poor returns. The *Investor's Monthly Manual* noted in February 1908, 'it is, perhaps, not surprising that the man who invests his money in Consols is often the least scientific of investors. His purpose is not to make the most of his funds, or to obtain a good rate of interest and an appreciation of capital, but simply to find a security which will give him no trouble, and on which the interest can never be passed and never be reduced. This frame of mind is, of course, not one to be rashly criticized, for any man who is not in touch with the markets and does not understand the movements of stocks and shares is far wiser to play for safety than to run the slightest risk in trying to increase his income.' The problem that investors faced in creating a balanced portfolio that would both reduce risk and maximize returns was that it was difficult to achieve precisely that. The *Investor's Monthly Manual* was well aware of the predicament that investors faced at this time, noting in 1909 that 'successful investment is not a question of arithmetic, for it depends on judgement, knowledge, experience, courage, and, last of all, good fortune'.[37]

The other problem was that investors were subject to mood swings from pessimism to optimism and back again. These reflected both current investment opportunities as well as sudden fads in the market. The *Investors' Review* included an article in 1896, entitled 'The Fever of Speculation and its risks: how the mood of the investor had been transformed over the last two years'. It commented on the fact that, 'Up to the end of 1894, it might be said that the public mind was still oppressed by the memory of the Baring crisis. Investors were up to then timid and anxious for the safety of their capital; but the year 1895 brought with it a remarkable change. The revival of speculation, first in the shares of Transvaal mining companies, and afterwards in various other directions, swiftly obliterated the recollection of past experiences and losses, and, from being timorous and careful, the monied classes throughout the country passed almost at once into a mood of overconfidence.'[38] Similarly, The *Investor's Monthly Manual* traced the speculative excitement in 1896 turning into a reaction in 1897, when losses on foreign securities led investors to

---

[36] Walker and Watson, *Investor's and Shareholder's Guide*, 262.
[37] *Investor's Monthly Manual*, September 1896, April 1897, February 1908, March 1909, October 1909.
[38] *Investors' Review*, July–December 1896.

favour the apparent safety of home industrials. In 1906, they followed investors switching from copper mining to motor car manufacturing and then to rubber planting. By 1910, the interest in rubber plantations had reappeared but was now accompanied by speculation in the shares of oil companies. Both were the product of the growth in motor car usage at home and abroad. In August 1911, they reflected on the longer-term changes undergone by investors since the beginning of the twentieth century: 'The last decade or so has seen a remarkable change in the habits of the investing public. The demand of today is for a return of 4½ to 5 per cent, or even more, on capital which at one time would have been put into 2½ or 3 per cent investments with perfect satisfaction. One result of the change has been the constant depreciation of high-class securities, until 2½ per cent investments no longer exist, so that there has been a levelling up process. Stocks which previously gave a speculative return are now on an investment basis, while gilt-edged investments, though unchanged as regards security, return a much more attractive figure.'[39] In many ways, this was only to be expected as the long period of deflation, which had begun in 1873, had ended in 1896 and in the following years prices rose year by year, though only to a modest degree. This had the effect of forcing investors to look for higher returns than those that had been acceptable in the past.

What emerges is that the behaviour of the investors was known to range from the ultra-cautious to the extreme risk-taker and from the knowledgeable to the ignorant. Investor behaviour also fluctuated between periods when only the safest options were considered to ones when the most speculative issues were favoured. However, in terms of perception it was neither the complexity nor variability of investors that mattered but the public's attitude towards them, for it was that which drove legislation in a democracy. Were investors seen as nothing more than greedy gamblers whose losses acted as a warning to others? Were they seen as naïve fools easily duped by unscrupulous financiers, whose arrest and prosecution provided a means of exposing fraudulent practices and protecting others from the consequences? Were they seen as innocent victims exposed to the crooked activities of insiders unless protected in some way? Were they seen as financial wizards whose command of knowledge and expertise allowed them to become wealthy through an informed choice of stocks and shares? All these were possibilities given the transformation of both the investing public and the securities they bought and sold between the middle of the nineteenth century and the First World War.

If investors were seen as either greedy gamblers or financial wizards, the need to protect them from themselves would be limited. Greedy gamblers were incapable of being saved, as they would always find a means of exercising their

---

[39] *Investor's Monthly Manual*, September 1896, April 1897, March 1906, February, March 1910, August 1911.

craving, whether it was at the card table, on the race track, in the casino or through the stock exchange. At the other extreme there was no need to intervene on behalf of financial wizards as they were capable of looking after themselves, even if they did experience the occasional loss. However, that left the two other categories. Naïve fools who lost their money at the hands of a skilful financier could be expected to generate both sympathy and demands for some kind of intervention. That depended, though, upon what type of fool they were seen to be. There was a world of difference between the small investor, who could not be expected to be aware of the ploys of a financial insider or an unscrupulous advisor, and the wealthy investor, whose gullibility left them exposed to the persuasive rhetoric of their friends and relatives. The former could expect sympathy and demands for intervention while the latter could not, being expected to learn from their own mistakes. Finally, if investors were increasingly perceived as innocent victims, whose losses at the hands of financial crooks impoverished both them and society as a whole, sympathy would be widespread and demands for intervention irresistible. Public opinion did matter but the question remains: what was the opinion of the public?

Certainly, this period did experience a growing public awareness of investors and their activities, especially when it involved the buying and selling of securities, as this received the greatest media attention. Not only did general newspapers increase their coverage of financial matters but the number that specialized in investment rose from just 19 in 1874 to 109 in 1914. These included the *Financial News*, established in 1884, and its rival, the *Financial Times*, which appeared in 1888.[40] These competed for readers by discussing the merits of individual securities and providing in-depth coverage of market activity. By personalizing and sensationalizing investment activity these newspapers attracted the interest of investors in a way that older journals, such as the *Economist*, never had, much to their annoyance.[41] Oscar Wilde, for example, noted the public's delight in reading these newspaper stories in his 1895 play, *An Ideal Husband*.[42] Due to the avid interest of investors in the publicity given to investments in the press, financiers found it worthwhile to bribe editors so as to obtain a newspaper's endorsement of their projects.[43]

[40] Porter, D. 1986. '"A trusted guide of the investing public": Harry Marks and the *Financial News*, 1884–1916'. *Business History* 28(1): 1–4.

[41] *Economist*, 25 January 1890.

[42] Wilde, O. 1899. *An Ideal Husband*. London: Leonard Smithers and Co. Reprinted 2000 in *The Importance of Being Earnest and Other Plays*, edited by R.A. Cave. London: Penguin, 197.

[43] Kynaston, D. 1988. *The Financial Times: A Centenary History*. London: Vintage, 47–8; Porter, '"A trusted guide"', 1; Armstrong, J. 1986. 'Hooley and the Bovril Company'. *Business History* 28(1): 20.

PERCEPTION

Faced with this information about investors what was the public perception, and did it change over time? One method of identifying this is to discover how investors were portrayed in contemporary novels. This use of novels is different from the way that they are used by literary scholars.[44] There the emphasis can be on comparing and contrasting the views expressed by the individual author in their fictional output and their actions and circumstances as an investor. This has been done by Nancy Henry in a recent investigation into female novelists in the Victorian era.[45] Other literary scholars use the words of the novel to identify broader and deeper currents of meaning about society as a whole at the time. There are also those who are steeped in literary scholarship seeking to explain what is written not in terms of the author or contemporary society but in relation to previous fiction.[46] All these approaches have merit and the use of novels to inform perceptions about contemporary investors has grown rapidly over the years.[47] However, the approach taken here is a narrow one as it restricts itself to references in novels to ordinary investors and ignores the activities of bankers, company promoters, and financiers. This does lead to the exclusion of a lot of material as novelists were much more interested in 'frauds, swindles, and bubbles', because of their dramatic possibilities, than the comments about those who invested.[48] Dickens and Trollope, for example, largely focus on what is done to investors by fraudulent financiers rather than the investors themselves, while Gaskell's purpose is to trace the reversal of personal fortune that can come from a bank

[44] For an excellent example of the use of literary evidence for historical purposes, see Taylor, J. 2006. *Creating Capitalism: Joint-Stock Enterprise in British Politics and Culture, 1800–1870.* Woodbridge: Boydell and Brewer.

[45] See Henry, N. 2007. '"Ladies do it?": Victorian women investors in fact and fiction'. In *Victorian Literature and Finance*, edited by F. O'Gorman. Oxford: Oxford University Press, 111–32. Other recent contributions to this growing field include Henry, N. and C. Schmitt eds. 2009. *Victorian Investments: New Perspectives on Finance and Culture.* Bloomington and Indianapolis, IN: Indiana University Press; Poovey, M. 2008. *Genres of the Credit Economy: Mediating Value in Eighteenth and Nineteenth-Century Britain.* Chicago, IL: University of Chicago Press.

[46] For two examples of this approach, see Bratlinger, P. 1996. *Fictions of the State: Culture and Credit in Britain, 1694–1994.* Ithaca, NY: Cornell University Press; Knezevic, B. 2003. *Figures of Finance Capitalism: Writing, Class and Capital in the Age of Dickens.* London: Routledge.

[47] For a number of examples, see Reed, J.R.. 1984. 'A friend to Mammon: speculation in Victorian literature'. *Victorian Studies* 27(2): 179–202; Schmitt, C., N. Henry, and A. Arondekar eds. 2002. 'Special Issue: Victorian Investments'. *Victorian Studies* 45(2); Poovey, M. ed. 2003. *The Financial System in Nineteenth-Century Britain.* Oxford: Oxford University Press; Rutterford, J. and J. Maltby 2006. '"Frank must marry for money": men, women and property in the novels of Anthony Trollope'. *Accounting Historians Journal* 33(2): 169–99. Henry and Schmitt eds. *Victorian Investments.*

[48] Henry, '"Ladies do it"', 113.

failure.[49] It is only to be expected that those who profited from the losses of others would be viewed with hostility but the question is whether their victims deserved sympathy or not. Secondly, the aim is to select novels by date of publication rather than by author or subject matter. The purpose of that is to establish how investors were regarded at particular moments in time and identify changes that took place. Was there an observable impact of the changing nature of the investing public and investment opportunities on the public's perception of investors?[50] In this way, novels are being used as a prism to capture contemporary public opinion that escapes detection by other means. However, the reliance on novels as testimony is tested by use of government inquiries, such as those into the Stock Exchange and foreign loans in the 1870s, and the comments in the investment manuals that began to proliferate thereafter. These allow conclusions to be drawn about how investors and their actions were being judged over the Victorian and Edwardian eras. This testimony should not be taken as an accurate representation of the behaviour of investors. That can only be achieved through investigating and analysing the actual decisions made and relating them to the opportunities available and the outcomes achieved. Instead, the intention here is to discover what the public thought at any one time, whether rightly or wrongly.

Prior to the railway mania investors were seen as comprising two distinct groups, as in the views expressed in Thackeray's *The History of Samuel Titmarsh and the Great Hoggarty Diamond*, which appeared in 1841. The first were those who believed in the merits of what they had bought and deserved sympathy, but no more, if they were swindled out of their money. The second were those who speculated in the hope of making a quick profit, and they were considered nothing more than gamblers.[51] With the collapse of the railway mania in the mid-1840s, many investors experienced losses, having been sucked into the speculation either through their own greed or the advice of others.[52] However, this did not produce any noticeable change in the public perception of investors. In Robert Bell's, novel, *The Ladder of Gold*, which appeared in 1850, it was noted that, 'the mass of the speculators were ruined; and a few crafty hands had amassed enormous wealth'. The fault was seen to lie with those who speculated not the promotion of railway companies, and so

---

[49] See Dickens, C. 1857. *Little Dorrit*. London: Bradbury and Evans; Gaskell, E. 1853. *Cranford*. London: Chapman and Hall; and Trollope, A. 1874. *The Way We Live Now*. London: Chapman and Hall.

[50] I have tried to do this for the City. See Michie, R.C. 2009. *Guilty Money: The City of London in Victorian and Edwardian Culture, 1815–1914*. London: Pickering and Chatto.

[51] Thackeray, W.M. 1841. *The History of Samuel Titmarsh and the Great Hoggarty Diamond*. London: Bradbury and Evans, 9, 32–3, 46, 50–1, 66, 74–5, 78–82, 91–4.

[52] For reactions to the Railway Mania, see Henry, '"Ladies do it"', 123.

those who had gambled and lost had only themselves to blame.[53] Confirming this continuing perception of most investors as greedy gamblers are the descriptions in Charles Lever's 1859 novel, *Davenport Dunn*. 'Dunn's house was a sort of Bourse, where shares were trafficked in, and securities bought and sold, with an eagerness none the less that the fingers that held them wore gloves fastened with rubies and emeralds. . . . All were eagerly bent upon lists of stocks and shares, and no words were heard save such as told of rise or fall – the alternations of that chance which makes or mars humanity.'[54] Investors such as these had only themselves to blame when the schemes collapsed. They also had the wealth to withstand the losses.

By the 1860s, there was a growing awareness of how naïve were many investors, in the wake of the numerous new companies that appeared after the Limited Liability acts of the 1850s. Those acts did protect investors from the consequences of bankruptcy, as had been portrayed by Charlotte Riddell in her 1864 novel, *George Geith*.[55] Conversely, it may have removed a restraint on their behaviour as the only loss was the value of the investment made, plus any unpaid element. The highly popular novelist, Mrs Henry Wood, picked up on that in her 1864 book, *Oswald Cray*. When Caroline, the wife of Dr Cray, inherited £4000 she was persuaded by her husband to buy shares in The Great Wheal Bang Mining Company because of the expectation that it would lead to a fortune. 'An utter tyro in business matters, in the ways of a needy world, imbued with unbounded faith in her husband, Caroline Cray listened to all with eager and credulous ears. Little more than a child, she could be as easily persuaded as a child, and she became as anxious to realise the good fortune as Mark. . . . In her inexperience, she knew nothing of those miserable calamities – failure, deceit, hope deferred. Not that her husband was purposely deceiving her: he fully believed in the good he spoke of. Mark Cray's was one of those sanguine roving natures which see an immediate fortune in every new scheme brought to them – if it be only wild enough.' Despite the personal tragedy experienced by Dr Cray and his wife, when the mine failed, the responsibility for any loss was seen to lie with the decisions they both took. They had gambled and had lost.[56]

The continuing expansion in joint-stock enterprise in the 1870s and 1880s did little to change this perception of investors. In Anthony Trollope's *The Prime Minister*, published in 1876, those who invested in the shares of

---

[53] Bell, R. 1850. *The Ladder of Gold: An English Story*. London: G. Routledge, 201, 302–3, 306–11, 315, 366–7, 398, 437.

[54] Lever, C. 1859. *Davenport Dunn or The Man and the Day*. Volume 3. London: Chapman, 104–5, 118–20.

[55] Trafford, F.G. (Charlotte Riddell) 1864. *George Geith of Fen Court*. London: R. Bentley and Son, 8, 12–13, 17, 21–2, 25, 55, 88, 106, 114–15, 139, 161.

[56] Wood, Mrs H. (Ellen) 1864. *Oswald Cray: A Novel*. London: Macmillan, 250–2, 282–7, 294–5, 330–40, 343–8, 416, 444–8, 450–4.

joint-stock companies were seen as 'asses'. Only 'land, or . . . Three per Cents' could be relied upon.[57] The consequences for those who departed from safe and tried investments were spelled out in Besant and Rice's novel, *The Golden Butterfly*, which was published in 1877. Lawrence Colquhoun placed his wealth and that of his guardian in the hands of Gabriel Cassilis, a City financier. 'Colquhoun was not the man to trouble about money. He was safe in the hands of this great and successful capitalist; he gave no thought to any risk; he congratulated himself on his cleverness in persuading the financier to take the money for him . . . why not get eight and nine per cent, if you can?' His lawyer, Joseph Jagenal, told him why: 'it isn't safe, and because you ought not to expect it'. Only consols and railways were safe, and so when all the money was lost the cause was seen to be greed, and a willingness to speculate.[58]

What did change was an appreciation of why investors were willing to take increased risks. Mrs Wood had spelt this out earlier. 'If you never had the chance of going to bed at night a poor man, and waking up in the morning with a greater fortune than could be counted, you might have it now. You had only to enter largely into the Great Wheal Bang Mining Company, become the successful possessor of a number of its shares, and the thing was accomplished.'[59] Wilkie Collins also developed this theme in an 1878 short story, *The Haunted Hotel*. When a retired nurse discovered she has been left £400 she sought advice from her employer on how to invest it. '"If you put your hundred pounds into the Funds, you will get between three and four pounds a year." The nurse shook her head. 'Three or four pounds a year? That won't do. I want more than that. Look here Master Henry. I don't care about this bit of money – I never did like the man who has left it to me, though he was your brother. If I lost it all tomorrow, I shouldn't break my heart; I'm well enough off, as it is, for the rest of my days. They say you're a speculator. Put me in for a good thing, there's a dear. Neck-or-nothing-and that for the Funds!" She snapped her fingers to express her contempt for security of investment at three per cent. Henry produced the prospectus of the Venetian Hotel Company. . . . The nurse took out her spectacles. "Six per cent guaranteed," she read, "and the Directors have every reason to believe that ten per cent, or more, will be ultimately realised to the shareholders by the hotel. Put me into that, Master Henry"'.[60] This did not mean that investors could expect sympathy for a loss, only an understanding why they had been willing to gamble.

The other change developing in the 1880s was the recognition that those investing in stocks and shares did not, inevitably, lose their money, if advice

---

[57] Trollope, A. 1876. *The Prime Minister*. Volumes 1 and 2. London: Chapman and Hall. Vol. 1, 12, 307; Vol. 2, 110–11, 117, 126–9, 134–6, 140.
[58] Besant, W. and J. Rice 1877. *The Golden Butterfly*. London: Tinsley Bros., 47, 130–2, 141, 165, 175, 228–9, 285, 490.
[59] Wood, *Oswald Cray*, 250–2, 282–7, 294–5, 330–40, 343–8, 416, 444–8, 450–4.
[60] Collins, W. 1878. *The Haunted Hotel*. London: Chatto and Windus, 151.

was taken and care was taken. This comes across in Samuel Butler's novel *The Way of All Flesh*, which dates from the 1880s. After losing £5000 speculating on the Stock Exchange, Pontifex placed what remained of his fortune in railway shares. These increased in value from £15,000 in 1850 to over £140,000 by 1882.[61] In contrast, those who were inclined to gamble in more exotic investments, especially the shares of foreign companies, continued to be seen as nothing more than gamblers. According to the English novelist but long-time US resident, A.C. Gunter, in his 1892 novel, *Miss Dividends*, 'of all the speculators of many nations who have invested in American securities, stocks, bonds, mining properties and beer interests, none have so rashly and so lavishly squandered their money as the speculators of merry England'.[62] Among those foreign speculations mines were especially prominent. Frederick Wicks, in his 1892 novel, *The Veiled Hand*, wrote that the Great Coradell Copper Mine, a South African mining enterprise, appealed to the gambler. 'As a rule there was not much of the widow and orphan associated with the business, but merely an aggregation of those thirsters after cent, per cent, who, in their pursuit of wealth, neglect the first principles of commerce, that high interest means bad security, and that in the City you should trust no one further than you can see him.' The public had thus only themselves to blame if they believed the promises expressed in the prospectus. These promises drew forth 'the gaping millions, and in their train came trooping impecunious politicians, the dregs of the Court, and every phase of the later nineteenth century greed, which specially exhibited itself in an absorbing desire to reap without sowing, and to gather without even putting the hand to the sickle, to say nothing of the plough'.[63] There was a decided lack of sympathy for the investors in this. As Oscar Wilde put it, to some an investment was 'a commonplace Stock Exchange swindle', whereas to others it was 'a brilliant, daring speculation', and each was given complete freedom to make their own choice.[64]

A change in the way the investor was perceived did seem to take place in the aftermath of the mania for gold mining shares that gripped the nation in the mid-1890s. The early accounts from South Africa had dampened expectations by stressing the risks involved, such as that from Randolph Churchill, when touring the country in 1892. 'What I have seen since I commenced my travels in South Africa has led me to the conclusion that no more unwise or unsafe speculation exists than the investment of money in exploration syndicates.' That judgement then changed to one of immense optimism as the extent of

[61] Butler, S. 1903. *The Way of all Flesh*. London: Grant Richards, 264, 273–4, 316–17, 370–1, 381, 419. (Although the novel was published in 1903, the author stopped work on it in 1884.)
[62] Gunter, A.C. 1892. *Miss Dividends: A Novel*. London: G. Routledge and Sons, 104.
[63] Wicks, F. 1892. *The Veiled Hand: A Novel of the Sixties, the Seventies, and the Eighties*. London: Eden and Co., 177–9, 181–6, 189–93, 202–5.
[64] Wilde, *An ideal husband*, 193.

the gold deposits became known. The mining engineer, Reunert, reported in 1893 that South Africa had 'opportunities for profitable investments such as no other country can offer'. That was followed up by financial experts, like Goldman in 1895–6, who claimed that the 'Witwatersrand gold mines probably present a better field for the investment of capital than is to be found in any other industry, since the value of the product remains constant.... The investor having decided upon what interest he expects to get as return for his capital, can with a regular dividend paying company, fairly regard some Witwatersrand gold mines in the light of annuities, etc., suitable for capital investment.'[65] Inevitably, most gold mining companies disappointed investors either because of unrealistic expectations, high development costs, or outright fraud, and this produced a public backlash. This can be seen in Headon Hill's 1896 novel, *Guilty Gold*. A company promoter called Vardon, persuaded innocent investors to buy shares in a South African gold mine through false claims in the prospectus, bribing newspaper journalists, and rigging the market. When this was exposed an American, Professor Drax, who had helped to uncover the plot, made a plea for investor protection. 'You can't expect folk that are without guile themselves to see a serpent in every rose bush that's dressed up as sweet as most of these swindling companies are. It's the fault, I reckon, of your British Legislature for allowing them to rampage around unchecked. Why, it's the popular opinion in this country that in the States all men are cheats and boodle-mongers; but I tell you, sir, that such a thief as this man Vardon wouldn't be able to live amongst us – let alone making a living off us – for a single month. We've got thieves and rogues galore, but we don't allow systems of organised robbery.'[66]

This suggests a transformation in public opinion. However, Headon Hill's view was not the only one heard at the time. Another was Francis Gribble, and he was less inclined to see those speculating in gold mining shares as innocent victims. In his novel, *The Lower Life*, which also appeared in 1896, he gives the impressions of two women who were appalled by the scenes outside the door of the Stock Exchange. 'A stationary row of men lined the pavement in front of it for a distance of twenty or thirty yards. They stood at the very edge of the kerb, with one foot in the gutter, so as not to block the traffic, and their eyes were fixed on the swing-door, watching the men who bustled in and out of it.

---

[65] Churchill, R.S. 1892. *Men, Mines and Animals in South Africa*. London: Sampson, Low and Co., 236; Reunert, T. 1893. *Diamonds and Gold in South Africa*. Cape Town: J.C. Rutta and Co., 120; Goldman, C.S. 1895. *South African Mines*. Volume 1. London: Effingham Wilson and Co., v, xiv–xv. For an example of a highly successful gold mining investment, see the *Investor's Monthly Manual*, 28 February 1893.

[66] Hill, H. 1896. *Guilty Gold: A Romance of Financial Fraud and City Crime*. London: C. Arthur Pearson, 78, 116, 351–3. Interestingly, in an American novel of 1909 US company promoters were blamed for defrauding US investors, see McCutcheon, G.B. 1909. *Brewster's Millions*. London: Collier and Co., 19.

Newspaper-boys tried to sell them the financial weeklies. A burly constable occasionally said, "Move on, please! Keep the pavement clear!" but in a deferential tone of voice, as though he knew that he had moneyed men to deal with, and must not be peremptory.' Such men were seen as no better than gamblers in a casino, who had only themselves to blame for their losses.[67] As the aftermath of the gold mining boom faded, public opinion took an even more cynical view of investors, as emerges from George Gissing's 1897 novel, *The Whirlpool*. In that there is a reported conversation between two investors, Harvey Rolfe and his friend Cecil Morphew. '"You don't speculate at all?" Morphew asked. "Shouldn't know how to go about it, replied the other in his deeper note." . . . "Wouldn't you be much more comfortable", said Rolfe, rather bluntly, "if you had your money in some other kind of security?" to which Morphew replied "Ah, but dear sir, twelve and a half per cent – twelve and a half! I hold preference shares of the original issue." Rolfe's parting comment to Morphew was that "Then I'm afraid you must take your chance."'[68]

Some investors were seen to take risks and others did not, and each had to accept the consequences of their own actions. Though a few were seen as wizards of finance, the perception of investors remained that they were either greedy gamblers or gullible fools. The perception that they were innocent victims flowered briefly after the mining boom and then quickly faded away, as can be seen in the 1904 novel *Sharks*, by Thorne and Custance. Though a number of investors of different types are noted, the nature of the main company being promoted reveals the enduring image of the investor as greedy and gullible. This concerned the promotion of The Lost Continent Recovery Company, which proposed to raise Atlantis from the seabed. According to Mr Blaber, who wrote the prospectus, 'It amuses me to think, as I sit in some obscure tavern up a dingy court, that the words written by my pen are charming the gold from the pockets of greedy people all over England, that my words can sway and move the huge crowd of people who are dying to get rich without working!'[69] In 1909, H. Rider Haggard published a novel, *The Yellow God*, which included a company, Sahara Ltd, which intended to flood the desert and so create an inland sea. It was believed that it would attract 'the speculative parson and the maiden lady who likes a flutter'.[70] In another 1909 novel, *A Change in the Cabinet* by Hilaire Belloc, an almost identical

[67] Gribble, F. 1896. *The Lower Life*. London: A.D. Innes and Co., 91–3, 100–1, 108–9, 118–20, 126–9, 137, 142, 149, 192, 195–7, 236–7.

[68] Gissing, G. 1897. *The Whirlpool*. London: Lawrence and Bullen, 6–10.

[69] Thorne, G. and L. Custance 1904. *Sharks: A Fantastic Novel for Business Men and their Families*. London: Greening and Co., 2–15, 20–3, 30–3, 50–5, 144–5, 156–7, 180–1, 188–9, 226–9, 232–5, 278–9, 298–9, 340–5.

[70] Haggard, H.R. 1909. *The Yellow God: An Idol of Africa*. London: Cassell and Co., 1–18, 20, 22, 33–4, 40, 42, 48, 51–3, 86, 89, 116.

description of investors was given. They were either 'country parsons' or 'ladies with far more money than knowledge what to do with it'.[71]

By referring to clergymen and women as the typical investor, novelists were portraying them as coming from those groups within society who were most divorced from the realities of business life, and thus most willing to trust the advice they were being given or the promises made in prospectuses. In Annie Swan's 1894 novel, *The Strait Gate*, it was a parson that had placed his life savings in a foreign mine, leaving his widow dependent upon her sons when he died and the company failed.[72] However, the view of women as the investors most likely to be duped into making an unwise investment was not one that went unchallenged. In Gissing's 1895 novel, *In The Year of the Jubilee*, it was a woman who was seen as a careful investor whereas in *Will Warburton*, dating from 1905, it was a man that rashly speculated in shares.[73] This contrast between the man seduced by the prospect of gain and the woman worried about the possibility of loss is also one that comes through starkly in Grace Pettman's 1912 novel, *A Study in Gold*. Despite the opposition of his daughter, Mark St Leonard decided to invest his entire fortune in the shares of companies promoted by the City financier, Otto-Smith. He told her that '"You are a woman – and women know nothing about finance whatever! It is your place to make the world beautiful and charming for the men who transact business. . . . I have no doubt in his hands my fortune would soon increase tenfold!" Margaret gazed at her father in startled fashion. There was a new expression in his eye – was it the covetous gleam of one who longed to add gold to gold.' Margaret, who was familiar with the dangers of speculative investments, persuaded her father to settle a little money on her and her mother. This was invested in bank shares, which she considered both safe and generated a good income. It was on this income that the family lived when the rest of the fortune was lost.[74] Though there was to be no redemption for the man of god as a careful investor, women were perceived as both risk-takers and risk-avoiders when it came to securities.

Whatever the gender or occupation of the investor, the view was commonplace that those who gambled lost their money while those that invested wisely were rewarded. Increasingly this perception of wise investment in shares was coming to the fore, especially when conducted by or on behalf of women. In Arnold Bennett's novel, *Anna of the Five Towns*, which appeared in 1902, Anna Tellwright's fortune had grown from £18,000 in government stock to

---

[71] Belloc, H. 1909. *A Change in the Cabinet*. London: Methuen, 99–104.

[72] Swan, A.S. 1894. *The Strait Gate*. London: S.W. Partridge and Co., 1–13.

[73] Gissing, G. 1895. *In the Year of the Jubilee*. London: Lawrence and Bullen, 4–5; Gissing, G. 1905. *Will Warburton: A Romance of Real Life*. London: Archibald Constable and Co., 18, 91, 96–100.

[74] Pettman, G. 1912. *A Study in Gold*. London: S.W. Partridge and Co., 101, 104, 115–17, 121–3, 126, 146–50, 157 165, 171, 201, 204–5, 207–8.

£48,000 through her father switching it from Consols to joint-stock company shares.[75] In E.M. Forster's 1910 novel, *Howards End*, the Schlegel sisters lived comfortably because 'the Foreign Things did admirably' while 'the Nottingham and Derby declined with the steady dignity of which only Home Rails are capable'.[76] A similar outcome is found in E. Phillips Oppenheim's 1912 novel, *Havoc*. An opera star, Mademoiselle Louise Idaile, trusts her fortune to a stockbroker, Laverick, and within a few weeks her portfolio had shown a profit of nearly £1600.[77] Leaving money to look after itself by placing it in Consols or 'Home Rails' was increasingly seen as foolish as investing in the shares of dubious foreign mines. Instead, a wise investor was one who took advice and was content with a steady income and modest gains. Among those wise investors it was women who were seen as more willing to take advice than men, and so benefit as a result.

Summing up this pre-war perception of investors was Hilaire Belloc who thought that 'the investing public was a queer thing!' in his 1910 novel, *Pongo and the Bull*. What this suggested was that contemporaries were aware that investors defied easy generalization and stereotyping because they contained so many different types, whether they were male or female, old or young, rich or poor. He also went on to observe how fickle they were, noting that for investors, 'there was a hair's breadth between full confidence and panic'.[78] That would also make it difficult for contemporaries to have a fixed view of investors as they were not constant in their behaviour. Despite the emergence of an investing public that increasingly exposed itself to the risks of corporate securities, and the widely reported abuses they were exposed to, there was no sign that attitudes towards them changed much between the 1840s and the years before the First World War. The perception of investors as the gullible and the gamblers remained throughout, while attitudes that saw them as the innocent and the clever waxed and waned depending on current circumstances. The one change that did seem to have happened is that it was important for the ordinary investor to take advice when making decisions for it was those that chased whatever was fashionable or stuck to the tried and tested that lost out. It appeared a lot easier to warn investors about what to avoid, and to criticize them for taking undue risks, than to suggest what a sound portfolio should comprise once the certainties of Consols or UK railways had disappeared.

---

[75] Bennett, A. 1902. *Anna of the Five Towns*. London: Methuen, 41–5, 64–6, 109, 111.

[76] Forster, E.M. 1910. *Howards End*. London: Edward Arnold, 139–40.

[77] Oppenheim, E.P. 1912. *Havoc*. London: Hodder and Stoughton, 62–8, 74, 98–9, 105, 116, 118, 236, 289–90, 314–15, 320–1, 329–30, 342–5.

[78] Belloc, H. 1910. *Pongo and the Bull*. London: Constable and Co., 74.

EXPLANATION

One of the reasons why investors generated so little sympathy among the public in the years before the First World War was that they remained a privileged and wealthy minority within British society.[79] A degree of sympathy existed for the widow who was reduced to poverty through an unwise investment, especially when it was the result of fraud or poor advice, but that did not extend to investors in general for any sustained period.[80] In addition, the public were also aware that these investors had access to a growing army of professionals offering impartial investment advice. The company promoter, H. Osborne O'Hagan, observed that 'a financier of any standing has, as a rule, a large clientele ready to follow him, knowing . . . he will not have taken up . . . the concern unless he believed . . . it would reflect credit on him'.[81] Guides were also published that gave sensible information about investment. When the *Investors' Review* appeared in 1892 its aim was to enable 'those who have money to invest to have an intelligent perception of what they are doing'.[82] It was not new to the field. As early as 1869, Bartlett and Chapman were recommending investors to concentrate upon those joint-stock companies about which they possessed some specialist knowledge.[83] In 1870, the *Stock Exchange Review* concluded that railways and life insurance companies were good investments, while *Phillips' Investors' Manual* favoured bank shares in 1887.[84] A Banker's Daughter, writing in 1891, suggested a diversified portfolio comprising the bonds of railways and utilities.[85] In 1893 S.F. Van Oss, editor of the investment manual, *Fenn on the Funds*, told his readers to focus first on safety, secondly return on capital, thirdly on marketability and fourthly on stability.[86]

This advice also included numerous warnings about risky investments. The *Stock Exchange Observer* almost pleaded with its readership in 1875 when it wrote, 'if only people would exercise reasonable caution, they would

---

[79] Mulhall, M.G. 1896. *Industries and Wealth of Nations*. London: Longmans Green, 100; Chiozza Money, L.G. 1910. *Riches and Poverty*. London: Methuen, 47, 79. However, see also the evidence presented in Chapter 8 of this volume.

[80] For this point, see Rutterford and Maltby, '"The widow, the clergyman and the reckless"', 120.

[81] O'Hagan, H.O. 1929. *Leaves from my Life*. London: John Lane, 255–7.

[82] *Investors' Review*, July–December 1892, 262.

[83] Bartlett and Chapman, *A Handy-Book*, 1, 5, 169, 187.

[84] *Stock Exchange Review*, October 1870; *Phillips' Investors' Manual*. London, 1887, 173.

[85] A Banker's Daughter 1891. *A Guide to the Unprotected in Every-Day Matters relating to Property and Income*, 6th edition. London: Macmillan, 1–4, 88. This went through many editions.

[86] van Oss, S.F. 1893. *American Railroads and British Investors*. London: Effingham Wilson and Co., 138–9.

not be despoiled of their money'.[87] The *Financial Register and Stock Exchange Manual* for 1877 observed that, 'dazzled by brilliant prospectus, or duped by deliberate untruth, a large proportion of English investors have too readily parted with their money, now almost as hopelessly lost to them as if they had cast it into the sea'.[88] The *Stock and Share Review* for February 1884 expressed a similar opinion: 'there seem to be plenty of people left in the world who will risk their money in all sorts of doubtful undertaking, if only a sufficiently high rate of interest is promised'.[89] In 1887, *Phillips' Investors' Manual* concluded that 'if ordinary shareholders would but exercise the same amount of caution, and make the same searching investigation before investing their capital no matter how small, in any undertaking, as they would if they contemplated entering into private partnerships, nine-tenths of them would never invest a shilling in the schemes so imprudently advertised and puffed in prospectuses'.[90] Walker and Watson expressed a similar warning in 1894. 'Companies making a good start and going on uninterruptedly to a listing success, are, unfortunately, so decidedly in the minority that, as a rule, the cautious investor would be well advised – unless possessed of special knowledge – to subscribe for nothing new, but to confine his attention to undertakings that have already got over the distempers incidental to the start of life and established their claim to the confidence of the public'.[91] The *'Money-Maker' Manuals for Investors*, which appeared in 1901, also cautioned investors against purchasing the shares of companies either trying to develop a new technology or process or open up a mine, seeing this as no better than gambling. 'Industrials and mining shares are the lodestars that usually attract the small investor; the bait being either the small nominal value, or otherwise a big dividend'.[92] Again, in 1909 the *Investor's Monthly Manual* concluded that 'investment, especially investment in a new company, is carried out by most people with so little information that loss or profit is reduced to a matter of bad or good luck'.[93]

[87] *Stock Exchange Observer*, 9 February 1875.
[88] *Financial Register and Stock Exchange Manual*, 1877, vii.
[89] *Stock and Share Review*, February 1884.
[90] *Phillips' Investors' Manual*, London, 1887, 31.
[91] Walker and Watson, *Investor's and Shareholder's Guide*, 109–10, 175–6, 267.
[92] Anon 1901. *The 'Money-Maker' Manuals for Investors. Number 1: How to Commence Investing*. London: Publisher unknown, 30, 39; Anon 1901. *The 'Money-Maker' Manuals for Investors. Number 2: A New Dictionary of Mining Terms*. London: Publisher unknown, 1, 14; Anon 1901. *The 'Money-Maker' Manuals for Investors. Number 4: Scientific Investment*. London: Publisher unknown, 57.
[93] *Investor's Monthly Manual*, November 1909.

CONCLUSION

Given the advice and warnings, pressure for government intervention in the shape of legal protection for investors was muted prior to the First World War. There was no general outcry to redress an obvious abuse as is evident from contemporary fiction. Instead, what took place were slow and incremental changes in response to specific complaints. The Bankruptcy Laws were reformed, for example, with the introduction of improved administration, auditing and professional accounting by 1883. Company law was tightened up so as to improve disclosure and make directors more liable for their actions. The 1900 Companies Act introduced regulations for the wording and issuing of prospectuses, and the allotment of shares. These amendments did provide investors with a limited degree of protection from the most blatant claims made in prospectuses and by company directors about current performance, upon which investors based their decisions.[94] However, institutions such as the Stock Exchange were left to regulate themselves and they continued to give priority to the interests of members not the investing public. The Stock Exchange provided a fair and orderly market but was little concerned with the merits or otherwise of the companies whose shares were traded there.[95] What transformed this situation was the First World War. Events during the war changed the relationship between the government and investors and between the Stock Exchange and the investors. During the war, for example, the government sequestered the US$ holdings of British investors, so as to finance purchases in the United States, as well as pressurizing the London Stock Exchange not to provide a market for certain securities. At the same time, the London Stock Exchange became much more responsive to government influence and modified the way its markets operated so as to make speculation much more difficult to conduct.[96] These created precedents for the post-war world as they provided evidence of how certain practices could be outlawed, suppressed, or curtailed through governmental and institutional intervention. As early as 1916, the experienced financial journalist, Hartley Withers, noted that attitudes towards investor protection were changing.[97] There was now an expectation that

---

[94] Ramage, R.W. 1982. *The Companies Acts: Table A 1856–1981.* London: Butterworths, vii–ix.

[95] Hein, *The British Companies Acts*, 129–32; Cottrell, P.L. 1980. *Industrial Finance, 1830–1914: The Finance and Organization of English Manufacturing Industry.* London: Methuen, 41–2; Markham Lester, V. 1995. *Victorian Insolvency: Bankruptcy, Imprisonment for Debt, and Company Winding-up in Nineteenth-Century England.* Oxford: Oxford University Press, 2, 289; Kynaston, *The Financial Times*, 51; Armstrong, 'The rise and fall', 115.

[96] See Michie, *The London Stock Exchange*, chapter 4.

[97] Withers, H. 1916. *International Finance.* London: John Murray, 169–70.

either the government or the Stock Exchange would intervene to protect investors.[98]

The war had also made Britain a nation of investors as the public at large subscribed to the successive issues of war loan, believing it was their patriotic duty to do so. Writing in 1918, Comyns Carr, an expert on company law, was in no doubt what the result was. 'We have seen during the war a remarkably widespread diffusion of money, and a wonderful growth in the habit of investment, among classes of the population to whom both are a novelty. It is computed that no less than 13,000,000 people are directly interested in various forms of Government war securities. After the war it is expected that a large number of people who never were investors before will be willing to entrust their savings to commercial companies, but will not be very well equipped to select those which are worthy of their confidence. Simultaneously, there will be a large crop of new schemes appealing for public support, mostly bona fide, but offering unique opportunity to the fraudulent and over-sanguine'.[99] At the time he was ignored but events were to prove him right. Many of these new investors were soon drawn towards joint-stock company shares forcing amendments to the Companies Acts in 1928/9. By the mid-1930s, a company such as ICI had a total of 124,690 shareholders while Imperial Tobacco had 94,690 destroying any belief that they were owned by investors who were well informed about the business in which they held shares. In addition, investors continued to be drawn into smaller and more speculative concerns offering the prospects of large capital gains.

In the wake of the Wall Street Crash, many investors in company shares experienced large losses fuelling pressure for a fundamental reform of investor protection, either through legislation or intervention by the Stock Exchange. This came to a head with complaints about the high-pressure techniques being employed by some brokers in the 1930s to sell overvalued or worthless shares to investors. An investigation into this practice, known as share-pushing, was ordered by the government. This then led to legislation in 1939 to ban such practices and provide investors with a greater degree of protection so far afforded by either the civil or criminal law. Such legislation passed with almost no opposition, as the *Banker* observed with some surprise. 'If there is one trade which vitally concerns the City of London, it is the business of dealing in securities. One might reasonably have expected, therefore, that the introduction of a new law to regulate dealings in securities would have been followed by City interests with the closest attention. Instead, the passage through the various stages of the so-called Prevention of Fraud (Investments) Bill, alias share-pushing Bill, has so far been watched by the many important groups

---

[98] Samuel, *Shareholders' Money*, 4–5, 9, 14, 67, 111, 329.
[99] PP 1918 VII (9138) *Report of the Company Law Amendment Committee*. Reservation by Mr A.S. Comyns Carr, 13–14. See also the Chapter 8 in this volume.

whom it closely concerns with a calm verging on apathy.[100] This Act was then amended in 1944 and 1958 before being replaced by the all-embracing legislation of 1986 and the Financial Services and Markets Act of 2000. In addition the Companies Acts were also amended in 1947/8, 1980, and 1985, while insider trading was made a criminal offence in 1985.[101] The result was to eliminate most of the flagrant abuses associated with the issue and trading of shares. In the process, the company promoter disappeared from the financial scene.

Despite being regarded by many as 'a den of gamblers and a casino', the London Stock Exchange also acquired a public role from the 1930s onwards, according to the journalist Oscar Hobson. He noted in July 1947 that 'it has imposed a more stringent disciplinary code on its members. It has tightened up its regulations for the granting of permission to deal in new issues of stocks and shares'.[102] These changes allowed the *Banker* to claim that the London Stock Exchange lay at the heart of investor protection as early as April 1947. 'The real safeguard for the investing public is the conservative administration of the "House" as a body and the high reputation of individual firms'.[103] The London Stock Exchange even introduced a compensation scheme for those investors who had lost money as result of the actions of its members. This was under active discussion from the mid-1930s onwards and had been agreed to by 1938 but the outbreak of the Second World War prevented its introduction. It eventually appeared in 1950. Until the 'Big Bang' in 1986, the London Stock Exchange occupied a central role in safeguarding the interests of investors. It controlled those securities to which it gave an official quotation, so eliminating most of the speculative issues on which investors had lost money in the past. It supervised the behaviour of its members so protecting investors from fraudulent behaviour. It monitored market activity and so both detected and punished insider trading long before it became a criminal offence.[104] Combined with legislation, the result was that investors did enjoy a growing degree of protection after 1945, long before the passing of the Financial Services Act in 1986.

It was a fundamental change in the size and composition of the investing population, as a result of the First World War, that changed the public's attitude towards investors, creating the belief that they were innocent victims of financial fraudsters. This was combined with a transformation in the balance between *laissez faire* and state intervention, which became even more pronounced after the Second World War. The result was to modify

[100] 'The Share-Pushing Bill'. *Banker*, January 1939, 9–10.
[101] Fisher et al. *The Law of Investor Protection*; Powell, *Issues and Offers*, 3, 5, 131.
[102] Hobson, O.R. 1947. 'The Stock Exchange and the public'. *Banker*, July, 31–2.
[103] 'The Future of the Stock Exchange'. *Banker*, April 1947, 21.
[104] Michie, *The London Stock Exchange*, 174–7, 207–8, 382.

the past practice of both governments and financial institutions and force steps to be taken to protect investors from the consequences of their own actions. Thus, the exposure of the wrongdoings of bankers, company promoters, and other inhabitants of the City of London, as was evident in the pre-1914 literature, was not sufficient to produce anything more than a slow, partial, and gradual tightening up of company laws. Self regulation remained the order of the day and the maxim of 'caveat emptor' (let the buyer beware) prevailed. The absence of any real sympathy towards investors as a class, which is evident in the pre-1914 fiction, is testimony to the fact that they continued to be held responsible for their own actions. There was a prevailing realism that people would gamble whatever was done to prevent it and that the only people harmed as a result was the individual and their immediate family. The mass participation in investment that took place during the First World War, and then the mass participation in conflict that took place during the Second, changed both British society and attitudes towards investors. Out of that came investor protection, not the publicity given to abuses by Victorian and Edwardian novelists.[105]

---

[105] Robb, G. 1992. *White-Collar Crime in Modern England: Financial Fraud and Business Morality, 1845–1929*. Cambridge: Cambridge University Press, 156–7. See also Lee, T.A. and R.H. Parker eds. 1979. *The Evolution of Corporate Financial Reporting*. Sunbury-on-Thames: T. Nelson.

8

The Evidence for 'Democratization' of Share Ownership in Great Britain in the Early Twentieth Century

Josephine Maltby, Janette Rutterford, David R. Green,
Steven Ainscough, and Carien van Mourik

INTRODUCTION

From the start of the twentieth century, commentators began to suggest that shareholding in Britain was becoming 'democratized' in the sense that a larger number of individuals from a widening social spectrum were beginning to own shares. E.T. Powell's study of the newly opened Selfridges department store, for example, noted that shareholders included 'a cabinet maker, a gas collector, a clerk, a nurse, a housekeeper, a school mistress, and a governess', each of whom represented 'a class of the community to whom investment was a word of unknown meaning, and the process itself an unprobed mystery, fifty years ago'.[1] Further evidence of the apparent diffusion of share ownership comes from the numbers of individuals involved and the size of shareholdings. In a series of articles published in 1926 and 1927, the *Economist* argued that industry was financed by 'innumerable small shareholders'.[2] The journal's survey of one holding out of 100 in very large companies found that 34.6 per cent of shareholders held less than £100 capital and 85 per cent less than £500. An additional sample of one holding in 40 moderate-sized companies showed that 37.8 per cent of shareholders held less than £100 nominal and 87.8 per cent had less than £500.[3] One-third of investors held less

[1] Cheffins, B.R. 2008. *Corporate Ownership and Control: British Business Transformed.* Oxford: Oxford University Press, 191, quoting Powell, E.T. 1910. *The Mechanism of the City.* London: P.S. King and Son, 127.
[2] *Economist*, 18 December 1926: 1054–5; 25 December 1926: 108–9; and 1 January 1927: 12–13.
[3] Ibid., 18 December 1926: 1055.

than £100 and the *Economist* concluded that in the sample of companies it had selected, shareholders were 'a very numerous body, running in some cases into the tens of thousands'.[4]

Views about the widening social spectrum of investors and the scale of holdings are paralleled by the growth in the absolute numbers of shareholders themselves. For railway shares alone, Board of Trade statistics showed that between 1886 and 1902 the number of holders went up from 546,000 to 800,000, nearly half of them owning ordinary shares, and Clapham suggested that by 1914 there were some 900,000 shareholders in UK and Irish railways and about 300,000 bank shareholders.[5] Cheffins has summarized more recent estimates, citing Jefferys' claim that between the 1860s and the early twentieth century, the number of British shareholders rose from under 50,000 to between 250,000 and 500,000, and Michie's view that between 1870 and 1914 the number of 'serious owners' of securities went up from 250,000 to 1 million.[6] However, despite Powell's opinion and the estimates cited above, Cheffins concludes that investment was 'an activity largely reserved for the wealthy'.[7] He points out that Michie's estimate of 1 million shareholders by the First World War represents only 2.2 per cent of the population, and that Inland Revenue data for 1913/14 showed that nearly 55 per cent of the shares, stocks, and funds held by individuals at the time of their death belonged to estates worth £50,000 or more. From this he concludes that it was the already wealthy who were expanding their portfolios to add shares, rather than the less affluent that were moving into the market.

These estimates of increased share ownership raise some important questions about the nature of the investors and the kinds of shares they invested in. Several studies have considered the extent to which the choice of shares widened and whether different kinds of investors showed a preference for different levels of risk.[8] But less attention has been paid to addressing which social classes invested in company securities. Did the increase in shareholder numbers result from investment activity outside the pool of the affluent elite, or was it simply a movement by the latter away from traditional assets such as land, mortgages, and government securities? This chapter investigates the

---

[4] Ibid., 1 January 1927: 13.

[5] Board of Trade 1903. *Return Showing Holders of Debentures, Preferred and Ordinary Stocks of Railways in the United Kingdom 16 December 1902*. London: His Majesty's Stationery Office; *Investors' Monthly Manual*, January 1887: 3; Clapham, J.H. 1938. *An Economic History of Modern Britain*. Volume 3. Cambridge: Cambridge University Press, 289.

[6] Cheffins, *Corporate Ownership and Control*, 191–2. See also Michie's Chapter in this volume (Chapter 7).

[7] Cheffins, Corporate Ownership and Control, 191–2.

[8] See, for instance, Turner, J.D. 2009. 'Wider share ownership? Investors in English and Welsh bank shares in the nineteenth century'. *Economic History Review* 62(s1): 167–92; Rutterford, J. and J. Maltby 2007. '"The nesting instinct": women investors and risk in England, 1700–1930'. *Accounting History* 12(3): 305–27; and Chapter 9 in this volume.

democratization process – the extent to which share ownership spread beyond the affluent classes – by drawing on evidence from the 1870s to the 1930s based on contemporary opinion, share records, and other forms of savings and investment activity. We begin by examining the role of savings banks, employee schemes for share ownership, and the purchase of government war bonds, all of which, to a greater or lesser extent, drew in working-class and lower middle-class investors to the financial sector. We then examine the extent to which these new groups of savers and investors became involved in share ownership, using fresh empirical evidence that links occupational categories with shareholding in a variety of companies that represented a cross section of the British economy.

NINETEENTH-CENTURY SAVINGS

In the course of the nineteenth century, especially as real wages began to rise from the 1850s onwards, working-class savings schemes grew in popularity. Friendly societies, first established during the seventeenth century, were important both as sources of social support and as a means of encouraging savings for welfare purposes – for instance, for use in case of injury, illness, unemployment, or old age. In terms of membership, their popularity doubled between the 1880s and 1913 with a movement away from the small and often short-lived societies based in public houses or neighbourhoods to larger national organizations such as the Oddfellows, whose contribution towards health insurance remained important until the advent of the National Health Service.[9] During the nineteenth century, door-to-door weekly collection of premiums made insurance more accessible to working-class households.[10] Insurance of various kinds – for health and for the costs of burial, especially of babies and young children – was energetically pursued, with the lowest paid households contributing for the latter when they could afford no other types of savings.[11] There was also a wide variety of savings schemes for clothing or food, such as the Christmas goose clubs, that were often local and informal – many of which operated as so-called 'deposit and dividing'

[9] Johnson, P. 1985. *Saving and Spending: The Working-Class Economy in Britain 1870–1939.* Oxford: Clarendon Press: 48–9; Lemire, B. 2005. *The Business of Everyday Life: Gender, Practice and Social Politics in England.* Manchester: Manchester University Press.

[10] Burton, D., D. Knights, A. Leyshon, C. Alferoff, and P. Signoretta 2005. 'Consumption denied? The decline of industrial branch insurance'. *Journal of Consumer Culture* 5(2): 181.

[11] See, for example, Reeves, M.P. 1913. *Round About a Pound a Week.* London: G. Bell and Sons and also Oren, L. 1973. 'The welfare of women in labouring families: England 1860–1950'. *Feminist Studies* 1(3/4): 107–25.

societies.[12] Nor was saving merely confined to men: some contemporaries commented on the propensity of married women to save despite their lack of ownership rights before the Married Women's Property Acts of 1870 and 1882. In 1838, for instance, a Berkshire vicar told the House of Lords committee on the Poor Law Amendment Act that 'every woman in my parish who has a large family is a subscriber' to a penny-a-week clothing club.[13]

Other forms of savings were also available to the working class. At the end of the eighteenth century, the first savings banks specifically for the use of the working class were established. These attracted government support and intervention from an early stage, with the 1817 Act for the Protection and Encouragement of Banks for Savings in England. This provided for savings bank deposits to be placed with Commissioners of the National Debt at 4.5 per cent interest – 'a substantial premium' on the rate for government stock. Investors were allowed to deposit £100 in first year, then £50 annually.[14] By the end of 1817, there were 101 savings banks in England and Wales rising to 541 by 1839 and 645 by 1861. Estimates of the number of savers in these banks varied but may have reached nearly three quarters of a million by 1839 and over 1.6 million by 1861, as shown in Table 8.1. Additional savings accounts were provided nationwide by the foundation in 1861 of the Post Office Savings Bank and Table 8.1 shows how the number of such accounts grew rapidly, reaching over 11 million by 1908. According to one contemporary estimate, by 1910 there were at least 13 million individual depositors in both sets of banks, or about one in every three of the entire population of the United Kingdom.[15] Other estimates are more conservative, suggesting that the number of working-class savers in these banks had risen to over 7.2 million by 1911.[16] In either case, however, the increase reflected a very significant rise in the number of savers in these types of banks. These numbers were paralleled by the amount of deposits that flowed into the savings banks, as shown in Table 8.2, which rose from nearly £29 million in 1850 to £187 million by 1900 and £241.5 million by the eve of the First World War.

Supporters of savings banks argued that habits of thrift and personal responsibility had wider social implications. Thomas Chalmers, for example, writing in 1841, suggested that savers would beget 'a sense of propriety . . . a stake and an interest in the social order, in the peace and stability of the

[12] Gosden, P.H. 1973. *Self-Help: Voluntary Associations in Nineteenth-Century Britain*. London: B.T. Batsford, 105.

[13] PP 1837–8 XIX (719) *Select Committee of the House of Lords on the Operation of the Poor Law Amendment Act, Report, Minutes of Evidence*, 101.

[14] Moss, M. and I. Russell 1994. *An Invaluable Treasure: A History of the TSB*. London: Weidenfeld and Nicolson, 34.

[15] Cargill, A. 1910. *Memorial of the Centenary of Savings Banks*. Edinburgh: Constable, 17.

[16] See Boyer, G.R. 2009. 'Insecurity, safety nets and self-help in Victorian and Edwardian Britain'. In *Human Capital and Institutions: A Long-Run View*, edited by D. Eltis, F.D. Lewis, and K.L. Sokoloff. Cambridge: Cambridge University Press, 77.

Table 8.1 Numbers of savings banks and savings banks accounts in the United Kingdom, 1819–1908

Estimates for 1819–61

Year	Number of savings banks	Number of accounts
1819	359	unknown
1829	476	409,714
1839	541	748,393
1849	579	1,087,354
1859	625	1,503,916
1861	645	1,643,822

Estimates for 1862–1908

Year	Number of Post Office savings banks	Number of accounts
1862	2535	178,499
1881	6513	2,607,612
1900	13,341	8,439,983
1908	15,257	11,018,251

Source: Cargill, A. 1910. *Memorial of the Centenary of Savings Banks*. Edinburgh: Constable, 17.

Table 8.2 Estimates of savings banks deposits in the United Kingdom, 1830–1913

Year	Trustee savings bank deposits (£million)	Post Office savings bank deposits (£million)	Total savings bank deposits (£million)
1830	14.6	—	14.6
1835	17.4	—	17.4
1840	23.5	—	23.5
1845	30.7	—	30.7
1850	28.9	—	28.9
1855	34.3	—	34.3
1860	41.3	—	41.3
1865	38.7	6.5	45.2
1870	38.0	15.1	53.1
1875	42.4	25.2	67.6
1880	44.0	33.7	77.7
1885	46.4	47.7	94.1
1890	43.6	67.6	111.2
1895	45.3	97.9	143.2
1900	51.5	135.5	187.0
1905	52.7	152.1	204.8
1910	52.3	168.9	221.2
1913	54.3	187.2	341.5

Source: Boyer, G.R. 2009. 'Insecurity, safety nets and self-help in Victorian and Edwardian Britain'. In *Human Capital and Institutions: A Long-Run View*, edited by D. Eltis, F.D. Lewis, and K.L. Sokoloff. Cambridge: Cambridge University Press, 62.

commonwealth'.[17] There is a continuing debate, however, about the extent to which these banks managed to attract working-class savers. A survey of their customer base in 1853 found that the largest group consisted of 'tradesmen and their assistants, small farmers, clerks, mechanics and artisans . . . and their wives'.[18] The implication was that it was the middle and lower middle classes rather than manual workers who chose savings banks. Subsequent scholarship has failed to resolve the extent to which one class or another made use of savings banks. Horne notes that it was 'rumoured' that the wealthy used English banks, via trusts or (illegally) depositing in more than one bank, but concludes that the majority of savers in the 1840s and 1850s were 'people of small means'.[19] Pollock emphasizes the importance of working-class savers in the Glasgow Savings Bank later in the century, with fewer than 10 per cent of new depositors in 1881 coming from the clerical or professional classes.[20] By contrast, Ó Gráda, for instance, points to evidence that Irish banks in the early nineteenth century were largely used by the better-off via accounts for trusts or by members of middle-class families who opened accounts for each of their children up to the maximum amount permitted annually.[21]

An alternative form of savings, and one that also tied workers more closely to the fortunes of an enterprise, was share ownership. However, there is little evidence that the government found working-class investment in shares to be as desirable it had done in relation to the savings banks. Certainly, Jefferys refers to the expectation in the early Victorian period that limited liability would draw 'labour and capital classes together in the same happy enterprise'.[22] The Select Committee on Investments for the Savings of the Middle and Working Classes, set up in 1850 to simplify the law for 'unfettering the energies of trade', reported on the desirability of encouraging workmen to 'combine . . . in industrial undertakings'.[23] But this was associated with the promotion of small businesses by artisans or the availability of savings opportunities for people with moderate amounts of savings; the Committee was looking for ways to promote the establishment of small businesses but not to stimulate investment by workers

[17] Chalmers, T. 1841. *On the Sufficiency of the Parochial System, without a Poor Rate, for the Right Management of the Poor*. Glasgow: William Collins, 28.

[18] Moss and Russell, *An Invaluable Treasure*, 53.

[19] Horne, O.H. 1947. *A History of Savings Banks*. Oxford: Oxford University Press.

[20] Pollock, G.D. 2007. 'Aspects of thrift in East End Glasgow: new accounts at the Bridgeton Cross branch of the Savings Bank of Glasgow, 1881'. *International Review of Scottish Studies* 32(1): 117–48.

[21] Ó Gráda, C. 2008. 'The early history of Irish savings banks'. Centre for Economic Research, University College Dublin, *Working Paper Series WP08/04*.

[22] Jefferys, J.B. 1938. 'Trends in business organisation in Great Britain since 1856, with special reference to the financial structure of companies, the mechanism of investment and the relations between the shareholder and the company'. Unpublished PhD Thesis, University of London, 55.

[23] PP 1850 XIX (508) *Select Committee on Investments for Savings of Middle and Working Classes, Report*, iii.

in the large ones that employed them. Although limited liability was viewed as a 'mechanism for reforming society through the sharing of capital', there was no concerted support for bringing the working classes into companies as shareholders with the same rights as their employers.[24] The argument was that it was beyond their skill and judgement to play a role in corporate governance. It was, as the jurist Leone Levi noted, 'incompatible with the character of an operative . . . (to) . . . inspect accounts, attend meetings (and) exercise a certain amount of control' as a partner or shareholder in the enterprise would do.[25] Where employee share ownership did occur, it was the result of a variety of strategies within businesses, rather than any government attempt to spread shareholding among a wider social group.

EMPLOYEE SHARE OWNERSHIP: PROFIT-SHARING AND 'CO-PARTNERSHIP'

In the period covered here, there were two different types of employee share ownership: cooperative ownership and profit-sharing/co-partnership schemes. These differed in their implications for employee shareholders and for the companies in which they operated. Cooperative ownership produced shareholders who closely monitored company performance and used their voting powers. Co-partnership schemes, as outlined below, conferred different levels of control on employee shareholders.

A leading example of cooperative ownership of limited companies was provided by the 'Oldham Limiteds', the East Lancashire cotton mills established after the Companies Acts of 1855 and 1862, the numbers of which grew dramatically in the boom between 1873 and 1875. Substantial employee share ownership was encouraged by a democratic voting structure – one shareholder one vote – rather than the plutocratic method that gave more votes to large shareholders, which was becoming common in other companies.[26] Widespread ownership of shares in the Oldham Limiteds also stimulated considerable employee interest in company activity, including avid attention

---

[24] Cited in Loftus, D. 2009. 'Limited liability, market democracy, and the social organization of production in mid-nineteenth-century Britain'. In *Victorian Investments: New Perspectives on Finance and Culture*, edited by N. Henry and C. Schmitt. Bloomington and Indianapolis, IN: Indiana University Press, 79–97.

[25] Ibid., 96.

[26] Toms, J.S. 2002. 'The rise of modern accounting and the fall of the public company: the Lancashire cotton mills 1870–1914'. *Accounting, Organizations and Society* 27(1/2): 61–84. For a discussion of the more general popularity of this voting system, see Dunlavy, C. 1998. 'Corporate governance in nineteenth-century Europe and the United States: the case of shareholder voting rights'. In *Corporate Governance: The State of the Art of Emerging Research*, edited by K.J. Hopt, H. Kanda, M. Roe, E. Wymeersch, and S. Prigge. Oxford: Clarendon Press, 5–39.

to news in the local press about corporate performance.[27] But these links were eroded in the latter part of the century. A depression in the cotton market, and hence in share prices, resulted in large blocks of shares in these companies being acquired by outside investors: by 1898–1907 just over 5 per cent of shares were held by company workers compared with 22 per cent in the years from 1874 to 1876.[28]

However, share ownership of this cooperative type was unusual; employee share ownership was more normally the result of one of a variety of methods of profit-sharing offered by employers in the nineteenth and early twentieth centuries. There were two main approaches to employee participation over this period. 'Profit-sharing' was often used to describe both, but more precisely this applied to the payment of an agreed share of profits as a cash bonus, usually as a contribution to a savings account or as superannuation. Employee share ownership was more accurately denoted by 'co-partnership' – the schemes which enabled the employee to acquire shares in the enterprise. Reviewing the situation in 1912, Fay argued that co-partnership could be distinguished from profit-sharing only 'in degree rather than in kind'. Co-partnership, he noted, was 'less of an isolated material advantage occurring once a year . . . (but) . . . more of a starting-point for ties and interests which shall permanently modify the status of the employee'.[29] Employees might receive shares by the conversion of some or all of a company's profit into shares. Alternatively, shares might be available to them in other ways, through, for example, the gift of free shares, often as a reward for good performance, or by the chance to buy on advantageous terms.[30]

To examine the creation and operation of 'ties and interests', Fay concentrated on two schemes: the Lever Bros. Co-partnership Trust, set up in 1909, and the South Metropolitan Gas Company scheme that had begun in 1889 and which by 1912 had been taken up by 35 other gas companies. Lever Bros. appointed trustees who, at their own discretion, allocated partnership certificates to employees, entitling them to a dividend of 10 per cent on profits after a 5 per cent dividend had been paid to ordinary shareholders. On the employee's retirement, the certificates would be converted to 'preferential certificates' attracting a 5 per cent dividend. Workers forfeited their certificates if they went on strike or left Lever Bros. for another employer. The South Metropolitan scheme was closely linked to the workers' bonus, half of which was credited to a savings account and the other half invested in the company's ordinary stock. As the price of gas fell, the shareholder dividend and the scheme bonus rose. In 1912, South Metropolitan was offering a bonus of

---

[27] Toms, 'The rise of modern accounting', 74.
[28] Ibid., 68.
[29] Fay, C.R. 1912. 'Co-partnership in industry'. *Economic Journal* 22(88): 530.
[30] Ibid.

8.25 per cent but for other gas companies, 5 per cent was more usual. Whilst Lever Bros. certificates were allotted at trustees' discretion, the gas scheme was available to all workers, and those who left employment could either take the stock or cash it in. The schemes had different impacts on corporate governance: the Lever certificates entitled employees to a dividend only, whilst the gas scheme was linked with a co-partnership committee – 'a channel of communication between the management and the men' – and also with employee representation.[31] Two workmen and one clerk served on the South Metropolitan board of directors.[32]

Fay's opinion about the benefits for workers was more generous to the South Metropolitan scheme than to that operated by Lever Bros. The Lever certificates did not carry a return unless the company had been able to pay out an adequate dividend to shareholders, and the employee could forfeit their entitlement for unsatisfactory behaviour. Control remained firmly with the employer and 'in ungenerous or imprudent hands' might simply produce 'a large pile of scrip' with no transfer value.[33] In 1899, the chairman of South Metropolitan claimed that co-partnership had improved performance, kept down wage costs and also 'entirely destroyed the power of the trades unions in the company's works'.[34] The columnist reporting his speech pointed out that the legal penalties for gas workers who broke a contract with their employer were also likely to have had an effect on their behaviour. But Fay concurred with the chairman's verdict: the combination of stock ownership and board representation was a remedy for an age where 'the more personal relation of the earlier days gives way to the soullessness of the joint-stock company'.[35]

Certainly, co-partnership was a popular topic in the period immediately before the First World War. In 1912, a Conservative MP introduced a bill to promote its adoption but it did not get past a second reading.[36] Parliamentary debates repeated the issues raised by the South Metropolitan scheme: did co-partnership give workers closer involvement with the company, or was it used as a means of penalizing trade union activity and enforcing compliance with management requirements? There is no clear-cut answer to this question, although Matthews suggests that a relationship existed between labour troubles and the growth of profit-sharing throughout the later nineteenth and early twentieth centuries.[37] According to figures collected by the Ministry of Labour in 1919, shown in Table 8.3. The peaks of new schemes appear to have occurred in the

---

[31] Fay, 'Co-partnership in industy', 539.   [32] Ibid., 540.   [33] Ibid., 533.

[34] 'Z' 1899. 'Successful profit-sharing'. *Economic Journal* 9(36): 585–8.

[35] Fay, 'Co-partnership in industry', 540.

[36] Hansard. House of Commons Debates, 12 June 1912, vol. 39, cc870–2.

[37] Matthews, D. 1989. 'The British experience of profit-sharing'. *Economic History Review* 42(4): 439–64. See also Hatton, T.J. 1988. 'Profit sharing in British industry, 1865–1913'. *International Journal of Industrial Organization* 6(1): 69–90, on the relationship between the 'new unionism' of 1889 and the 'sharp increase' in profit-sharing.

Table 8.3 Profit-sharing and co-partnership schemes in the United Kingdom, 1860–1920

Period during which started	Total number of schemes started in period	Schemes still in existence in 1920
To 1870	20	3
1871–80	18	5
1881–90	79	14
1891–1900	77	14
1901–10	80	51
1911–18	77	66
1919 (10 months)	29	29
Total	380	182

Source: PP 1920 XXIII (157) *Profit-sharing and Labour Co-partnership. Ministry of Labour (Intelligence and Statistics Department). Report on Profit-sharing and Labour Co-partnership in the United Kingdom*, 66–7.

years from 1882 to 1892, when new unionism was gathering strength, and between 1908 and 1909 and again from 1912 to 1914.[38] Following a lull during the First World War, a further set of new schemes was launched, the timing of which Ramsay suggests coincided with a period of challenge with management authority. In total 29 new schemes were launched in a period of 10 months, compared with an average of 8 per year between 1901 and 1910 and 10 per year from 1911 to 1918. The surge in the number of schemes was associated with a variety of factors that pitted workers against management, including the growth of trades union membership from two to five million between 1911 and 1919, a vigorous shop stewards' movement and public resentment over wartime profiteering.[39]

Figures complied by the Ministry of Labour shown in Table 8.4, record that of the 380 schemes started between 1870 and 1919, only 182 were still in existence in 1920. Further details were available for 165 of the extant schemes and for these the report identified a number of key features. Their popularity varied between industries. The 36 'gas undertakings' comprised the largest group of companies running schemes covering in total 33,000 employees. However, the largest firms participating in these arrangements were in shipbuilding and engineering where 11 companies had schemes involving over 81,000 workers. Banking and insurance, textile trades, warehouse and retail trades were the next largest groups, with a total of 45 firms running schemes for more than 51,000 employees. The average size of the schemes overall was fewer than 1500 people which suggests that many were run by private

[38] Church, R.A. 1971. 'Profit-sharing and labour relations in England in the nineteenth century'. *International Review of Labour History* 16(1): 2–16.
[39] Ramsay, H. 1977. 'Cycles of control: worker participation in sociological and historical perspective'. *Sociology* 11(3): 481–506.

Table 8.4 Existing schemes of profit-sharing or labour co-partnership, summarized by form of bonus payment and period in which started

Form of bonus payment	Date schemes started						
	Up to and including 1880	1881–90	1891–1900	1901–5	1906–10	1911–15	1916–19	Total
Panel A: including gas companies' schemes								
S.	—	—	1	—	7	2	5	15
C.S.	—	—	—	2	—	—	2	4
W.S.	—	—	1	1	5	3	—	10
P.S.	—	1	1	1	1	—	—	4
S.W.	—	—	—	—	5	6	—	11
S.P.	—	—	—	—	2	3	—	5
Others	8	13	11	8	19	37	37	133
Total	8	14	14	12	39	51	44	182
Panel B: excluding gas companies' schemes								
S	—	—	—	—	—	—	—	—
C.S.	—	—	—	2	—	—	2	4
P.S.	—	—	1	—	—	—	—	1
S.W.	—	—	—	—	—	1	—	1
Others	8	13	12	8	20	37	42	140
Total	8	13	13	10	20	38	44	146

Key:
S.: invested in the capital of the undertaking;
C.S.: partly cash, partly capital;
W.S.: partly credited to a savings/deposit account, partly capital;
P.S.: paid partly to a provident fund, partly in capital;
S.W.: capital up to a certain amount, then partly capital, partly credited to a savings/deposit account;
S.P.: capital up to a certain amount, then partly capital, partly credited to a provident fund.

Source: PP 1920 XXIII (157) *Profit-sharing and Labour Co-partnership. Ministry of Labour (Intelligence and Statistics Department). Report on Profit-sharing and Labour Co-partnership in the United Kingdom*, 166.

companies that offered profit rather than share-based participation. This is borne out by Table 8.4 which analyses the 182 schemes in existence in 1920 according to the way in which employees benefited, first including and then excluding the single largest sector, the gas industry. It is apparent that share schemes were less popular than those distributing a profit share: in total, only 49 companies out of 182 paid benefits wholly or partly as shares but when gas companies are removed, only 6 out of 146 did so.

Co-partnership schemes continued into the 1920s, although the pace of formation abated. By 1929, there was a total of 330 profit-sharing schemes in existence with 260,000 employees entitled to participate. Of these, 69 issued shares and 32 others converted bonus payments directly into shares. The *Ministry of Labour Gazette*, reporting on these schemes, noted that the share-issuing companies employed 187,000 workers, but only 37,000 of these participated – not because of the conditions attached to ownership but because 'only a minority of the employees have been able, or have wished, to take advantage of the facilities offered'.[40] In subsequent years, employee share ownership continued but there was no evidence of a rising tide of popularity. Profit-sharing schemes appear to have declined in the 1930s, perhaps, as Jones argues, because of employers' preference for amenity welfare provision, such as health care, canteens, and social funds, or as a result of the economic recession following the Wall Street crash.[41] Survival of these schemes seemed to be linked more to the characteristics and attitudes of particular employers and their relationships with employees rather than with a trend towards closer involvement between workers and managers.[42]

But did co-partnership schemes turn workers into shareholders? Employee rights in the shares they were allotted did not always equate to those given to outside investors, as noted in Fay's discussion of schemes like that of Lever Bros. The 1920 Ministry of Labour report noted that the proportion of votes commanded by employee shareholders under these schemes was almost negligible but, echoing Fay, it argued that employees were still efficiently kept in touch via regular meetings or co-partnership committees.[43] This was a major difference from the status of cooperative shareholders like those of the Oldham Limiteds, who monitored company performance via the local press and could use a democratic voting structure to exert control. The important thing, as *The Times* had asserted in an editorial in 1903, was to persuade employees that 'the real interests of employer and employed are identical'.[44] For advocates of co-partnership, this did not mean turning employees into shareholders who could vote on matters of corporate governance but linking their financial interests as closely as possible with those of the company. Nevertheless, although two-thirds of the companies identified in 1920 as operating profit-sharing schemes were private ones, the 1920 report also noted that a large proportion of the schemes started in 1919 were in public companies.[45] This opens the possibility that employee share schemes could have operated as a way of drawing a wider group of non-traditional investors into the stock market.

---

[40] Anon 1930. 'Profit-sharing and co-partnership in 1929'. *Ministry of Labour Gazette*, July, 238–41.

[41] Jones, H. 1983. 'Employers' welfare schemes and industrial relations in inter-war Britain'. *Business History* 25(1): 61.

[42] Hatton, 'Profit sharing in British industry', 88.

[43] PP 1920 XXIII (157) *Profit-sharing and labour co-partnership. Ministry of Labour (Intelligence and Statistics Department). Report on profit-sharing and labour co-partnership in the United Kingdom. Report on Profit-sharing and Labour Co-partnership in the United Kingdom*, 25–6.

[44] *The Times*, 9 May 1903, 11, col. E.

[45] PP 1920 XXIII (157) *Profit-Sharing and Labour Co-Partnership*, 16.

SELLING SHARES TO THE GENERAL PUBLIC

In addition to the possibility that employees who participated in company share schemes could have traded their shares on the open market, there was also the attempt by some companies to market their shares directly to the general public. Thames Iron Works, for instance, in 1899 used 49 national and provincial newspapers to advertise an issue of 200,000 irredeemable 4 per cent debentures and 300,000 5 per cent cumulative preference shares, some aimed in particular at its customers.[46] Claudius Ash & Sons Ltd, which dealt in dental products, decided that their 1913 new issue would be allotted preferentially to existing shareholders and to members of the dental profession.[47] Similarly, when the building firm Trollope, Colls & Co. made a share issue in 1913, Everard Hambro, their banker, wrote to Trollope that he 'hoped and believed that a great number of your customers and merchants would subscribe to the shares at issue'.[48]

Such customers, of course, might be part of an existing business network but equally others could have come from a wider range of investors, enticed to purchase shares in companies with widely known brand names. It was, for instance, announced at the first public general meeting of Boots in 1892 that, although the company was not listed, its preference shares would be sold over the counter. Jesse Boot and a small circle of his business and professional friends held the ordinary shares that provided voting rights: the preference issue offered a chance to 'bind the public to the concern' as investors as well as customers although they did not confer any rights to vote on matters of corporate governance. These shares were inexpensive, priced at 21s, and carried a 10 per cent dividend. More than 9000 out of the 10,000 shares had been sold 18 months later.[49] Boots made efforts to appeal directly to people unfamiliar with the investment market. The shares were advertised in local newspapers and popular magazines, such as *Titbits*, encouraging potential new investors with comments like 'The preference shares are . . . a favourite investment with customers who have small savings which they desire to invest safely at a fair rate of interest'.[50] When J. Lyons & Co. in 1920 made an issue of one million 8 per cent preference shares in order to expand, the chairman announced at the annual general meeting that 'the applications of share-holders and staff (would) receive due consideration by the board . . . [We]

---

[46] Rutterford, J. 2006. 'The merchant banker, the broker and the company chairman: a new issue case study'. *Accounting, Business and Financial History* 16(1): 45–68.

[47] Claudius Ash & Sons Limited: Prospectus, Guildhall Library MS/18000/Applications for listing file, 1913.

[48] Quoted by Rutterford, 'The merchant banker, the broker and the company chairman', 60.

[49] Chapman, S.D. 1974. *Jesse Boot of Boots the Chemist: A Study in Business History*. London: Hodder and Stoughton, 125–7.

[50] *Titbits*, 28 June 1902, quoted in Chapman, *Jesse Boot*, 128.

intend, as hitherto, to assist our employees with advances when desired. Our last issue was heavily oversubscribed by the thousands of applicants who desired a holding'.[51]

But the enthusiastic marketing does not seem to have contributed to a very wide distribution of shares. In 1894, Jesse Boot was disappointed. He had hoped for 1000 small investors, each with £10 of shares, but his marketing had produced only 360 shareholders.[52] Boot's reluctance to divulge information may have contributed to this unenthusiastic take-up of shares. In 1899, for instance, the journal *Finance* complained that a prospectus for a new Boots subsidiary divulged 'no evidence of the vendor's ability to guarantee the dividend . . . we dislike the company heartily and recommend our readers to ignore it'.[53] It does not, however, appear that other retail companies took this approach. Lipton's, for instance, was a chain of several hundred grocers when it became a limited company in 1898. The result of conversion was that Lipton Ltd proudly reported at its statutory general meeting that it had 74,000 shareholders – 'the largest number of shareholders . . . of any undertaking whatever in the country'.[54] Press coverage and reputation clearly helped to spark public interest. The *New York Times*, for example, reported 'an extraordinary rush' for its shares which 'extended to the West End, where ladies of title, officers and public men were among the people who besieged Sir TL, imploring him to take their money'.[55]

WARTIME SAVINGS AND A POST-WAR EFFECT?

Whilst initiatives to widen the share owning population continued to be promoted, other potentially important influences on investment were also taking place, notably the major impact on savings of the War Loan issued by the British government after 1916. It was estimated by May 1918 that 'some 16¾ million' individuals had invested in the British War Loan.[56] War savings certificates were intended to appeal to the less affluent or experienced investor and the government based its design on the lengthy deliberations of the Committee on War Loans for the Small Investor.[57] The certificates cost 15s 6d and were redeemable after five years for £1, representing 5.47 per cent annual interest, which was free of tax. No more than 500 could be bought by an individual. By 1918, there were over 40,000 War Savings Associations with

---

[51] *Economist*, 19 June 1920, 1357.   [52] Chapman, *Jesse Boot*, 127.   [53] Ibid., 128.
[54] *Economist*, 4 June 1898, 847.
[55] Waugh, A. 1951. *The Lipton Story, a Centennial Biography*. London: Cassell, 93.
[56] *Economist*, 25 May 1918, 913.
[57] Wormell, J. 2000. *The Management of the National Debt of the United Kingdom, 1900–1932*. London: Routledge, 126–36, 369.

a weekly subscribing membership of over 7,000,000 people. The Associations were run on a voluntary basis and operated at local level, including at workplaces, churches, shops, social groups, clubs, men's and women's organizations, and in as many as 10,000 schools.[58]

Advertising of the certificates emphasized that they were intended for people who did not normally invest. A typical poster, issued by the War Savings Committee in 1916, carrying the slogan 'If you cannot fight, lend your money', depicted two plainly dressed women and an elderly man in a Post Office queue.[59] Another from 1918 showed two workmen discussing War Savings in their meal break; the caption quoted one telling the other 'It's Worth While! That's Why'.[60] Such advertising also sought to draw new kinds of investors into purchasing War Bonds. A financial journalist writing in 1917 noted that small investors in particular would benefit from the new opportunity, commenting that 'The Government has given to them not only the necessary facilities for the safe investment of small sums, but, what is even more important, they have advertised the fact far and wide'.[61] Two female journalists also writing in 1917 predicted that women especially would learn from their experience:

> The War Loans have brought to the individual notice of women sound schemes for the investment of their money, the prospectuses of which . . . were simply and clearly written, with the particular aim of interesting and attracting the embryo investor. Indeed, many women received their first lesson in investment from these prospectuses, which patriotism compelled them to study, and the interest thus aroused will not entirely disappear after the War.[62]

Whether patriotism, opportunity or advertising was the prime motive for purchase, the take-up of certificates was exceptionally large: 140 million were sold between 1916 and 1918 and by June 1929, 918 million certificates had been sold, representing a cash investment of £720 million. Allowing for conversions and withdrawals, the balance outstanding at that date was still £483 million.[63] Moreover, the 1920 Ministry of Labour report on profit-sharing, outlined above, noted that 'the habit of saving thus formed may work to the advantage of the employer's own thrift or investment schemes in the long run'.[64] War Loans, it implied, might have contributed to a very widespread awareness of different ways in which to invest savings.

[58] Fraser, H. 1918. *Women and War Work*. New York, NY: G. Arnold Shaw.

[59] Imperial War Museum IWM PST 10350.

[60] Ibid 3594.

[61] Stiles, C.R. 1917. 'The war's lesson for investors'. *Financial Review of Reviews*, March, 49.

[62] Greig, J. and M. Gibson 1917. 'Women and investment'. *Financial Review of Reviews*, June, 174–82.

[63] Wright, A. 1930. 'The state and the small investor'. *Financial Review of Reviews*, January, 31–7.

[64] PP 1920 XXIII (157) *Profit-Sharing and Labour Co-Partnership*, 30.

'INTO THE HOMES OF EVERYONE' – DEMOCRATIZATION AFTER 1919

The post-war period saw, in addition to a boom in profit-sharing schemes, a surge in share issues driven largely by a massive increase in new company formations. In 1919, 860 public companies were registered, and in 1920 the number was 1261.[65] The conclusion drawn by a variety of commentators was that this would lead to the diffusion of shareholding at all social levels. In a lecture at the University of London in 1920, Hartley Withers, editor of the *Economist*, commented that 'finance and financial questions had become democratised'. He quoted the claim by the chairman of the War Savings Committee that the number of UK savers had increased from a pre-war total of 340,000 holders of government securities to 20 million. The new level of national debt, he argued, 'had brought financial questions really into the homes of everyone, and in a way quite new to this generation'.[66] In similar fashion the press also helped to create a new space for the discussion of financial matters that was equally important in bringing them to the attention of a wider reading public. Writing in 1919, for example, Powell noted the proliferation of financial journalism, the existence of 'great daily journals devoted entirely to finance and keeping a close eye on the needs of the small investor', the availability of official information issued by the London Stock Exchange, and the 'really colossal expansion of the activities of the provincial Exchanges'.[67] The question that remains is to what extent this diffusion of knowledge translated into a diffusion of ownership and it is this that the remainder of the chapter seeks to address.

THE DEMOCRATIZATION OF INVESTMENT? ANALYSING SHAREHOLDERS' OCCUPATIONS

In 1927, the *Accountant* reprinted an article on 'The diffusion of capital ownership', originally published in the *Westminster Bank Review*, that dealt with 'the actual incidence of capital ownership in Great Britain – a subject on which scientific data in the past have been exceedingly meagre'.[68] It found that savings were 'by no means the sole prerogative of the well-to-do', and drew on a variety of sources to support its argument. It quoted the 1926 report of the National Savings Committee that found that half the £375.5 million holdings

[65] Essex-Crosby, A. 1938. 'Joint stock companies in Great Britain 1890–1930'. Unpublished M.Comm. Thesis, University of London.

[66] *Accountant*, 7 February 1920, 167.

[67] Powell, E.T. 1919. 'The democratisation of investment'. *Financial Review of Reviews*, September, 249.

[68] *Accountant*, 19 March 1927, 439.

were 'to be accredited to the small investor'.[69] It also noted the chairman's speech at the 1926 annual general meeting of Westminster Bank Ltd which recorded that £60 million of banking capital was owned by 275,000 shareholders, an average holding of under £220.[70] In other words, there was a view that investment had spread further down the social and wealth-holding hierarchy than perhaps had been the case in earlier decades.

The extent to which the expansion of shareholding was based on attracting new kinds of investors, or merely represented a change in the way that traditional shareholders behaved, remains an open question. As Cheffins has suggested, there is a possibility that rather than spread to new groups of shareholders, investment may have remained the preserve of the wealthy. In this case, the expansion of ownership might be attributed to existing investors who chose to spread their shareholding activities over a wide range of securities. This would have resulted in the dispersal noted by the *Economist* in 1929.[71] In order to determine whether the social make-up of shareholders widened, it is necessary to explore their occupational status. Support for the democratization thesis would arise if the post-war group of shareholders included a comparatively large proportion of shareholders from non-traditional backgrounds drawn from the lower middle and working classes.

To address this question, the remainder of this chapter explores the relationships between occupations and shareholding, based on a major study of 261 company share records for the period from 1870 to 1935.[72] The data are taken from a sample of 47 companies in seven different sectors and include information on the identity and occupational and marital status of shareholders drawn either from the share registers maintained continuously by companies or the Form Es they returned annually to the Registrar of Companies. In total, the study includes details of 33,848 individual shareholdings, based on a random sample of all shareholders in these companies.[73]

Occupations were recorded and grouped according to the HISCO system of classification.[74] This scheme has been developed by historians and sociologists

---

[69] Ibid., 440.   [70] Ibid.

[71] *Economist*, 30 March 1929, 691.

[72] The project was entitled 'Women Investors in England and Wales 1870 to 1930' and was funded by the UK Economic and Social Research Council, grant number RES 000-23-1435. Further details are available at http://www.womeninvestors.org.uk (site accessed 23 June 2010).

[73] For further discussion of the sample and sampling methodology, see Rutterford, J., D.R. Green, J. Maltby, and A. Owens 2011. 'Who comprised the nation of shareholders? Gender and investment in Great Britain c.1870–1935'. *Economic History Review* 64(1): 157–87; Rutterford, J., J. Maltby, D.R. Green, and A. Owens 2009. 'Researching shareholding and investment in England and Wales: approaches, sources and methods'. *Accounting History* 14(2): 269–92.

[74] See The History of Work Information System website – http://historyofwork.iisg.nl (site accessed 23 June 2010) – for an outline of the development of the scheme and van Leeuwen, M. H.D., I. Maas, and A. Miles 2007. *HISCO Historical International Standard Classification of Occupations*. Leuven: Leuven University Press.

to allow the classification of occupational titles into an organized system, based on evidence drawn from a number of European countries. HISCO allows occupations to be divided into nine 'major' groups including: (1) professional, technical, and related trades; (2) administrative and managerial; (3) clerical and related trades; (4) sales; (5) services; (6) agricultural, animal husbandry, forestry, fishermen, and hunters; (7) production and related workers; (8) transport equipment operators; and (9) labourers. In addition, a further group of elite shareholders was defined for this study based on the appellation of 'Gentleman' or 'Esquire' noted in the share records. The reason for doing so is because relatively large numbers of shareholders were defined in these terms. However, the term 'Gentleman' is ambiguous and may have been used as an indicator of social class, as a substitute for providing an occupation, or as an indication that the shareholder was 'a man of money and leisure . . . a socially respectable person who has no specific occupation or profession'.[75] It may also have been used to indicate an individual who had retired from business or some other occupation.

Using information provided in the share records, it was possible to classify the occupations of 14,524 individual holdings, or 57.1 per cent of the total number of shareholdings in the sample, into one of the nine groups outlined above plus the elite category, as shown in Table 8.5. This overall percentage declined over time from 78.5 per cent of entries in the 1870s to 46.8 per cent by the 1930s, decreasing as the average number of shareholdings per share record increased.[76] A significant number of shareholdings had no occupational category provided, most of which belonged to women whose marital status was often recorded in place of any occupational information. Of the 14,524

Table 8.5 Number of shareholdings with known and unknown HISCO codings

Decade	Unknown	Known	Total	Known (% total)
1870–9	174	651	825	78.9
1880–9	528	1352	1880	71.9
1890–9	1285	2710	3995	67.8
1900–10	2539	3838	6377	60.2
1910–19	3510	4100	7610	53.9
1920–9	3579	4117	7696	53.5
1930–9	2909	2556	5465	46.8
Total	14,524	19,324	33,848	57.1

Source: see text.

[75] Definitions are taken from *Oxford English Dictionary*, 2nd edition. Oxford: Oxford University Press, 1989.

[76] See Rutterford et al., 'Who comprised?' table 2.

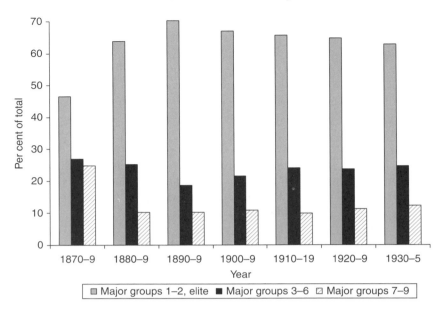

Figure 8.1 Composition of shareholders by HISCO major group, 1870–1935

Source: see text.

Note: A small number of shareholders were classified under HISCO major groups 10–12; these are not shown here. For further discussion of HISCO classification, see text.

shareholdings without an occupation noted, 11,176 or 76.9 per cent belonged to women. Female occupations were provided in 15.4 per cent of holdings in the 1870s but fell to a mere 2.7 per cent by the 1930s, possibly because the number of married women shareholders who were not in any form of paid employment increased over the period.[77] By contrast, the occupational recording of male shareholdings was much higher, ranging from 94.6 per cent of holdings in the 1870s to 87.0 per cent by the 1930s. Much of the decline in the overall recording of shareholder occupations, therefore, was due to the growing number of women shareholders – a phenomenon that we have noted elsewhere.[78]

If the argument about the democratization of shareholdings is to be believed, then the HISCO evidence should show a switch away from the elite and professional categories and towards occupational groups more typical of lower middle-class and working-class investors. Figure 8.1 shows the categories amalgamated into three broad groups: the first (major groups 1 to 2 and elite) includes the group consisting of titled investors, landed gentry, gentlemen, professionals, company directors, and owners, those in senior

[77] Ibid., table 5.   [78] See Rutterford et al., 'Who comprised?'

Table 8.6 Type of shareholding by HISCO major groups

Decade	% HISCO 1–2 elite	% HISCO 3–6	% HISCO 7–9
Ordinary shares (*N* = 11,683)			
1870–9	52.5	32.5	15.0
1880–9	64.2	27.1	8.7
1890–9	71.4	19.5	9.0
1900–10	68.9	22.2	8.9
1910–19	69.1	24.1	6.8
1920–9	75.0	19.2	5.8
1930–9	72.0	20.9	7.1
Preference shares (*N* = 5905)			
1870–9	n/a	n/a	n/a
1880–9	81.3	18.1	0.7
1890–9	82.2	15.9	1.9
1900–10	77.9	16.1	5.9
1910–19	76.8	18.3	4.9
1920–9	71.9	20.5	7.6
1930–9	64.0	24.2	11.8
Fixed interest securities (*N* = 1736)			
1870–9	79.7	14.4	5.9
1880–9	70.4	24.8	4.8
1890–9	88.5	8.2	3.4
1900–10	83.6	12.0	4.4
1910–19	86.8	9.1	4.2
1920–9	82.1	11.5	6.4
1930–9	100.0	0.0	0.0

Source: see text and Rutterford, J., J. Maltby, D.R. Green, and A. Owens 2009. 'Researching shareholding and investment in England and Wales: approaches, sources and methods'. *Accounting History* 14(2): 269–92.

administrative roles together with teachers and men in holy orders; the second (major groups 3–6) comprises primarily middle-ranking employees, in particular clerks; and the third (major groups 7–9) includes, *inter alia*, servants, labourers, factory workers, and miners. Contrary to the belief that the social spectrum of shareholding widened, the evidence shows that there was no decline in the importance of the top group over time. Indeed the importance of this category increased from the 1870s to the 1900s and then stabilized. Middle-ranking investors also declined from the 1870s and those at the lower end of the social spectrum always remained below 10 per cent throughout the period.

Although there is little evidence from the HISCO classifications for any democratization of the investor population, nevertheless the story is rather more complex than at first appears, particularly when share type is included in the analysis. Table 8.6 considers changes in occupational groupings broken down by type of shareholding. For ordinary shares, the top shareholder category increased in importance over the period, from 52.5 per cent of known occupation holdings in the 1870s to 72.0 per cent by the 1930s. This group also increased its share of holdings of fixed-interest securities. However, a stronger case for democratization can be proposed for preference shares, with this top category falling from 81.3 per cent in the 1880s to 64.0 per cent in the 1930s. In contrast, over the same period the middle-ranking category increased in importance from 18.1 to 24.2 per cent in the 1930s and the lower category rose from less than 1 to 11.8 per cent. Only with preference shares, therefore, do we see any sign of diffusion of holdings amongst a wider range of investors. Part of the explanation for this trend refers to the growing popularity of preference shares, noted above, in the later nineteenth and early twentieth centuries. Between 1885 and 1915, a sample of some 2500 British companies found that preference shares rose from 12.2 to 30 per cent of issued capital.[79] They offered the issuing companies funding without dilution of control, as they were often shares without voting rights, and they gave shareholders a guaranteed return, without the risks potentially attached to equity. This was likely to appeal particularly to new or inexperienced and non-traditional investors, which helps to explain why this type of share attracted investors from a wider social spectrum than was the case with ordinary shares.

Of course, the large number of 'unknowns' prevents clear conclusions being drawn and there were different experiences in individual companies. For example, the registers of some companies, such as the City of Ely Gas Company and J.S. Fry, the chocolate manufacturers, suggest the increasing importance of the lower occupational groups over time. In Bon Marché, for example, a London retail department store, this group of investors disappear as holders of ordinary shares in 1923 but they subsequently reappear as preference shareholders. In Boots, between 1893 and 1930 the lower group maintains its importance for preference shareholding but for the Ceylon Cocoa and Rubber Company it falls sharply over time. However, with the sole exception of preference issues, the evidence does not show any general, consistent, and growing trend for non-traditional investors to buy shares.

CONCLUSION

The evidence provided by companies' share records and summarized above does not suggest a consistent shift in the social class of share ownership over the period under review. Where investors are classified in company records, the professional, managerial, and 'gentleman' categories remain predominant.

---

[79] See Essex-Crosby, 'Joint stock companies in Great Britain'.

The democratization of investment ownership does not appear to have increased over the later nineteenth and early twentieth centuries, despite the arguments put forward by several commentators at the time. This final section of the chapter discusses why democratization failed and the reasons why it was nevertheless claimed to have occurred.

Several factors may have contributed to the failure of democratization. One important reason was the lack of continuing support for co-partnership schemes which, had they been pursued more vigorously and spread more widely, had considerable potential for promoting the take-up of shares by company employees. They were aimed directly at workers, without the need for them to use intermediaries, such as stockbrokers, to make investments. They were also often offered at less than market price, or might not necessarily have required a cash payment. However, profit-sharing schemes of all types were fragile creations for which 'the probability of abandonment increased with the duration of the scheme' and their success was more likely to be related to the context of particular firms than to the benefits they offered in general.[80] For these reasons, it is unlikely that company schemes acted as a way of popularizing share ownership outside the setting of the employing firm.

The suggestion was also made that investment in war bonds was likely to have encouraged wider share ownership. It was indeed the case that War Loans had been successfully promoted in settings where traditional investments were not available, such as schools, shops, and social clubs. But it seems likely that their effect was to encourage further investment in government stock, rather than in private company shares. Savings certificates remained attractive after the First World War and were, as Wormell pointed out, 'protected against depreciation (and) repayable on demand' at a time when other types of security, a senior Treasury official commented in 1932, were 'under a cloud'.[81] Purchase of shares for individuals was also more tightly in the hands of stockbrokers in the United Kingdom than in the United States, where a national distribution system was in operation by the late 1920s. A sophisticated system of marketing of securities across the United States had been put in place, building on both the strategies adopted in the First World War to sell Liberty Bonds and on corporate strategies to sell shares to customers and employees.[82] The United Kingdom did not make a similar use of War Savings as a starting-point for share ownership.

Leaving aside any increase in real wealth that might have been directed into savings and investments, as the population of Great Britain increased from

[80] Hatton, 'Profit sharing in British industry', 69.
[81] Wormell, *Management of the National Debt*, 610, 629.
[82] Ott, J. 2007. 'From new proprietorship to new era: marking a shareholders' democracy in the United States, 1919–1929'. Economic Department Colloquium, New School for Social Research (New York), unpublished paper.

26.7 to 44.8 million between 1871 and 1931, a rise of 68 per cent, similar growth in the population of shareholders might also have been expected.[83] Shareholder numbers, though, did not increase over the period in line with population growth. What did change was the average size of shareholding, and there was an increase in the percentages of small shareholders in any one company, as noted by the *Economist* in the series of articles published in 1926 and 1927 that pointed out the growing numbers of investors holding less than £500 or £100.[84] This paradox can be explained by diversification, as investors sought to spread risk across a larger number of shares, the number varying according to the wealth of the individual.[85] This trend was further encouraged by companies that made small issues of a variety of shares, such as the different types of preference shares issued by Boots and J. Lyons noted above. The availability of these new shares to existing shareholders via rights issues made it possible for investors to take up a wider range of small holdings.

Contrary to popular belief, therefore, both at the time and since, the evidence for democratization of the shareholding population is relatively thin. The pattern identified by the *Economist* in 1926 and 1927 seems not to have been the arrival in the share market of a new group of non-traditional investors, but rather a change in behaviour by the classes who had been investors from the mid- to late nineteenth century onwards. Despite the growing numbers of lower middle-class and working-class savers, and the limited attempt to promote various employee schemes, in terms of social class the democratization of share ownership remained confined largely to holders of preference shares. To the extent that this type of share issue grew in importance, so too did the social composition of the shareholding population widen, both in relation to gender and occupational group. But outside this limited expansion, for the period under consideration the socio-economic composition of the nation of shareholders hardly changed at all.

---

[83] Mitchell, B.R. and P. Deane 1962. *Abstract of British Historical Statistics*. Cambridge: Cambridge University Press, 6.

[84] *Economist*, 18 December 1926: 1054–5; 25 December 1926: 1108–9; 1 January 1927: 12–13.

[85] See Lowenfeld, H. 1909. *All About Investment*, 2nd edition. London: Financial Review of Reviews, 270.

9

Shareholder Liability, Risk Aversion, and Investment Returns in Nineteenth-Century British Banking

Graeme G. Acheson and John D. Turner

INTRODUCTION

The British equity market experienced rapid growth in the nineteenth century, with the capitalization of the London market alone growing from approximately £45 million in 1825 to £285 million in 1870.[1] Accompanying this market growth was the increasing democratization of share ownership, with the newly politically enfranchised and increasingly prosperous middle classes investing their savings in the equity markets rather than in low-yielding Consols.[2] However, many equity securities in this nascent market had features such as extended shareholder liability (where a shareholder's liability for the firm's debt was extended beyond their investment of capital in the firm) and high share denominations, both of which may have discouraged such individuals from investing in equity.[3] Extended shareholder

Thanks to the Economic and Social Research Council (Award Number: RES-000-22-1391) for financial support. Research assistance was provided by Jonny McCollum, Lei Qu, and Nadia Vanteeva. Thanks also to Qing Ye for her invaluable input to this chapter. John Turner also acknowledges financial support provided by the trustees of the Houblon-Norman Fund and a British Academy Grant (G-36598).

[1] Estimates are from Acheson, G.G., C.R. Hickson, J.D. Turner, and Q. Ye 2009. 'Rule Britannia!: British stock market returns, 1825–1870'. *Journal of Economic History* 69(4): 1107–37. These figures ignore foreign railways. Grossman, R.S. 2002. 'New indices of British equity prices, 1870–1913'. *Journal of Economic History* 62(1): 121–46 estimates the total value of the London and regional equity markets in 1870 to be *c.* £ 750m.

[2] Gayer, A.D., W.W. Rostow, and J.A. Schwartz 1953. *The Growth and Fluctuation of the British Economy*. Oxford: Clarendon Press, 377, 380, 410. For further discussion of this theme, see Chapter 8 in this volume.

[3] On this issue, see Jefferys, J.B. 1946. 'The denomination and character of shares, 1855–1885'. *Economic History Review* 16(1): 45–55; and Jefferys, J.B. 1977. *Business Organisation in Great*

liability, as well as making diversification more costly, may have discouraged some of these new investors from acquiring such stock due to the large potential downside arising from the liability.[4] Extensions of shareholder liability were most common in the banking, finance, and insurance sectors.[5] In these areas it was common for companies to have unlimited shareholder liability and shares with permanent uncalled capital.[6] In the first instance, this chapter examines the prevalence and nature of extended shareholder liability in banking, the largest of these three sectors. It then goes on to explore the extent to which women, arguably the most risk-averse investor category, invested in bank stock. Using evidence from the shareholder constituencies of 23 banks, we find that women's ownership of unlimited liability bank stock was substantial in the second half of the nineteenth century. This raises the intriguing question as to why risk-averse investors owned such stock. Three possibilities are investigated. The first explanation is that bank stock was de facto limited and therefore was not overly risky. However, we argue that legal and company-level institutional mechanisms prevented bank stock from being or becoming de facto limited. The second explanation investigated is that bank stock was less risky than other types of stock because banks were governed in a very prudent and conservative fashion due to the presence of extended liability. However, the experience of bank failures and risk measures calculated using a version of the Capital Asset Pricing Model suggest that this may not have been the case. The final explanation which is explored is that bank stock paid higher returns than other stock, and thus offered risk-averse investors a sufficient risk premium to encourage them to invest in the shares. Using share price and dividend data for the period 1825–70, we find that bank stock earned higher returns than the overall market, thus compensating investors for the downside risk which they faced.

This chapter is structured as follows. Section 2 examines the evolution of shareholder liability in British banking. Section 3 examines the extent to which women were present in the shareholder constituencies of joint-stock banks in the second half of the nineteenth century. The fourth section analyses the

---

Britain 1856–1914. New York, NY: Arno Press. High share denominations may have made it costly for investors to hold diversified portfolios, thus increasing their risk. See Hickson, C.R. and J.D. Turner 2003. 'Shareholder liability regimes in English banking: the impact upon the market for shares'. *European Review of Economic History* 7(1): 99–125.

[4] Kaisanlahti, T.H. 2006. 'Extended liability of shareholders'. *Journal of Corporate Law Studies* 6(1): 139–63.

[5] See Jefferys, 'The denomination and character' and Hickson, C.R., J.D. Turner, and Q. Ye 2011. 'The rate of return on equity across industrial sectors on the British equity market, 1825–70'. *Economic History Review* published online 18 February 2011.

[6] Investors in new railways typically faced extensions of liability beyond paid-up capital as the railway company only required a small proportion of nominal capital to be initially paid in. However, as railway construction progressed, the uncalled proportion of capital was gradually called up until there was nothing left unpaid on the shares.

various explanations as to why bank stock was popular with risk-averse investors such as women. The final section summarizes our findings.

THE EVOLUTION OF SHAREHOLDER LIABILITY IN BRITISH BANKING

In the mid-1820s, only the owners of the five publicly chartered banks enjoyed the privilege of limited liability; that is the liability of shareholders to creditors was limited to the capital they had invested in the bank.[7] Under the influence of the common law, other banks in Britain were restricted to the partnership organizational form, with the consequence that bank owners had unlimited liability.[8] In other words, a bank owner was liable for the debts of their bank right down to their last sixpence should the bank fail. Following the post-Napoleonic-war financial turmoil, legislation was enacted which permitted joint-stock banks to incorporate.[9] However, the shareholders of British joint-stock banks still faced unlimited liability. In contrast, up until the 1862 Companies Act, double shareholder liability was usually made a condition of the grant of a charter to an overseas or colonial bank by the Board of Trade.[10] The Board of Trade may have found it expedient to grant such privileges to colonial and overseas banks because of the contribution they made to imperial expansion. Alternatively, British investors may have been very reluctant to invest in an unlimited liability bank operating in distant lands.

Unlimited liability appears to have played an important role in assuring bank depositors (and note-holders) as to the safety of their bank.[11] The personal wealth of shareholders would have given confidence to depositors and note-holders that their funds would not be expropriated because, as noted

---

[7] Bank of England (1694), Bank of Scotland (1695), Royal Bank of Scotland (1727), British Linen Company Bank (1746), Bank of Ireland (1783).

[8] A consequence of the flexibility of Scottish partnership law was that banks in Scotland enjoyed a quasi-joint-stock form in the eighteenth century. See Munn, C.W. 1981. *The Scottish Provincial Banking Companies, 1747–1864*. Edinburgh: John Donald Publishers.

[9] Irish Banking Co-partnership Regulation Act, 1825, 6 Geo. IV, c.42; Banking Co-partnership Act, 1826, 7 Geo. IV, c.46.

[10] Double liability meant that a shareholder's liability for the debts of the bank were twice what they had invested in the bank; see Hunt, B.C. 1936. *The Development of the Business Corporation in England, 1800–1867*. Cambridge, MA: Harvard University Press, 59. See also Baster, A.S.J. 1977. *The International Banks*. New York, NY: Staples Press, 10; Jones, G. 1993. *British Multinational Banking, 1830–1990*. Oxford: Clarendon Press, 18–20.

[11] See Hickson, C.R. and J.D. Turner 2004. 'Free banking and the stability of early joint-stock banking'. *Cambridge Journal of Economics* 28(6): 903–19; Hickson, C.R. and J.D. Turner 2003. 'The trading of unlimited liability bank shares in nineteenth-century Ireland: the Bagehot Hypothesis'. *Journal of Economic History* 63(4): 931–58; Hickson and Turner, 'Shareholder liability regimes'.

Table 9.1 Capital of English banks (1874)

	Unlimited liability banks	Limited liability banks
Uncalled capital/liabilities to public (%)		
Mean	24.8	64.8
Median	13.9	50.6
Standard deviation	31.4	37.6
Paid-up capital/liabilities to public (%)		
Mean	13.4	29.6
Median	10.1	25.2
Standard deviation	8.5	22.3
Paid-up capital + shareholder reserves/liabilities to public (%)		
Mean	20.3	37.2
Median	15.8	30.5
Standard deviation	12.4	24.5
Total shareholder resources/liabilities to public (%)		
Mean	45.0	100.1
Median	31.9	88.4
Standard deviation	39.7	53.3
N	30	33

Source: Authors' calculations based on data contained in Dun, 'The banking institutions'.

Note: Only 63 English banks issued financial reports. Of these, only 55 reported the breakdown of their assets. All the major banks issued reports, and therefore, only small banks are omitted from the above ratios. Total shareholder resources comprise uncalled capital, paid-up capital, and shareholder reserves. The difference in means for each variable is statistically significant with *p*-values equal to zero in each case.

above, in the event of bank failure, shareholders were liable right down to their last 'acre and sixpence'.[12] Indeed, banks were initially excluded from the provisions of the Joint Stock Companies Act of 1856, which granted businesses the freedom to adopt limited liability, due principally to concerns about depositor safety.[13] It was only after the passage of legislation in 1857 and 1858 that banks were permitted to adopt limited liability. Subsequently, by 1875, there were 42 relatively small limited liability banks in England, one in Ireland and none in Scotland.[14] Yet significantly, the majority of the established banks did not adopt limited liability for a further two decades.[15] One explanation given by a contemporary banking expert was that unlimited

---

[12] Indeed, one would expect that depositors would be risk averse, and would therefore require high levels of aggregate shareholder wealth before they would deposit their money.

[13] Joint Stock Companies Act, 1856, 19 & 20 Vict. c.47. On this point, see Alborn, T.L. 1998. *Conceiving Companies: Joint-Stock Politics in Victorian England*. London: Routledge, 129.

[14] Dun, J. 1876. 'The banking institutions, bullion reserves, and non-legal-tender note circulation of the United Kingdom statistically investigated'. *Journal of the Statistical Society* 39(1): 26.

[15] Sayers, R.S. 1957. *Lloyds Bank in the History of English Banking*. Oxford: Clarendon Press, 222.

liability was 'thought by the shareholders more conducive to profit, and by the depositors, more likely to give safety'.[16] He went on to argue that

> unlimited banks had an enormous advantage over their competitors in the struggle for deposits. A depositor would be much more likely to trust his money with a bank whose shareholders he knew must yield up to him the uttermost farthing that they possessed, in making good losses should the bank fail, than with a bank whose shareholders were liable only to the amount uncalled on their shares.[17]

These newly established limited liability banks, in order to compete with their unlimited rivals, had to assure depositors as to the security of their deposits. As can be seen from Table 9.1, as a proportion of liabilities to the public, limited banks had substantially more uncalled capital, paid-up capital, and shareholder reserves.[18] Indeed, it is notable that for the average limited bank, liabilities to the public were matched on a one-for-one basis by shareholder resources.[19] The uncalled margin on shares was a form of extended liability, and, from the depositors' viewpoint, it was argued that it would have made the limited banks 'practically as safe as an unlimited bank'.[20]

Most established British banks converted to limited liability in the period 1879–83. The standard view is that the failure of the City of Glasgow Bank in October 1878 and the subsequent bankruptcy of 1565 of its 1819 shareholders undermined confidence in the unlimited liability joint-stock bank.[21] As a result of this failure, there was a concern that shares in unlimited banks would no longer be held by wealthy individuals. For example, a contemporary law professor suggested that 'fear has been entertained that in consequence of

---

[16] Wilson, A. 1879. *Banking Reform: An Essay on the Prominent Dangers and the Remedies they Demand.* London: Longmans, Green and Co., 69.

[17] Wilson, *Banking Reform*, 71. A similar view is given in Crick, W.F. and J.E. Wadsworth 1936. *A Hundred Years of Joint Stock Banking.* London: Hodder and Stoughton, 31.

[18] Shareholder reserves are problematic for students of British banking because many banks held 'hidden reserves', which acted as a buffer in difficult times, without the knowledge of depositors. It was believed that disclosure of fluctuations in these reserves could undermine depositor confidence at vital times.

[19] Thirteen out of the 33 limited banks in our sample have ratios of total shareholder resources/liabilities to the public exceeding 1. Some 29 out of the 33 banks have ratios exceeding 0.5; the ratios of the remaining four banks are: 0.46, 0.34, 0.29, and 0.25.

[20] Dun, 'The banking institutions', 28.

[21] Checkland, S. 1975. *Scottish Banking: A History, 1695–1973.* Glasgow: Collins, 471; Evans, L.T. and N.C. Quigley 1995. 'Shareholder liability regimes, principal-agent relationships, and banking industry performance'. *Journal of Law and Economics* 38(2): 497–520; White, L.H. 1995. *Free Banking in Britain: Theory, Experience and Debate 1800–1845*, 2nd edition. London: Institute of Economic Affairs, 501 and 507; Collins, M. 1989. 'The banking crisis of 1878'. *Economic History Review* 42(4): 504–27. The City of Glasgow failure has been described as 'the last serious deposit bank failure in the UK'. See Collins, M. 1991. *Banks and Industrial Finance in Britain, 1800–1939.* Cambridge: Cambridge University Press.

recent disasters not a few wealthy shareholders in our unlimited banks may be led to throw aside their excessive responsibility by the sale of their shares'.[22] This sentiment was also expressed at the time by the Chairman of the London and County Bank who stated that, 'it is simple nonsense that people will, after they consider the matter, continue to hold shares in an unlimited bank'.[23] This more sceptical view was also articulated in a communication to the Editor of the *Bankers' Magazine*, where it was argued that 'no wealthy man will on any account hold a share in an unlimited bank, and therefore the proprietary and consequently the standing of the bank will deteriorate, and once on the descent the fall will be rapid'.[24] Of course the end result of this would be that 'unlimited liability would be no security at all'.[25] In turn, this would undermine depositor confidence in the safety of their bank.[26]

Evans and Quigley have suggested that the City of Glasgow failure revealed to depositors that the shares of unlimited liability banks had been diffused to shareholders of modest means, and this provided an impetus for banks to move to limited liability.[27] However, their view has several flaws. First, no depositor lost any money as a result of the failure. Second, a recent study provides evidence that the ownership of bank stock had not been diffused to owners of modest means prior to the failure.[28] Third, there was strong opposition against moving to limited liability from bank directors and the general public.[29]

An alternative explanation as to why banks converted to limited liability at this time is that depositors were now given implicit protection by the Bank of England. After Bagehot's *Lombard Street* was published in 1873, 'every student of the subject was brought up on the doctrine that the Bank had an inescapable duty as lender of last resort irrespective of anything said in the Bank Charter Act'.[30] However, the Bagehotian lender of last resort did not provide implicit

[22] Levi, L. 1880. 'The reconstruction of joint stock banks on the principle of limited liability'. *The Bankers' Magazine* 40: 468–79.

[23] Gregory, T.E. 1936. *The Westminster Bank Through a Century*, Volume 1. London: Westminster Bank, 212.

[24] Anon 1880. 'Reasons in favour of limited liability for joint-stock banks'. *The Bankers' Magazine* 40: 55–9.

[25] Ibid., 56.

[26] Clapham, J.H. 1944. *The Bank of England: A History*. London: Cambridge University Press, 311.

[27] Evans and Quigley, 'Shareholder liability regimes', 507.

[28] See Acheson, G.G. and J.D. Turner 2008. 'The death blow to unlimited liability in Victorian Britain: the City of Glasgow failure'. *Explorations in Economic History* 45(3): 235–53. Furthermore, George Rae, the famous banking expert, believed that the fear of wealthy shareholders rapidly exiting banks was greatly exaggerated. See Rae, G. 1885. *The Country Banker: His Clients, Cares, and Work From an Experience of Forty Years*. London: John Murray, 257.

[29] Sykes, J. 1926. *The Amalgamation Movement in English Banking, 1825–1924*. London: P.S. King and Son, 38.

[30] Sayers, R.S. 1976. *The Bank of England: 1891–1944*. Cambridge: Cambridge University Press, 3. However, it is claimed that up until 1914, bankers faced uncertainty as to 'whether and

deposit insurance, rather it provided liquidity support at a penal rate to banks with suitable collateral.[31] Even though the Bank of England led the bailout of Barings in 1890 and cajoled other banks into contributing to the bailout package, there is little evidence to suggest that it would have done the same for the majority of joint-stock banks.

A further explanation as to why banks only converted to limited liability at this time was that the Companies Act of 1879 aided the conversion to limited liability of the established joint-stock banks.[32] The provisions of this Act enabled banks to adopt limited liability and concurrently provide adequate security to depositors by creating 'reserve liability', whereby the unpaid portion of bank shares was to be divided into two parts, one being callable at the directors' discretion, and the other callable *only* in the event of bankruptcy.[33] In reality, reserve liability was a form of extended liability, which made shareholders liable for a multiple of paid-up capital. George Rae, one of the architects of reserve liability, stated that the idea of the 1879 Act was to enable banks to 'set aside and hypothecate a certain portion of its registered capital, as an inalienable fund for the protection of its depositors'.[34]

By 1884, 80 joint-stock banks had moved from unlimited liability to reserve liability, with only nine banks maintaining their unlimited status. The average and median reserve liability as a multiple of paid-up capital were 2.963 and 2.825, respectively.[35] Although not every bank had reserve liability, the largest banks typically did, and, in England, most of the smaller limited banks were subsumed into these larger entities during the amalgamation process.[36]

Although reserve liability as well as uncalled capital may have provided credible alternatives to unlimited liability, the assurance they gave depositors

---

when and how the Bank might so act to check a crisis'; see Pressnell, L. 1970. 'Cartels and competition in British banking: a background study'. *Banca Nazionale Del Lavoro Quarterly Review* 95(4): 379.

[31] Capie, F. 1995. 'Commercial banking in Britain between the wars'. In *Banking, Currency, and Finance in Europe between the Wars*, edited by C.H. Feinstein. Oxford: Clarendon Press, 401.

[32] The Companies Act, 1879, 42 & 43 Vict., c.76. On this theme, see Crick and Wadsworth, *Hundred Years*, 33. Gregory, *Westminster Bank*, volume 1, 206.

[33] Levi, 'The reconstruction of joint stock banks'. Indeed, reserve liability was generally viewed as a compromise between those who wanted pure limited liability and those wanting unlimited liability; see Collins, M. 1988. *Money and Banking in the United Kingdom: A History*. London: Croom Helm, 101.

[34] Rae, *The Country Banker*, 258.

[35] Figures calculated from data contained in the *Banking Almanac and Yearbook*, 1885.

[36] Barclays Bank, which eventually became one of the 'Big Five' banks, did not have reserve liability as it was only formed in 1896. See Matthews, P.W. and A.W. Tuke 1926. *History of Barclays Bank Limited*. London: Blades, East and Blades; and Ackrill, M. and L. Hannah 2001. *Barclays: The Business of Banking 1690–1996*. Cambridge: Cambridge University Press, chapter 1. However, it had more capital and reserves than its rivals. For example, in 1915, its paid-up capital plus shareholder reserves:deposits ratio was 8.4 per cent, compared to an average of 7.5 per cent for the other members of the 'Big Five'.

Table 9.2 Liability regimes and shareholders in British banking, 1849–89

	1849	1869	1889
England and Wales			
Number limited liability banks (state-charter)	1	1	1
Number unlimited liability joint-stock banks	113	73	2
Number limited liability joint-stock banks	—	41	40
Number reserve liability joint-stock banks	—	—	62
Number of shareholders	22,031	40,583	95,701
Ireland			
Number limited liability banks (state-charter)	1	1	1
Number unlimited liability joint-stock banks	10	7	0
Number limited liability joint-stock banks	—	1	0
Number reserve liability joint-stock banks	—	—	8
Number of shareholders	3,083	8,487	20,226
Scotland			
Number limited liability banks (state-charter)	3	3	3
Number unlimited liability joint-stock banks	18	9	0
Number limited liability joint-stock banks	—	0	0
Number reserve liability joint-stock banks	—	—	7
Number of shareholders	11,157	10,865	19,192

Source: Banking Almanac and Yearbook, 1850, 1870, 1890.

Note: Shareholder numbers were not reported for a small proportion of banks.

may have been substantially weakened during the first two decades of the twentieth century. Firstly, the growth of shareholder numbers may have undermined the credibility and feasibility of reserve liability and uncalled capital.[37] Secondly, the numerous amalgamation schemes typically led to the writing-down of reserve liability and uncalled capital.[38] By 1937, only six relatively small British banks still had reserve liability, with the Deputy Governor of the Bank of England being sceptical as to its value, arguing that it was 'a survival from the time when banks were smaller and numerous; today a bank could not in a crisis make a call on shareholders without aggravating the crisis'.[39]

[37] In 1921, shareholder numbers of the 'Big Five' were as follows: Barclays (46,500), Lloyds (56,000), London Joint City and Midland (52,052), London County Westminster and Parr's (74,000), National Provincial and Union Bank of England (38,000); figures are taken from the *Bankers' Almanac and Yearbook*, 1921. Notably, Holden's evidence to the Colwyn Committee indicated that due to the amalgamation process, small shareholders had actually increased their importance in the ownership of British banks. Unsurprisingly, the majority of shareholders were individuals of modest means; see Sykes, *The Amalgamation Movement*, 141.

[38] Treasury Committee on Bank Amalgamations 1918. *Report of the Treasury Committee on Bank Amalgamations*. London: His Majesty's Stationery Office, 5. For example, the amalgamation of the National Provincial Bank of England with the Union of London and Smith's Bank lead to a reduction of 48 per cent in the reserve liability of the Union's shareholders.

[39] Bank of England Archives (BoE hereafter) C48/61 – Capital of the Bank of Scotland – secret memo dated 27 October 1937. The six banks were Martins, Williams Deacon's, District, National, Bank of Scotland, and Commercial Bank of Scotland.

In summary, as can be seen from Table 9.2, during the nineteenth century, the large number of investors in British banks faced a variety of shareholder liability regimes. Indeed, the number of banks which had *pure* limited liability was essentially restricted to the five chartered banks as the other limited banks in Table 9.2 usually had uncalled capital. The vast majority of bank shareholders faced unlimited liability until the early 1880s, and even after the general limitation of liability, shareholder liability was still extended beyond paid-up capital in the form of reserve liability and uncalled capital.

WOMEN'S OWNERSHIP OF BANK STOCK

If an investor is risk averse, they will prefer the actuarial value of a gamble with certainty rather than the gamble itself.[40] This does not mean that risk-averse individuals do not take risk; it simply means that they need to be offered a higher risk premium than other individuals to bear a certain level of risk. Women have long been recognized as one of the most risk-averse group of investors.[41] This was particularly evident in the nineteenth century when the equity market was in its infancy, and female investors were generally reluctant to invest.[42] This does not mean that women investors did not take risk, but that they needed a higher risk premium than other investors before they would invest in risky equity. One would therefore expect to see few female shareholders in the constituencies of British joint-stock banks as investors in such companies potentially stood to lose all their wealth in the event of bankruptcy. Recent research by Lucy Newton and Philip Cottrell has concurred with this perspective by suggesting that females were not that common among English joint-stock bank shareholders.[43] However, they argue that this should not be taken as an indication of timidity or their aversion to risk. Rather it appears

---

[40] In other words, a risk-averse investor will prefer £10 for sure rather than a gamble with the following payoffs: £100 (10 per cent of the time) and £0 (90 per cent of the time).

[41] Dwyer, P.D., J.H. Gilkeson, and J.A. List 2002. 'Gender differences in revealed risk taking: Evidence from mutual fund investors'. *Economics Letters* 76(2): 151–8; Bajtelsmit, V.L. and A. Bernasek 1999. 'Gender differences in defined contribution pension decisions'. *Financial Services Review* 8(1): 1–10; Rutterford, J. and J. Maltby. 2006. '"The widow, the clergyman and the reckless": women investors in England 1830–1914'. *Feminist Economics* 12(1/2): 113; Jianako-poulos, N.A. and A. Bernasek 1998. 'Are women more risk averse?' *Economic Inquiry* 36(4): 620–1; Rutterford, J. and J. Maltby. 2007. '"The nesting instinct": women and investment risk in an historical context'. *Accounting History* 12(3): 306–7.

[42] Newton, L. and P.L. Cottrell 2006. 'Female investors in the first English and Welsh commercial joint-stock banks'. *Accounting, Business and Financial History* 16(2): 326 and 332; Reed, M.C. 1975. *Investment in Railways in Britain 1820–1844: A Study in the Development of the Capital Market*. Oxford: Oxford University Press, 203–4; Rutterford and Maltby, '"The nesting instinct"', 306–7.

[43] Newton and Cottrell, 'Female investors'.

Table 9.3 Female ownership of bank shares in the second half of the nineteenth century

Bank (year established)	Sample year	Female shareholders	
		% of total owners	% of total capital
London-based banks			
London Joint Stock Bank (1836)	1856	30.3	17.4
London & County Bank (1836)	1878	31.9	—
National Provincial Bank of England (1833)	1878	35.4	—
Union Bank of London (1839)	1878	29.4	—
English provincial banks			
Huddersfield Banking Co. (1827)	1847	17.1	10.3
Barnsley Banking Co. (1831)	1851	8.8	7.3
Bank of Westmorland (1833)	1853	10.3	23.3
Wilts & Dorset (1836)	1853	13.6	10.0
Manchester & Liverpool District Bank (1829)	1856	24.5	—
Sheffield & Rotherham Banking Co. (1836)	1856	7.9	3.0
Swadedale & Wensleydale Banking Co. (1836)	1856	21.1	11.5
Birmingham & Midland (1836)	1859	15.3	6.8
Wilts & Dorset (1836)	1860	27.5	—
Yorkshire Banking Co. (1843)	1864	20.2	11.8
Birmingham Town & District (1836)	1866	26.6	—
North and South Wales Bank (1836)	1874	26.3	16.4
Bank of Liverpool (1831)	1879	25.7	12.3
Manchester & Liverpool District Bank (1829)	1882	26.8	—
North and South Wales Bank (1836)	1890	26.1	23.9
Bank of Liverpool (1831)	1894	28.6	15.1
Irish banks			
Ulster Banking Co. (1836)	1878	32.2	27.0
	1892	39.3	31.7
Scottish public banks			
Bank of Scotland (1695)	1878	30.8	—
Royal Bank of Scotland (1727)	1878	27.9	—
Scottish joint-stock banks			
Caledonian Banking Co. (1838)	1878	28.8	20.9
City of Glasgow Bank (1839)	1878	15.7	8.9
Clydesdale Bank (1838)	1878	29.3	—
National Bank of Scotland (1825)	1878	34.2	—

Source: Acheson and Turner, 'The impact of limited liability': Ulster Banking Co. (1892). Acheson and Turner, 'The death blow to unlimited liability': Bank of Scotland (1878); Royal Bank of Scotland (1878); National Bank of Scotland (1878); City of Glasgow Bank (1878); Clydesdale Bank (1878); Caledonian Banking Co. (1878); Ulster Banking Co. (1878); North and South Wales Bank (1874); National Provincial Bank of England (1878); London & County Bank (1878); Union Bank of London (1878). Cottrell and Newton, 'Female investors': Bank of Westmorland (1853); Barnsley Banking Co. (1851); Birmingham & Midland (1859); Huddersfield Banking Co. (1847); London Joint Stock Bank (1856); Sheffield & Rotherham Banking Co. (1856); Swadedale & Wensleydale Banking Co. (1856); Wilts & Dorset (1853); Yorkshire Banking Co. (1864). Turner, J.D. 2009. 'Wider share ownership? Investors in English and Welsh Bank shares in the nineteenth century'. *Economic History Review* 62(s1): 167–92: Bank of Liverpool (1879, 1894); Birmingham Town & District (1866); Manchester & Liverpool District Bank (1856 and 1882); Wilts & Dorset (1860); North and South Wales Bank (1890).

that female investors may have been crowded out of bank constituencies by local commercial and industrial interests.[44]

Similarly, it appears that female investors were not that common amongst the constituencies of Scottish joint-stock banks even by the mid-1840s.[45] Notably, however, they were much more frequently found amongst the constituencies of the limited liability public banks in Scotland. This difference could again be explained by female investors being crowded out of the joint-stock banks which were established to meet the needs of the rapidly expanding commercial and industrial sector. Alternatively, female investors may have been exhibiting their high risk aversion by steering clear of the shares of the recently formed unlimited liability joint-stock banks. Another possible reason as to why females were not common amongst the constituencies of early unlimited joint-stock banks is that bank promoters only wanted wealthy businessmen, landowners, professionals, and gentry in the shareholding population so as to assure note-holders and depositors of a bank's good-standing and trustworthiness.

Although female shareholders may not have been prevalent in the constituencies of early joint-stock banks, we can observe from Table 9.3 that female ownership of joint-stock bank shares was substantial by the 1850s. The average constituency in the 1850s consisted of close to 17.3 per cent female shareholders, holding 11.3 per cent of the capital. As can be seen from Table 9.3, the proportion of female shareholders in banks had expanded greatly by the 1870s – females constituted 31.6 per cent of the average shareholder constituency.

In contrast to the substantial number of female shareholders in many joint-stock constituencies by the 1870s, only 15.7 per cent of the City of Glasgow Bank's shareholders were women, and they only owned 8.9 per cent of the bank's capital. Unlike its peers, this Glasgow bank was an aggressive and high-risk institution right from its inception.[46] For example, the bank typically carried few secondary reserves, it was active in international financing via the discount market, it invested a great deal in an American railroad and in a New Zealand land speculation company, and its loan portfolio was heavily concentrated, with many loans having inadequate collateral.[47] It also appears that the City of Glasgow Bank was viewed by its peers as a risky institution.[48] Hence, it is maybe not surprising that females invested less in the shares of this bank than they did in the stock of other banks.

---

[44] Newton and Cottrell, 'Female investors', 319.

[45] Acheson, G.G. and J.D. Turner forthcoming. 'Investor behaviour in a nascent capital market: Scottish bank shareholders in the nineteenth century'. *Economic History Review.*

[46] Checkland, *Scottish Banking*, 469; French, E.A. 1985. *Unlimited Liability: The Case of the City of Glasgow Bank*. London: Certified Accountant Publications, 8.

[47] Checkland, *Scottish Banking*, 470–1; French, *Unlimited Liability*, 8.

[48] See Wilson, *Banking Reform*, 52; Clapham, *The Bank of England*, Volume 2, 309.

Table 9.3 also contains two public Scottish banks, which had limited liability from their inception. One can clearly see that these banks had similar levels of females in their ownership constituency in 1878 as their Scottish joint-stock counterparts (apart from the City of Glasgow Bank). This would suggest that the unlimited liability of the joint-stock banks did not discourage females from investing in large numbers. However, Table 9.3 also contains the proportion of females in shareholder constituencies for three banks in the 1890s, which had had limited liability for at least 12 years. Although the Bank of Liverpool sees some slight increase in terms of the proportion of owners and capital, the female ownership of the North and South Wales Bank increases from 16.4 to 23.9 per cent of capital by 1890, and by 1892, nearly 40 per cent of Ulster Bank shareholders are female. These increases could be due to women investors viewing the shares of these banks as being less risky. Alternatively, a supply-side explanation is more likely in that the removal of unlimited liability permitted these banks to open their ownership to individuals from a broader social and wealth spectrum.[49]

At the outset of this section, we stated that from a theoretical perspective one would not typically expect risk-averse individuals such as females to invest in stock which carried unlimited liability. However, the evidence presented above suggests that they did – females were by far the largest socio-occupational group in most joint-stock banks by the 1870s. The next section will attempt to explain this phenomenon.

RISK AND RETURN

Banks were de facto limited

One possibility as to why risk-averse investors were happy to own bank stock is that banks may have been de facto limited. In other words, stock in extended liability banks may have been owned by individuals whose wealth consisted only of their investment in the bank's stock. Indeed, it appears that some contemporaries believed that this was the case. For example, William Clay, the parliamentarian, argued that 'unlimited liability has a tendency to deter persons of fortune, intelligence, and respectability, from becoming partners or managers of joint-stock banks'.[50] Similarly, General Austin, managing

[49] Acheson, G.G. and J. D. Turner 2006. 'The impact of limited liability on ownership and control: Irish banking, 1877–1914'. *Economic History Review* 59(2): 320–46.

[50] Clay, W. 1837. *Speech of William Clay, Esq., M.P. on Moving for the Appointment of a Committee to Inquire into the Operation of the Act Permitting the Establishment of Joint-stock Banks. To Which are Added, Reflections on Limited Liability, Paid-up Capital, and Publicity of*

director of the North of England Bank, and a witness before the parliamentary joint-stock bank committees, argued that:

> unlimited liability discourages a great many wealthy persons from taking shares. A party reasons with himself very justly, why should I, who have property, subject my property to loss on the chance of trifling dividends I can obtain in a bank? If the liability was limited, he would not so view it; there would be a better class of shareholders.[51]

These views were repeated a couple of decades later by the famous polymath Walter Bagehot. For example, in 1856, he wrote that: 'we enact that every person joining a bank shall be liable for every sixpence contained in it, to his last acre and shilling. The consequence is that persons who join banks have very commonly but few acres and shillings.'[52]

Importantly, it is unlikely that banks were established with low-wealth shareholders because to do so would have meant either having to hold large amounts of idle funds at a huge opportunity cost to assure depositors and note-holders, or paying a very high risk premium to depositors and note-holders. As ownership in these unlimited liability joint-stock banks was freely transferable, a dynamic may have existed where shares, although initially in the hands of wealthy owners, could have eventually ended up in the hands of the impecunious classes, resulting in diminished depositor safety. Consequently, unless banks could credibly commit that ownership would not unravel, rational depositors and note-holders, foreseeing an unravelling of ownership, would at the foundation of the bank require a compensatory risk premium.[53] Hence the cost of unravelling would be borne by the founding shareholders. However, the vetting of candidate shareholders by directors would have constrained the dilution of aggregate shareholder wealth over time.[54] This vetting policy meant that directors had to approve every subscriber for the initial offering, every investor who purchased shares on the secondary market, and every individual who was bequeathed or given shares in the bank. Such vetting was only credible if the directors were themselves very wealthy owners as they would have had substantial incentives to prevent low-wealth individuals becoming shareholders.[55] Although this vetting mechanism could have potentially collapsed when the probability of

---

Accounts, as Applied to Such Institutions; With Some Remarks on an Article on Joint-stock Companies in the Last Number of the Edinburgh Review. London: James Ridgway and Sons, 117.

[51] PP 1836 LX (591), *Report from the Select Committee on Joint Stock Banks*, evidence of Austin q. 2129.

[52] Bagehot, W. 1856. 'Unfettered banking'. *Saturday Review*, 1 November.

[53] See Acheson and Turner, 'The City of Glasgow'.

[54] Banks' deeds of settlement imposed upon directors the obligation to vet all share transfers. See Hickson and Turner, 'The trading of unlimited liability bank shares'.

[55] Ibid.

bankruptcy increased, the English and Irish joint-stock banking legislation had a post-sale-extended liability clause which acted to prevent opportunistic share dumping.[56] This clause made shareholders liable for a bank's debts for three years after selling their ownership stake. In Scotland, previous owners of unlimited liability joint-stock shares were held liable for debts incurred during their tenure if existing owners were unable to cover these losses from their own personal assets.[57] Established English, Irish, and Scottish banks which registered as unlimited liability companies under the Companies Act of 1862 were able to reduce their post-sale extended liability requirement to one year.

As with unlimited liability, one potential problem with reserve liability is that bank shares could end up in the hands of individuals who have inadequate wealth to cover their extended liability.[58] However, George Rae recognized that

> Directors have the power to make this [shareholders that have adequate wealth to meet all calls] an indispensable condition of proprietorship: they are empowered by your Deed of Settlement to reject, as a shareholder, anyone of whom they do not approve . . . if it is not exercised, portions of the stock may gradually drift into the hands of persons of insufficient substance.[59]

Oral evidence presented to the National Monetary Commission in the United States suggested that bank directors were careful in admitting individuals into ownership, and they frequently rejected transfers to unsuitable individuals.[60] In addition, under the Companies Act of 1862, past members of banks were liable for all unpaid capital (including reserve liability) for up to one year after they ceased to be a shareholder.[61] Nevertheless, given that reserve liability was a pro rata extended liability regime, there may have been less of an incentive for bank directors to vet share transfers than there was under unlimited liability, as their own potential liability in the event of bankruptcy was now limited to the amount of capital they held.

Recent evidence on the shareholder constituencies of unlimited liability joint-stock banks suggests that the above mechanisms were effective in preventing a deterioration of aggregate shareholder quality. Charles Hickson and John Turner in their study of Irish bank shareholders find that wealthy directors ensured that bank ownership was not dispersed into the hands of

---

[56] See Hickson and Turner, 'Shareholder Liability Regimes'.

[57] Bell, G.J. 1858. *Commentaries on the Laws of Scotland*, 6th edition. Edinburgh: T. and T. Clark, 224.

[58] Levi, 'The reconstruction of joint stock banks', 476.

[59] Rae, *The Country Banker*, 233.

[60] Withers, H. and R.H.I. Palgrave 1910. *The English Banking System*. Washington, DC: Government Printing Office, 93.

[61] Plumptre, C.C.M. 1882. *Grant's Treatise on the Law Relating to Bankers and Banking Companies*. London: Butterworths, 507.

low-wealth individuals.[62] Similarly, Graeme Acheson and John Turner find that the quality of shareholder constituencies in large English and Scottish banks did not deteriorate in the decades before the City of Glasgow failure.[63] The same authors also find that after the Ulster Bank moved to reserve liability, no shareholders had less wealth than their maximum potential call under reserve liability.[64] All this evidence would therefore suggest that banks with extended shareholder liability were not de facto limited.

Bank stock was less risky

One possibility as to why risk-averse investors were willing to hold unlimited liability bank stock was that it was less risky than other types of stock. Although this appears to be counterintuitive, there may be theoretical reasons why unlimited liability actually reduces risk-taking. As directors were the wealthiest owners and therefore had the most to lose in the event of a bank collapse, it is likely that they would manage the bank in a very conservative fashion by maintaining high reserves and lending short-term only to the most secure of borrowers. Thus, the wealthier the directors, the more likely it would be for the bank to be run in a conservative manner, and the less likely it would be for it to fail, thus making the bank's stock potentially more attractive to risk-averse investors.

Once liability is limited to some fixed proportion of paid-up capital, the above incentive structure changes. Under such regimes, a wealthy owner's liability was now determined by the number of shares they owned. This therefore made them less likely to participate in bank governance as their entire wealth was no longer in jeopardy from bad managerial decision-making.[65] Consequently, less wealthy owners emerge as directors. As a result, such banks were likely to be run in a less conservative manner than their unlimited counterparts, making the bank's stock potentially less attractive to risk-averse investors. Nevertheless, there remains a substantial check on managerial risk-taking relative to pure limited liability banks.

The collapse of several prominent unlimited liability banks calls into question the suggestion that extended liability stock was less risky. One of the first major collapses of an unlimited liability bank was in 1836 when the Agricultural and Commercial Bank of Ireland failed, resulting in calls upon its shareholders in order to reimburse its depositors. However, the Agricultural and Commercial Bank was something of a fraudulent enterprise with most of

---

[62] Hickson and Turner, 'The trading of unlimited liability bank shares'.
[63] Acheson and Turner, 'The City of Glasgow'.
[64] Acheson and Turner, 'The impact of limited liability', 337.
[65] Ibid. 342–3.

its board of directors comprising of individuals with very little personal wealth to lose.[66] It is therefore unsurprising that this institution adopted an incautious approach to banking. Such failures of unlimited liability banks were not confined to this formative period. Indeed, later collapses resulted in large calls being made upon shareholders. For example, the Western Bank of Scotland failure in November 1857 resulted in its stockholders paying £36 for every share they held to cover the deficit between the bank's assets and liabilities.[67] As a consequence, on average the stockholders had to pay £816. The failure of the Birmingham Banking Company in 1866 resulted in its shareholders paying out £9 per share, with the average shareholder paying £380.[68] Finally, the most infamous collapse of an unlimited bank occurred in October 1878, when the City of Glasgow Bank closed its doors. Such was the extent of the bank's losses that the deficit between its assets and liabilities was £613 per share. The first call of £500 per share was made at the start of December 1878, and it resulted in the financial ruin of 599 shareholders. A final call of £2250 per share was made in April 1878. After this final call, only 254 of the original 1819 shareholders were solvent.[69] The *Economist* magazine outlined the extent of the human suffering caused by the failure of this bank:

> In hundreds and thousands of cases homes have been broken up, health and life destroyed, dismay and ruin spread over towns and parishes, sons and daughters left penniless – by the wickedness and folly which perverted a public trust in so infamous a manner.[70]

A recent study of this bank suggests that it was an aggressive and risk-loving institution unlike most of its counterparts.[71] The ultimate source of this bank's risky nature can be partially attributed to the incentive structure of its board – several of its members were heavily indebted to the bank.[72]

These several cases of banks collapsing and shareholders having to cover losses out of their own wealth might, however, be the exception rather than the rule. It is quite possible that these banks were at the extreme end of the spectrum in terms of risk-taking and most other banks were conservative. Therefore, in order to test the overall riskiness of the banking sector in

---

[66] Hickson, C.R. and J.D. Turner 2005. 'The genesis of corporate governance: nineteenth-century Irish joint-stock banks'. *Business History* 47(2): 184.

[67] On the failure of this banks, see Campbell, R. 1955. 'Edinburgh banks and the Western Bank of Scotland'. *Scottish Journal of Political Economy* 2(1): 133–48; Checkland, *Scottish Banking*, 466–76.

[68] Holmes, A.R. and E. Greene 1986. *Midland: 150 Years of Banking Business*. London: B.T. Batsford, 46.

[69] Checkland, *Scottish Banking*, 471.

[70] Anon 1879. 'City of Glasgow Bank – Progress and details of the liquidation'. *Economist*, 1480.

[71] Acheson and Turner, 'The City of Glasgow'.

[72] HBOS Archives, City of Glasgow Bank List of Shareholders and Portraits of Directors.

the heyday of extended liability banking, we use a new dataset constructed from the *Course of the Exchange*.[73] This dataset contains monthly prices for most equities traded on the London Stock Exchange in the period 1825–70, which enables us to see how risky bank equity was compared to the overall market. Although this dataset does not contain many of the banks which had stock traded on the various regional stock markets, it does contain most of the overseas and colonial banks which had stock traded in Britain.

Table 9.4 Estimates of risk of bank stocks quoted on London Stock Exchange, 1825–70

Beta of portfolio weighted by market capitalization	0.836
Beta of unweighted portfolio	0.832
Number of banks in bank portfolio	111
Number of bank stocks in portfolio	138
Number of companies in market portfolio	681
Number of stocks in market portfolio	1015

Source: Hickson et al., 'The rate of return on equity'.

As can be seen from Table 9.4, there are 681 companies in the market portfolio and 111 in the portfolio of bank stocks. Close to a quarter of these banks had unlimited liability, about a fifth had double shareholder liability, and 89 banks had uncalled capital. Only five of the 111 banks did not have any form of extended liability.

In order to measure the relative riskiness of the banking sector we use the *ex post* version of the Capital Asset Pricing Model. We tested the following:

$$R_{bt} - R_{ft} = a_t + \beta_b(R_{mt} - R_{ft}) + \epsilon_{pt}$$

where R_{bt} is the rate of return on the bank portfolio at time t, R_{ft} is the rate of return on a risk-free asset at time t, R_{mt} is the return on the market portfolio at time t, and ϵ_{pt} is a random error term. The β_b (beta) coefficient measures the risk of a portfolio relative to the market. Leads and lags were introduced to correct for the thin trading problem.[74] Monthly returns on 3 per cent Consols were used as a proxy for the risk-free rate.[75]

Table 9.4 reports the beta estimates for portfolios of bank stock weighted by market capitalization and equally weighted portfolios. The beta estimates for

---

[73] See Acheson et al., 'Rule Britannia!', for the details.

[74] Dimson, E. 1979. 'Risk measurement when shares are subject to infrequent trading'. *Journal of Financial Economics* 7(2): 197–226; Scholes, M. and J. Williams 1977. 'Estimating betas from nonsynchronous data'. *Journal of Financial Economics* 5(3): 309–27.

[75] Consol prices were obtained from the *Course of the Exchange*.

both portfolios imply that the banking sector is marginally less risky than the overall market. Consequently, as bank stocks are only slightly less risky than the overall market, this cannot fully explain the popularity of bank shares amongst risk-averse investors.

Portfolio diversification is usually an optimal strategy used by investors to reduce their risk. However, the risk associated with liability extensions cannot be diversified away. Indeed, diversification is not an optimal strategy in the presence of extended liability as each share with extended liability added to the portfolio increases the joint probability of a call on an investor's wealth.

Bank stock earned higher returns

Thus far we have established that extended liability bank shares were not de facto limited and that they were not substantially less risky than other shares. Consequently, we are left with one obvious explanation as to why they were popular with risk-averse investors: they gave investors a relatively high risk-adjusted return compared to other assets.[76] In order to test this, we again draw from the dataset upon which Table 9.4 is based which was constructed using share prices from the *Course of the Exchange*.

From Figure 9.1, we can see that after 1825, banks constituted an increasing proportion of the London market, with a huge increase occurring between 1833 and 1836, following the 1833 liberalization of banking incorporation law.

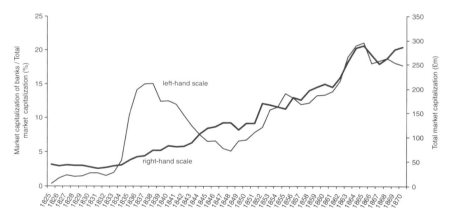

Figure 9.1 Market capitalization of the London market, 1825–70.

Source: Hickson et al., 'The rate of return'.

---

[76] Newton and Cottrell, 'Female investors' suggest that high dividends made bank stock attractive to female investors.

Table 9.5 Summary statistics for stock market and banking sector annual total returns in Britain, 1825–70

	Overall market		Banking sector	
	MC	UN	MC	UN
Panel A: Total return (%)				
Mean	9.28	10.16	10.75	13.12
Coefficient of variation	0.94	1.00	1.80	1.77
Dividend yield	51.40	51.50	48.90	38.50
Capital appreciation	48.60	48.50	51.10	61.50
Panel B: Attrition-adjusted return (%)				
Attrition strategy I				
Mean	6.11	3.38	8.32	7.33
Attrition strategy II				
Mean	6.98	6.00	9.48	10.75
Attrition strategy III				
Mean	7.34	6.72	9.85	11.36

Source: Hickson et al., 'The rate of return on equity'.

Note: MC, weighted by market capitalization; UN, unweighted. All means are arithmetic means.

The fall in banks' share of market capitalization after 1838 is due to the disappearance of several banks as well as to the rise of the railway sector. After the end of the railway mania, banks' share of market capitalization rises steadily and in line with the growth of overall market capitalization. These figures, however, underestimate the true position of banks as they do not contain most Irish, Scottish, and many English provincial joint-stock banks. However, as Figure 9.1 illustrates, even with these omissions, banking was an important sector within the London equity market.

Statistics for annual calendar total returns for the overall market and banking sector are reported in Table 9.5. Total returns include capital appreciation and dividends, and are either equally weighted (unweighted) or weighted by market capitalization. In order to adjust for survivorship bias, several 'strategies' are employed, with Attrition Strategy 1 being the most severe and Attrition Strategy 3 being the least severe.[77]

As can be observed from Table 9.5, the returns on the banking sector were higher than those on the overall market, with the arithmetic mean for both weighting strategies being higher for banking than the market. Notably, as can be seen from Panel B, dividends constituted a large part of total weighted returns for both banks and the overall market.

---

[77] See Acheson et al., 'Rule Britannia!', for the details.

One possible reason for the higher returns in the banking sector is that the estimate suffers from a greater survivorship bias than the overall market; in other words proportionally more banks entered bankruptcy than the market norm. However, as we can observe from Panel B of Table 9.5, the banking sector still earns a higher return even when the most stringent attrition strategy is applied. Once less stringent (and more realistic) strategies are simulated, the difference between the returns on the market and the returns on the banking sector are actually greater than the unadjusted returns.

Another possible reason for the difference in returns between bank stocks and the market is that the extended liability of bank stocks made them relatively illiquid, and that investors needed a premium to compensate them for this. However, recent work on the secondary market for bank stock suggests that bank shares were relatively liquid in the nineteenth century, and that limiting liability had little impact on their marketability.[78]

CONCLUSION

The evidence presented above suggests that shares in extended liability banks were popular investments even with risk-averse investors such as women. For example, by the 1870s, women constituted close to one-third of owners in most large unlimited liability joint-stock banks, and, as noted above, this did not differ much from the limited liability Scottish public banks.

In order to explain the large number of risk-averse individuals who owned bank stock, we examined the credibility of extended liability, the riskiness of bank stock, and the returns generated by bank stock relative to those of the market. Our evidence suggests that the demand for bank stock by risk-averse investors cannot be explained by liability being de facto limited. Furthermore, bank stock was not substantially less risky than other stock. On the other hand, our evidence strongly suggests that the demand for bank stock by risk-averse investors may have been largely determined by the returns earned relative to the overall market. In other words, the large risk premium on bank shares was sufficiently high to attract risk-averse investors.

Although banks with extended liability had to pay a premium to raise their equity capital, the existence of liability extensions no doubt lowered their cost of debt capital and provided assurances to customers that deposits would be

---

[78] See Acheson, G.G. and J.D. Turner 2008. 'The secondary market for bank shares in nineteenth-century Britain'. *Financial History Review* 15(2): 123–52; and Hickson, C.R., J.D. Turner, and C. McCann 2005. 'Much ado about nothing: the introduction of limited liability and the market for nineteenth-century Irish bank stock'. *Explorations in Economic History* 42(3): 459–76.

repaid and policies would be honoured. This raises the question as to how their cost of capital and their customers were affected whenever these institutions eventually became pure limited liability companies. Of key importance is depositors were assured that their bank would not expropriate them by risk-shifting at their expense. These, however, are questions for future research.

10

The Shareholders' 'Dog' that did not Bark: Contested Takeover Bids in Long-Run Comparative Perspective

Leslie Hannah

SHAREHOLDER RIGHTS AND THE TAKEOVER BID

The development of widespread public shareholding described in other chapters in this book had potentially profound consequences for corporate boards and the ways that they controlled companies. This was especially the case in Britain and France, where the separation of ownership from control had advanced furthest in the nineteenth century. Even in those countries, like Germany, Japan, and the United States, in which developments of stock exchanges were initially slower, there were significant sectors in which ownership had become divorced from control. In Britain, shareholder rights to information (with corporate accounts only legally required for many companies from 1900), to voting power (with preference shares often having no votes or only fractional votes), and to listing rules protections (enforced by the London Stock Exchange Committee) were only slowly being reinforced in the period from 1870 to 1930. This chapter examines the delayed development of takeover bids as a mechanism for further reinforcing shareholder rights. This important consequence of dispersed share ownership has been the focus of much modern discussion by economists, but has received little historical attention. The argument here is that more dispersed ownership, improved information dissemination and changes in corporate governance, stock exchange listing rules, and company legislation all played a role in permitting open competitive bidding to develop – albeit at varied paces in different countries – even though bankers and company directors often opposed and for long periods successfully suppressed such developments that challenged their prerogatives.

There are many words in English for mergers – acquisitions, consolidations, bids, combinations, fusions, takeovers, amalgamations, or the global financiers' shorthand 'M & A' – but none of them alone conveys a key analytical distinction: that between *agreed* transactions and *contested* ones. Most – probably approaching 99 per cent until recently – of the tens of thousands of mergers that have taken place – were *agreed*. Irrespective of whether the merger was initiated collectively, or by one firm, or by an investment banker, company promoter, merger broker or another third party, the controllers (the board) of the 'target' company concurred in the view that the amalgamation should take place. The much rarer *contested* takeover bid is now thought of as a distinctively Anglo-Saxon (American and British Commonwealth) institution, vigorously promoting shareholder value maximization, and only recently (and still sometimes reluctantly) accepted in continental Europe and Japan.[1] However, even at the height of the hostile takeover boom of the 1980s – when names of corporate raiders like Carl Icahn and T. Boone Pickens were regular features in the financial press – the proportion of US deals that were contested was only 14 per cent and fell to 4 per cent in the 1990s.[2]

Why, then, are such unusual bids important to shareholders and to the wider economy? A *contestable* market for corporate control may be critical in conditions of concentrated monopolies and entrenched managerial control.[3] If large firms control a considerable proportion of national assets, the competitive processes of differential growth, in which agreed mergers and de-mergers, together with the internal growth of efficient firms and the decline and eventual bankruptcy of the inefficient, may only work in the long run and with suboptimal slowness. A different kind of competition – that for control of corporate assets in the capital market via direct bids for shareholder votes, leading to their rapid transfer to more efficient managers – can supplement the

---

[1] The 'contest' is essentially between the would-be acquirer and the incumbent board of the target firm, although there may sometimes be a secondary contest among rival acquirers. Approximate equivalents in French, German, and Japanese, respectively, are *offre publique d'achat, feindliche Übernahmeangebote*, and *TOB* (takeover-bid or *kabushiki kokai kaitsuke*). Somewhat ruder words, like *nottoriya* (hijacking) and *Heuschrecker* (locusts), are also sometimes used.

[2] Andrade, G., M. Mitchell, and E. Stafford et al. 2001. 'New evidence and perspectives on mergers'. *Journal of Economic Perspectives* 15(2): 106. They argue that the proportion of contested bids subsided because US corporate governance – weaknesses in which caused the hostile bids – had been improved in response to the threat of bids.

[3] Note that there can be a *market* in corporate control, even with entrenched boards, who may be swayed to act in the interest of shareholders and recommend the takeover due to a sufficiently high financial offer or other persuasive arguments. A *contestable* market in corporate control is one in which bidders have the realistic further option of buying control in the market and/or appealing directly to the shareholder owners. Another aspect of a contestable market is that shareholders may disagree with an incumbent board's recommendation of an offer and attempt to obtain a higher price than the board is willing to recommend. Of course, the distinction between contested and agreed bids is not absolute: a contest may lead to a modified offer and agreement.

constrained resource allocation process of oligopolistic product markets, resulting in a more rapid convergence on a more efficient outcome.[4] Shareholders in managerial firms may find it difficult to exercise their nominal voting control, as they are widely dispersed, but outside bidders may be able to galvanize their powers for clearly articulated and constructive ends. Takeover bids will likely be especially important where local corporate governance traditions favour the relatively untrammelled 'dictatorship of the CEO', found everywhere, but perhaps most notably in the United States. They may be less important where there are alternative restraints on management powers such as supervisory boards separate from full-time management, banker control, chairmen independent of CEOs, independent nominating and audit committees, large block-holders, or activist shareholder board nomination lobbies with rights.[5]

THE EXTENT OF THE SEPARATION OF OWNERSHIP FROM CONTROL

There are, of course, many causes of mergers, but the only *necessary* condition for *contested* takeover bids is that the control of the acquired corporation should be separated from its ownership. Specifically, the board of the acquired company must own, or represent, fewer than 50 per cent of the votes (and in practice, in view of the inertia of some shareholders, often considerably below 50 per cent); and the board must also be united in exercising those votes. Otherwise, the possibility of outsiders obtaining control without the incumbent board's agreement is, by definition, zero.[6] This is a trivially obvious proposition, but since boards with majority voting control were and, in many countries still are, common, it has accounted for much of the historical and contemporary absence of takeover activity. Yet, equally obviously,

---

[4] The classic statement is Manne, H.G. 1965. 'Mergers and the market for corporate control'. *Journal of Political Economy* 73(2): 110–20; see also Jensen, M.C. 1988. 'Takeovers: their causes and consequences'. *Journal of Economic Perspectives* 2(1): 21–48.

[5] For a view of the US situation, see Holmstrom, B. and S.N. Kaplan 2001. 'Corporate governance and merger activity in the United States: making sense of the 1980s and 1990s'. *Journal of Economic Perspectives* 15(2): 121–44.

[6] Of course, the proportion of votes exercisable may not be the same as the proportion of capital held, due to non-voting capital (such as bonds and debentures), differential voting rights (such as A and B shares, management, founders', deferred or preferred shares, tiered or capped votes), conditional voting rights (voting trusts or non-voting preferred stock with votes contingent on events such as capital issues or dividend payments), proxy rules (directors – and particularly bank directors or the chairman – may vote wider shareholdings than their own) or pyramiding (a hierarchy of subsidiaries in which only the top level has 50+ per cent board control).

ownership is now divorced from control in many companies and, throughout the twentieth century, this has probably been true of most corporations with ordinary shares listed on major stock exchanges. In Britain, the majority of companies by the early twentieth century had significantly dispersed owner- ship. Yet for most of the century, takeover bids for such corporations have been rare and, in some countries, still remain so.

Typically, a British-listed company in 1900 had only about 13 per cent board ownership, a French company around 17 per cent, with American and German companies perhaps as much as 33 per cent.[7] If the necessary condi- tion of ownership divorced from control were a sufficient (or even the major) reason for the emergence of contested takeover bidding, one would have expected Britain and France to have experienced more widespread bidding around 1900 than Germany and the United States. Yet no such suggestion appears remotely plausible. Indeed, I know of no French contested takeover

---

[7] Hannah, L. 2007. 'The "Divorce" of ownership and control from 1900 onwards: recalibrat- ing imagined global trends'. *Business History* 49(4): 404–38. See also the essays in the special issue of *Enterprise and Society* on corporate governance 8(3) 2007 and Davis, L. 1966. 'The capital markets and industrial concentration: the US and UK, a comparative study'. *Economic History Review* 19(2): 255–72. If the interesting rebuttal by Brian Cheffins and Steven Bank of my estimates of the divorce of ownership from control in Britain relative to the United States is correct, the present chapter would require significant revision; see Cheffins, B.R. and S. Bank 2009. 'Is Berle and Means really a myth?' *Business History Review* 83(3): 443–74. They provide convincing evidence that opinions on the historical facts have been widely divergent, but fail to draw the obvious lesson that believable statements on long-run trends in board ownership cannot be based on such opinions or on unrepresentative samples using the unstandardized measures that they extensively cite. They offer no methodological critique of the suggested standardizations of cross-country and diachronic comparisons by myself and by Holderness, C.G., R.S. Kroszner, and D.P. Sheehan 1999. 'Were the good old days that good? Changes in managerial stock ownership since the Great Depression'. *Journal of Finance* 54(2): 435–69. Nor do they offer any new quantitative evidence, or recognize that discussions of the matter can only sensibly be conducted in *relative and quantified* terms, since to some commentators a 5 per cent holding shows massive owner–director influence, while to others the identical figure betokens a clear separation of management control from ownership. In a later study, James Foreman-Peck and Leslie Hannah exploit a newly rediscovered contemporary data source covering over 2000 UK companies in 1911, finding that, on various standardized definitions, ownership was then more divorced from control than in the United States in the 1930s or 1990s, or than in the United Kingdom in the 1990s. See Foreman-Peck, J. and L. Hannah 2010. 'The twentieth- century divorce of ownership from control: the facts and some consequences'. Paper presented at 2nd EURHISTOCK conference, Judge Business School, University of Cambridge, Cambridge. The timings of US and UK developments were thus quite different, with the United Kingdom developing an early lead, though the long-run outcomes were almost identical. Despite Cheffins and Bank's misleading title, I have never questioned Berle and Means' convincing description of a massively increasing dispersion of US stock ownership during the first three decades of the twentieth century: implying sharply lower owner control in 1930 than the initially much higher 1900 US level. On the contrary, for my own proposition – that Britain was already nearer the classic separation of ownership from control in 1900, while the United States then still main- tained more personal capitalism – to be true, Berle and Means must also be substantially right.

bid around 1900, whereas examples are evident in several other European countries and Japan, while the United States appears to have more – rather than, as would be predicted, less – contested bids than anywhere else at that time.[8] It is clear, then, that we must look beyond the necessary but trivial determinant of the relative national incidence of the divorce of ownership from control, to other conditions, for understanding the earlier chronological and geographical incidence of the phenomenon of the contested takeover bid.

INFORMATION AND VOTING RULES:
WHY WERE THERE TAKEOVER BIDS IN SOME
RAILWAYS BUT NOT OTHERS?

One variable restricting contested takeovers is the availability of information about quoted companies: it is riskier to bid for large and complex companies if there is no reliable public information on their underlying balance sheet assets and current profitability.[9] Hence, the improvement of accounting information by legislative intervention in the United States in the 1930s (the establishment of the Securities and Exchange Commission) and in the United Kingdom in the 1940s (the 1947 Companies Act), substantially increased the confidence of outside bidders.[10] The quality of information available to public investors in Japan and continental Europe appears to have lagged after the Second World War, though when Anglo-Saxon investors and investment banks moved into those markets, in the later decades of the twentieth century, and when their companies increasingly sought supplementary stock exchange listings in London and New York (thus requiring adherence to the latters' accounting standards, involving, typically large, restatements of profits and reserves), the information arguably improved and takeover bidding slowly emerged.

For the decades before the 1930s, however, disclosure rules were at least as strong in continental Europe, Japan, and Britain as in the United States,

---

[8] See also Bonin, H. 2010. 'Les offensives boursières en France'. Unpublished paper, Bordeaux.

[9] Exceptions emphasized in the contemporary literature are post-1945 corporations in which published book values were so obviously below true values, as a result of wartime inflation, that, if stock exchange values did not reflect this, it was a good idea to bid, irrespective of the reliability of currently available balance sheet information. Yet since wartime and post-war inflations were chronic in Japan, Germany, Italy, and France, and relatively minor in Britain and the United States, this model would predict higher levels of takeover activity in the former than the latter. Since the opposite patently occurred, such obvious mis-valuations cannot have been the major cause of differences in the national incidence of contested bidding.

[10] Hannah, L. 1974. 'Takeover bids in Britain before 1950: an exercise in business "pre-history"'. *Business History* 16(1): 65–77.

indeed in some cases were stronger.[11] In 1900, for example, 43 per cent of the largest quoted US industrials, including leading firms such as Standard Oil, Singer Manufacturing, and Anaconda, did not even issue balance sheets or income statements to shareholders, though this situation gradually improved until publication was decisively imposed by legislative intervention in 1933. Yet there is no evidence of higher takeover activity in Europe and Japan than in the United States before the 1930s.

However, the railway sector in the United States did, at an earlier stage, have exceptionally good disclosure standards, particularly after the Interstate Commerce Commission required accounts publication (though not external audit) from its inception in 1890 and, later, specified standard accounts. The railway sector was also identified by Adolf Berle and Gardiner Means as the industry which led the divorce of ownership from control in the United States, so the two major determinants of contested bidding so far identified would lead us to predict a high level of contemporary bidding in that sector, even if there was little contested bidding in other US industries.[12] The narratives of US corporate reorganizations around the turn of the century reveal precisely such a pattern. In the industrial sector, large mergers like US Steel or International Harvester were typically by the agreement of incumbent boards orchestrated by investment bankers. However, in the railway sector – then the biggest section of the New York Stock Exchange – Vanderbilt, Moore, Rockefeller, Harriman, Hill, Morgan, Gould, and others competed for corporate control of major lines and the profits of reorganizing and integrating regional and transcontinental systems. Of course, some consolidation in railways also occurred by agreement, but many examples of contested bids – attempting and sometimes succeeding in unseating the incumbent board – can be identified. The most notorious was the battle between Hill and Harriman for the control of the Great Northern Railway in 1901, which Hill won with the support of the Morgan and Schiff banking houses which were represented on his board.[13]

Yet if bids occurred in US railroads, because of ownership being divorced from control and exceptionally good information disclosure, why did the same

[11] Sylla, R. and G.D. Smith 1995. 'Information and capital market regulation in Anglo-American finance'. In *Anglo-American Financial Systems*, edited by M.D. Bordo and R. Sylla. New York, NY: Irwin, 179–205; Hannah, L. 2007. 'Pioneering modern corporate governance: a view from London in 1900'. *Enterprise and Society* 8(3): 642–86.

[12] Berle, A.A. and G.C. Means 1991. *The Modern Corporation and Private Property* (originally published 1932). New Brunswick, NJ: Transactions Publishers.

[13] See Cleveland, F.A. and F.W. Powell 1912. *Railroad Finance*. New York, NY: Appleton, 273–321 for a clear contemporary discussion of the market in railroad control. In the case of the Great Northern, the board successfully defeated the hostile bid (but only by Morgan's son buying the critical last few shares on the London market to get above 50 per cent of the votes). Another, in this case successful, bid was the contemporary takeover of the Louisville & Nashville Railroad, see Meade, E.S. 1910. *Corporation Finance*. New York, NY: Appleton, 278.

not happen elsewhere? In some countries – like Germany, Russia, Belgium, Austria-Hungary, Italy, Australia, and post-1905 Japan – the answer is obvious: their railways (or substantial parts of the sector) were state-owned and hence controlled by bureaucratic hierarchies answerable only to the state. In these instances their non-voting state bondholders had no say in the matter. Yet some local lines in such countries were privately owned, and in France and Britain, and many African, American, and Asian countries, railways were publicly quoted and widely held.[14] Indeed the divorce of ownership and control had gone further in these railways compared with the United States and accounting disclosure standards by railways were generally quite high.

Why then did takeover bids not emerge in these non-US railways, as theory and US precedent predicts they should have done? The answer appears to be in the nature of the corporate governance rules in railways, which were typically very different – more 'modern', or, as Colleen Dunlavy has described it, more 'plutocratic' – in the United States than those that still survived elsewhere. In the nineteenth-century United States, voting rules had earlier often conformed to the European practice, but by 1900 railway and other company voting rules generally followed the modern norm: one share, one vote. It was thus possible for someone purchasing the majority of a railway company's shares to control its management. Elsewhere, however, the voting rule for railways remained typically what Dunlavy describes as 'democratic' (one shareholder, one vote) or what that great designer of many US institutions, Alexander Hamilton, called 'the prudent mean' (tiered voting rights, declining proportionately with the numbers of shares held).[15] Almost all British railways, for example, had adopted a tiered voting structure, which restricted the powers of large holders, as provided by the 1845 Railway Clauses Act and recommended for other companies in various Companies Acts. For example, each £100 of stock held up to £1000 might have one vote, each further £500 up to £10,000 one vote, and beyond that there would be only one vote per £1000 of stock. Some financial institutions and other companies in Britain, France, and elsewhere adopted similar tiered voting rules or the even more stringent capped voting, in which shares above the cap simply forfeited their voting rights, though this seems to have been relatively uncommon everywhere in manufacturing, mining, and other service companies.[16] Of the

---

[14] Hannah, 'The divorce of ownership', 407–10, 423.

[15] Dunlavy, C. 1998. 'Corporate governance in nineteenth-century Europe and the United States: the case of shareholder voting rights'. In *Corporate Governance: The State of the Art of Emerging Research*, edited by K.J. Hopt, H. Kanda, M. Roe, E. Wymeersch, and S. Prigge. Oxford: Clarendon Press, 5–39. See also Hilt, E. 2008. 'When did ownership separate from control?'. *Journal of Economic History* 68(3): 645–85. The literature is unclear on why the United States pioneered the abandonment of 'democracy' in the corporate world.

[16] We know little about the reasons for this differentiation in the evolution of voting rules by industry. In Britain, the model clauses in the various Companies Acts recommended a similar

335 independent, British-owned companies with more than £1 million nominal share capital listed in the *Investor's Year Book* for 1912, 21 per cent still had tiered voting rights and 14 per cent had capped voting rights, and these tended to be concentrated in railways and financials which had the most widely dispersed shareholdings.[17] I know of no evidence that such rules were introduced to inhibit takeover-bidding. Rather, their prime motivation appears to have been to protect small shareholders and inhibit insider abuse. Blocking bids was, in fact, their accidental by-product when, for example, the earliest railways, some of which were initially financed by banks, public authorities or controlling entrepreneurs, were pioneering widespread shareholding.[18]

Unlike in the United States, anyone who successfully bought the majority of shares in companies with such tiered voting rules could not thereby acquire control: typically they would still only have a minority of votes and would still be dependent on the support of many small and medium shareholders if they wished to unseat the incumbent board. A takeover bid was, therefore, simply ineffective in securing control. That such voting rules inhibited contested takeover bids is confirmed by the contrasting behaviour of the few railways which exceptionally followed US voting rules. For example, not all London tramways and underground railways adopted the 1845 Railway Clauses Act, and an American syndicate, organized by the Speyer Brothers' investment bank, was able successfully to acquire pyramided control over much of the London transport system.[19] It is clear that in such companies with widely

voting structure for all companies to that generally required for railways by the 1845 Railway Clauses Act. However, most manufacturing and mining companies, even if basing their articles on the model clauses, deleted that voting provision. In Russia, exceptionally, the general company legislation banned majority voting completely. Nevertheless, some companies, such as Singer Manufacturing, are known to have circumvented this by the use of dummy nominee shareholdings. Richard Jordan and Francis Gore-Brown suggest this circumvention through multiple nominees was possible in Britain, though I have not encountered cases of it happening; see Jordan, R. and F. Gore-Brown 1892. *A Handy Book on the Formation, Management and Winding-Up of Joint-Stock Companies*. London: Jordan, 25. In Japan, the Jugo Bank takeover of the Nippon Railway in 1898 also used such tactics prompting the adoption in the 1899 company law of US-style plutocratic voting as the norm for new companies. See Miwa, Y. and J.M. Ramseyer 2000. 'Corporate governance in transitional economies: lessons from the pre-war Japanese cotton textile industry'. *Journal of Legal Studies* 29(1): 199.

[17] This is based on my calculation from voting rules described in *Stock Exchange Official Intelligence*. Forty-two per cent of the 335 firms had equal voting rights for all shares (the modern norm). Many of the remainder restricted preference shareholders' votes to fractions or special circumstances.

[18] Early railways were sometimes founded by small consortia of engineers, local landowners, and bankers, but very rapidly appealed to a wider body of shareholders for funds. By the 1840s, some British railways were very widely held and by the 1850s the London Stock Exchange was also funding foreign railways. Similar developments took place in Paris and New York.

[19] Lowenfeld, H. 1907. *Investment: An Exact Science*. London: Financial Review of Reviews, 35–6; Barker, T.C. and M. Robbins 1974. *London Transport: A History*. London: George Allen and Unwin, 60. The Metropolitan District Railway (like the independent Central London Railway) had tiered voting under 1845 Railway Clauses Act rules, though the US syndicate still

dispersed shareholding and appropriate voting rules, reorganization on something approaching the US plutocratic model could happen.

If voting rules inhibited takeover bids for most other railways in Britain, we might expect inefficiency to result from the failure to gain advantages from integration, when incumbent directors used their powers to resist moves that would compromise their own control.[20] It was, however, possible to implement mergers in companies with the normal Franco-British railway governance structure by legislation imposed on the companies by governments (or by private acts of parliament) promoting integration. Indeed, compared to the United States, such legislatively led amalgamations were more advanced in France by 1885 – when there were essentially six privately owned regional railway monopolies – and in Britain by 1921 – when four private regional railway monopolies were created.[21] Some US railway managers even looked enviously at such examples. It remains a matter of debate, however, whether a US-style, more decentralized and contestable market in corporate control might have produced more insistent pressures for improved managerial performance from entrenched incumbents. It might also have focused attention earlier on the more profitable areas of integration and innovation than unchallenged monopolistic companies with entrenched boards.[22]

Businessmen, in general, expected to continue running their firms even after an initial public offering (IPO) in which they had sold significant ownership stakes to the wider public. They hated any hint of a new world of takeovers that threatened their control. Even in the United States, there were serious doubts about some aspects of the contestable market in corporate control that railway entrepreneurs were pioneering. Investment bankers like Morgan, as we have seen, were themselves involved in contesting control of railways but they, together with many of their clients, were somewhat less

---

managed to gain control by massive purchases in the market swaying incumbent management to support them. Other subsidiaries of the Underground Electric Railway (the US-controlled holding company) had equal, not tiered, voting, with most capital raised by non-voting shares, bonds and notes, and control vested in voting shares substantially controlled by UER and the Speyer syndicate, with rights to residual profits.

[20] Perhaps the clearest case of something similar argued in the literature is for British electric utilities from *c.*1905 to *c.*1930, where private and municipal companies failed to integrate, but this was caused by incompatible public/private ownership structures and regulatory rules and their incumbency entrenchment effects, rather than by voting rules. See Hannah, L. 1979. *Electricity before Nationalisation.* London: Macmillan.

[21] There were, of course, also some legal procedures inhibiting railway mergers in the United States, notably the antitrust laws.

[22] There are extensive and somewhat inconclusive contemporary and historical literatures on the relative efficiency of European and American railroad managements, which might benefit from a fuller consideration of this point. See, for example, Hoff, W. and F. Schwabach 1906. *North American Railroads.* New York, NY: Germania; Crafts, N., T. Leunig, and A. Mulatu 2008. 'Were British railway companies well-managed in the early twentieth century?' *Economic History Review* 61(4): 842–66.

enthusiastic when corporate raiders threatened their own control. This was especially problematic when they were reconstructing railways that had been too heavily geared, poorly managed, and received inadequate investment for the massively increased demands being placed upon them. Their essential work of corporate reconstruction would, they felt, be compromised if a dissident board member or an outsider bought a majority of shares in the market and unseated the professional railway managers and finance directors or corporate treasurers they had put in place to initiate changes.[23]

One tool they used to insulate the incumbent management from the threat of takeover in such circumstances was the voting trust, though others, such as interlocking shareholdings, were also used. Morgan, for example, in his 1890s railway reconstructions refused to provide the urgently required restructuring finance unless the existing shareholders placed their votes in a trust which he and his financing syndicate members controlled. Thus, even though he had less than a majority of the voting shares, he was able temporarily to suspend the operation of the market for corporate control. Although typically such trusts only ran for five years, they were renewable, sometimes automatically if certain targets had not been met, though on occasions subject to continuing shareholder approval. The voting trust was one of the first new legal devices to be widely used to inhibit the market for corporate control in the United States and it was common in the sector where companies were at most risk of contested bidding: that is, turn-of-the-century railways. Morgan and other bankers appearing before the Pujo Committee in 1913 explicitly stated that they saw the function of the voting trusts they had created as a substitute for the European 'democratic' voting rules, which, as we have seen, inhibited contested bids for railways.[24]

The main difference between the bidding technique then and that in modern capital markets was that shares were bought over a period and at a variety of prices, rather than a public offer being formally made at a fixed price to all shareholders. Paradoxically, gradual takeovers were easier if the shares were not too widely held because the bidder could approach some known major shareholders directly and build up a significant holding secretly, before entering the wider market. This technique avoided bidding up the market price too rapidly by marginal purchases in relatively thin public markets.[25] One factor facilitating such approaches was the public availability of shareholder lists, but US businesses were not generally obliged to provide

[23] Tufano, P. 1997. 'Business failure, judicial intervention and financial innovation: restructuring US railroads in the nineteenth century'. *Business History Review* 71(1): 1–40.

[24] Pujo Committee 1913. *Money Trust Investigation: Hearings*. Washington, DC: Government Printing Office, 1058–60, 1970–2.

[25] It should be noted that in many listed companies a substantial proportion of stock was still held by the original vendors (not all of whom gained board positions). Even the most widely held public companies then numbered their shareholders in the thousands or tens of thousands (not

these.[26] In some cases, bidders came to the conclusion that they should try to get hold of some directors' shareholdings too, in order to sidestep the inevitable inertia of many small holders of stock who were not easily identified.[27] In such cases, of course, unless one significant holder–director could be persuaded to double-cross his board colleagues, the bid ceased to be contested and, by definition, was agreed.

OTHER SECTORS: TAKEOVER DEFENCES AND 'GRIT' IN THE TAKEOVER MECHANISM

It remains to be explained why other European and US business sectors, where ownership was divorced from control and accounting disclosure was of above-average quality, did not emulate the US railway sector in developing an active market in corporate control.[28] In mining and manufacturing, incumbent boards – in this sector more than others, typically the founding entrepreneurs, their families, associates, and heirs – often retained more than 50 per cent of the votes and thus contested bidding was much less universally feasible than after the Second World War, when ownership had generally become more dispersed.[29] Perhaps one reason that families everywhere were keen to maintain a controlling block was that it was perfectly obvious what could happen if they relaxed their grip. When the Gruson family incautiously issued most of the capital of their family armaments firm on the Berlin Stock Exchange, at their first annual general meeting in 1892, they discovered that Fritz Krupp had simply bought a controlling stake in the market. The family were unceremoniously booted off the board and Krupp took over, the once-quoted firm becoming a subsidiary of his unquoted family firm. This was a financial stretch even for such a large family firm, but Krupp

---

the hundreds of thousands which became more common from the 1920s) and large shareholding blocks by non-directors could have been common.

[26] In Delaware and New Jersey, for example, laws allowed boards to keep shareholder lists confidential. Bearer shares, whose owners were unknown unless, for example, they identified themselves by attending shareholder meetings, dominated German shareholding. However, in Britain shareholder lists for companies registered under the Companies Acts were publicly updated annually at Somerset House, while in Japan they were often published as an appendix to corporate annual reports.

[27] Cases of open public bids at a uniform price direct to shareholders in the modern manner appear rare, though such public offers were frequently made with the support and recommendation of the incumbent board.

[28] The financial sector is not considered here, but contested bids were very rare there, partly for reputational reasons. See Hannah, 'The divorce of ownership', 412–14, 424; and O'Sullivan, M. 2007. 'The expansion of the US stock market, 1885–1930: historical facts and theoretical fashions'. *Enterprise and Society* 8(3): 519–20.

[29] Hannah, 'The divorce of ownership', 414–21.

re-financed his purchase in 1893 with a 24 million Deutsche Mark (US $6 million) bond issue, secured on Gruson's Magdeburg properties.[30] Unsurprisingly, many German industrialists, when floating their companies, were thereafter careful to retain control and issue only a minority of voting shares to the public.

Britain was the exception. Family firms were not permitted to float their ordinary shares on public markets without giving up majority voting control. The London Stock Exchange and some provincial exchanges required that at least two-thirds of any listed security must be subscribed in the public issue, with the vendors retaining no more than a third. Like Gruson's, British firms were apparently the most defenceless against outside bidders.[31] Yet, despite this compulsory share dispersion, the possible threat of takeover does not seem to have prevented families from seeking stock exchange flotations. Indeed, the London Stock Exchange was, at this time, the largest in the world and companies on it had ownership typically widely separated from control. The explanation seems to be that British incumbent boards could deploy alternative anti-takeover defences that were as powerful as board majority shareholding. One important anti-takeover defence in the British corporate armoury was barred to German firms by legislation passed in 1884 which forbade new share issues with differential voting rights.[32] In Britain this was not banned, so a common form of anti-takeover defence was to issue non-voting preference shares (and/or non-voting bonds): the two-thirds rule applied separately to each class of capital, not to the company overall.[33] In one extreme case, Maple & Co., the board issued not only vote-less preference but also management (sometimes called founders'), shares with 500 times the voting power of ordinary shares, so they held 40 per cent of the votes with only 3 per cent of the capital! The more favoured option, however, was to issue preference shares with restricted voting rights. Among independent British-owned companies with more than £1 million capital listed in the 1912

---

[30] Manchester, W. 1968. *The Arms of Krupp 1587–1968*. Boston, MA: Little Brown, 207; *Saling's Börsenpapiere*, 1900–1. Berlin: Verlag für Börsen und Finanzliteratur, 341.

[31] The only other stock exchange I have encountered copying the British model of discouraging majority family ownership was Shanghai, where expatriate Britons founded the exchange. The 'two-thirds' rule was not relaxed in Britain until the late 1940s. Even at the present time the average free float in German listed companies is only at the level already required by the London Stock Exchange in the nineteenth century; see Swann, C. 2000. 'The weak will become prey'. *Financial Times*, 30 June, 4.

[32] Though in the 1920s the German provision was relaxed and unequal voting rights became more common there too. In France, preference shares were also effectively outlawed by a provision that they could only be issued with the unanimous consent of existing shareholders, though this provision was relaxed in 1902, widening the possibility of non-voting preference shares there, though they were still not extensively adopted. Non-voting bonds were also legal in most countries, though they appear to have been relatively uncommon at this period in Berlin.

[33] The purpose of the London two-thirds listing rule was, of course, to encourage liquid share-trading and inhibit corners, not to facilitate takeover bids.

Investor's Year Book which issued two or more classes of share, 44 per cent restricted the voting rights of some (usually preference) shareholders, so the directors retained a larger proportion of votes than they did of the share capital.[34] Some companies listed only debentures, with no voting rights at all, the directors retaining complete control of the unlisted ordinaries.[35] Even so, the proportion of British boards with full voting control remained quite limited, by either contemporary standards abroad or even by modern British or American standards.

Other anti-takeover defences included voting trusts, limited proxy rights, interlocking shareholdings, and pyramiding. Where shares with unequal votes were banned, as in Germany, other anti-takeover defences were used, although this did not apply to firms that predated the 1884 legislation. Bonds could, of course, be issued – as elsewhere – without votes, but the German market for corporate bonds at this time was, in fact, relatively small. The main German method of retaining control seems to have been via ownership of a large block of shares, the method banned by the London listing rule. However, rapidly expanding firms found this difficult. In 1902, the Siemens family was faced with having to issue such a large quantity of new capital to fund its agreed merger with the Schuckert electrical enterprise it would have reduced the family's share of the corporate capital to below their controlling 53 per cent stake. The family overcame the problem by creating a pyramid structure that retained its majority control of the peak controlling capital, while much of the outside capital had its votes neutralized in controlled subsidiaries.[36] In Japan, the incumbent management were kicked out of the cotton firm Kanegafuchi Boseki in 1905 by an outside bidder, but succeeded in returning with Yasuda Bank support in 1908. A new statute in 1921 protected the management from further outsider intervention by insisting that two senior posts be held by those with five years' experience in the company.[37]

In the United States, family firms often shunned the more public markets, like the New York Stock Exchange, which from 1895 increasingly required

---

[34] These are based on my calculations from the *Investors' Year Book*. Even so, boards with more than 50 per cent of the votes were extremely rare in Britain by 1911, and the majority of boards of companies capitalized at £1 million or more had less than 5 per cent of the votes.

[35] I found only three independent listed British-owned companies with more than £1 million share capital that listed *only* debentures in 1911: Charringtons, the brewers, Gilbeys, the gin distillers and wine merchants, and S. Pearson & Son, the public works contractors. However, this was more common among smaller companies, especially breweries.

[36] Siemens, G. 1957. *History of the House of Siemens. Volume 1, The Era of Free Enterprise.* Freiburg: Adler, 192–7, 329–30; Joly, H. 2003. 'Ende des Familienkapitalismus'. In *Die deutsche Wirtschaftselite im 20. Jahrhundert*, edited by V.R. Berghahn, S. Unger, and D. Ziegler. Essen: Klartext, 75–91.

[37] Miwa and Ramseyer, 'Corporate governance in transitional economies', 198.

transparency in accounting on the European model. Instead they preferred to use the New York curb, which had no publicity requirements on accounts and permitted families to sell and buy in the market without providing information about the changing levels of their shareholdings.[38] From the 1890s, banks such as J.P. Morgan increasingly made public issues for industrials on the New York Stock Exchange of the kind which had long been common in Europe, though typically on a somewhat larger scale: the average size of listed companies in New York-listed companies was three times that quoted on the leading European exchanges. Yet, even in such cases, the families often retained a majority of the capital and the votes; while in cases where the dominant family may not have been able to maintain control, voting trusts were also often created to restrict the voting powers of outside shareholders.

There were some US-listed companies where neither voting trusts nor board majorities existed, most famously the widely held US Steel Corporation, from its foundation in 1901 the world's largest quoted industrial company. Of course, giant size itself was, in this period – and, indeed, at any time before the 1980s boom in competitive financing of leveraged deals – an effective takeover defence. Probably only one person – J.P. Morgan – was at this time capable of raising enough outside capital to bid for voting control of US Steel and he already had substantial influence over its board appointments and corporate policymaking.[39] Perhaps for these reasons, I have not been able to trace any contested outside bids for listed American industrial companies in this early period, of the kind that occasionally happened in British, German, and Japanese industrial and commercial companies or in US railways.

Sometimes contested bids succeeded even in the nineteenth century. Although the directors of Provident Insurance and Trust (a Natal insurer) recommended acceptance of a bid from Imperial Assurance in 1894, it was a rival bid from Commercial Union (a British insurance group) – of only 3.5 per cent more – that won the shareholders' direct approval.[40] However, even in 'Anglo-Saxon' countries it was more usual for shareholders to follow their boards' recommendations.[41] Most boards that lacked a voting majority ruled their companies securely, without effective shareholder challenge, unless they were egregiously corrupt or ineffective, and, even then, shareholder rights were more likely to be asserted in meetings via shareholder investigating

---

[38] Among the major firms not listed on the New York Stock Exchange but trading on the curb were Standard Oil, Singer, Procter and Gamble (after delisting in 1903), and Eastman Kodak.

[39] John D. Rockefeller was also personally rich enough to bid for a majority of the voting stock and held some, but he had already decided to sell his iron ore interests to the steel colossus and concentrate his voting power in oil, copper, and railroads.

[40] Liveing, E. 1961. *A Century of Insurance: The Commercial Union Group of Insurance Companies, 1861–1961*. London: Witherby, 63–4.

[41] Cases of shareholders resisting such recommendations are rare, but see Hannah, 'Takeover bids in Britain', 70 for a 1935 British example.

committees than by outside contested bidding. Boards were occasionally willing to give up the perquisites of office, even in some circumstances where they disagreed with the objectives of the bidder but saw that shareholders would benefit from the attractive price offered.[42] In other cases, they were not willing to recommend a bid in such circumstances. The solutions adopted by those wishing to force through such bids reflected the power of incumbent boards in such conditions of poor information. One solution was what would now be considered a bribe to the directors to recommend the offer to shareholders, thus greatly increasing the likelihood of acceptance and perhaps reducing the overall price, relative to the purchase of shares in the market. Thus British directors of acquired firms not offered seats on the acquirer's board were sometimes pensioned off with a fee for several years after their displacement, in return for a recommendation that shareholders accept the offer.[43] In the United States, Morgan persuaded the stockholders in existing quoted companies to merge to form US Steel by obtaining the endorsement of the incumbent directors by offering them participation in an underwriting syndicate (whose excessive underwriting fee was undisclosed to other stockholders in the offer document).[44] Thus, effectively the insider director–stockholders were offered a higher price than other stockholders, though that particular strategy of undisclosed inducement was already illegal in the United Kingdom, and other forms were occasionally already considered unethical, while not explicitly barred.

LATER DEVELOPMENTS: FROM PERVASIVE CONSTRAINTS TO OPEN CONTESTS

During the first half of the twentieth century, the use of anti-takeover defences proliferated. Incumbent boards' dislike of takeovers was, understandably, a universal phenomenon. In an atmosphere of rising nationalism following the Versailles settlement, many new and old European countries introduced takeover defences explicitly designed to prevent foreign control.[45] Pyramiding

---

[42] Hannah, 'Takeover bids in Britain', 69 for some inter-war examples.   [43] Ibid., 72, nn. 5 and 6.

[44] Hannah, L. 2007. 'What did Morgan's men really do?'. *University of Tokyo CIRJE Discussion Paper* F-465.

[45] Some of these defences – for example, requiring a majority of national directors on the board or restricting the votes of controlling shareholders – date back to the nineteenth century, though in countries such as the Netherlands or Russia they were sometimes circumvented by using dummy directors or shareholders. Small European countries, such as Sweden or Switzerland, or newly independent ones like the successor states of the Hapsburg Empire, were particularly prone to nationalist restrictions and 'nostrification'. Even in the United States and the United Kingdom, there were selective nostrifications (such as the squeezing out of British–Italian capital to create Radio Corporation of America, ostensibly on national security grounds).

was widely used in US utilities as a means of entrenching control of founding entrepreneurs and their families. Even some of the most widely held US corporations, which had once appeared too large to be taken over, deemed it wise to discourage the activity. The Pennsylvania Railroad, for example, formed a voting trust to more securely entrench its professional management. AT&T, faced with its largest shareholder (who owned 5 per cent of the firm) challenging the incumbent management, initiated a programme of worker and customer shareholding, aimed partly at dispersing shares among such holders, who were perceived as more loyal.[46] In the United States, by the 1920s, as share ownership was becoming as widely dispersed as it had been in Europe at an earlier stage, non-voting shares were becoming so commonly used to entrench ownership and control – the most notable case being Dillon Read's issue for Dodge Motor Co. – that the New York Stock Exchange attempted a ban on them, in favour of equal treatment for all shareholders.[47] Yet new dominant firms such as Ford were able, as they went public and endowed their charities with non-voting stock in the mid-century decades, to devise voting structures that preserved family voting control.[48] Few outsiders were willing to finance a proxy fight, which managers could defend using the company's own resources. Berle and Means therefore referred to shareholders' voting rights as practically inoperative: 'a right to revolution rather than a method of control'.[49] Revolution was not, generally, a modern American taste: boards were almost perfectly secure.

In 1920s, continental Europe, nationalism and currency instability created an *Uberfremdungsgefahr* and many boards – in Belgium, Holland, and France as well as in Germany – used fear of foreign takeover as a cover for entrenching their own powers by issuing privileged voting stock.[50] In Britain, there was both legislation and stock exchange regulation – based on elementary beliefs in shareholder rights, rather than explicit endorsement of the virtues of bids – to prevent directors resisting their own removal in the event of outsiders obtaining majority control.[51] This should have encouraged bids. Yet in Britain,

---

[46] Lipartito, K. and Y. Morii 2008. 'Rethinking the separation of ownership from management in American history'. Paper presented to the Social Science History Conference, Miami, FL.

[47] The London Stock Exchange tolerated them for somewhat longer (though discouraged them from the 1950s on). On the other hand, the German legal ban was relaxed in the 1920s.

[48] Even today the Ford family has 40 per cent of the votes, while owning only 4 per cent of the capital.

[49] Berle, A.A. and C.G. Means 1931. 'Corporation'. In *International Encyclopedia of the Social Sciences*, Volume 4, edited by E.R.A. Seligman. New York, NY: The Macmillan Company, 420.

[50] Lamal. E. 1930. *Une Enquête surles actions a vote privilégié en Belgique*. Brussels: Lamertin, 1–9, 45.

[51] Hannah, 'Takeover bids in Britain', 69, n. 5 for examples around 1929, and 67, for an example of directors failing to change articles of association to thwart a takeover. See Ingall, G.D. and G. Withers 1904. *The Stock Exchange*. London: Arnold, 73, for pre-1914 takeover bids in British mining enterprises.

too, there was also a widespread view that challenging the considered stance of a corporate board was culturally unacceptable and the few who ignored such widely accepted norms seriously risked failing to win shareholder approval.[52] Max Aitken bought a controlling majority of Rolls-Royce shares in the market in 1912 on behalf of a financial group, but when they failed to persuade the incumbent board to adopt their favoured policies, they, apparently graciously, accepted the directors' alternative strategy.[53]

Richard Roberts has described how this cultural and legal norm first changed in 1950s Britain.[54] As improving information, increasing divorce of ownership from control and other factors led some entrepreneurs to flout these established conventions, the view of politicians, the City establishment, and the Bank of England about these new corporate raiders initially remained traditional. Winston Churchill was outraged that his favourite hotel, the Savoy, was threatened by takeover and demanded action to prevent it! 'This kind of manoeuvre may mean the break-up of businesses which are making an important contribution to the nation's needs', a Bank of England memorandum on the subject dutifully concluded. Its solemnly authoritative and defensive language could easily be mistaken for a recent pronouncement of Japan's Keidanren business association about an interloping bidder like Livedoor! Yet, critically, Bank of England officials later came to the more considered view that bidders had a useful economic function – 'Directors generally have only themselves to blame if they are dispossessed by more enterprising rivals' – and laid the foundation of later policy by recommending self-regulation by a City Working Party rather than legislative intervention. By 1967, this had resulted in the acceptance by British and foreign investment banks in London of a voluntary code of behaviour in merger negotiations, which proved highly effective in protecting the rights of shareholders and weakening those of directors. Whereas in the United States, smart corporate lawyers funded by incumbent boards were endlessly innovative in devising corporate defences against takeover – such as so-called 'poison pills' – in Britain the Takeover Panel, as the Working Party soon became known, responded rapidly and flexibly to veto any such subterfuges. Paradoxically, self-regulation by financiers, which survived in relation to takeover bids despite its progressive abandonment elsewhere, proved more effective than the rule of law in preserving this aspect of the rights of shareholders against incumbent management. The result was the development in Britain of the

---

[52] Hannah, 'Takeover bids in Britain', 67, 70, n. 6, 72–3.

[53] Lloyd, I. 1978. *Rolls-Royce: The Growth of a Company*. London: Macmillan, 39–41.

[54] Roberts, R. 1992. 'Regulatory responses to the market for corporate control in Britain in the 1950s'. *Business History* 34(1): 183–200. See also Cheffins, B.R. 2008. *Corporate Ownership and Control: British Business Transformed*. Oxford: Oxford University Press, 333–6, 360–70.

most fluid and open market in corporate control of anywhere in the world, while in the United States, resistance to takeovers remained more feasible.[55]

In recent decades, contested takeover bidding has again become common. The United States is usually considered the most enthusiastic in following the United Kingdom, partly as a consequence of the courts restricting some takeover defences. Continental Europe has also seen more bids. In Germany, Thyssen's bid for Rheinstahl is commonly considered the pivotal change.[56] In France, bids also developed in the late 1960s, with about thirty cases, including the BSN-Saint Gobain contest.[57] By the current count of Citibank's survey, contested takeover bids are now more common in Europe than in the United States.[58] In Japan, 'greenmailings' increased in the 1970s and 1980s and more contested bids have recently occurred, though the country remains one of the least hospitable markets for hostile bids.[59]

One important innovation of the last few decades, which has removed size as a barrier to contested takeover, is the development of highly leveraged deals, underwritten by private equity firms and banks. Managers with modest personal stakes but formidable reputations (for good strategic sense and effective execution) can now realistically challenge incumbent boards. While it was difficult in the past to contemplate a bid for a firm as big as US Steel, or more recently, ICI, that is no longer the case.

CONCLUSION: THE AMBIGUOUS CONSEQUENCES

Whether contested takeovers are best left relatively unconstrained (as in Britain) or should be subject in some degree to social, political, or cultural control (as in many other countries) is an open question, which cannot be resolved here. Alfred Chandler's conclusion was, however, clear and unmistakeable: contested takeover bids of the sort experienced in the United States

---

[55] While increasing competition in the 1980s compromised this British tradition of self-regulation, in takeovers, foreign investment banks (including the major American players) operating in London respected the British rules rather than challenging them.

[56] Breiding, W.D. 1974. *Ubernahmeangebote im amerikanischen Börse und Gesellschaftsrecht*. Unpublished PhD Thesis, University of Kiel, 11.

[57] von Kapff, K. 1975. *Ubernahmeangebote in England und Frankreich*. Unpublished PhD Thesis, University of Augsburg, 160; Bonin, 'Offensives boursières'.

[58] Politi, J. 2007. 'Hostile takeovers make a comeback'. *Financial Times*, 28 November, special report on corporate finance, 1.

[59] Kester. W.C. 1991. *Japanese Takeovers: The Global Contest for Corporate Control*. Boston, MA: Harvard Business School Press; Milhaupt, C.J. 2005. 'In the shadow of Delaware? The rise of hostile takeovers in Japan'. *Columbia Law Review* 105(7): 2171–216; Jackson, G. and H. Miyajima 2006. 'Varieties of takeover markets: comparing mergers and acquisitions in Japan with Europe and the USA'. Unpublished paper.

compromised the development of organizational capabilities in managerial enterprises. Even though contested bids were relatively few in number, they posed grave risks to America's carefully nurtured pre-eminence in the industrial world.[60] It is possible that he was, at least partly, right, though America's pre-eminence proved much more secure than Chandler feared, partly, in the view of some American economists, because of the successful jolt administered to the complacency of inefficient Chandlerian managerial hierarchies by contested bidding.[61]

Sceptical views about bids – similar to Chandler's – have been more the norm in Japan and continental Europe, as similar features of the market for corporate control have developed there. Such views are still widely shared, despite evidence that some contested bids, private equity deals, and related elements of 'Anglo-Saxon capitalism' appear to have helped their economies overcome some of their alleged recent institutional sclerosis. The *Economist*, in the context of discussing the recent bid for Solid Group, quoted Atsushi Saito, President of the Tokyo Stock Exchange, as saying: 'It is difficult to assert that companies are owned by their shareholders.'[62] Chandler would have loved this: when questioned by a journalist about American corporate governance and shareholder democracy, he said: 'If you really believe – this is where I get upset – that the function of the firm is to give dividends to shareholders, we're going to end up worse than Britain.'[63]

Academic research is not entirely unsupportive of such sceptical views on the merits of contested bids reinforcing shareholder control, though the benefits to the shareholders of target companies in the post-war United Kingdom are clear enough: a 20–30 per cent premium on the pre-bid price.[64] Yet historical analyses of mergers suggest many fail, while acquired firms are *not* the least well performing, which calls into doubt the effectiveness

---

[60] Chandler, A.D. 1992. 'Managerial enterprise and competitive capabilities'. *Business History* 34(1): 1–41. This is the full version of an article summarized in Chandler, A.D. 1990. 'The enduring logic of industrial success'. *Harvard Business Review* 90(2): 130–40.

[61] Andrade et al., 'New evidence and perspectives on mergers', 104–20; Holmstrom and Kaplan, 'Corporate governance and merger activity', 121–44.

[62] *Economist*, 22 December 2007, 110. In Germany, Werner Seifert, head of the Deutsche Börse, expressed similar sentiments in a famous book, *Invasion of the Locusts*, but he was subsequently removed from his position by foreign investors for his performance. It is still difficult – if not completely impossible – to imagine that happening in Japan! Seifert's book was published in German: Seifert, W.G. and H-J. Voth 2006. *Invasion der Heuschrecken. Intrigen – Machtkämpfe – Marktmanipulation. Wie Hedge Fonds die Deutschland AG attackieren*. Berlin: Econ.

[63] Interview with *Financial World*, cited in Parker, W.N. 1991. 'The scale and scope of Alfred, D. Chandler, Jr'. *Journal of Economic History* 51(4): 958–63.

[64] Franks, J.R. and R.S. Harris 1989. 'Shareholder wealth effects of corporate takeovers: the UK experience 1955–1985'. *Journal of Financial Economics* 23(2): 225–49.

of this market discipline.[65] Even some Chicago-style free marketeers perceive difficulties – free-rider problems, 'imperialist' rather than value-maximizing motivations of acquiring managers, the winner's curse, overturning of implicit contracts – with the contested market for control.[66] It is not easy to accept the view – that investment bankers miraculously appear to get away with – that in one decade a merger is required to achieve the benefits of diversification and economies of scope, while, a few years later, managers who do not demerge those very same businesses and focus on their 'core' activities are considered strategically incompetent. The only consistent feature of such recommendations is the large investment banking fees that both transactions require! More recently, there is some evidence that the successful acquirers are not so much the more effective managers as those (foolishly, it now increasingly appears) willing to take higher leverage risks: such people are not necessarily those best qualified to control corporate assets.

The issue of the desirability of takeover bids as a means to improve the quality of corporate management to whom shareholders delegate their ownership rights therefore remains as contested and controversial as at its birth – or perhaps, more accurately, stillbirth – in the nineteenth century, and rightly so. What is good for Goldman Sachs is not necessarily good for the United States, or, indeed, for the global economy, though it sometimes will be. Probably the partners of Goldman Sachs are more capable than politicians of knowing the appropriate financial structure for enterprises. It is unclear whether they – and other investment bankers operating in an environment of asymmetric information – have always been correctly motivated to implement such optima. The current global financial crisis prompts reasonable doubt on the matter.

---

[65] Singh, A. 1975. 'Takeovers, economic natural selection and the theory of the firm'. *Economic Journal* 85(339): 497–515. However, such tests are not decisive: the absence of any correlation could mean that the threat of takeover is so effective that it pervasively disciplines incumbent boards to more effective performance, irrespective of whether they are themselves subject to a bid; see Hannah, L. and J.A. Kay 1977. *Concentration in Modern Industry: Theory, Measurement and the UK Experience*. London: Macmillan, 124–5.

[66] See the various contributions, especially that by Andre Shleifer and Robert Vishny, to the special 1988 edition of the *Journal of Economic Perspectives* 2(1), edited by H.R. Varian.

11

Wealth, Investment, and Global Finance: International Financial Centres, 1870–1930

Youssef Cassis

International financial centres have been a major source of wealth accumulation and an essential channel for investment – hence their relevance to the themes of this book. A financial centre can be defined as an intermediation process between a surplus and deficit of capital. Indeed, a leading London merchant banker once considered that 'all they [financial centres] require is a surplus of capital, a roughly offsetting deficit of capital and an intermediator or intermediation process'.[1] Put another way, a financial centre can be considered as the grouping together, in a given urban space, of a certain number of financial services; or, in a more functional way, as the place where intermediaries coordinate financial transactions and arrange for payments to be settled. This geographical concentration can chiefly be explained by external economies – in other words, the benefits deriving from the liquidity and efficiency of markets, the diversity and complementarity of financial activities, professional services, technological expertise, and access to high-quality information.

The object of this chapter is to provide a broad framework within which issues considered in previous chapters of this book – the relationships between knowledge, investment and risk, regional and social variations in wealth-holding, and companies and investors – can be set in context. It primarily deals with London, the financial centre of the world between 1870 and 1914 and in many respects still in the lead after the First World War; and with New York, the main port of entry for British overseas investment before 1914 and the leading centre for foreign lending. By the 1920s, New York was also

---

This chapter is mainly based on my recent book Cassis, Y. 2006. *Capitals of Capital: A History of International Financial Centres, 1780–2005.* Cambridge: Cambridge University Press.

[1] Scholey, D. 1987. 'Essential features of international financial centres'. In *International Financial Centres: Structure, Achievements and Prospects*, Swiss Bankers' Association, Proceedings of the 40th International Summer School, Interlaken/Basel, 12.

London's main rival. The chapter takes a chronological approach, starting with the globalized economy between 1870 and 1914, before discussing the shock of the First World War and then considering the post-war financial order of the 1920s. A final section draws some general conclusions.

THE FIRST GLOBALIZATION
OF THE WORLD ECONOMY

The political and economic environment prior to 1914 was particularly conducive to the rapid development of international financial centres. In many respects, it was truly a golden age for them and one that they would not encounter again before the late twentieth century. With the financing of international trade, their main activities revolved around foreign investment; in other words, essentially issuing securities on behalf of governments and companies abroad, and trading these securities on the secondary markets. This period has often and rightly been characterized as the first era of globalization. Exported capital reached hitherto unheard of – and even undreamt of – sums; it was invested in the four corners of the world and used to finance a multitude of public and private activities. And international financial centres became far more closely integrated, owing to the much faster transmission of information and the free circulation of capital – as witnessed by the harmonization of the prices of stock traded simultaneously in several centres and the strong international convergence of interest rates.[2]

Even if globalization is, by definition, a global phenomenon, it takes place within the framework of an economic order that hinges on a dominant economy. Between 1870 and 1914, the dominant economy was Great Britain.[3] However, even by the start of this period, Britain was no longer the world's largest economy. It had been overtaken by the United States in terms of total national income by 1870 and in terms of per capita income shortly before 1914.[4] Nor was Britain the world's foremost industrial power: it had been

---

[2] See Neal, L. 1985. 'Integration of international capital markets: quantitative evidence from the eighteenth to the twentieth centuries'. *Journal of Economic History* 45(2): 219–26; Homer, S. and R. Sylla 1996. *A History of Interest Rates*, 3rd edition. New Brunswick, NJ: Rutgers University Press.

[3] On Great Britain's dominant position before 1914, see Crouzet, F. 1978. *L'économie de la Grande-Bretagne victorienne*. Paris: Belin, 17–25.

[4] In 1870 the United Kingdom's GDP, measured in dollars of 1985, came to $82 billion and that of the United States to $90 billion. In 1913 the figures were $184 billion and $472 billion, respectively. Even in terms of per capita income, while Britain retained a small lead over the United States in 1870 ($2610 compared with $2247), this was no longer the case on the eve of the war ($4024 compared with $4854). Maddison, A. 1991. *Dynamic Forces in Capitalist Development*. Oxford: Oxford University Press, 6–7.

overtaken by the United States around 1880 and by Germany around 1905, even though its level of industrialization, measured in terms of per capita industrial production, was probably still the highest in the world. The fact that Britain remained the dominant economy until 1914 was thanks to the leadership that it retained in numerous fields of activity, such as foreign trade, services, and finance on the one hand, and to its key position in the system of multilateral trade on the other.

London's position as the financial centre of the world meant that it played a key role in the global economy. The City had held the top position among the international financial centres since the beginning of the nineteenth century. Its position was strengthened from 1870s onwards and for about forty years the City was the hub of international financial relations. The strengthening was of a quantitative nature, whether measured in terms of financial capacity (Britain was by far the largest exporter of capital, with a stock of foreign investment reaching some $18.3 billion, about 42 per cent of the world's total, in 1913, as against $8.7 billion, 20 per cent, for France); size of its financial institutions (10 of the world's 25 largest largest commercial banks in 1913 were based in London) and markets (the London Stock Exchange was nearly twice as large as the Paris Bourse, its immediate follower); or multinational banking (London was home to 31 multinational British banks with 1387 foreign branches in 1913, nearly three times as many as French and German banks, and host to 30 foreign banks, as against 15 in Paris).[5] But, and even more significantly, the strengthening was also qualitative. Between 1870 and 1914, the City of London became the first modern financial centre, where an unrivalled range of hitherto unavailable, or at least hard-to-find, services were provided. At the risk of oversimplifying the complexity and richness of the City's texture, the most significant amongst them will be highlighted, especially with respect to wealth and investment.

THE MECHANISM OF THE CITY

The first such service was commercial banking. The City's financial predominance was assured by a combination of financial institutions whose operating mechanisms were highly integrated. The lynchpins of the mechanism were the clearing banks. Their banking services – short-term loans to private and corporate customers and discounting – provided the cash credit which fuelled the entire system, especially the money and financial markets. They also acted as London agent for foreign banks, holding their London deposits

---

[5] United Nations, 1949. *International Capital Movements during the Interwar Period.* New York, NY: United Nations. On the number of banking institutions in different financial centres, see Jones, G. 1993. *British Multinational Banking, 1830–1990.* Oxford: Clarendon Press.

and undertaking various transactions on their behalf, especially on the money market.[6] The clearing banks enjoyed tremendous growth during the period, mainly as a result of an intense amalgamation movement leading by 1914 to the formation of a dozen London-based banks, with a national network of branches, controlling about two-thirds of the country's deposits, four of which – Midland, Lloyds, Westminster, and National Provincial – ranked amongst the world's top 10.[7] Another service was trade finance. More than any other activity, the financing of world trade lay at the heart of the City's international calling. The volume of acceptances on the London market grew from approximately £50 or £60 million in 1875 to some £140 million in 1913; in other words, by more than 120 per cent. This activity remained the prerogative of the merchant banks, which held 70 per cent of the market on the eve of the First World War.[8] It was these banks that accepted, or upon which were directly drawn, bills of exchange, generally for three months, that constituted the main instrument for financing international trade. The good reputation of the merchant banks turned these bills of exchange into negotiable instruments. Well before they reached their maturity dates, they were discounted, also by specialized banking houses – the discount houses – which then resold them to various British or foreign banks present in the City; and thus these bills lay at the heart of the huge discount market that existed in London and in which the banks of the entire world took part, whether directly or indirectly. From then on, 'Lombard Street belonged to the whole world'.[9] On the eve of the war, there were nearly £350 million worth of bills in circulation, the bulk of them in the form of bills of exchange, but a growing proportion of them in riskier finance bills.

The issuing of loans and equities on behalf of foreign government and companies remained the City's most prestigious activity. A rough measure of the growth of the business, and of the City's prominence in the field, is given by the volume of capital exports from Britain. The merchant banks – above all such houses as Rothschilds, Barings, Morgan Grenfell, or Schroders – also succeeded in keeping control over this activity offering, on average, 40 per cent of these issues to the public between 1870 and 1914.[10] Foreign issues

---

[6] Battilossi, S. 2000. 'Financial innovation and the golden age of international banking: 1890–1931 and 1958–81'. *Financial History Review* 7(2): 150–1; Flandreau, M. and F. Gallice 2005. 'Paris, London and the international money market: lessons from Paribas, 1885–1913'. In *London and Paris as International Financial Centres in the Twentieth Century*, edited by Y. Cassis and E. Bussière. Oxford: Oxford University Press, 79–106.

[7] Cottrell, P.L. 1998. 'Aspects of commercial banking in northern and central Europe, 1880–1931'. In *International Banking in an Age of Transition*, edited by S. Kinsey and L. Newton. Aldershot: Ashgate, 109.

[8] Chapman, S.D. 1984. *The Rise of Merchant Banking*. London: Allen and Unwin.

[9] King, W.T.C. 1936. *A History of the London Discount Market*. London: Routledge.

[10] Hall, A.R. 1963. *The London Capital Market and Australia, 1870–1914*. Canberra, ACT: Australian National University.

represented some two-thirds of all new issues in the two decades preceding the First World War. Britain was then investing more abroad than at home. Capital outflows represented on average 40 per cent of available savings between 1880 and 1914, reaching 67 per cent at their peak, in the years 1906–14. Forty per cent of foreign investment went to the British Empire, the largest part being allocated to India and the settler colonies of Canada, South Africa, Australia, and New Zealand. A similar proportion was invested in railways bonds and over a third in government bonds.[11]

The City's pulse beat to the rhythm of its markets, headed by the London Stock Exchange, where the nominal value of the securities listed there went from £2.3 billion in 1873 to £11.3 billion in 1913; in other words, more than the New York Stock Exchange and the Paris Bourse combined.[12] As evidence of its highly cosmopolitan character, foreign stocks, which represented between 35 and 40 per cent of the total in 1873, exceeded 50 per cent from 1893 onwards. By 1914, one-third of all negotiable instruments in the world were quoted on the London Stock Exchange.[13] The functioning of the market was based on the separation of roles between jobbers and brokers. The jobbers were securities traders who earned their profit from the difference between the purchase price and the selling price. But they could not buy or sell securities directly from the public, which did not have direct access to the Stock Exchange. For all its transactions, the public, whether individuals or companies, was obliged to go through a broker who, in return for a commission, would negotiate with the jobber. The separation between brokers and jobbers offered guarantees of security to the public, since the broker with whom it dealt made no profit on the difference between the purchase price and the selling price and competition between jobbers assured clients of a narrow margin between the two prices.[14] Apart from functioning as a market organized for trading negotiable stocks, and even more so for speculating on these stocks, the London Stock Exchange represented an important outlet for short-term funds. The City's various financial institutions used the possibility of investing short term on the stock exchange, by buying and reselling

[11] See Simon, M. 1968. 'The pattern of new British portfolio investment, 1865–1914'. In *The Export of Capital from Britain 1870–1914*, edited by A.R. Hall. London: Methuen, 15–44; Edelstein, M. 1982. *Overseas Investment in the Age of High Imperialism: The United Kingdom 1850–1914*. London: Methuen; Davis, L. and R. Huttenback 1988. *Mammon and the Pursuit of Empire: The Economics of British Imperialism*. Abridged edition. Cambridge: Cambridge University Press. For a useful synthesis, see Pollard, S. 1989. *Britain's Prime and Britain's Decline The British Economy 1870–1914*. London: Edward Arnold, 58–114.

[12] Michie, R. 1999. *The London Stock Exchange: A History*. Oxford: Oxford University Press, 88.

[13] Davis, L. and L. Neal 1998. 'Micro rules and macro outcomes: the impact of micro structures on the efficiency of security exchanges, London, New York and Paris, 1800–1914'. *American Economic Review* 88(2): 40–5.

[14] See Michie, *The London Stock Exchange*; Kynaston, D. 1983. 'The London Stock Exchange, 1870–1914: an institutional history'. Unpublished PhD Thesis, University of London.

securities over short periods to obtain slightly higher yields than the money market's discount rate. These transactions were risky nevertheless, and the banks tended increasingly to lend these funds to brokers and jobbers, who, at their own risk, placed them themselves. In 1914, half of the very short-term credit granted by both the British and foreign banks in London were loans to members of the stock exchange, backed by securities pledged as collateral.[15]

The Bank of England stood on top of the entire edifice. However, the 'conductor' of the world's monetary system found it increasingly difficult to control the money market – because of the very expansion of this market and the new power of the clearing banks. No longer able to control the market merely by adjusting its discount rate, it had to resort to other means of making its interest rate effective. In particular, it borrowed on the market in order to raise the price of money and thus attract gold to London and, in times of crisis, it relied on support from the central banks, especially the Banque de France.[16]

INVESTMENT AND INVESTORS

The City offered a wide range of investment services. Individual investors dominated the stock market, their estimated number rising from 250,000 in 1870 to one million in 1914.[17] By then, some 70 per cent of securities were held by the richest segment of society, those with a fortune of £20,000 or more.[18] The diversification of assets for small investors was the *raison d'être* of a new kind of financial institution that appeared on the scene in the 1870s – the investment trust.[19] In England, the Foreign and Colonial Government Trust, founded in 1868 and specializing in foreign and colonial government bonds, was the first to apply the principles of the investment trust – namely spreading risk by purchasing large numbers of different stocks and by using a part of the

---

[15] Michie, *The London Stock Exchange*, 133–5. In fact, buying on the stock exchange was essentially done on the basis of loans, in a proportion that reached 80 per cent in the mid-1890s and even 90 per cent 15 years later, so much so that at the beginning of August 1914, brokers and jobbers owed more than £80 million to the City's banks and other financial institutions.

[16] Sayers, R.S. 1976. *The Bank of England 1891–1944*. Cambridge: Cambridge University Press.

[17] Jeffreys, J.B. 1977. *Business Organization in Great Britain 1856–1914*. New York, NY: Arno Press, 385–6. Clapham, J. 1938. *An Economic History of Modern Britain*. Volume 3. Cambridge: Cambridge University Press, 289. For further discussion of the numbers of investors, see Chapters 7 and 8 in this volume.

[18] Hall, *The London Capital Market*, 39.

[19] See Cassis, Y. 1990. 'The emergence of a new financial institution: investment trusts in Britain 1870–1939'. In *Capitalism in a Mature Economy: Financial Institutions, Capital Exports and British Industry*, edited by J.J. van Helten and Y. Cassis. Aldershot: Ashgate, 139–58.

surplus as a redemption fund to reimburse the initial capital. Its issue leaflet claimed that under its proposal: 'a capitalist who at any time within the last twenty or thirty years had invested, say £1,000,000 in 10 or 12 stocks selected with ordinary prudence, would...not only have received a high rate of interest, but by this time have received back his original capital by the action of the drawings and sinking fund, and held the greater part of his stock for nothing'.[20]

Investment trusts thus acted as a collective capitalist. They invested their shareholders' capital and paid them a dividend based on the average yield of their diversified investment as well as the gains from a few other operations. Their investments usually exceeded the amount of their share capital as, in addition to issuing debentures, they borrowed from the banks, pledging their capital as security. They also participated in underwriting syndicates and granted long – and medium-term loans to other companies.[21] Investment trusts experienced rapid growth in the late 1880s, with the nominal capital of all investment trusts quoted on the stock exchange growing from nearly £5 million in 1887 to some £50 million in 1890. They were profoundly shaken in the early 1890s, following the Baring crisis, and held responsible for all the fraudulent transactions associated with setting up limited liability companies. But they eventually won acceptance, as a new wave of creation took place after 1905. Their assets reached £90 million in 1913, mainly invested in foreign stock, primarily American. As a class of security, they represented, together with mortgage and land companies, 1.4 per cent of the nominal value of all securities quoted on the London Stock Exchange.[22]

Insurance was another of the City's great specialities. In addition to providing insurance services, insurance companies collected vast funds and played a growing role in the financial markets. Their assets increased fivefold between 1870 and 1914, while their portfolio became far more diversified, with a spectacular increase in foreign investment (from 7 to 40 per cent) and in the proportion of stocks of private companies (from 13 to nearly 40 per cent) to the detriment of insurance companies' traditional types of investment – government securities, loans to local authorities, and British railways.[23] The marine insurance market remained dominated by Lloyd's of London. Through

[20] Cited by Powell, E.T. 1915. *The Evolution of the Money Market*. London: Cass and Co., 467.

[21] A good case study is provided by Michie, R.C. 1983. 'Crisis and opportunity: the formation and operation of the British Assets Trust 1897–1914'. *Business History* 25(2): 125–47.

[22] Michie, *The London Stock Exchange*, 89. This percentage was comparable to that of Indian railways, telegraphs and telephones, and breweries and distilleries; though lower than Imperial railways, banks and discount companies, or iron and steel, each representing between 3 and 3.5 per cent.

[23] These changes implied that insurance companies were far more active on the stock exchange: 60 per cent of their investment went through the London Stock Exchange in 1913, compared with 25 per cent in 1880. See Supple, B. 1970. *The Royal Exchange Assurance: A History of British Insurance 1720–1970*. Oxford: Oxford University Press.

brokers it brought together insurance buyers and insurers willing to under-write the risk. Underwriting syndicates were led by insurance professionals but were mostly made up of Lloyd's members, commonly known as 'Names': they received a share of the syndicate's profits but, in the event of bankruptcy, were liable with their entire fortune.

The City's activities required professional services, especially legal and accounting: in 1891 about 700 accountancy and 2000 law firms were in operation there, though the figures include a vast majority of tiny firms that had no involvement at all in international activities on the London market.[24] International activities tended to be concentrated in the hands of a few key companies, such as Freshfield & Sons, Ashurst, Morris & Crisp, and Slaughter and May among the law firms; and Deloitte & Co., Price Waterhouse, and Cooper Brothers among the chartered accountants, which all grew in impor-tance during the period. Financial information was also abundantly available in the City, whether through the diverse though not always unbiased financial press, the advice of a stockbroker, or informal channels – not least through the innumerable private firms, both large and small (bankers, merchants, finan-ciers, stockbrokers, insurers, arbitragers, and brokers in the various commod-ity markets) all gathered within the square mile. This geographical concentration of expertise constituted one of the main characteristics of the City. It was a world unto itself, where people met continuously and where contacts were made orally among businessmen.

FOREIGN INVESTMENT IN THE UNITED STATES: THE ROLE OF NEW YORK

New York's accession to the rank of foremost international financial centre took a different route from that followed by London. The city became a major financial centre as an entry point into a capital-importing country rather than as an exit point from a capital-exporting country, and it mostly kept this status until 1914.[25] New York did not yet fulfil all the functions of a global interna-tional financial centre, but its importance became increasingly decisive be-cause of the total amount of foreign investment in the United States, the dynamism of the US economy and the city's position as the country's financial centre. On the eve of the First World War, the United States was the top destination for overseas investment, having accumulated some $7 billion

---

[24] Kynaston, D. 1995. *The City of London, Volume 2: Golden Years 1890–1914*. London: Chatto and Windus, 21.

[25] See Davis, L. and R. Cull 1994. *International Capital Markets and American Economic Growth 1820–1914*. Cambridge: Cambridge University Press.

worth of liabilities, of which nearly two-thirds were from British creditors. On the London Stock Exchange, US railways were the most popular type of security, making up 18.1 per cent of the nominal value of all quoted securities, ahead of foreign governments' bonds (14.9 per cent) and UK railways (12.7 per cent).[26] New York's international role began to grow as the first foreign issues were introduced at the beginning of the twentieth century, but it was still dependent upon the City of London for the financing of a good part of American foreign trade, and for obtaining liquid assets and, ultimately, gold.

The investment banks formed the cornerstone of New York's financial centre. The most important among them – J.P. Morgan & Co., Kuhn, Loeb & Co. – were those that had the closest links to foreign financial centres, above all the City of London, thereby illustrating Wall Street's national and international roles. Most of them had been founded in the first half of the nineteenth century, but really took off from the 1870s, above all in the national context, due to them financing the railways during the 1870s and 1880s and the large limited liability manufacturing companies in the 1890s. They also grew as a consequence of the sweeping trend towards mergers at the turn of the twentieth century. The investment banks' main task was to supply these firms with capital, usually through public issues. Yet the investment banks' activities also took place in an international context, as a larger or smaller proportion of the capital that they raised actually came from Europe, primarily Britain.[27] The predominance of the New York Stock Exchange over the other US stock exchanges dates back to the telecommunications revolution (telegraph, ticker tape in 1867, and then telephone in 1878). Its share of the nominal value of the securities listed on all the American stock exchanges reached 45 per cent in 1912, but 69 per cent of the total number of shares sold in the country in 1910 – and even 91 per cent (in value) for bonds.[28] As a result of its strict membership criteria, the New York Stock Exchange was driven to specialize in a certain type of stock – that of large American companies with solid reputations (railways and later large manufacturing companies). Another crucial role of the New York Stock Exchange was in attracting short-term funds, especially from banks and insurance companies. In the absence of a discount market modelled on London's, these funds made their way to the Stock Exchange.

---

[26] Michie, *The London Stock Exchange*, 89.

[27] See Carosso, V. 1970. *Investment Banking in America: A History*. Cambridge, MA: Harvard University Press.

[28] Michie, R. 1987. *The London and New York Stock Exchanges, 1850–1914*. London: Allen and Unwin, 168–70.

THE FIRST WORLD WAR

International financial centres prosper in times of peace, not in times of war. Indeed for most bankers and financiers, the war meant a marked decrease in their activities, owing to disruptions in the trading of goods, services, and capital among countries, as well as to growing state intervention in economic and financial affairs. Foreign issues were prohibited or subject to control by all belligerents. And yet, international capital flows did not cease during the war – far from it. Between 1914 and 1918, debts totalling nearly £4 billion pounds or $19.4 billion – in other words an amount equivalent to the stock of British foreign assets on the eve of the war – were incurred among the Allies. The two main creditor countries were the United States ($9.2 billion) and the United Kingdom ($8.5 billion), with France ($1.7 billion) trailing far behind. But only the United States never needed to take out loans abroad during the hostilities. The British had to borrow $4.2 billion and the French $2.7 billion from the United States, the French also having to obtain loans for a more or less equivalent amount, namely $2.5 billion, from the British. The other Allies merely borrowed.[29]

These loans were essentially contracted between governments and did not activate the mechanisms usually associated with credit transfers between the international financial centres. France, for example, borrowed $2.9 billion from the American government compared with only $336 million from the banks, and $2.1 billion from the British government, compared with $625 million from the banks, including the Bank of England.[30] Only a few intermediaries and privileged partners were involved in these operations, most of which were managed from New York and London. One banking house dominated these operations: J.P. Morgan & Co. The New York bank took over the syndicate responsible for issuing the first Anglo-French loan for $500 million in October 1915 and four more loans amounting to a total of $950 million on behalf of Britain in 1916 and 1917.[31] The United States started to lend directly to London after entering the war in April 1917.

In the field of financial activities, the most important transformation brought about by the war was the dramatic growth in state borrowing. In Britain, the national debt increased from £700 million at the beginning of the war to £7.5 billion at the end. The assets of the big British banks mainly

[29] Kindleberger, C. 1993. *A Financial History of Western Europe*, 2nd edition. New York, NY: Oxford University Press.

[30] Artaud, D. 1977. 'Les dettes de guerre de la France, 1919–1929'. In *La position internationale de la France. Aspects économiques et financiers, XIXe–XXe siècles*, edited by M. Lévy-Leboyer. Paris: EHESS, 313–18.

[31] Burk, K. 1990. *Morgan Grenfell 1838–1988: The Biography of a Merchant Bank*. Oxford: Oxford University Press; Chernow, R. 1989. *The House of Morgan: An American Banking Dynasty and the Rise of Modern Finance*. London: Simon and Schuster.

comprised Treasury Bonds and similar stocks at that time. On the London Stock Exchange, government securities regained the part that they had played at the dawn of the first phase of globalization, exceeding 30 per cent of the nominal value of all quoted securities in 1920, compared with 11.5 per cent in 1913.[32] Stock-market transactions were themselves disrupted by restrictions like the ban on arbitrage operations.

The world economic order in 1918 was very different from what it had been four years earlier, especially with regards to the financial capacity of particular states, and thus that of the main financial centres that they hosted. The great victor was the United States, which in a few years changed from a debtor country to a creditor country – from having net private liabilities in excess of $3 billion 1913 to having net assets of $4.5 billion in 1919. Europe was no longer the world's banker. Britain, France, and Germany together lost more than a third of their foreign investment; in other words, some $12 billion. But the gaps between the three countries were far more significant than the Old Continent's collective destiny. Germany lost nearly all its foreign assets, France most of them – probably three-quarters of its assets in Europe, mainly in Russia – and Britain only a part, chiefly the $3 billion worth of American stock that it was obliged to sell.[33] Moreover, opportunities for building up their portfolio of foreign stocks again were limited. Germany, burdened with reparations, became a huge importer of capital. France was crippled until 1926 by the weakness of the franc, capital flight, and reconstruction requirements. Britain, on the other hand, found it increasingly difficult to regain its role of exporter of long-term capital because of the constraints weighing down its balance of payments, especially due to the loss of competitiveness of its staple industries. Financial centres were also operating in a much less stable monetary environment. The gold standard, which had underpinned the international monetary system since the 1880s, stopped functioning at the beginning of the conflict. Restoring it proved difficult, not least because of rampant inflation and hyperinflation. Even though restoration was finally achieved between 1924 and 1926, amidst efforts and crisis, the system never worked entirely satisfactorily until its final collapse in 1931.[34]

---

[32] Michie, *The London Stock Exchange*, 184.

[33] Feinstein, C. and K. Watson 1995. 'Private international capital flows in Europe in the inter-war period'. In *Banking, Currency and Finance in Europe between the Wars*, edited by C. Feinstein. Oxford: Oxford University Press, 98.

[34] See Eichengreen, B. 1995. *Golden Fetters: The Gold Standard and the Great Depression 1919–1939*. Oxford: Oxford University Press.

THE PERSISTENCE OF THE CITY

London's influence had indisputably been on the wane since 1914, mainly as a result of the reduction in British assets abroad, the large increase in the public debt, and the slump in the old British export industries. Crucially, this loss of influence occurred just as competition from New York was becoming keener. Nevertheless, at the end of the Great War, London still held some aces: unrivalled expertise, solid and well-established networks and client bases, considerable openness to the world and also, though to a lesser extent than New York, by no means insignificant financial capabilities, especially in relation to its stock of capital invested abroad, which still ranked first in the world. These were advantages that the British were determined to deploy to conserve for the City the top place that it had occupied before the war. In their view, this necessitated the return of the pound to the gold standard at its pre-war parity, an exchange rate usually considered as overvalued. The decision was nonetheless taken in April 1925.[35]

Overall, London remained the world's leading financial centre in the 1920s, even if it had to share this role with New York. It was in most respects a more international financial centre offering a far more comprehensive range of activities than New York. In this way, the situation was not so different from what it had been before 1914, except for placing foreign issues, the capital henceforth coming from the other side of the Atlantic. US investment capacity greatly exceeded Britain's potential, so that during the second half of the 1920s foreign issues placed in New York generally exceeded those offered in London by 50 per cent. They amounted to respectively $969 million and $592 million in 1924, to $1337 million and $676 million in 1927, and to $671 million and $457 million in 1929.[36] London suffered from restrictions placed on foreign loans, officially until 1919, then unofficially until 1925, on top of which came the handicap of a 2 per cent stamp duty. But foreign issues took off again in the second half of the 1920s, both on behalf of traditional clients, such as the governments of the Dominions, especially Australia, and new-comers such as big German companies.[37] Moreover, the United Kingdom remained the largest holder of long-term foreign investment in the inter-war

---

[35] On the pound's return to the gold standard, see also Moggridge, D.E. 1972. *British Monetary Policy, 1924–1931*. Cambridge: Cambridge University Press; Howson, S. 1975. *Domestic Monetary Management in Britain, 1919–1939*. Cambridge: Cambridge University Press; Sayers, *The Bank of England*; Eichengreen, *Golden Fetters*; Kynaston, D. 1999. *The City of London, Volume 3: Illusions of Gold, 1914–1945*. London: Chatto and Windus.

[36] Burk, K. 1992. 'Money and power: the shift from Great Britain to the United States'. In *Finance and Financiers in European History*, edited by Y. Cassis. Cambridge: Cambridge University Press, 364.

[37] Cottrell, P.L. 2005. 'Established connections and new opportunities: London as an international financial centre, 1914–1958'. In *London and Paris as International Financial Centres in the Twentieth Century*, edited by Y. Cassis and E. Bussière. Oxford: Oxford University Press, 161–4.

years, with $22.9 billion in 1938, as against $11.5 billion for the United States.[38]

Elsewhere, the City retained all or part of the advantage that it had enjoyed before 1914, particularly in financing international trade, the draft on London remaining, despite competition from New York, the preferred instrument for financing international trade. Consequently, the London money market recovered a great deal of its dynamism and, above all, its attraction for investing funds on a short-term basis – not only in the form of bills of exchange, which traditionally constituted its backbone, but also in the form of short-term Treasury Bonds that were especially popular at the time.[39] The clearing banks, dubbed the 'Big Five' following the 1918 mergers, became giant companies, the three most important amongst them – Barclays, Midland, and Lloyds – being at that time the largest banks in the world. On the foreign exchange market, a field of activity that developed considerably in the climate of monetary instability following the war, the City established its predominance from the very outset, thanks to its high concentration of banks from all over the world. The main foreign banking houses continued to maintain a presence in London (except for the large German banks) with, in total, 55 foreign banks having a branch or a representative office in the City in 1930. Moreover, the City's influence exerted internationally through multinational banks based in London grew during the 1920s – the British banks' total number of foreign branches increased from 1387 to 2253 between 1913 and 1928 and remained far more intense than that of any other financial centre.[40]

While openness to the world remained one of London's characteristics during the 1920s, a retreat to domestic financial business was nonetheless clearly perceptible. Foreign issues dropped to below half the total, whereas they had represented more than two-thirds before 1914. The stock exchange also mirrored this new state of affairs. By 1933, British government bonds represented 35.3 per cent of the nominal value of quoted securities, American railways only 7.7 per cent.[41] The merchant banks suffered from the scarcity of foreign issues on the London market and even though they kept control over those that remained, they started turning their attention to domestic issues. These tensions were reflected by the position of the Bank of England. While its international presence contributed to the prestige and influence of the City in the world – one of the avowed goals of its governor, Montagu Norman – the Bank had far greater difficulties in fulfilling its role as the guardian of the country's gold reserves.[42]

---

[38] Feinstein and Watson, 'Private International Capital Flows', 97.
[39] Scammell, W.M. 1968. *The London Discount Market*. London: Elek Books, 192–219.
[40] Jones, *British Multinational Banking*.   [41] Michie, *London Stock Exchange*, 184.
[42] Sayers, *Bank of England*.

THE RISE OF WALL STREET

As the war drew to a close, New York seemed ready to take up the torch of the world's financial centre from London: US foreign trade finance was freeing itself from London's control; acceptances in dollars were posing a serious challenge to those in sterling; the huge expansion of the US merchant navy during the war led to the parallel development of marine insurance; the national banks started expanding overseas, though they had mainly retreated to their home territory by 1925; and, of course, the United States lent heavily abroad.[43]

The change that hauled New York up to the top of the international hierarchy of financial centres was the export of capital – thanks to the American public's newly acquired enthusiasm for foreign stocks, combined with an abundance of savings in the United States and the east coast investment banks' expertise and networks of relationships. US foreign investment mainly flowed to Europe (41 per cent), ahead of Canada (25 per cent), Latin America (22 per cent) and Asia (12 per cent), with a very marked preference for public bonds that made up more than 95 per cent of issues between 1920 and 1929. These large-scale international financial operations essentially continued to be the preserve of the investment banks and the national banks that had dominated the stage even before 1914, the main difference being that from then on they acted far more as intermediaries between American savers and foreign debtors than between European investors and American companies. The responsibilities taken on by the Federal Reserve of New York reflected the USA's financial capital's new status and at the same time helped its influence grow. Its governor from 1914 to 1928, Benjamin Strong, certainly contributed to this both on the national level – his influence spread throughout the Federal Reserve System – and abroad. The Federal Reserve played its role to the full, as during the famous summit on Long Island in July 1927, at the end of which the Fed lowered its discount rate and conducted vast open-market operations to ease pressure on the Bank of England's gold reserves.[44]

However, in spite of its new world role, New York remained just as much an American financial centre as a truly international one. Foreign issues played a secondary role – unlike in London before 1914 and even in the 1920s – despite

---

[43] The banks were permitted by the Edge Act of 1919 to set up joint-stock companies to develop their international business. On overseas lending, see Wilkins, M. 1999. 'Cosmopolitan finance in the 1920s: New York's emergence as an international financial centre'. In *The State, the Financial System and Economic Modernization*, edited by R. Sylla, R. Tilly, and G. Tortella. Cambridge: Cambridge University Press, 271–90.

[44] Chandler, L.V. 1958, *Benjamin Strong, Central Banker*. Washington, DC: The Brookings Institute; Clay, H. 1957. *Lord Norman*. London: Macmillan; Eichengreen, *Golden Fetters*; Roberts, P. 2000. 'Benjamin Strong, the Federal Reserve and the limits to interwar American nationalism'. *Economic Quarterly* 86(2): 61–98.

the enthusiasm that they aroused among American investors.[45] The main changes undergone by New York after the war were mainly connected with the incredible boom in issues of American stock. The 1920s saw a period of strong industrial growth, of modernized production and management methods, and of mergers and acquisitions, with companies resorting far more to the capital market than to bank loans to finance themselves. The democratization of share ownership went hand in hand with this strengthening of the stock market. Moreover, there were still far more numerous and tempting investment opportunities in domestic securities within the United States than in Europe and foreign capital continued to be invested in the American economy. Apart from long-term investments, which went from $3 to $5.8 billion between 1918 and 1929, New York became the favoured market for the short-term deposit of foreign funds, which increased from $1.7 billion in 1925 to $3.6 billion in 1929.[46] The New York Stock Exchange mirrored this state of affairs. On the one hand, foreign investors, particularly European, were attracted by American stocks, especially with the bullish trend that marked the decade and saw shares almost triple and those of public utilities, the most popular, more than quadruple between 1919 and 1929. On the other hand, the liquid assets of foreign banks supplied short-term loans to brokers, which constituted the bulk of the New York money market, where prices reached new heights with the speculative fever of the end of the decade.

This interaction between national and international business was one of the main characteristics of the New York financial centre, which differentiated it from the City. While international issues handled in the two large financial centres attracted capital from all over the world, New York was far more successful than London in attracting funds looking to be invested in the domestic economy. The New York centre's tremendous vitality in the 1920s came to an end with the Wall Street stock-market crash of October 1929.

CONCLUDING REMARKS

How to explain the success of international financial centres? Contemporary economic and financial literature has identified conditions that are necessary, if not sufficient, for their development. The most important and most frequently

---

[45] In the 1920s, foreign issues in New York fluctuated between 15 and 18 per cent of the total amount of new issues, including domestic ones, with troughs of 10 per cent in 1923 and 6 per cent in 1929.

[46] See Wilkins, *Foreign Investment*, 184; Jollife, M.L. 1935. *The United States as a Financial Centre 1919–1933*. Cardiff: University of Wales Press, 112.

debated of these include: stability of political institutions; strength of the currency; sufficient savings that can readily be invested abroad; powerful financial institutions; firm, but not intrusive, state supervision; a light tax burden; a highly skilled workforce; efficient means of communication; and plentiful, reliable, and widely accessible information. This list may not be exhaustive, but it is hard to refute it. And yet, these short- and medium-term conditions do not take into account longer-term historical explanations. Two of them seem particularly relevant to the period considered in this chapter. The first is the economic power of the country that hosts it: London and New York successively ranked top in world finance, and at the same time were the financial centres of the dominant national economy of the day. The second is the impact of wars, sometimes irrespective of the outcome, victory or defeat – the City came out of the First World War weakened and its decline seemed irreversible after the Second, while New York's rise was undoubtedly hastened by two world wars.

This broad overview of the world's leading financial centres has underlined how the various services offered to investors enabled financial resources to be channelled across the world during the first era of globalization. International financial centres fulfilled their task mainly by cooperating, but also by competing, with each other. Bankers and financiers operating in these centres, while offering investing opportunities to the wealthy, also built large fortunes for themselves, on a scale rarely matched in other business activities. Did the international activities of the main financial centres solely benefit the bankers and financiers who stood at the helm? In spite of the recent crisis, hosting a large international financial centre is nowadays seen as being particularly beneficial to the host country. The question was seen in a somewhat different light before 1914 – in terms of the country's trade and financial balance. In the case of the City, British political and economic leaders were very keenly aware how vitally important the income from its financial activities and that of some other centres – like Liverpool or Glasgow – was in maintaining the British balance of payments. In fact, since the income from commercial services, insurance, and the merchant navy counterbalanced the traditional trade deficit, the balance of goods and services was stable on the eve of the war; so much so that the surplus on the British current account was entirely due to interest and dividends drawn from overseas investment, which exceeded £100 million net at the beginning of the century, and it was these that fed the flow of foreign investment.[47]

Dissenting voices have denounced the negative effects of capital exports on national growth, though recent research has shown that capital exports barely

---

[47] Traditionally referring to trade balance in the broader sense of the word, excluding factor incomes.

affected the economies of the core industrial countries.[48] But was this also the case for those on the periphery? On the whole, there is little doubt that capital transfers played a positive role in their economic development. There were, of course, major differences among countries and regions depending on the period. Government loans were certainly not always put to productive use, whether in connection with military expenditure or, more often, with servicing an already contracted debt. The bankers and financiers in the main financial centres often 'forced' weak states to borrow beyond their means. It is, nevertheless, a fact that significant achievements were made, especially in infrastructure: railways, roads, docks, ports, power stations, and urban development. These achievements enabled natural resources to be developed and exported, thus stimulating economic growth; and only foreign capital could ensure their success. But at what price? Did the indebtedness of borrowing countries lead to their loss of political independence or other forms of 'informal' domination? The question not only preoccupied contemporaries but lay at the heart of debates on imperialism for several generations. These debates have lost some of their significance in the last 25 years, though they should not be readily dismissed: capital exports were not the main factor behind colonial expansion, but political and financial interests were closely interwoven; and the value systems of the City and other leading financial centres were deeply marked by the imperialist culture of the day.

In the end, investors – men and women – were major protagonists in the activities of international financial centres, and the financial services the latter offered were the main channel through which investments were made. How efficiently did investors use financial institutions and markets? How did they interact with bankers, brokers, and financiers? Was their behaviour passive or active? These questions are central to any inquiry of wealth and investment and some answers to them have been offered in other chapters of this book. They remind us that international financial centres lie at the heart of understanding the changing relationships between men, women, and money.

---

[48] Pollard, S. 1985. 'Capital exports, 1870–1914: harmful or beneficial?' *Economic History Review* 38(4): 489–514.

Bibliography

A Banker's Daughter 1891. *A Guide to the Unprotected in Every-Day Matters relating to Property and Income*, 6th edition. London: Macmillan.

Acheson, G.G. and J.D. Turner 2006. 'The impact of limited liability on ownership and control: Irish banking, 1877–1914'. *Economic History Review* 59(2): 320–46.

—— —— 2007. '"Canny investors?" The investment behaviour of Scottish bank shareholders in the nineteenth century'. European Business History Association, conference paper.

—— —— 2008a. 'The death blow to unlimited liability in Victorian Britain: The City of Glasgow failure'. *Explorations in Economic History* 45(3): 235–53.

—— —— 2008b. 'The secondary market for bank shares in nineteenth-century Britain'. *Financial History Review* 15(2): 123–52.

—— —— 2011. 'Investor behaviour in a nascent capital market: Scottish bank shareholders in the nineteenth century'. *Economic History Review* 64(1): 188–213.

—— C.R. Hickson, J.D. Turner and Q. Ye 2009. 'Rule Britannia!: British stock market returns, 1825–1870'. *Journal of Economic History* 69(4): 1107–37.

Ackrill, M. and L. Hannah 2001. *Barclays: The Business of Banking 1690–1996*. Cambridge: Cambridge University Press.

Alborn, T.L. 1998. *Conceiving Companies: Joint-Stock Politics in Victorian England*. London: Routledge.

Allen, R. 2001. 'The great divergence in European wages and prices from the Middle Ages to the First World War'. *Explorations in Economic History* 38(4): 411–47.

Alter, G., C. Goldin, and E. Rotell 1994. 'The savings of ordinary Americans: the Philadelphia Savings Fund Society in the mid-nineteenth century'. *Journal of Economic History* 54(4): 735–67.

Anderson, G.L. 1976. *Victorian Clerks*. Manchester: Manchester University Press.

—— 1977. 'The social economy of late Victorian clerks'. In *The Lower Middle Class in Britain*, edited by G. Crossick. London: Croom Helm, 113–33.

Anderson, M. 1990. 'The social implications of demographic change'. In *The Cambridge Social History of Britain 1750–1950*, Volume 2, edited by F.M.L. Thompson. Cambridge: Cambridge University Press, 1–70.

Ando, A. and F. Modigliani 1963. 'The life cycle hypothesis of saving: aggregate implications and tests'. *American Economic Review* 53(1): 55–84.

Andrade, G., M. Mitchell, and E. Stafford 2001. 'New evidence and perspectives on mergers'. *Journal of Economic Perspectives* 15(2): 103–20.

Anon 1879. 'City of Glasgow Bank – progress and details of the liquidation'. *Economist*: 1480.

—— 1880. 'Reasons in favour of limited liability for joint-stock banks'. *The Banker's Magazine* 40: 55–9.

—— 1901a. *The 'Money-Maker' Manuals for Investors. Number 1: How to Commence Investing*. London: Publisher unknown.

Anon 1901b. *The 'Money-Maker' Manuals for Investors. Number 2: A New Dictionary of Mining Terms.* London: Publisher unknown.

—— 1901c. *The 'Money-Maker' Manuals for Investors. Number 4: Scientific Investment.* London: Publisher unknown.

—— 1930. 'Profit-sharing and co-partnership in 1929'. *Ministry of Labour Gazette* July: 238–41.

Armstrong, J. 1986. 'Hooley and the Bovril Company'. *Business History* 28(1): 18–34.

—— 1990. 'The rise and fall of the company promoter and the financing of British industry'. In *Capitalism in a Mature Economy: Financial Institutions, Capital Exports and British Industry, 1870–1939*, edited by J.J. van Helten and Y. Cassis. Aldershot: Edward Elgar Publishing, 115–38.

Artaud, D. 1977. 'Les dettes de guerre de la France, 1919–1929'. In *La position internationale de la France. Aspects économiques et financiers, XIXe–XXe siècles*, edited by M. Lévy-Leboyer. Paris: EHESS, 313–18.

Atack, J. and F. Bateman 1981. 'Egalitarianism, inequality and age: the rural north in 1860'. *Journal of Economic History* 41(1): 85–93.

Atkinson, A.B. and A.J. Harrison 1978. *The Distribution of Personal Wealth in Britain.* Cambridge: Cambridge University Press.

Auwers, L. 1979. 'History from the mean – up, down and around: a review essay'. *Historical Methods* 12(1): 39–45.

Bacchi, C. 1986. 'The "woman question" in South Australia'. In *The Flinders History of South Australia: Social History*, edited by E. Richards. Adelaide, SA: Wakefield Press, 403–32.

Backhouse, C.B. 1988. 'Married women's property law in nineteenth-century Canada'. *Law and History Review* 6(2): 211–57.

Bagehot, W. 1856. 'Unfettered banking'. *Saturday Review* 1 November.

Baines, D. and R. Woods 2004. 'Population and regional development'. In *The Cambridge Economic History of Modern Britain. Volume 2: Economic Maturity, 1860–1939*, edited by R. Floud and P. Johnson. Cambridge: Cambridge University Press, 25–55.

Bajtelsmit, V.L. and A. Bernasek 1999. 'Gender differences in defined contribution pension decisions'. *Financial Services Review* 8(1): 1–10.

Baker, A.H. 1990. *An Introduction to English Legal History.* London: Butterworths.

Banks, J.A. 1954. *Prosperity and Parenthood: A Study of Family Planning Among the Victorian Middle Classes.* London: Routledge and Kegan Paul.

Barker, T.C. and M. Robbins 1974. *London Transport: A History.* London: George Allen and Unwin.

Bartlett, W. and H. Chapman 1869. *A Handy-Book for Investors: Comprising a Sketch of the Rise, Progress, and Present Character of every Species of Investment, British, Colonial, and Foreign; Including an Estimate of their Comparative Safety and Profit.* London: Effingham Wilson.

Basch, N. 1979. 'Invisible women: the legal fiction of marital unity in nineteenth-century America'. *Feminist Studies* 5(2): 346–66.

Baskerville, P. 1999. 'Women and investment in late-nineteenth-century urban Canada: Victoria and Hamilton, 1880–1901'. *Canadian Historical Review* 80(2): 191–218.

—— 2008. *A Silent Revolution? Gender and Wealth in English Canada 1860–1930*. Montreal, QC: McGill-Queen's University Press.

Baster, A.S.J. 1977. *The International Banks*. New York, NY: Staples Press.

Battilossi, S. 2000. 'Financial innovation and the golden age of international banking: 1890–1931 and 1958–81'. *Financial History Review* 7(2): 141–75.

Baxter, R.D. 1868. *National Income: The United Kingdom*. London: Macmillan.

Beachy, R., B. Craig, and A. Owens eds. 2006. *Women, Business and Finance in Nineteenth-Century Europe: Rethinking Separate Spheres*. Oxford: Berg.

Becker, G.S. and N. Tomes 1976. 'Child endowments and the quantity and quality of children'. *Journal of Political Economy* 84(4) Part 2: S143–62.

—— —— 1979. 'An equilibrium theory of the distribution of incomes and intergenerational mobility'. *Journal of Political Economy* 87(6): 1153–89.

Beckert, J. 2008. *Inherited Wealth*. Princeton, NJ: Princeton University Press.

Beeton, S. 1870. *Beeton's Guide Book to the Stock Exchange and Money Market with Hints to Investors and the Chances of Speculation*. London: Ward, Lock, Tyler.

Bell, G.J. 1858. *Commentaries on the Laws of Scotland*, 6th edition. Edinburgh: T. and T. Clark.

Bell, G.M. 1846. *A Guide to the Investment of Capital; or how to Lay out Money with Safety and Profit. Being a Popular Exposition of the Various Descriptions of Securities, with Hints for the Guidance of Capitalists*. London: C. Mitchell.

Bell, R. 1850. *The Ladder of Gold: An English Story*. London: G. Routledge.

Belloc, H. 1909. *A Change in the Cabinet*. London: Methuen.

—— 1910. *Pongo and the Bull*. London: Constable and Co.

Bennett, A. 1902. *Anna of the Five Towns*. London: Methuen.

Berg, M. 1993. 'Women's property and the industrial revolution'. *Journal of Interdisciplinary History* 24(2): 233–50.

Berle, A.A. and C.G. Means 1931. 'Corporation'. In *International Encyclopedia of the Social Sciences*, Volume 4, edited by E.R.A. Seligman. New York, NY: The Macmillan Company.

—— —— 1991. *The Modern Corporation and Private Property* (originally published 1932). New Brunswick, NJ: Transactions Publishers.

Bernheim, B.D., A. Shleifer, and L.H. Summers 1985. 'The strategic bequest motive'. *Journal of Political Economy* 93(6): 1045–76.

Besant, W. and J. Rice 1877. *The Golden Butterfly*. London: Tinsley Bros.

Bishop, J. 1858. *The English Laws of Landlords, Tenants and Lodgers*. London: Effingham Wilson.

Black, I.S. 1995. 'Money, information and space: banking in early-nineteenth-century England and Wales'. *Journal of Historical Geography* 21(4): 398–412.

Bloom, D., D. Canning, and B. Graham 2003. 'Longevity and life-cycle savings'. *Scandinavian Journal of Economics* 105(3): 319–38.

Blumin, S.M. 1989. *The Emergence of the Middle Class: Social Experience in the American City, 1760–1900*. Cambridge: Cambridge University Press.

Board of Trade 1903. *Return Showing Holders of Debentures, Preferred and Ordinary Stocks of Railways in the United Kingdom 16 December 1902*. London: His Majesty's Stationery Office.

Bonin, H. 2010. 'Les offensives boursières en France'. Unpublished paper, Bordeaux.

Bourdieu, J., G. Postel-Vinay, and A. Suwo-Eisenmann 2008. 'Aging women and family wealth'. *Social Science History* 32(2): 143–74.

Bourguignon, F. and C. Morrisson 2002. 'Inequality among world citizens, 1820–1992'. *American Economic Review* 92(4): 727–44.

Bowley, A.L. 1920. *The Change in the Distribution of the National Income, 1880–1913*. Oxford: Clarendon Press.

Boyer, G.R. 2004. 'Living standards 1860–1939'. In *The Cambridge Economic History of Modern Britain. Volume 2: Economic Maturity, 1860–1939*, edited by R. Floud and P. Johnson. Cambridge: Cambridge University Press, 280–313.

—— 2009. 'Insecurity, safety nets, and self-help in Victorian and Edwardian Britain'. In *Human Capital and Institutions: A Long-Run View*, edited by D. Eltis, F.D. Lewis, and K.L. Sokoloff. Cambridge: Cambridge University Press, 46–90.

Bradbury, B. 1979. 'The family economy and work in an industrializing city: Montreal in the 1870s'. *Historical Papers: Canadian Historical Association* 14(1): 71–96.

Bratlinger, P. 1996. *Fictions of the State: Culture and Credit in Britain, 1694–1994*. Ithaca, NY: Cornell University Press.

Breiding, W.D. 1974. *Ubernahmeangebote im amerikanischen Börse und Gesellschafts-recht*. Unpublished Ph.D. Thesis, University of Kiel.

Broadberry, S. 2004. 'Human capital and skills'. In *The Cambridge Economic History of Modern Britain. Volume 2: Economic Maturity, 1860–1939*, edited by R. Floud and P. Johnson. Cambridge: Cambridge University Press, 56–73.

Buchinsky, M. and B. Pollack 1993. 'The emergence of a national capital market in England, 1710–1880'. *Journal of Economic History* 53(1): 1–24.

Burk, K. 1990. *Morgan Grenfell, 1838–1988: The Biography of a Merchant Bank*. Oxford: Oxford University Press.

—— 1992. 'Money and power: the shift from Great Britain to the United States'. In *Finance and Financiers in European History*, edited by Y. Cassis. Cambridge: Cambridge University Press, 359–70.

Burley, D.G. 1994. *A Particular Condition in Life: Self-Employment and Social Mobility in mid-Victorian, Brantford, Ontario*. Montreal, QC: McGill-Queen's University Press.

Burton, D., D. Knights, A. Leyshon, C. Alferoff, and P. Signoretta 2005. 'Consumption denied? The decline of industrial branch insurance'. *Journal of Consumer Culture* 5(2): 181–205.

Butler, S. 1903. *The Way of all Flesh*. London: Grant Richards.

Butlin, N. 1962. *Australian Domestic Product: Investment and Foreign Borrowing, 1861–1938/39*. Cambridge: Cambridge University Press.

Buxton, S. and G.S. Barnes 1890. *A Handbook to the Death Duties*. London: John Murray.

Cain, P.J. and A.G. Hopkins 2001. *British Imperialism, 1688–2000*, 2nd edition. Harlow: Longman.

Cairncross, A.K. 1953. *Home and Foreign Investment, 1870–1913*. Cambridge: Cambridge University Press.

Campbell, R. 1955. 'Edinburgh banks and the Western Bank of Scotland'. *Scottish Journal of Political Economy* 2(1): 133–48.

Cannadine, D. 1977. 'Aristocratic indebtedness in the nineteenth century: the case re-opened'. *Economic History Review* 30(4): 624–50.

—— 1980. *Lords and Landlords: The Aristocracy and the Towns, 1774–1967.* Leicester: Leicester University Press.

Capie, F. 1995. 'Commercial banking in Britain between the wars'. In *Banking, Currency, and Finance in Europe between the Wars,* edited by C.H. Feinstein Oxford: Clarendon Press, 395–413.

Cargill, A. 1910. *Memorial of the Centenary of Savings Banks.* Edinburgh: Constable.

Carosso, V. 1970. *Investment Banking in America: A History.* Cambridge, MA: Harvard University Press.

Carter, S., R. Ransom, and R. Sutch 2004. 'Family matters: the life-cycle transition and the antebellum American fertility decline'. In *History Matters: Essays on Economic Growth, Technology, and Demographic Change,* edited by T. Guinnane, W. Sundstrom, and W. Whatley. Stanford, CA: Stanford University Press, 271–327.

Cassis, Y. 1990. 'The emergence of a new financial institution: investment trusts in Britain 1870–1939'. In *Capitalism in a Mature Economy: Financial Institutions, Capital Exports and British Industry,* edited by J.J. van Helten and Y. Cassis. Aldershot: Ashgate, 139–58.

—— 2006. *Capitals of Capital: A History of International Financial Centres, 1780–2005.* Cambridge: Cambridge University Press.

Castles, A.C. 1963. 'The reception and statutes of English law in Australia'. *The Adelaide Law Review* 2(1): 1–21.

Caves, R.E. 1971. 'Export-led growth and the new economic history'. In *Trade, Balance of Payments and Growth,* edited by J.N. Bhagwati, R.W. Jones, R.A. Mundell, and J. Vanek. Amsterdam: North-Holland, 403–42.

Central Statistical Office 1968. *Standard Industrial Classification.* London: Central Statistical Office.

Chalmers, T. 1841. *On the Sufficiency of the Parochial System, without a Poor Rate, for the Right Management of the Poor.* Glasgow: William Collins.

Chambers, E.J. and D.F. Gordon 1966. 'Primary products and economic growth: an empirical measurement'. *Journal of Political Economy* 74(4): 315–32.

Chambers, L. 1997. *Married Women and the Law of Property in Victorian Ontario.* Toronto, ON: Osgoode Society for Canadian Legal History, University of Toronto Press.

Chandler, A.D. 1990. 'The enduring logic of industrial success'. *Harvard Business Review* 90(2): 130–40.

Chandler, L.V. 1958. *Benjamin Strong, Central Banker.* Washington, DC: The Brookings Institute.

Chapman, S.D. 1974. *Jesse Boot of Boots the Chemist: A Study in Business History.* London: Hodder and Stoughton.

—— 1984. *The Rise of Merchant Banking.* London: Allen and Unwin.

Checkland, S. 1975. *Scottish Banking: A History, 1695–1973.* Glasgow: Collins.

Cheffins, B.R. 2008. *Corporate Ownership and Control: British Business Transformed.* Oxford: Oxford University Press.

—— S. Bank 2009. 'Is Berle and Means really a myth?' *Business History Review* 83(3): 443–74.

Chernow, R. 1989. *The House of Morgan: An American Banking Dynasty and the Rise of Modern Finance*. London: Simon and Schuster.

Chiozza Money, L.G. 1910. *Riches and Poverty*. London: Methuen.

Church, R.A. 1971. 'Profit-sharing and labour relations in England in the nineteenth century'. *International Review of Labour History* 16(1): 2–16.

Churchill, R.S. 1892. *Men, Mines and Animals in South Africa*. London: Sampson Low and Co.

Clapham, J.H. 1938. *An Economic History of Modern Britain*, Volume 3. Cambridge: Cambridge University Press.

—— 1944. *The Bank of England: A History*. London: Cambridge University Press.

Clark, G. 2007. *A Farewell to Alms: A Brief Economic History of the World*. Princeton, NJ: Princeton University Press.

Clarke, M. 1999. *Citizens' Financial Futures: The Regulation of Retail Investment Financial Services in Britain*. Aldershot: Ashgate.

Clay, H. 1957. *Lord Norman*. London: Macmillan.

Clay, W. 1837. *Speech of William Clay, Esq., M.P. on Moving for the Appointment of a Committee to Inquire into the Operation of the Act Permitting the Establishment of Joint-stock Banks. To Which are Added, Reflections on Limited Liability, Paid-up Capital, and Publicity of Accounts, as Applied to Such Institutions; With Some Remarks on an Article on Joint-stock Companies in the Last Number of the Edinburgh Review*. London: James Ridgway and Sons.

Cleveland, F.A. and F.W. Powell 1912. *Railroad Finance*. New York, NY: Appleton.

Cleveland, W.S. 1979. 'Robust locally weighted regression and smoothing scatterplots'. *Journal of the American Statistical Association* 74(368): 829–36.

—— 1985. *The Elements of Graphing*. Monterey, CA: Wadsworth.

—— 1993. *Visualizing Data*. Summit, NJ: Hobart.

Coghlan, T.A. 1896. *A Statistical Account of the Seven Colonies of Australasia, 1895–6*, 6th issue. Sydney, NSW: Government Printers.

Cohen, D. 2006. *Household Gods: The British and their Possessions*. London: Yale University Press.

Cohen, M. 1988. *Women's Work, Markets and Economic Development in Nineteenth-Century Ontario*. Toronto, ON: University of Toronto Press.

Collinge, M. 1987. 'Probate valuations and the death duty registers: some comments'. *Bulletin of the Institute of Historical Research* 60(142): 240–5.

Collins, M. 1988. *Money and Banking in the United Kingdom: A History*. London: Croom Helm.

—— 1989. 'The banking crisis of 1878'. *Economic History Review* 42(4): 504–27.

—— 1991. *Banks and Industrial Finance in Britain, 1800–1939*. Cambridge: Cambridge University Press.

Collins, W. 1878. *The Haunted Hotel*. London: Chatto and Windus.

Combs, M.B. 2004. 'Wives and household wealth: the impact of the 1870 British Married Women's Property Act on wealth-holding and share of household resources'. *Continuity and Change* 19(1): 141–63.

—— 2005. 'A measure of legal independence: the 1870 Married Women's Property Act and the wealth-holding patterns of British wives'. *Journal of Economic History* 65(4): 1028–57.

—— 2006. '*Cui Bono*?: the 1870 British Married Women's Property Act, bargaining power, and the distribution of resources within marriage'. *Feminist Economics* 12(1/2): 51–83.

—— 2010. 'A nation of shopkeepers?' Fordham University discussion paper.

Conley, T.G. and D.W. Galenson 1998. 'Nativity and wealth in mid-nineteenth century cities'. *Journal of Economic History* 58(2): 468–93.

Cottrell, P.L. 1980. *Industrial Finance, 1830–1914: The Finance and Organization of English Manufacturing Industry*. London: Methuen.

—— 1998. 'Aspects of commercial banking in northern and central Europe, 1880–1931'. In *International Banking in an Age of Transition: Globalisation, Automation, Banks and their Archives*, edited by S. Kinsey and L. Newton. Aldershot: Ashgate, 119–29.

—— 2004. 'Domestic finance 1860–1914'. In *The Cambridge Economic History of Modern Britain. Volume 2: Economic Maturity, 1860–1939*, edited by R. Floud and P. Johnson. Cambridge: Cambridge University Press, 253–79.

—— 2005. 'Established connections and new opportunities: London as an international financial centre, 1914–1958'. In *London and Paris as International Financial Centres in the Twentieth Century*, edited by Y. Cassis and E. Bussière. Oxford: Oxford University Press, 153–82.

Cox, J. 1988a. *Affection Defying the Power of Death: Wills, Probate and Death Duty Records*. London: Federation of Family History Societies.

—— 1988b. *Wills, Inventories and Death Duties: A Provisional Guide*. London: Public Record Office.

Crafts, N., T. Leunig, and A. Mulatu 2008. 'Were British railway companies well-managed in the early twentieth century?' *Economic History Review* 61(4): 842–66.

Crick, W.F. and J.E. Wadsworth 1936. *A Hundred Years of Joint Stock Banking*. London: Hodder and Stoughton.

Cross, F. 1854. *Hints to all About How to Rent, Buy or Build House Property*. London: Nelson.

Crossick, G. 1977. 'The emergence of the lower middle class in Britain: a discussion'. In *The Lower Middle Class in Britain*, edited by G. Crossick. London: Croom Helm, 11–60.

Crossick, G. ed. 1977. *The Lower Middle Class in Britain*. London: Croom Helm.

Crossick, G. 2000. 'Meanings of property and the world of the petite bourgeoisie'. In *Urban Fortunes: Property and Inheritance in the Town*, edited by J. Stobart and A. Owens. Aldershot: Ashgate, 50–78.

—— H-G. Haupt eds. 1984. *Shopkeepers and Master Artisans in Nineteenth-Century Europe*. London: Methuen.

Crouzet, F. 1978. *L'économie de la Grande-Bretagne victorienne*. Paris: Belin.

Darroch, G.A. 1983. 'Early industrialization and inequality in Toronto, 1861–1899'. *Labour/Le Travail* 11(Spring): 31–61.

Daunton, M. 1977. *Coal Metropolis: Cardiff, 1870–1914*. Leicester: Leicester University Press.

Daunton, M. 1989. '"Gentlemanly Capitalism" and British industry, 1820–1914'. *Past and Present* 122: 119–58.

—— 1991. 'Reply: "Gentlemanly Capitalism" and British industry, 1820–1914'. *Past and Present* 132: 170–87.

—— 2001. *Trusting Leviathan: The Politics of Taxation in Britain 1799–1914.* Cambridge: Cambridge University Press.

—— 2008. *State and Market in Victorian Britain.* Woodbridge: Boydell and Brewer.

Davidoff, L. 1973. *The Best Circles: Women and Society in Victorian England.* Totowa, NJ: Rowman and Littlefield.

—— 1990. 'The family in Britain'. In *The Cambridge Social History of Britain, 1750–1950,* Volume 2, edited by F.M.L. Thompson. Cambridge: Cambridge University Press, 71–129.

—— C. Hall 2002. *Family Fortunes: Men and Women of the English Middle Class 1780–1850,* 2nd edition. London: Routledge.

—— B. Westover eds. 1986. *Our Work, Our Lives, Our Words: Women's History and Women's Work.* London: Macmillan Education.

Davies, J.B. 1981. 'Uncertain lifetime, consumption and dissaving in retirement'. *Journal of Political Economy* 89(3): 561–77.

Davis, L. 1966. 'The capital markets and industrial concentration: the US and UK, a comparative study'. *Economic History Review* 19(2): 255–72.

—— R.J. Cull 1994. *International Capital Markets and American Economic Growth 1820–1914.* Cambridge: Cambridge University Press.

—— R. Huttenback 1988. *Mammon and the Pursuit of Empire: The Economics of British Imperialism,* abridged edition. Cambridge: Cambridge University Press.

—— L. Neal 1998. 'Micro rules and macro outcomes: the impact of micro structures on the efficiency of security exchanges, London, New York and Paris, 1800–1914'. *American Economic Review* 88(2): 40–5.

Davis, M. 2001. *Late Victorian Holocausts: El Niño Famines and the Making of the Third World.* London: Verso.

Di Matteo, L. 1990. 'Wealth-holding in Wentworth County, Ontario, 1872–1892'. Unpublished Ph.D. Thesis, McMaster University.

—— 1991. 'The economic development of the Lakehead during the wheat boom era: 1900–1914'. *Ontario History* 83(3): 297–316.

—— 1992. 'Evidence on Lakehead economic activity from the Fort William building permits registers, 1907–1969'. *Thunder Bay Historical Museum Society Papers and Records* 20: 37–49.

—— 1993. 'Booming sector models, economic base analysis and export-led economic development: regional evidence from the Lakehead'. *Social Science History* 17(4): 593–617.

—— 1997. 'The determinants of wealth and asset holding in nineteenth-century Canada: evidence from microdata'. *Journal of Economic History* 57(4): 907–34.

—— 1998. 'Wealth accumulation and the life-cycle in economic history: implications of alternative approaches to data'. *Explorations in Economic History* 35(3): 296–324.

—— P.J. George 1992. 'Canadian wealth inequality in the late nineteenth century: a study of Wentworth County, Ontario, 1872–1902'. *Canadian Historical Review* 73(4): 453–83.

—— —— 1998. 'Patterns and determinants of wealth among probated decedents in Wentworth County, Ontario 1872–1902'. *Histoire sociale–Social History* 31(1): 1–33.

Dickens, C. 1857. *Little Dorrit*. London: Bradbury and Evans. Reprinted 1999, Oxford: Oxford University Press.

Digby, A. 1994. *Making a Medical Living: Doctors and Patients in the English Market for Medicine, 1720–1911*. Cambridge: Cambridge University Press.

Dimson, E. 1979. 'Risk measurement when shares are subject to infrequent trading'. *Journal of Financial Economics* 7(2): 197–226.

Doe, H. 2009. *Enterprising Women and Shipping in the Nineteenth Century*. Woodbridge: Boydell and Brewer.

—— 2010. 'Waiting for her ship to come in: the female investor in nineteenth-century shipping'. *Economic History Review* 63(1): 85–106.

Drummond, I.M. 1987. *Progress Without Planning: The Economic History of Ontario from Confederation to the Second World War*. Toronto, ON: University of Toronto Press.

Dun, J. 1876. 'The banking institutions, bullion reserves, and non-legal-tender note circulation of the United Kingdom statistically investigated'. *Journal of the Statistical Society* 39(1): 1–189.

Dunlavy, C. 1998. 'Corporate governance in nineteenth-century Europe and the United States: the case of shareholder voting rights'. In *Corporate Governance: The State of the Art of Emerging Research*, edited by K.J. Hopt, H. Kanda, M. Roe, E. Wymeersch, and S. Prigge. Oxford: Clarendon Press, 5–39.

Dwyer, P.D., J.H. Gilkeson, and J.A. List 2002. 'Gender differences in revealed risk taking: evidence from mutual fund investors'. *Economics Letters* 76(2): 151–8.

Earle, P. 1989. *The Making of the English Middle Class: Business, Society and Family Life in London, 1660–1730*. Berkeley, CA: University of California Press.

Edelstein, M. 1976. 'Realized rates of return of UK home and overseas portfolio investments in the Age of High Imperialism'. *Explorations in Economic History* 13(3): 283–329.

—— 1982. *Overseas Investment in the Age of High Imperialism: The United Kingdom 1850–1914*. London: Methuen.

—— 2004. 'Foreign investment, accumulation and Empire, 1860–1914'. In *The Cambridge Economic History of Modern Britain. Volume 2: Economic Maturity, 1860–1939*, edited by R. Floud and P. Johnson. Cambridge: Cambridge University Press, 190–226.

Eichengreen, B. 1995. *Golden Fetters: The Gold Standard and the Great Depression 1919–1939*. Oxford: Oxford University Press.

Elliott, B.S. 1985. 'Sources of bias in nineteenth-century Ontario wills'. *Histoire sociale–Social History* 18(35): 125–32.

Emery, G. 1993. *Facts of Life: The Social Construction of Vital Statistics, Ontario 1869–1952*. Montreal, QC: McGill-Queen's University Press.

Emery, J.C., K. Inwood, and H. Thille 2007. 'Hecksher-Ohlin in Canada: new estimates of regional wages and land prices'. *Australian Economic History Review* 47(1): 22–48.

English, B. 1984. 'Probate valuations and the death duty registers'. *Bulletin of the Institute of Historical Research* 57(135): 80–91.

English, B. 1987. 'Wealth at death in the nineteenth century: the death duty registers'. *Bulletin of the Institute of Historical Research* 60(142): 246–9.

Erickson, A.L. 1993. *Women and Property in Early Modern England*. London: Routledge.

Essex-Crosby, A. 1938. 'Joint stock companies in Great Britain 1890–1930'. Unpublished M.Comm. Thesis, University of London.

Evans, L.T. and N.C. Quigley 1995. 'Shareholder liability regimes, principal-agent relationships, and banking industry performance'. *Journal of Law and Economics* 38(2): 497–520.

Fay, C.R. 1912. 'Co-partnership in industry'. *Economic Journal* 22(88): 529–41.

Feinstein, C. and K. Watson 1995. 'Private international capital flows in Europe in the inter-war period'. In *Banking, Currency and Finance in Europe between the Wars*, edited by C. Feinstein. Oxford: Oxford University Press, 94–130.

Ferrie, J.P. 1994. 'The wealth accumulation of antebellum European immigrants to the U.S., 1840–1860'. *Journal of Economic History* 54(1): 1–33.

—— 1995. 'The entry into the U.S. labour market of antebellum European immigrants, 1840–1860'. *Explorations in Economic History* 34(3): 295–330.

—— 1999. *Yankees Now: Immigrants in the Antebellum U.S., 1840–1860*. New York, NY: Oxford University Press.

Fisher, J., J. Bewsey, M. Waters, and E. Ovey 2003. *The Law of Investor Protection*, 2nd edition. London: Sweet and Maxwell.

Flandreau, M. and F. Gallice 2005. 'Paris, London and the international money market: lessons from Paribas, 1885–1913'. In *London and Paris as International Financial Centres in the Twentieth Century*, edited by Y. Cassis and E. Bussière. Oxford: Oxford University Press, 79–106.

Floud, R. 1993. 'Britain, 1860–1914: a survey'. In *The Economic History of Britain Since 1700. Volume 2: 1860–1939*, edited by R. Floud and D.N. McCloskey. Cambridge: Cambridge University Press, 1–28.

Foreman-Peck, J. and L. Hannah 2010a. 'The twentieth-century divorce of ownership from control: the facts and some consequences'. Paper presented at 2nd EURHISTOCK conference, Judge Business School, University of Cambridge, Cambridge.

—— —— 2010b. 'UK Corporate Governance'. Paper presented at 2nd EURHISTOCK conference, Judge Business School, University of Cambridge, Cambridge.

Forster, E.M. 1910. *Howards End*. London: Edward Arnold.

Franks, J.R. and R.S. Harris 1989. 'Shareholder wealth effects of corporate takeovers: the UK experience 1955–1985'. *Journal of Financial Economics* 23(2): 225–49.

—— C. Mayer 1989. *Risk, Regulation and Investor Protection: The Case of Investment Management*. Oxford: Clarendon Press.

Fraser, H. 1918. *Women and War Work*. New York, NY: G. Arnold Shaw.

French, E.A. 1985. *Unlimited Liability: The Case of the City of Glasgow Bank*. London: Certified Accountant Publications.

Gagan, D. 1976. 'The indivisibility of land: a microanalysis of the system of inheritance in nineteenth-century Ontario'. *Journal of Economic History* 36(1): 126–41.

—— 1981. *Hopeful Travellers: Families, Land and Social Change in Mid-Victorian Peel County, Canada West*. Toronto, ON: University of Toronto Press.

Galenson, D.W. 1991. 'Economic opportunity on the urban frontier: nativity, work and wealth in early Chicago'. *Journal of Economic History* 51(3): 581–603.

Galsworthy, J. 2001. *The Forsyte Saga* (originally published 1906). Ware: Wordsworth Editions.

Galt, M.N. 1985. 'Wealth and Income in New Zealand 1870 to 1939'. Unpublished Ph.D. Thesis, Victoria University, Wellington.

Garrett, E., A. Reid, K. Schurer, and S. Szreter 2001. *Changing Family Size in England and Wales: Place, Class and Demography, 1891–1911*. Cambridge: Cambridge University Press.

Gaskell, E. 1853. *Cranford*. London: Chapman and Hall.

Gayer, A.D., W.W. Rostow, and A.J. Schwartz 1953. *The Growth and Fluctuation of the British Economy*. Oxford: Clarendon Press.

Gissing, G. 1895. *In the Year of the Jubilee*. London: Lawrence and Bullen.

—— 1897. *The Whirlpool*. London: Lawrence and Bullen.

—— 1905. *Will Warburton: A Romance of Real Life*. London: Archibald Constable and Co.

Goldman, C.S. 1895. *South African Mines*, Volume 1. London: Effingham Wilson and Co.

Goschen, G.J. 1905. *Essay and Addresses on Economic Questions, 1865–1893*. London: Edward Arnold.

Gosden, P.H. 1973. *Self-Help: Voluntary Associations in Nineteenth-Century Britain*. London: B.T. Batsford.

Grannum, K. and N. Taylor 2004. *Wills and Other Probate Records*. Kew: The National Archives.

Green, A.G. and M.C. Urquhart 1987. 'New estimates of output growth in Canada: measurement and interpretation'. In *Perspectives on Canadian Economic History*, edited by D. McCalla. Toronto, ON: Copp Clark Pitman, 158–75.

Green, D.R. and A. Owens 2003. 'Gentlewomanly capitalism? Spinsters, widows and wealth-holding in England and Wales, c.1800–1860'. *Economic History Review* 56(3): 510–36.

—— —— J. Maltby, and J. Rutterford 2009. 'Lives in the balance? Gender, age and assets in late-nineteenth-century England and Wales'. *Continuity and Change* 24(2): 307–35.

Gregory, T.E. 1936. *The Westminster Bank Through a Century*, Volume 1. London: Westminster Bank.

Gregson, M.E. 1996. 'Wealth accumulation and distribution in the Midwest in the late nineteenth century'. *Explorations in Economic History* 33(4): 524–38.

Greig, J. and M. Gibson. 1917. 'Women and investment'. *Financial Review of Reviews* June: 174—82.

Gribble, F. 1896. *The Lower Life*. London: A.D. Innes and Co.

Grossman, R.S. 2002. 'New indices of British equity prices, 1870–1913'. *Journal of Economic History* 62(1): 121–46.

Gunn, S. 1988. 'The "failure" of the British middle class: a critique'. In *The Culture of Capital: Art, Power and the Nineteenth-Century Middle Class*, edited by J. Wolff and J. Seed. Manchester: Manchester University Press, 17–44.

Gunn, S. 2000. *The Public Culture of the Victorian Middle Class: Ritual and Authority in the English Industrial City, 1840–1914*. Manchester: Manchester University Press.

—— R. Bell 2002. *Middle Classes: Their Rise and Sprawl*. London: Cassell.

Gunter, A.C. 1892. *Miss Dividends: A Novel*. London: G. Routledge and Sons.

Haggard, H.R. 1909. *The Yellow God: An Idol of Africa*. London: Cassell and Co.

Haines, M.R. and A.C. Goodman 1991. 'A home of one's own: aging and homeownership in the United States in the late nineteenth and early twentieth centuries'. *National Bureau of Economic Research, Working Paper Series on Historical Factors and Long-Run Growth* 21.

Hall, A.R. 1963. *The London Capital Market and Australia, 1870–1914*. Canberra, ACT: Australian National University.

Hamilton, G. 1999. 'Property rights and transaction costs in marriage: evidence from prenuptial contracts'. *Journal of Economic History* 59(1): 68–103.

Hannah, L. 1974. 'Takeover bids in Britain before 1950: an exercise in business "pre-history"'. *Business History* 16(1): 65–77.

—— 1979. *Electricity before Nationalisation*. London: Macmillan.

—— 1986. *Inventing Retirement: The Development of Occupational Pensions in Britain*. Cambridge: Cambridge University Press.

—— 2007a. 'Pioneering modern corporate governance: a view from London in 1900'. *Enterprise and Society* 8(3): 642–86.

—— 2007b. 'The "Divorce" of ownership from control from 1900 onwards: re-calibrating imagined global trends'. *Business History* 49(4): 404–38.

—— 2007c. 'What did Morgan's men really do?' *University of Tokyo CIRJE Discussion Paper* F-465.

—— J.A. Kay 1977. *Concentration in Modern Industry: Theory, Measurement and the UK Experience*. London: Macmillan.

Harris, W. and K.A. Lake 1906. 'Estimates of the realisable wealth of the United Kingdom based mostly on estate duty returns'. *Journal of the Royal Statistical Society* 69(4): 709–45.

Harrison, A.E. 1981. 'Joint-stock company flotation in the cycle, motor-vehicle and related industries, 1882–1914'. *Business History* 23(1): 165–90.

Harvey, D. 1989. *The Condition of Postmodernity: An Enquiry into the Origins of Cultural Change*. Oxford: Basil Blackwell.

Hatton, T.J. 1988. 'Profit sharing in British industry, 1865–1913'. *International Journal of Industrial Organization* 6(1): 69–90.

Hein, L.W. 1978. *The British Companies Acts and the Practice of Accountancy, 1844–1962*. New York, NY: Arno.

Heller, M. 2008. 'Work, income and stability: the late Victorian and Edwardian London male clerk revisited'. *Business History* 50(3): 253–71.

Henretta, J. 1978. 'Families and farms: mentalité in pre-industrial America'. *William and Mary Quarterly* 35(1): 3–32.

Henry, N. 2007. '"Ladies do it?": Victorian women investors in fact and fiction'. In *Victorian Literature and Finance*, edited by F. O'Gorman. Oxford: Oxford University Press, 111–32.

—— C. Schmitt eds. 2009. *Victorian Investments: New Perspectives on Finance and Culture*. Bloomington and Indianapolis, IN: Indiana University Press.

Herbert, C. 2002. 'Filthy lucre: Victorian ideas of money'. *Victorian Studies* 44(2): 185–213.

Herscovici, S. 1993. 'The distribution of wealth in nineteenth-century Boston: inequality among natives and immigrants, 1860'. *Explorations in Economic History* 30(3): 321–35.

—— 1998. 'Migration and economic mobility: wealth accumulation and occupational change among antebellum migrants and persisters'. *Journal of Economic History* 58(4): 927–56.

Hickson, C.R. and J.D. Turner 2003a. 'Shareholder liability regimes in English banking: the impact upon the market for shares'. *European Review of Economic History* 7(1): 99–125.

—— —— 2003b. 'The trading of unlimited liability bank shares in nineteenth-century Ireland: the Bagehot Hypothesis'. *Journal of Economic History* 63(4): 931–58.

—— —— 2004. 'Free banking and the stability of early joint-stock banking'. *Cambridge Journal of Economics* 28(6): 903–19.

—— —— 2005. 'The genesis of corporate governance: nineteenth-century Irish joint-stock banks'. *Business History* 47(2): 174–89.

—— —— C. McCann 2005. 'Much ado about nothing: the introduction of limited liability and the market for nineteenth-century Irish bank stock'. *Explorations in Economic History* 42(3): 459–76.

—— —— Q. Ye 2011. 'The rate of return on equity across industrial sectors on the British equity market, 1825–70'. *Economic History Review published online 18 February 2011.*

Hill, H. 1896. *Guilty Gold: A Romance of Financial Fraud and City Crime.* London: C. Arthur Pearson.

Hilt, E. 2008. 'When did ownership separate from control?' *Journal of Economic History* 68(3): 645–85.

Hirst, J.B. 1973. *Adelaide and the Country, 1870–1917: Their Social and Political Relationship.* Melbourne, VIC: Melbourne University Press.

Hobson, O.R. 1947. 'The stock exchange and the public'. *The Banker* July: 31–2.

Hoff, W. and F. Schwabach 1906. *North American Railroads.* New York, NY: Germania.

Hoffman, P.T., D. Jacks, P. Levin, and P. Lindert 2002. 'Real inequality in Europe since 1500'. *Journal of Economic History* 62(2): 322–55.

—— G. Postel-Vinay, and J-L. Rosenthal 2007. *Surviving Large Losses: Financial Crises, the Middle Class, and the Development of Capital Markets.* Cambridge, MA: Harvard University Press.

Holcombe, L. 1973. *Victorian Ladies at Work; Middle-Class Working Women in England and Wales, 1850–1914.* Toronto, ON: Archon Books.

—— 1983. *Wives and Property: Reform of the Married Women's Property Law in Nineteenth-Century England.* Toronto, ON: University of Toronto Press.

Holderness, C.G., R.S. Kroszner, and D.P. Sheehan 1999. 'Were the good old days that good? Changes in managerial stock ownership since the great depression'. *Journal of Finance* 54(2): 435–69.

Holmes, A.R. and E. Greene 1986. *Midland: 150 Years of Banking Business.* London: B.T. Batsford.

Holmstrom, B. and S.N. Kaplan 2001. 'Corporate governance and merger activity in the United States: making sense of the 1980s and 1990s'. *Journal of Economic Perspectives* 15(2): 121–44.

Homer, S. and R. Sylla. 1996. *A History of Interest Rates*, 3rd edition. New Brunswick, NJ: Rutgers University Press.

Horne, O.H. 1947. *A History of Savings Banks*. Oxford: Oxford University Press.

Horwitz, H. 1987. '"The mess of the middle class" revisited: the case of the "big bourgeoisie" of Augustan London'. *Continuity and Change* 2(2): 269–96.

Howell, A. 1880. *The Law and Practice as to Probate, Administration and Guardianship*. Toronto, ON: Carswell.

—— 1895. *Probate, Administration and Guardianship*, 2nd edition. Toronto, ON: Carswell.

Howson, S. 1975. *Domestic Monetary Management in Britain, 1919–1939*. Cambridge: Cambridge University Press.

Hunt, B.C. 1936. *The Development of the Business Corporation in England, 1800–1867*. Cambridge, MA: Harvard University Press.

Hurd, M. 1987. 'Savings of the elderly and desired bequests'. *American Economic Review* 77(3): 298–312.

Ingall, G.D. and G. Withers 1904. *The Stock Exchange*. London: Arnold.

Inwood, K. and S. Ingram 2000a. 'Property ownership by married women in Victorian Ontario'. Working Paper No. 2000-8, Department of Economics, University of Guelph, ON.

—— —— 2000b. 'The impact of married women's property legislation in Victorian Ontario'. *Dalhousie Law Journal* 23(2): 504–49.

—— S. van Sligtenhorst 2004. 'The social consequences of legal reform: women and property in a Canadian community'. *Continuity and Change* 19(1): 165–97.

Irving, R.J. 1976. *The North Eastern Railway Company, 1870–1914: An Economic History*. Leicester: Leicester University Press.

Jackson, G. and H. Miyajima 2006. 'Varieties of takeover markets: comparing mergers and acquisitions in Japan with Europe and the USA'. Unpublished paper.

Jacobsen, J.P. 2007. *The Economics of Gender*. Malden, MA: Blackwell Publishing.

Jefferys, J.B. 1938. 'Trends in business organisation in Great Britain since 1856, with special reference to the financial structure of companies, the mechanism of investment and the relationship between the shareholder and the company'. Unpublished Ph.D. Thesis, University of London.

—— 1946. 'The denomination and character of shares, 1855–1885'. *Economic History Review* 16(1): 45–55.

—— 1977. *Business Organisation in Great Britain 1856–1914*. New York, NY: Arno Press.

Jensen, M.C. 1988. 'Takeovers: their causes and consequences'. *Journal of Economic Perspectives* 2(1): 21–48.

Jianakopoulos, N.A. and A. Bernasek 1998. 'Are women more risk averse?' *Economic Inquiry* 36(4): 620–30.

Johns, L. 2006. 'The first female shareholders of the Bank of New South Wales: examination of shareholdings in Australia's first bank, 1817–1821'. *Accounting, Business and Financial History* 16(2): 293–314.

Johnson, P. 1985. *Saving and Spending: The Working-Class Economy in Britain 1870–1939.* Oxford: Clarendon Press.

—— 1994. 'The employment and retirement of older men in England and Wales, 1881–1991'. *Economic History Review* 47(1): 106–28.

—— 2009. *Making the Market: Victorian Origins of Corporate Capitalism.* Cambridge: Cambridge University Press.

Jollife, M.L. 1935. *The United States as a Financial Centre 1919–1933.* Cardiff: University of Wales Press.

Joly, H. 2003. 'Ende des Familienkapitalismus'. In *Die deutsche Wirtschaftselite im 20. Jahrhundert*, edited by V.R. Berghahn, S. Unger, and D. Ziegler. Essen: Klartext, 75–91.

Jones, G. 1993. *British Multinational Banking, 1830–1990.* Oxford: Clarendon Press.

Jones, H. 1983. 'Employers' welfare schemes and industrial relations in inter-war Britain'. *Business History* 25(1): 61–75.

—— 1986. 'South Australian women and politics'. In *The Flinders History of South Australia: Political History*, edited by D. Jaensch. Adelaide, SA: Wakefield Press, 414–47.

Jordan, R. and F. Gore-Brown 1892. *A Handy Book on the Formation, Management and Winding-Up of Joint-Stock Companies.* London: Jordan.

Kaisanlahti, T.H. 2006. 'Extended liability of shareholders'. *Journal of Corporate Law Studies* 6(1): 139–63.

Kay, A.C. 2009. *The Foundations of Female Entrepreneurship: Enterprise, Home and Household, London c.1800–1870.* Abingdon: Routledge.

Kearl, J.R. and C.L. Pope 1983. 'The life cycle in economic history'. *Journal of Economic History* 43(1): 149–58.

Kennedy, W.P. 1987. *Industrial Structure, Capital Markets and the Origins of British Decline.* Cambridge: Cambridge University Press.

Kessler, D. and A. Masson 1989. 'Bequest and wealth accumulation: are some pieces of the puzzle missing?' *Journal of Economic Perspectives* 3(3): 141–52.

Kester, W.C. 1991. *Japanese Takeovers: The Global Contest for Corporate Control.* Boston, MA: Harvard Business School Press.

Khan, Z. 1996. 'Married women's property laws and female commercial activity: evidence from United States patent records'. *Journal of Economic History* 56(2): 356–88.

Kidd, A. and D. Nicholls eds. 1998. *The Making of the British Middle Class? Studies in Regional and Cultural Diversity since the Eighteenth Century.* Stroud: Sutton.

—— —— 1999. *Gender, Civic Culture and Consumerism: Middle-Class Identity in Britain, 1800–1940.* Manchester: Manchester University Press.

Killick, J.R. and W.A. Thomas 1970. 'The provincial stock exchanges 1830–1870'. *Economic History Review* 23(1): 96–111.

Kindleberger, C. 1993. *A Financial History of Western Europe*, 2nd edition. New York, NY: Oxford University Press.

King, M. 1985. 'The economics of savings: a survey of recent contributions'. In *Frontiers in Economics*, edited by K.J. Arrow and S. Honkapohja. Oxford: Basil Blackwell, 227–327.

King, W.T.C. 1936. *A History of the London Discount Market.* London: Routledge.

Knezevic, B. 2003. *Figures of Finance Capitalism: Writing, Class and Capital in the Age of Dickens.* London: Routledge.

Knibbs, G.H. 1918. *The Private Wealth of Australia and its Growth as Ascertained by Various Methods Together with a Report of the War Census of 1915*. Melbourne, VIC: McCarron and Bird.

Kotlikoff, L. 1988. 'Intergenerational transfers and savings'. *Journal of Economic Perspectives* 2(2): 41–58.

Kynaston, D. 1983. 'The London Stock Exchange, 1870–1914: an institutional history'. Unpublished Ph.D. Thesis, University of London.

—— 1988. *The Financial Times: A Centenary History*. London: Vintage.

—— 1995. *The City of London, Volume 2: Golden Years 1890–1914*. London: Chatto and Windus.

—— 1999. *The City of London, Volume 3: Illusions of Gold 1914–1945*. London: Chatto and Windus.

Lamal, E. 1930. *Une Enquête sur les actions a vote privilégié en Belgique*. Brussels: Lamertin.

Laurence, E.A., J. Maltby, and J. Rutterford eds. 2009. *Women and Their Money 1700–1950: Essays on Women and Finance*. Abingdon: Routledge.

Lee, T.A. and R.H. Parker eds. 1979. *The Evolution of Corporate Financial Reporting*. Sunbury-on-Thames: T. Nelson.

Lemire, B. 2005. *The Business of Everyday Life: Gender, Practice and Social Politics in England*. Manchester: Manchester University Press.

Lever, C. 1859. *Davenport Dunn or The Man and the Day*, Volume 3. London: Chapman.

Levi, L. 1880. 'The reconstruction of joint stock banks on the principle of limited liability'. *The Bankers' Magazine* 40: 468–79.

Levitan, K. 2008. 'Redundancy, the "surplus woman" problem, and the British Census, 1851–1861'. *Women's History Review* 17(3): 359–76.

Lewis, F. 1975. 'The Canadian wheat boom and per capita income, new estimates'. *Journal of Political Economy* 83(6): 1249–57.

—— 1981. 'Farm settlement on the Canadian prairies 1898 to 1911'. *Journal of Economic History* 41(3): 517–35.

Lindert, P. 1981. 'An algorithm for probate sampling'. *Journal of Interdisciplinary History* 11(4): 649–68.

—— 1986. 'Unequal English wealth since 1670'. *Journal of Political Economy* 94(6): 1127–62.

—— 1989. 'Who owned Victorian England? The debate over landed wealth and inequality'. *Agricultural History* 61(4): 25–51.

—— 2000. 'Three centuries of inequality in Britain and America'. In *Handbook of Income Distribution*, Volume 1, edited by A.B. Atkinson and F. Bourguignon Amsterdam: Elsevier, 167–216.

Lipartito, K. and Y. Morii 2008. 'Rethinking the separation of ownership from management in American history'. Paper presented to the Social Science History Conference, Miami, FL.

Liveing, E. 1961. *A Century of Insurance: The Commercial Union Group of Insurance Companies, 1861–1961*. London: Witherby.

Lloyd, I. 1978. *Rolls-Royce: The Growth of a Company*. London: Macmillan.

Loftus, D. 2002. 'Capital and community: limited liability and attempts to democratize the market in mid-nineteenth-century England'. *Victorian Studies* 45(1): 93–120.

—— 2009. 'Limited liability, market democracy, and the social organization of production in mid-nineteenth-century Britain'. In *Victorian Investments: New Perspectives on Finance and Culture*, edited by N. Henry and C. Schmitt. Bloomington and Indianapolis, IN: Indiana University Press, 79–97.

Lomax, D.F. 1987. *London Markets after the Financial Services Act*. London: Butterworths.

Lowenfeld, H. 1907. *Investment: An Exact Science*. London: Financial Review of Reviews.

—— 1909. *All About Investment*, 2nd edition. London: Financial Review of Reviews.

Lundberg, S. and R.A. Pollak 2007. 'The American family and family economics'. *Journal of Economic Perspectives* 21(2): 3–26.

McCutcheon, G.B. 1909. *Brewster's Millions*. London: Collier and Co.

Mackinnon, A. 1984. *One Foot on the Ladder: Origins and Outcomes of Girls' Secondary Schooling in South Australia*. St Lucia, QLD: University of Queensland Press.

McMichael, P. 1984. *Settlers and the Agrarian Question. Foundations of Capitalism in Colonial Australia*. Cambridge: Cambridge University Press.

Maddala, G. 1997. *Introduction to Econometrics*. New York, NY: Wiley.

Maddison, A. 1964. *Economic Growth in the West: Comparative Experience in Europe and North America*. London: Routledge.

—— 1991. *Dynamic Forces in Capitalist Development*. Oxford: Oxford University Press.

—— 2003. *The World Economy: Historical Statistics*. Paris: OECD.

—— 2005. *Growth and Interaction in the World Economy*. Washington, DC: AEI.

Magee, L., A.L. Robb, and J.B. Burbridge 1998. 'On the use of sampling weights when estimating regression models with survey data'. *Journal of Econometrics* 84(2): 251–71.

Main, G.L. 1974. 'The correction of biases in colonial probate records'. *Historical Methods Newsletter* 8(December): 10–28.

Maltby, J. 1999. '"A Sort of Guide, Philosopher and Friend": the rise of the professional auditor in Britain'. *Accounting, Business and Financial History* 9(1): 29–50.

—— 2000. 'Was the 1947 Companies Act a response to a national crisis?' *Accounting History* 5(2): 31–60.

—— J. Rutterford 2006. '"She possessed her own fortune": women investors in the late nineteenth century to the early twentieth century'. *Business History* 48(2): 220–53.

—— —— eds. 2006. 'Women, accounting and investment'. (Special Issue) *Accounting, Business and Financial History* 16(1).

Manchester, W. 1968. *The Arms of Krupp, 1587–1968*. Boston, MA: Little Brown.

Manne, H.G. 1965. 'Mergers and the market for corporate control'. *Journal of Political Economy* 73(2): 110–20.

Markham Lester, V. 1995. *Victorian Insolvency: Bankruptcy, Imprisonment for Debt, and Company Winding-up in Nineteenth-Century England*. Oxford: Oxford University Press.

Marshall, A. 1920. *Principles of Economics*, first published 1890. London: Macmillan and Company.

Matthews, D. 1989. 'The British experience of profit-sharing'. *Economic History Review* 42(4): 439–64.

Matthews, P.W. and A.W. Tuke 1926. *History of Barclays Bank Limited*. London: Blades, East and Blades.

Mauro, P., N. Sussman, and Y. Yafeh 2007. *Emerging Markets and Financial Globalization: Sovereign Bond Spreads in 1870–1913 and Today*. Oxford: Oxford University Press.

Meade, E.S. 1910. *Corporation Finance*. New York, NY: Appleton.

Meinig, D.W. 1962. *On the Margins of the Good Earth. The South Australian Wheat Frontier, 1869–1884*. Adelaide, SA: Rigby Ltd.

Menchik, P. and M. David 1983. 'Income distribution, lifetime savings, and bequests'. *American Economic Review* 73(4): 672–90.

Michie, R.C. 1981. *Money, Mania and Markets: Investment, Company Formation and the Stock Exchange in Nineteenth-Century Scotland*. Edinburgh: John Donald.

—— 1983. 'Crisis and opportunity, the formation and operation of the British Assets Trust 1897–1914'. *Business History* 25(2): 125–47.

—— 1985. 'The London Stock Exchange and the British securities market, 1850–1913'. *Economic History Review* 38(1): 66–82.

—— 1987. *The London and New York Stock Exchanges, 1850–1914*. London: Allen and Unwin.

—— 1992. *The City of London: Continuity and Change since 1850*. London: Macmillan.

—— 1999. *The London Stock Exchange: A History*. Oxford: Oxford University Press.

—— 2006. *The Global Securities Market: A History*. Oxford: Oxford University Press.

—— 2009. *Guilty Money: The City of London in Victorian and Edwardian Culture, 1815–1914*. London: Pickering and Chatto.

—— P.A. Williamson eds. 2004. *The British Government and The City of London in the Twentieth Century*. Cambridge: Cambridge University Press.

Miles, A. 1999. *Social Mobility in Nineteenth and Early Twentieth-Century England*. Basingstoke: Palgrave.

Milhaupt, C.J. 2005. 'In the shadow of Delaware? The rise of hostile takeovers in Japan'. *Columbia Law Review* 105(7): 2171–216.

Mitchell, B.R. 1988. *British Historical Statistics*. Cambridge: Cambridge University Press.

—— P. Deane 1962. *Abstract of British Historical Statistics*. Cambridge: Cambridge University Press.

Miwa, Y. and J.M. Ramseyer 2000. 'Corporate governance in transitional economies: lessons from the pre-war Japanese cotton textile industry'. *Journal of Legal Studies* 29(1): 171–203.

Modigliani, F. 1966. 'The life-cycle hypothesis of saving, the demand for wealth and the supply of capital'. *Social Research* 33(1): 160–217.

—— 1988. 'The role of intergenerational transfers and life-cycle savings in the accumulation of wealth'. *Journal of Economic Perspectives* 2(1): 15–40.

Moggridge, D.E. 1972. *British Monetary Policy, 1924–1931*. Cambridge: Cambridge University Press.

Morris, R.J. 1976. 'In search of the urban middle class: record linkage and methodology, Leeds 1832'. *Urban History Yearbook* 1(3): 200–22.

—— 1979. 'The middle class and the property cycle during the industrial revolution'. In *The Search for Wealth and Stability: Essays in Honour of M.W. Flinn*, edited by T.C. Smout. London: Macmillan, 91–113.

—— 1980. 'Middle-class culture 1700–1914'. In *A History of Modern Leeds*, edited by D. Fraser. Manchester: Manchester University Press, 200–22.

—— 1983. 'The middle class and British towns and cities of the industrial revolution, 1780–1870'. In *The Pursuit of Urban History*, edited by D. Fraser and A. Sutcliffe. London: Edward Arnold, 286–305.

—— 1990. *Class, Sect and Party. The Making of the British Middle Class: Leeds 1820–1850*. Manchester: Manchester University Press.

—— 1994. 'Men, women, and property: the reform of the Married Women's Property Act 1870'. In *Landowners, Capitalists, and Entrepreneurs: Essays for Sir John Habakkuk*, edited by F.M.L. Thompson. Oxford: Oxford University Press, 171–92.

—— 2005. *Men, Women and Property in England, 1780–1870: A Social and Economic History of Family Strategies among the Leeds Middle Classes*. Cambridge: Cambridge University Press.

Morris, S. 1995. *Financial Services: Regulating Investment Business*, 2nd edition. London: FT Law and Tax.

Moss, M. and I. Russell 1994. *An Invaluable Treasure: A History of the TSB*. London: Weidenfeld and Nicolson.

Mulhall, M.G. 1896. *Industries and Wealth of Nations*. London: Longmans Green.

Munn, C.W. 1981. *The Scottish Provincial Banking Companies, 1747–1864*. Edinburgh: John Donald Publishers.

Nance, C. 1984. '"Making a better society?" Immigration to South Australia, 1836–1871'. *Journal of the Historical Society of South Australia* 12(1): 105–22.

Neal, L. 1985. 'Integration of international capital markets: quantitative evidence from the eighteenth to the twentieth centuries'. *Journal of Economic History* 45(2): 219–26.

Neufeld, E.P. 1972. *The Financial System of Canada: Its Growth and Development*. Toronto, ON: Macmillan.

Newton, L. and P.L. Cottrell 2006. 'Female investors in the first English and Welsh commercial joint-stock banks'. *Accounting, Business and Financial History* 16(2): 315–40.

Nicholas, T. 1999. 'Wealth making in nineteenth- and twentieth-century Britain: industry v. commerce and finance'. *Business History* 41(1): 16–36.

Norrie, K.H. 1975. 'The rate of settlement of the Canadian prairies'. *Journal of Economic History* 35(2): 410–27.

North, D.C. 1990. *Institutions, Institutional Change and Economic Performance*. Cambridge: Cambridge University Press.

Nugent, J. 1985. 'The old-age security motive for fertility'. *Population and Development Review* 11(1): 75–97.

Nunokawa, J. 1994. *The Afterlife of Property: Domestic Security and the Victorian Novel*. Princeton, NJ: Princeton University Press.

O'Brien, P. 1988. 'The costs and benefits of British imperialism, 1846–1914'. *Past and Present* 120: 147–62.

O'Gorman, F. ed. 2007. *Victorian Literature and Finance*. Oxford: Oxford University Press.

Ó Gráda, C. 2008. 'The early history of Irish savings banks'. *Centre for Economic Research, University College Dublin, working paper series* WP08/04.

O'Hagan, H.O. 1929. *Leaves from my Life*. London: John Lane.

O'Sullivan, M. 2007. 'The expansion of the US stock market, 1885–1930: historical facts and theoretical fashions'. *Enterprise and Society* 8(3): 489–542.

Offer, A. 1981. *Property and Politics, 1870–1914: Landownership, Law, Ideology and Urban Development in England*. Cambridge: Cambridge University Press.

—— 1983. 'Empire and social reform: British overseas investment and domestic politics, 1908–1914'. *Historical Journal* 26(1): 119–38.

Office of National Statistics 2002. *Decennial Life Tables – English Life Tables: Series DS*. http://www.statistics.gov.uk/STATBASE/Product.asp?vlnk=333 (site accessed: 15 June 2010).

Oppenheim, E.P. 1912. *Havoc*. London: Hodder and Stoughton.

Oren, L. 1973. 'The welfare of women in labouring families: England 1860–1950'. *Feminist Studies* 1(3/4): 107–25.

Osborne, B.S. 1980. 'Wills and inventories: records of life and death in a developing society'. *Families* 19(4): 235–47.

Ott, J. 2007. *From New Proprietorship to New Era: Marking a Shareholders' Democracy in the United States, 1919–1929*. Economic Department Colloquium, New School for Social Research (New York). Unpublished paper.

Owens, A., D.R. Green, C. Bailey, and A.C. Kay 2006. 'A measure of worth: probate valuations, personal wealth and indebtedness in England, 1810–40'. *Historical Research* 79(205): 383–403.

Paish, G. 1909. 'Our investments in 1908'. *The Statist* 2 January.

Parker, W.N. 1991. 'The scale and scope of Alfred D. Chandler, Jr'. *Journal of Economic History* 51(4): 958–63.

Pearson, R. 1992. 'Shareholder democracies? English stock companies and the politics of corporate governance during the industrial revolution'. *English Historical Review* 117(473): 840–66.

Perkin, H. 1989. *The Rise of Professional Society: England since 1880*. London: Routledge.

Pettman, G. 1912. *A Study in Gold*. London: S.W. Partridge and Co.

Pike, D. 1957. *Paradise of Dissent. South Australia, 1829–1857*. Melbourne, VIC: Melbourne University Press.

Plumptre, C.C.M. 1882. *Grant's Treatise on the Law Relating to Bankers and Banking Companies*. London: Butterworths.

Politi, J. 2007. 'Hostile takeovers make a comeback'. *Financial Times* 28 November, special report on corporate finance, 1.

Pollard, S. 1985. 'Capital exports, 1870–1914: harmful or beneficial?' *Economic History Review* 38(4): 489–514.

—— 1989. *Britain's Prime and Britain's Decline. The British Economy 1870–1914*. London: Edward Arnold.

Pollock, G.D. 2007. 'Aspects of thrift in East End Glasgow: new accounts at the Bridgeton Cross branch of the Savings Bank of Glasgow, 1881'. *International Review of Scottish Studies* 32 (1): 117–48.

Pomfret, R. 1981. *The Economic Development of Canada*. Agincourt, ON: Methuen.

—— 1993. *The Economic Development of Canada*, 2nd edition. Toronto, ON: Nelson.

Pooley, C. and M. Harmer 1999. *Property Ownership in Britain c.1850–1950: The Role of the Bradford Equitable Building Society and the Bingley Building Society in the Development of Homeownership*. Cambridge: Granta.

Poovey, M. 2003. 'Introduction'. In *The Financial System in Nineteenth-Century Britain*, edited by M. Poovey. Oxford: Oxford University Press, 1–33.

—— ed. 2003. *The Financial System in Nineteenth-Century Britain*. Oxford: Oxford University Press.

—— 2008. *Genres of the Credit Economy: Mediating Value in Eighteenth and Nineteenth-Century Britain*. Chicago, IL: The University of Chicago Press.

—— 2009. 'Writing about finance in Victorian England: disclosure and secrecy in the culture of investment'. In *Victorian Investments: New Perspectives on Finance and Culture*, edited by N. Henry and C. Schmitt. Bloomington and Indianapolis, IN: Indiana University Press, 39–57.

Pope, C. 1989. 'Households on the American frontier: the distribution of income and wealth in Utah 1850–1900'. In *Markets in History: Economic Studies of the Past*, edited by D. Galenson. New York, NY: Cambridge University Press, 148–89.

Porter, D. 1986. '"A trusted guide of the investing public": Harry Marks and the *Financial News*, 1884–1916'. *Business History* 28(1): 1–17.

Powell, E.T. 1910. *The Mechanism of the City*. London: P.S. King and Son.

—— 1915. *The Evolution of the Money Market*. London: Cass and Co.

—— 1919. 'The democratisation of investment'. *Financial Review of Reviews* September: 249.

Powell, J.L. 1988. *Issues and Offers of Company Securities: The New Regimes*. London: Sweet and Maxwell.

Preda, A. 2001. 'The rise of the popular investor: financial knowledge and investing in England and France 1840–1880'. *Sociological Quarterly* 42(2): 205–32.

—— 2009. *Framing Finance: The Boundaries of Markets and Modern Capitalism*. Chicago, IL: University of Chicago Press.

Pressnell, L. 1970. 'Cartels and competition in British banking: a background study'. *Banca Nazionale Del Lavoro Quarterly Review* 95(4): 373–405.

Prest, W., K. Round, and C. Fort eds. 2001. *The Wakefield Companion to South Australian History*. Adelaide, SA: Wakefield Press.

Pujo Committee 1913. *Money Trust Investigation: Hearings*. Washington, DC: Government Printing Office.

Quinn, S.E. 1992. *Statutes Revised on Commercial Law, 1695–1913*. Bray: Irish Law Publishing.

Rae, G. 1885. *The Country Banker: His Clients, Cares, and Work From an Experience of Forty Years*. London: John Murray.

Ramage, R.W. 1982. *The Companies Acts: Table A 1856–1981*. London: Butterworths.

Ramsay, H. 1977. 'Cycles of control: worker participation in sociological and historical perspective'. *Sociology* 11(3): 481–506.

Ransom, R. and R. Sutch 1986. 'The life-cycle transition: a preliminary report on wealth-holding in America'. In *Income and Wealth Distribution in Historical Perspective*, Volume 1. Utrecht: Rijksuniversiteit te Utrecht, 10.1–10.69.

Reed, J.R. 1984. 'A friend to Mammon: speculation in Victorian literature'. *Victorian Studies* 27(2): 179–202.

Reed, M.C. 1975. *Investment in Railways in Britain 1820–1844: A Study in the Development of the Capital Market*. Oxford: Oxford University Press.

Reeves, M.P. 1913. *Round About a Pound a Week*. London: G. Bell and Sons.

Reunert, T. 1893. *Diamonds and Gold in South Africa*. Cape Town, WC: J.C. Jutta and Co.

Richards, E. ed. 1986. *The Flinders History of South Australia: Social History*. Adelaide, SA: Wakefield Press.

Robb, G. 1992. *White-Collar Crime in Modern England: Financial Fraud and Business Morality, 1845–1929*. Cambridge: Cambridge University Press.

Roberts, P. 2000. 'Benjamin Strong, the Federal Reserve and the limits to interwar American nationalism'. *Economic Quarterly* 86(2): 61–98.

Roberts, R. 1992. 'Regulatory responses to the market for corporate control in Britain in the 1950s'. *Business History* 34(1): 183–200.

Roth, R. and G. Dinhobi eds. 2008. *Across the Borders: Financing the World's Railways in the Nineteenth and Twentieth Centuries*. Aldershot: Ashgate.

Routh, G. 1980. *Occupation and Pay in Great Britain, 1906–1979*, 2nd edition. London: Macmillan.

Rubinstein, W.D. 1971. 'Occupations among British millionaires, 1857–1969'. *Review of Income and Wealth* 17(4): 375–8.

—— 1977. 'The Victorian middle classes: wealth, occupation and geography'. *Economic History Review* 30(4): 602–23.

—— 1981. 'New men of wealth and the purchase of land in nineteenth-century Britain'. *Past and Present* 92: 125–47.

—— 1987. *Elites and the Wealthy in Modern British History: Essays in Economic and Social History*. Brighton: Harvester Wheatsheaf.

—— 1988. 'The size and distribution of the English middle classes in 1860'. *Historical Research* 61(144): 65–89.

—— 1991. '"Gentlemanly Capitalism" and British industry, 1820–1914'. *Past and Present* 132: 150–70.

—— 1992a. 'Cutting up rich: a reply to F.M.L. Thompson'. *Economic History Review* 45(2): 350–61.

—— 1992b. 'The structure of wealth-holding in Britain, 1809–39: a preliminary anatomy'. *Historical Research* 65(156): 74–89.

—— 1999. 'Response'. *Historical Research* 72(177): 88–91.

—— 2000. 'The role of London in Britain's wealth structure'. In *Urban Fortunes: Property and Inheritance in the Town, 1700–1900*, edited by J. Stobart and A. Owens. Aldershot: Ashgate, 131–48.

—— 2006. *Men of Property: The Very Wealthy in Britain since the Industrial Revolution*, 2nd edition. London: The Social Affairs Unit.

—— 2009. *Who Were the Rich? A Biographical Directory of British Wealth-holders, Volume 1: 1809–39*. London: The Social Affairs Unit.

Rutterford, J. 2006a. 'The merchant banker, the broker and the company chairman: a new issue case study'. *Accounting, Business and Financial History* 16(1): 45–68.

—— 2006b. 'The world was their oyster: international diversification pre-World War I'. In *Financial Strategy: Adding Stakeholder Value*, 2nd edition, edited by J. Rutterford, M. Upton, and D. Kodwani. Chichester: John Wiley, 5–24.

—— J. Maltby 2006a. '"Frank must marry for money": men, women and property in the novels of Anthony Trollope'. *Accounting Historians Journal* 33(2): 169–99.

—— —— 2006b. '"The widow, the clergyman and the reckless": women investors in England, 1830–1914'. *Feminist Economics* 12(1/2): 111–38.

—— —— 2007. '"The nesting instinct": women investors and risk in England, 1700–1930'. *Accounting History* 12(3): 305–27.

—— J. Maltby, D.R. Green, and A. Owens 2009. 'Researching shareholding and investment in England and Wales: approaches, sources and methods'. *Accounting History* 14(2): 269–92.

—— D.R. Green, J. Maltby, and A. Owens 2011. 'Who comprised the nation of shareholders? Gender and investment in Great Britain, c.1870–1935'. *Economic History Review* 64(1): 157–87.

Salmon, M. 1986. *Women and the Law of Property in Early America*. Chapel Hill, NC: University of North Carolina Press.

Samuel, H.B. 1933. *Shareholders' Money: An Analysis of Certain Defects in Company Legislation with Proposals for their Reform*. London: Pitman.

Sayers, R.S. 1957. *Lloyds Bank in the History of English Banking*. Oxford: Clarendon Press.

—— 1976. *The Bank of England, 1891–1944*. Cambridge: Cambridge University Press.

Scammel, W.M. 1968. *The London Discount Market*. London: Elek Books.

Schmitt, C., N. Henry, and A. Arondekar eds. 2002. 'Special Issue: Victorian Investments'. *Victorian Studies* 45(2).

Scholes, M. and J. Williams 1977. 'Estimating betas from nonsynchronous data'. *Journal of Financial Economics* 5(3): 309–27.

Scholey, D. 1987. 'Essential features of international financial centres' In *International Financial Centres: Structure, Achievements and Prospects*, Swiss Bankers' Association, Proceedings of the 40th International Summer School, Interlaken/Basel.

Scott, M. 1997. *Prerogative Court of Canterbury Wills and Other Probate Records*. Kew: Public Record Office.

Secretan, J.J. 1833. *Fortune's Epitome of Stocks and Public Funds*, 13th edition. London: Sherwood, Gilbert and Piper.

Seed, J. 1992. 'From "middling sort" to middle class in late-eighteenth and early-nineteenth-century England'. In *Social Orders and Social Classes in Europe since 1500: Studies in Social Stratification*, edited by M.L. Bush. London: Longman, 114–35.

Seifert, W.G. and H-J. Voth 2006. *Invasion der Heuschrecken. Intrigen – Machtkämpfe – Marktmanipulation. Wie Hedge Fonds die Deutschland AG attackieren*. Berlin: Econ.

Shammas, C. 1993. 'A new look at long-term trends in wealth inequality in the United States'. *American Historical Review* 98(2): 412–31.

—— 1994. 'Re-assessing the Married Women Property Acts'. *Journal of Women's History* 6(1): 9–30.

Shammas, C., M. Salmon, and M. Dahlin 1987. *Inheritance in America from Colonial Times to the Present*. New Brunswick, NJ: Rutgers University Press.

Shanahan, M. 1991. 'The distribution of personal wealth in South Australia, 1905–1915'. Unpublished Ph.D. Thesis, Flinders University of South Australia.

—— 1995. 'The distribution of personal wealth in South Australia, 1905–1915'. *Australian Economic History Review* 35(1): 82–111.

Shanley, M.L. 1989. *Feminism, Marriage, and the Law in Victorian England*. Princeton, NJ: Princeton University Press.

Siddiq, F.K. and J. Gwyn 1991. 'The importance of probate inventories in estimating the distribution of wealth'. *Nova Scotia Historical Review* 11(1): 103–17.

Siemens, G. 1957. *History of the House of Siemens. Volume 1, The Era of Free Enterprise*. Freiburg: Adler.

Simmel, G. 1907. *The Philosophy of Money (Philosophie des Geldes)*. Leipzig: Duncker und Humblot. Reprinted 2004, edited by D. Frisby, 3rd edition. London: Routledge.

—— 1991. 'Money in modern culture'. *Theory, Culture and Society* 8(3): 17–31.

Simon, M. 1968. 'The pattern of new British portfolio investment, 1865–1914'. In *The Export of Capital from Britain 1870–1914*, edited by A.R. Hall. London: Methuen, 15–44.

Sinclair, W.A. 1981. 'Women at work in Melbourne and Adelaide since 1871'. *Economic Record* 57(159): 344–53.

—— 1985. *The Process of Economic Development in Australia*. Melbourne, VIC: Lontgman Cheshire.

Singh, A. 1975. 'Takeovers, economic natural selection and the theory of the firm'. *Economic Journal* 85(339): 497–515.

Smiles, S. 1859. *Self Help*. London: John Murray.

—— 1875. *Thrift*. London: John Murray.

Smith, D.S. 1975. 'Under registration and bias in probate records: an analysis of data from eighteenth-century Hingham, Massachusetts'. *William and Mary Quarterly* 32(1): 100–10.

Soltow, L. 1972. 'The census of wealth of men in Australia in 1915 and in the United States in 1860 and 1870'. *Australian Economic History Review* 12(2): 125–41.

Spring, E. 1999. 'Businessmen and landowners re-engaged'. *Historical Research* 72(177): 77–88.

Staves, S. 1990. *Married Women's Separate Property in England, 1660–1883*. Cambridge, MA: Harvard University Press.

Steckel, R.H. 1990. 'Poverty and prosperity: a longitudinal study of wealth accumulation, 1850–1860'. *Review of Economics and Statistics* 72(2): 275–85.

—— C.M. Moehling 2001. 'Rising inequality: trends in the distribution of wealth in industrializing New England'. *Journal of Economic History* 61(1): 160–83.

Stiles, C.R. 1917. 'The war's lesson for investors'. *Financial Review of Reviews* March: 49.

Sundstrom, W. and P. David 1988. 'Old-age security motives, labour markets, and farm-family fertility in antebellum America'. *Explorations in Economic History* 25 (2): 164–97.

Supple, B. 1970. *The Royal Exchange Assurance: A History of British Insurance 1720–1970*. Oxford: Oxford University Press.

Sutch, R. 1991. 'All things reconsidered: the life-cycle perspective and the third task of economic history'. *Journal of Economic History* 51(2): 271–88.

Sutherland, A. 1968. *The Landowners*. London: Blond.

Swan, A.S. 1894. *The Strait Gate*. London: S.W. Partridge and Co.

Swann, C. 2000. 'The weak will become prey'. *Financial Times* 30 June: 4.

Sykes, J. 1926. *The Amalgamation Movement in English Banking, 1825–1924*. London: P.S. King and Son.

Sylla, R. and G.D. Smith 1995. 'Information and capital market regulation in Anglo-American finance'. In *Anglo-American Financial Systems*, edited by M.D. Bordo and R. Sylla. New York, NY: Irwin, 179–205.

Szreter, S. 1996. *Fertility, Class and Gender in Britain, 1860–1940*. Cambridge: Cambridge University Press.

Taylor, J. 2006. *Creating Capitalism: Joint-Stock Enterprise in British Politics and Culture, 1800–1870*. Woodbridge: Boydell and Brewer.

Thackeray, W.M. 1841. *The History of Samuel Titmarsh and the Great Hoggarty Diamond*. London: Bradbury and Evans.

Thane, P. 2000. *Old Age in English History: Past Experiences, Present Issues*. Oxford: Oxford University Press.

Thomas, M. 2004. 'The service sector'. In *The Cambridge Economic History of Modern Britain. Volume 2: Economic Maturity, 1860–1939*, edited by R. Floud and P. Johnson. Cambridge: Cambridge University Press, 99–132.

Thompson, F.M.L. 1990. 'Life after death: how successful nineteenth-century businessmen disposed of their fortunes'. *Economic History Review* 43(1): 40–61.

—— 1992. 'Stitching it together again'. *Economic History Review* 45(2): 362–75.

—— 2001. *Gentrification and the Enterprise Culture: Britain 1780–1980*. Oxford: Oxford University Press.

Thorne, G. and L. Custance 1904. *Sharks: A Fantastic Novel for Business Men and their Families*. London: Greening and Co.

Toms, J.S. 2002. 'The rise of modern accounting and the fall of the public company: the Lancashire cotton mills 1870–1914'. *Accounting, Organizations and Society* 27(1/2): 61–84.

Tonts, M. 2002. 'State policy and the yeoman ideal: agricultural development in Western Australia, 1890–1914'. *Landscape Research* 27(1): 103–15.

Trafford, F.G. (Charlotte Riddell) 1864. *George Geith of Fen Court*. London: R. Bentley and Son.

Treasury Committee on Bank Amalgamations 1918. *Report of the Treasury Committee on Bank Amalgamations*. London: His Majesty's Stationery Office.

Trollope, A. 1874. *The Way We Live Now*. London: Chapman and Hall.

—— 1876. *The Prime Minister*, Volumes 1 and 2. London: Chapman and Hall.

Tufano, P. 1997. 'Business failure, judicial intervention and financial innovation: restructuring US railroads in the nineteenth century'. *Business History Review* 71(1): 1–40.

Turner, J.D. 2009. 'Wider share ownership? Investors in English and Welsh bank shares in the nineteenth century'. *Economic History Review* 62(s1): 167–92.

Turrell, R. and J.J. van Helten 1986. 'The Rothschilds, the Exploration Company and mining finance'. *Business History* 28(1): 181–205.

United Nations 1949. *International Capital Movements during the Interwar Period*. New York, NY: United Nations.

Urquhart, M.C. 1986. 'New estimates of gross national product, Canada 1870–1926: some implications for Canadian development'. In *Long Term Factors in American Economic Growth*, Volume 51. NBER Conference on Research in Income and Wealth, edited by S.L. Engerman and R.E. Gallman. Chicago, IL: The University of Chicago Press, 9–94.

—— 1993. *Gross National Product, Canada 1870–1926: The Derivation of the Estimates*. Kingston, ON: McGill-Queen's University Press.

Vamplew, W., E. Richards, D. Jaensch, and J. Hancock 1986. *South Australian Historical Statistics*. Monograph 3. Sydney, NSW: University of New South Wales.

van Leeuwen, M.H.D., M. Ineke, and A. Miles 2007. *HISCO Historical International Standard Classification of Occupations*. Leuven: Leuven University Press.

van Oss, S.F. 1893. *American Railroads and British Investors*. London: Effingham Wilson and Co.

Vincent, J. ed. 1981. *The Later Derby Diaries: Home Rule, Liberal Unionism and Aristocratic Life in Late Victorian England*. Bristol: J.Vincent.

Vissink, H.G.A. 1985. *Economic and Financial Reporting in England and the Netherlands*. Assen and Maastricht: Van Gorcum.

Vizetelly, E.A. 1894. 'Introduction'. In E. Zola, *Money (L'Argent)*. London: Chatto and Windus.

von Kapff, K. 1975. *Ubernahmeangebot in England und Frankreich*. Unpublished Ph.D.Thesis, University of Augsburg.

Walker, J.D. and R.M. Watson. 1894. *Investor's and Shareholder's Guide*. Edinburgh: E. and S. Livingstone.

Walker, T.R. 2000. 'Economic opportunity on the urban frontier: wealth and nativity in early San Francisco'. *Explorations in Economic History* 37(3): 258–77.

Waugh, A. 1951. *The Lipton Story, a Centennial Biography*. London: Cassell.

Wedgwood, J. 1929. *The Economics of Inheritance*. London: George Routledge and Sons.

West, J. 1982. *Village Records*. London: Phillimore.

White, L.H. 1995. *Free Banking in Britain: Theory, Experience and Debate 1800–1845*, 2nd edition. London: Institute of Economic Affairs.

Wicks, F. 1892. *The Veiled Hand: A Novel of the Sixties, the Seventies, and the Eighties*. London: Eden and Co.

Wilde, O. 1899. *An Ideal Husband*. London: Leonard Smithers and Co. Reprinted 2000 in *The Importance of Being Earnest and Other Plays*, edited by R.A. Cave. London: Penguin, 175–274.

Wilkins, M. 1999. 'Cosmopolitan finance in the 1920s: New York's emergence as an international financial centre'. In *The State, the Financial System and Economic Modernization*, edited by R. Sylla, R. Tilly, and G. Tortella. Cambridge: Cambridge University Press, 271–90.

Williamson, J.G. 1998a. 'Growth, distribution and demography: some lessons from history'. *Explorations in Economic History* 35(3): 241–71.

—— 1998b. 'Real wages and relative factor prices in the Third World 1820–1940: the Mediterranean Basin'. *Discussion Paper Number 1842*, Harvard Institute of Economic Research, Harvard University: Cambridge MA.

Wilson, A. 1879. *Banking Reform: An Essay on the Prominent Dangers and the Remedies they Demand.* London: Longmans, Green and Co.

—— 1954. *The History of Unilever.* London: Cassell.

Wilson, J.F. 1997. 'The finance of municipal capital expenditure in England and Wales, 1870–1914'. *Financial History Review* 4(1): 31–50.

Winstanley, M.J. 1983. *The Shopkeeper's World: 1830–1914.* Manchester: Manchester University Press.

Withers, H. 1916. *International Finance.* London: John Murray.

—— R.H.I. Palgrave 1910. *The English Banking System.* Washington, DC: Government Printing Office.

Wood, Mrs H (Ellen) 1864. *Oswald Cray: A Novel.* London: Macmillan.

Woods, R. and P.R. Hinde 1987. 'Mortality in Victorian England: models and patterns'. *Journal of Interdisciplinary History* 18(1): 27–54.

Wormell, J. 2000. *The Management of the National Debt of the United Kingdom, 1900–1932.* London: Routledge.

Worsnop, J. 1990. 'A re-evaluation of "the problem of surplus women" in nineteenth-century England: the case of the 1851 census'. *Women's Studies International Forum* 13(1/2): 21–31.

Wright, A. 1930. 'The state and the small investor'. *Financial Review of Reviews* January: 31–7.

'Z'. 1899. 'Successful profit-sharing'. *Economic Journal* 9(36): 585–8.

Index